THE PRINCE OF TENNIS
VOL. 24
The SHONEN JUMP Manga Edition

STORY AND ART BY
TAKESHI KONOMI

Translation/Joe Yamazaki
Consultant/Michelle Pangilinan
Touch-up Art & Lettering/Vanessa Satone
Design/Sam Elzway
Editor/Leyla Aker

Editor in Chief, Books/Alvin Lu
Editor in Chief, Magazines/Marc Weidenbaum
VP of Publishing Licensing/Rika Inouye
VP of Sales/Gonzalo Ferreyra
Sr. VP of Marketing/Liza Coppola
Publisher/Hyoe Narita

Printed in the U.S.A.

Published by VIZ Media, LLC
P.O. Box 77010
San Francisco, CA 94107

SHONEN JUMP Manga Edition
10 9 8 7 6 5 4 3 2 1
First printing, March 2008

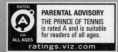

PARENTAL ADVISORY
THE PRINCE OF TENNIS
is rated A and is suitable
for readers of all ages.
ratings.viz.com

THE WORLD'S
MOST POPULAR MANGA

www.shonenjump.com

www.viz.com

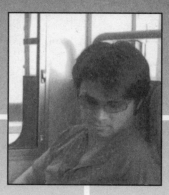

Finally! The movie's finally here! I'm so happy that all the hard work has paid off. See you in the theaters!!

– Takeshi Konomi, 2004

D0951463

About Takeshi Konomi

Takeshi Konomi exploded onto the manga scene with the incredible **THE PRINCE OF TENNIS**. His refined art style and sleek character designs proved popular with **Weekly Shonen Jump** readers, and **THE PRINCE OF TENNIS** became the number one sports manga in Japan almost overnight. Its cast of fascinating male tennis players attracted legions of female readers even though it was originally intended to be a boys' comic. The manga continues to be a success in Japan and has inspired a hit anime series, as well as several video games and mountains of merchandise.

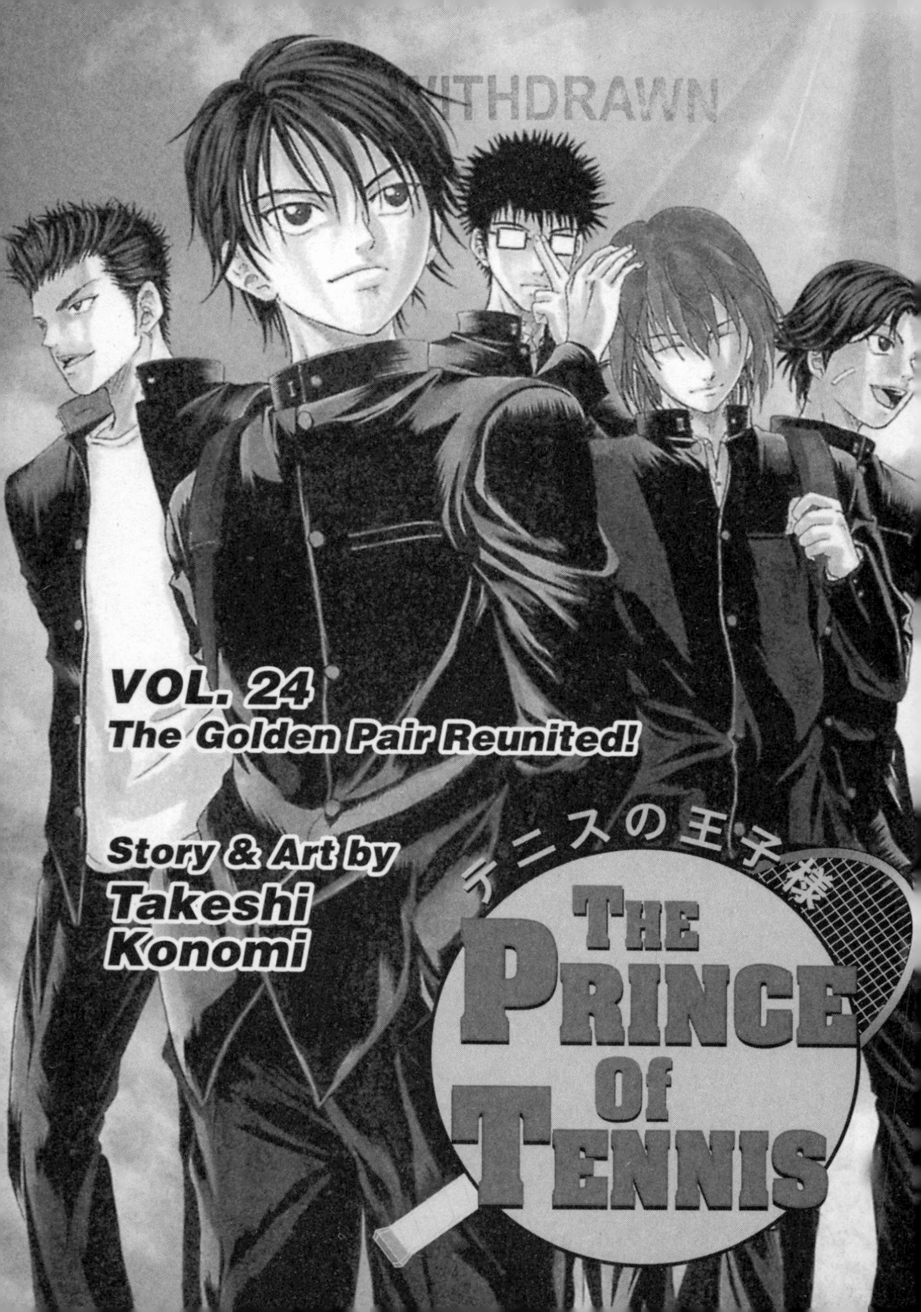
VOL. 24
The Golden Pair Reunited!
Story & Art by
Takeshi
Konomi
テニスの王子様
THE
PRINCE
OF
TENNIS

ENNIS CLUB

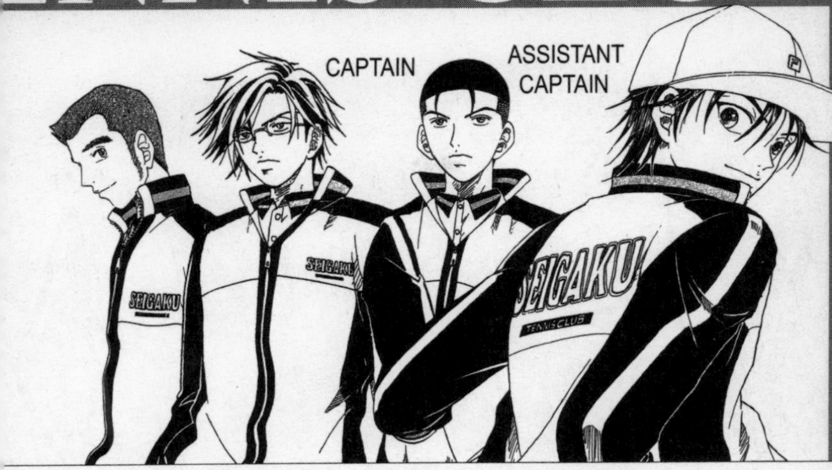
CAPTAIN
ASSISTANT CAPTAIN
SEIGAKU
SEIGAKU
SEIGAKU
TENNIS CLUB

• TAKASHI KAWAMURA • KUNIMITSU TEZUKA • SHUICHIRO OISHI • RYOMA ECHIZEN •

STORY & CHARACTERS

Seishun Academy student Ryoma Echizen is a tennis prodigy with wins in four consecutive U.S. Junior tournaments under his belt. Then he became a starter as a 7th grader and led his team to the District Preliminaries! Despite a few mishaps, Seishun won the District Prelims and City Tournament, and even earned a ticket to the Kanto Tournament.

After defeating Midoriyama and Rokkaku to reach the tournament finals, Seishun is now up against the number-one ranked Rikkai, a team full of national-level players. Their spirits are high, but despite a good game from their No. 2 Doubles pairing of Momo and Kaoru, they lose the opening match. Now the play comes around to No. 1 Doubles: Eiji and Shuichiro. With Shuichiro's return from injury, the Golden Pair is reunited!

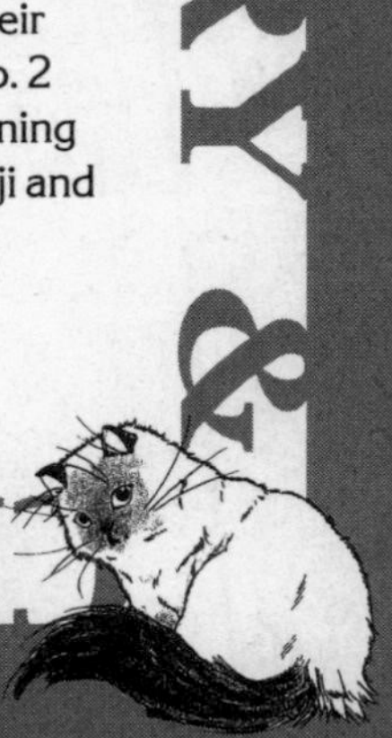

SEIGAKU T

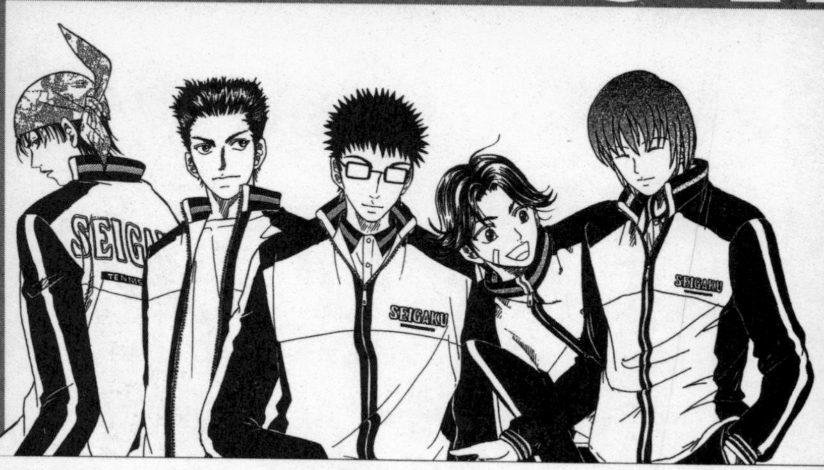
SEIGAKU
SEIGAKU
SEIGAKU

• KAORU KAIDO • TAKESHI MOMOSHIRO • SADAHARU INUI • EIJI KIKUMARU • SHUSUKE FUJI •

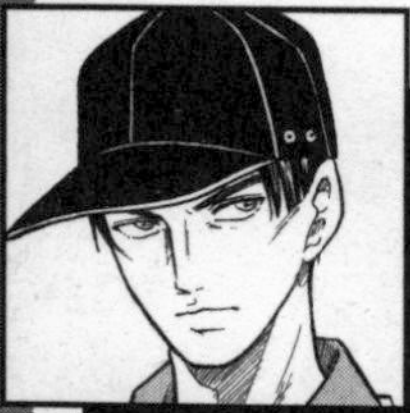
RIKKAI
GENICHIRO SANADA

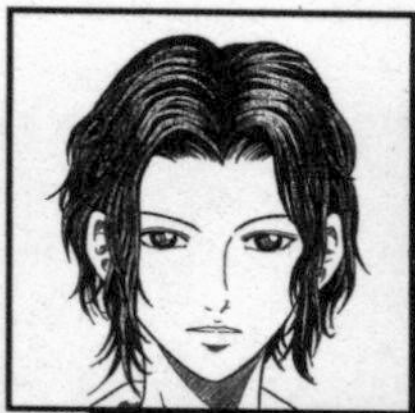
RIKKAI
SEIICHI YUKIMURA

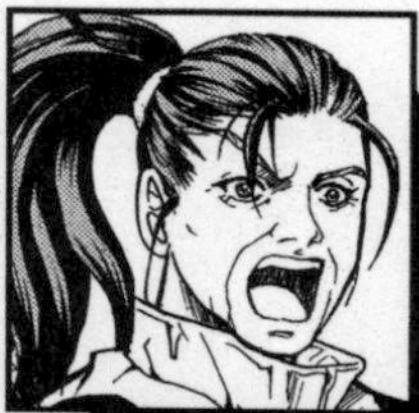
SEISHUN ACADEMY TENNIS COACH
SUMIRE RYUZAKI

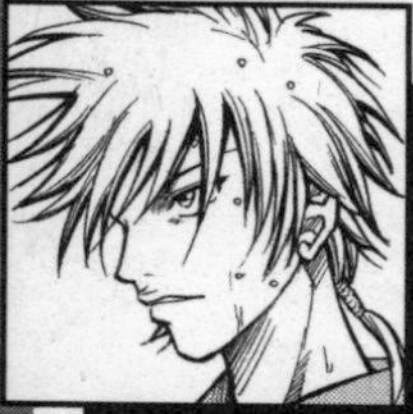
RIKKAI
MASAHARU NIO

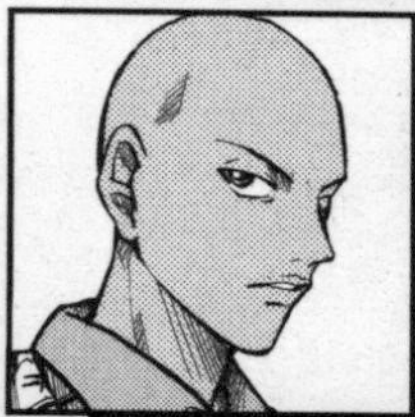
RIKKAI
JACKAL KUWAHARA

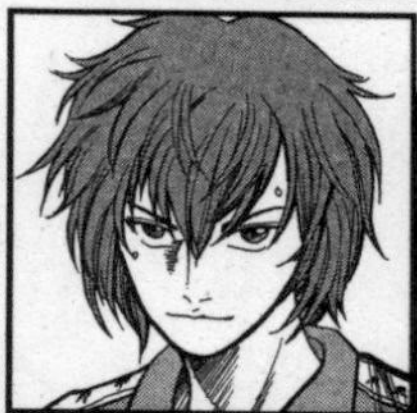
RIKKAI
BUNTA MARUI

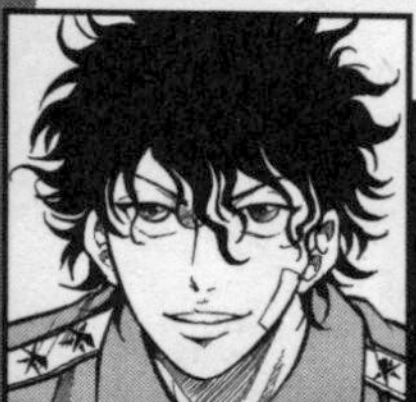
RIKKAI
AKAYA KIRIHARA

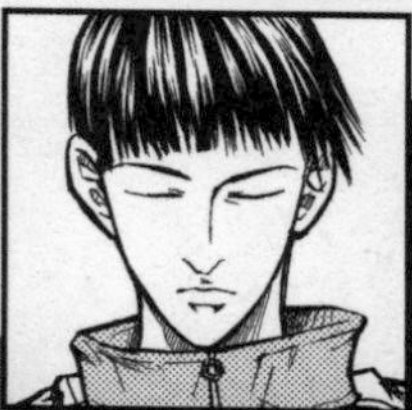
RIKKAI
RENJI YANAGI

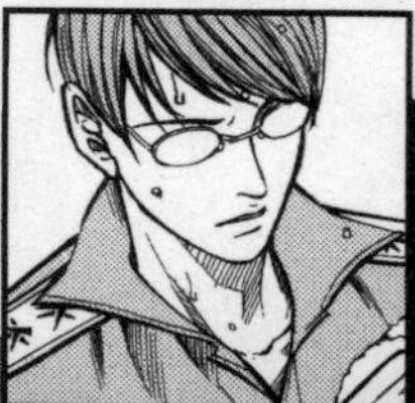
RIKKAI
HIROSHI YAGYU

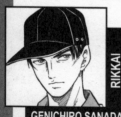

CONTENTS

Vol. 24
The Golden Pair Reunited!

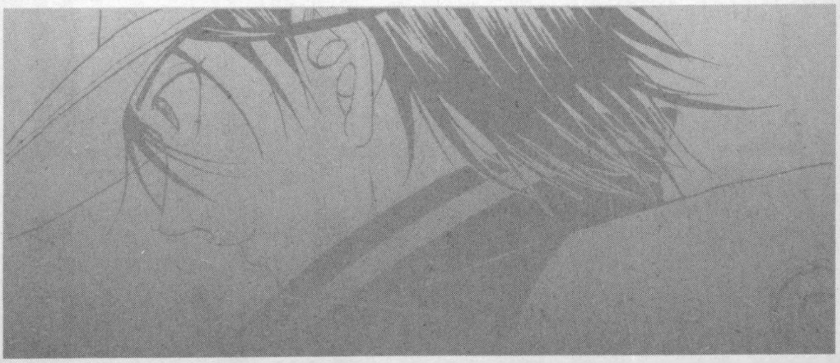

GENIUS 202: THE GOLDEN PAIR REUNITED!

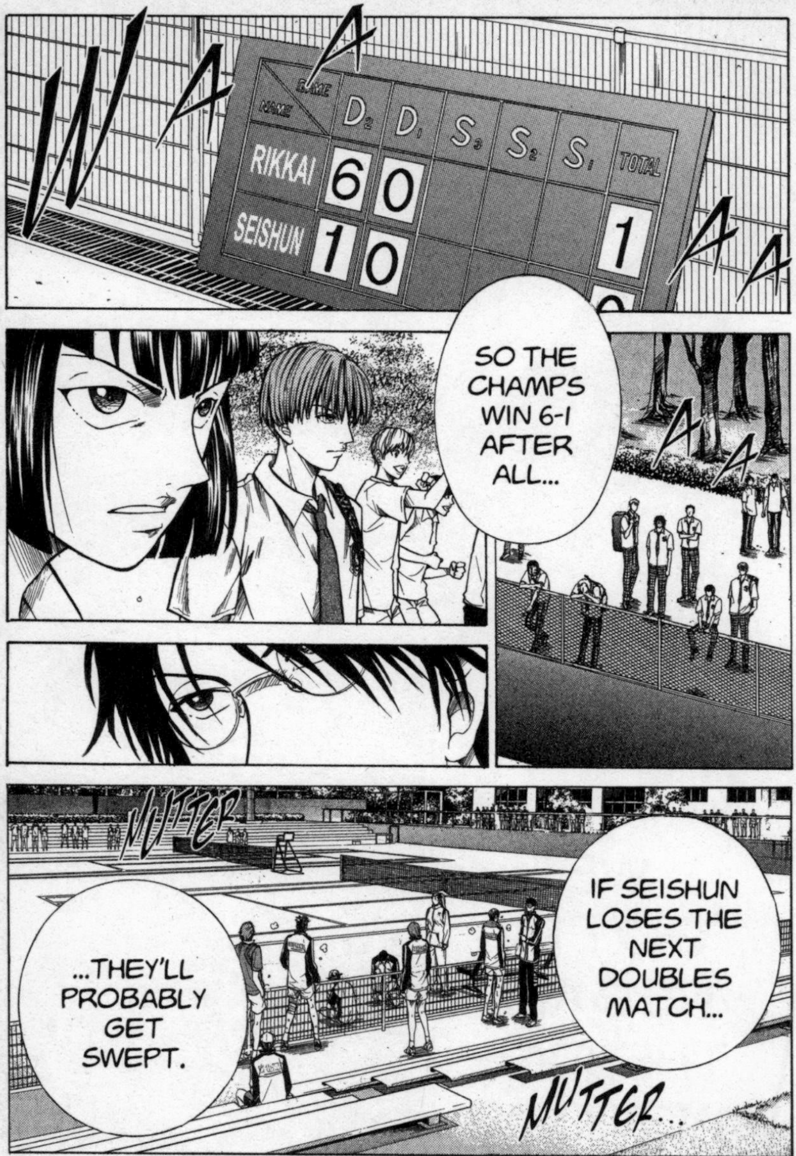
WAA
GAME
NAME
D2 D1 S3 S2 S1 TOTAL
RIKKAI 6 0
SEISHUN 1 0 1
AA
AA
SO THE CHAMPS WIN 6-1 AFTER ALL...
MUTTER
IF SEISHUN LOSES THE NEXT DOUBLES MATCH...
...THEY'LL PROBABLY GET SWEPT.
MUTTER...

GENIUS 202:
THE GOLDEN PAIR REUNITED!

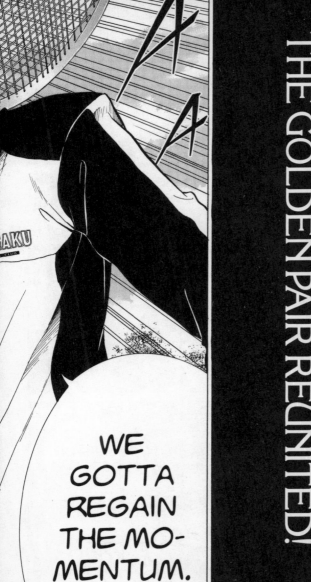

WE GOTTA REGAIN THE MO-MENTUM.

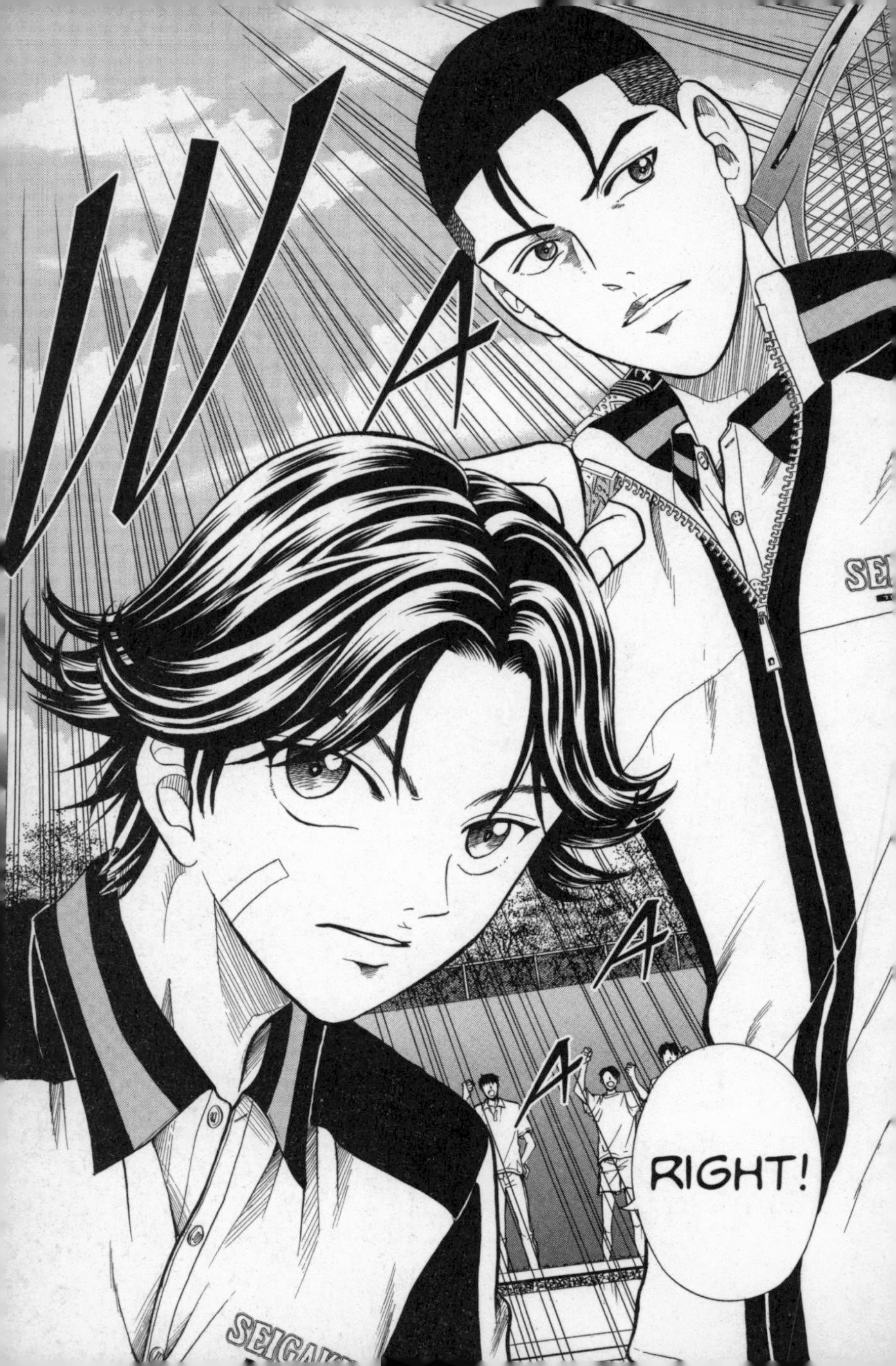
WAAA
RIGHT!

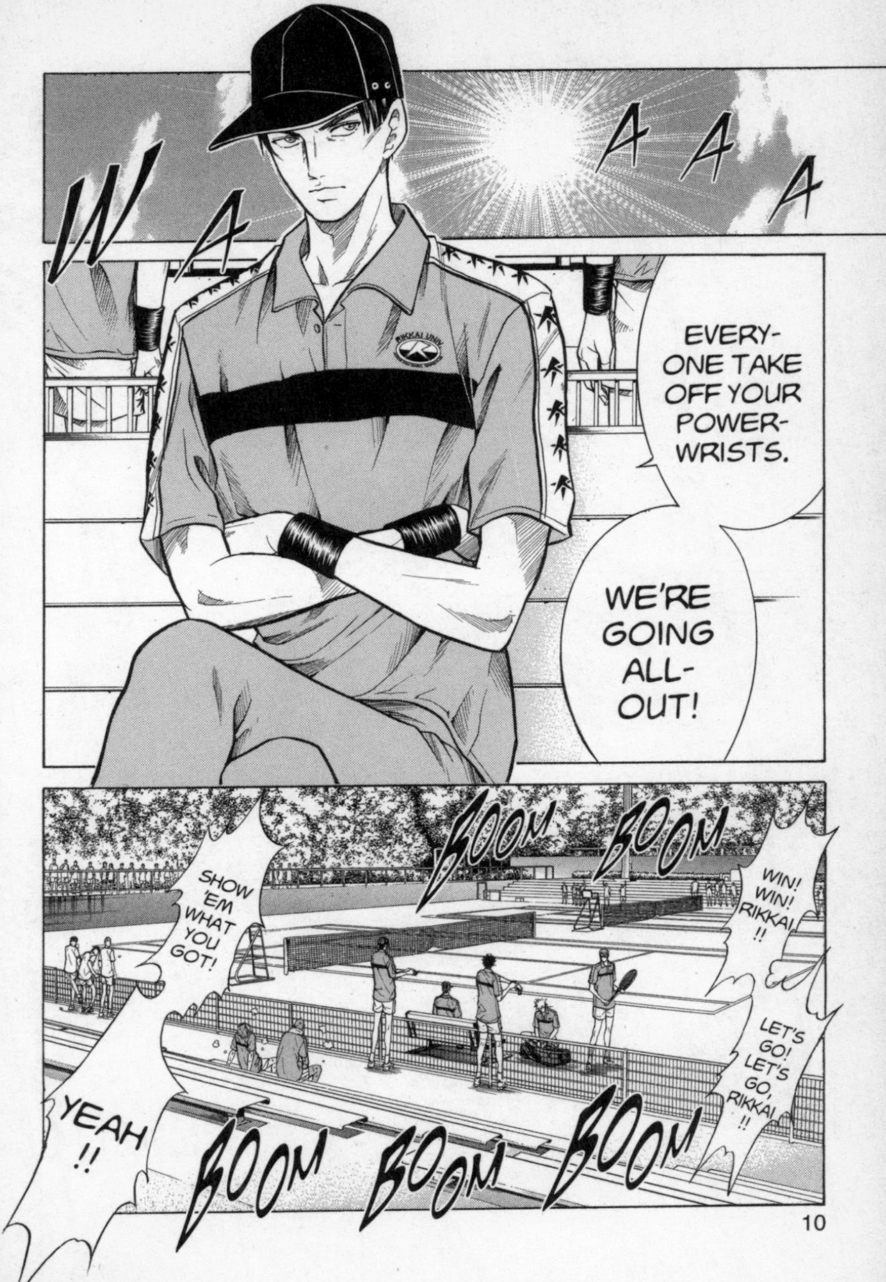
WAAAA
EVERY-ONE TAKE OFF YOUR POWER-WRISTS.
WE'RE GOING ALL-OUT!
WIN! WIN! RIKKAI!!
BOOM BOOM
SHOW 'EM WHAT YOU GOT!
LET'S GO! LET'S GO, RIKKAI!!
BOOM BOOM BOOM
YEAH!!

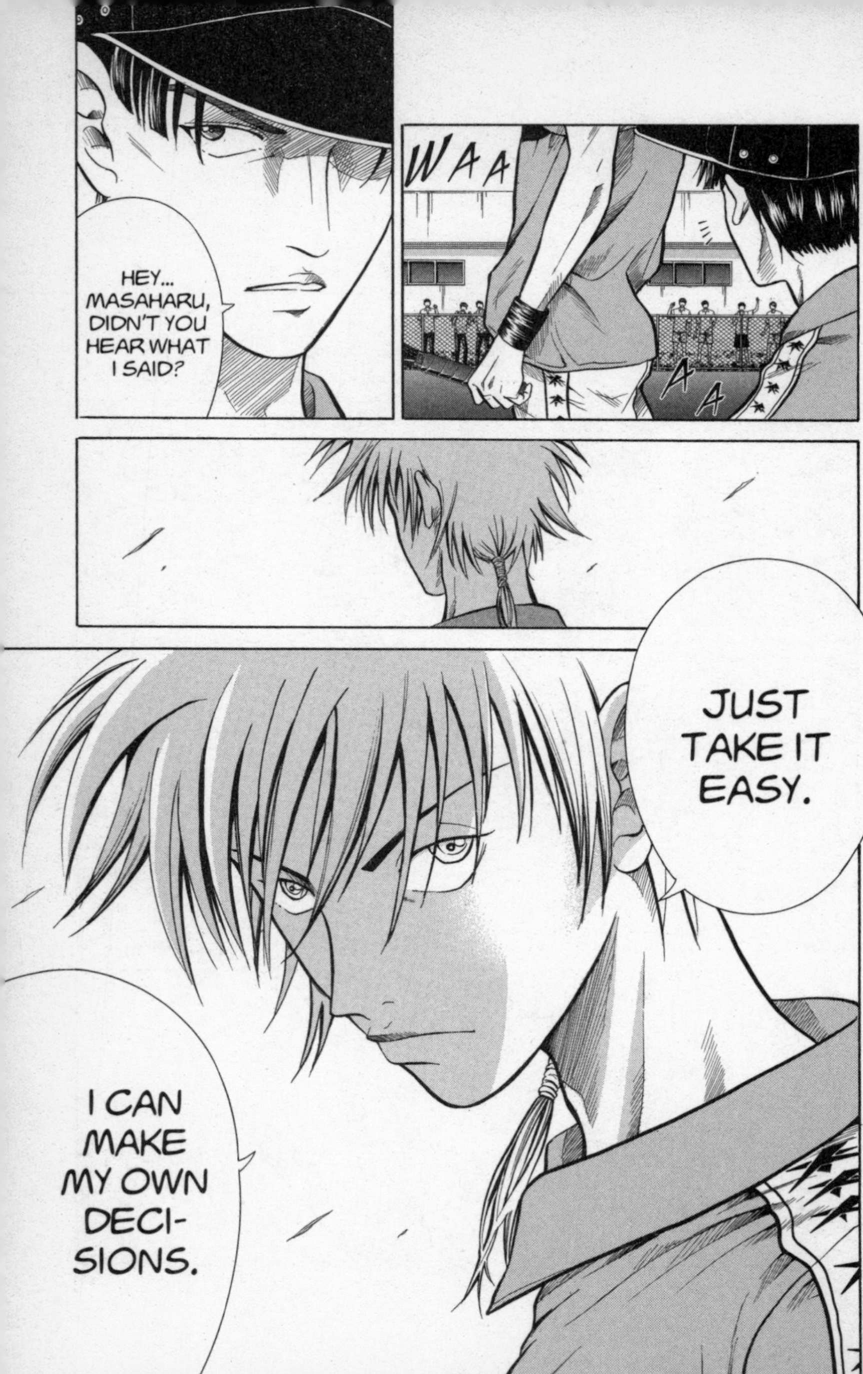
WAA
AA
HEY... MASAHARU, DIDN'T YOU HEAR WHAT I SAID?
JUST TAKE IT EASY.
I CAN MAKE MY OWN DECI-SIONS.

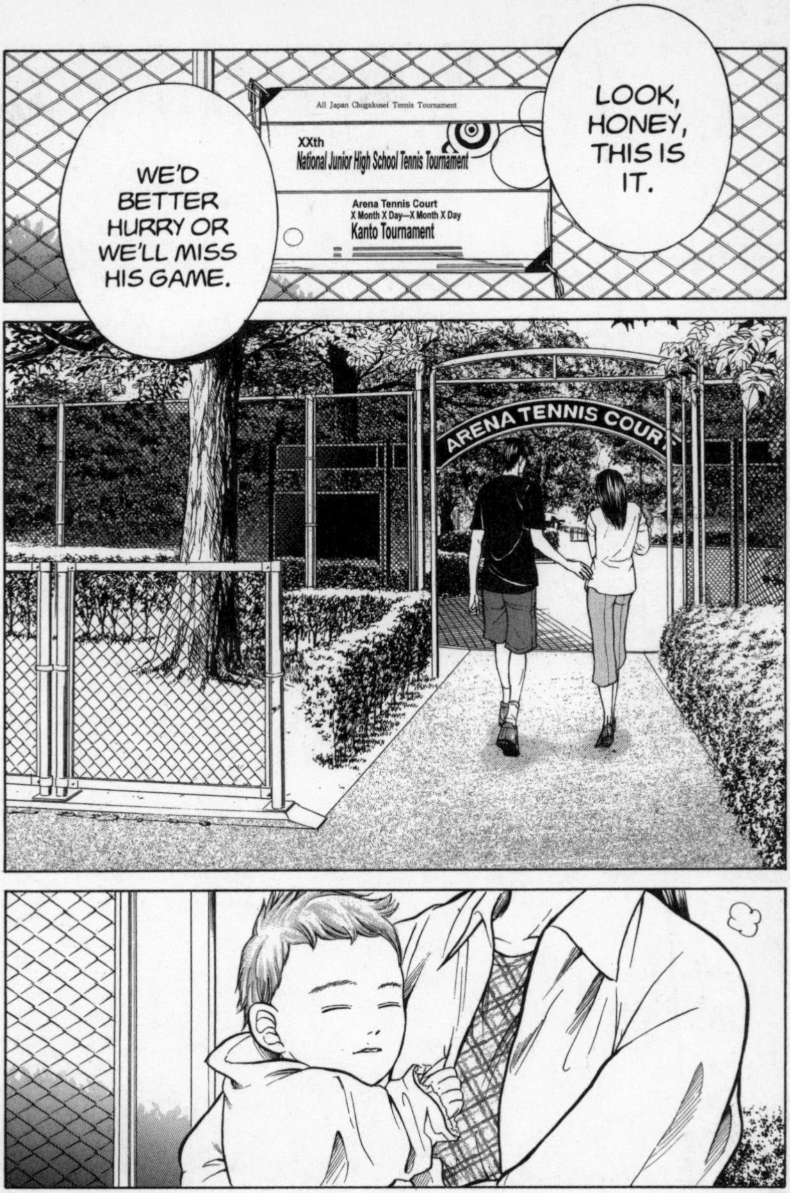
LOOK, HONEY, THIS IS IT.
All Japan Chugakusei Tennis Tournament
XXth National Junior High School Tennis Tournament
Arena Tennis Court
X Month X Day—X Month X Day
Kanto Tournament
WE'D BETTER HURRY OR WE'LL MISS HIS GAME.
ARENA TENNIS COURT

READ THIS WAY

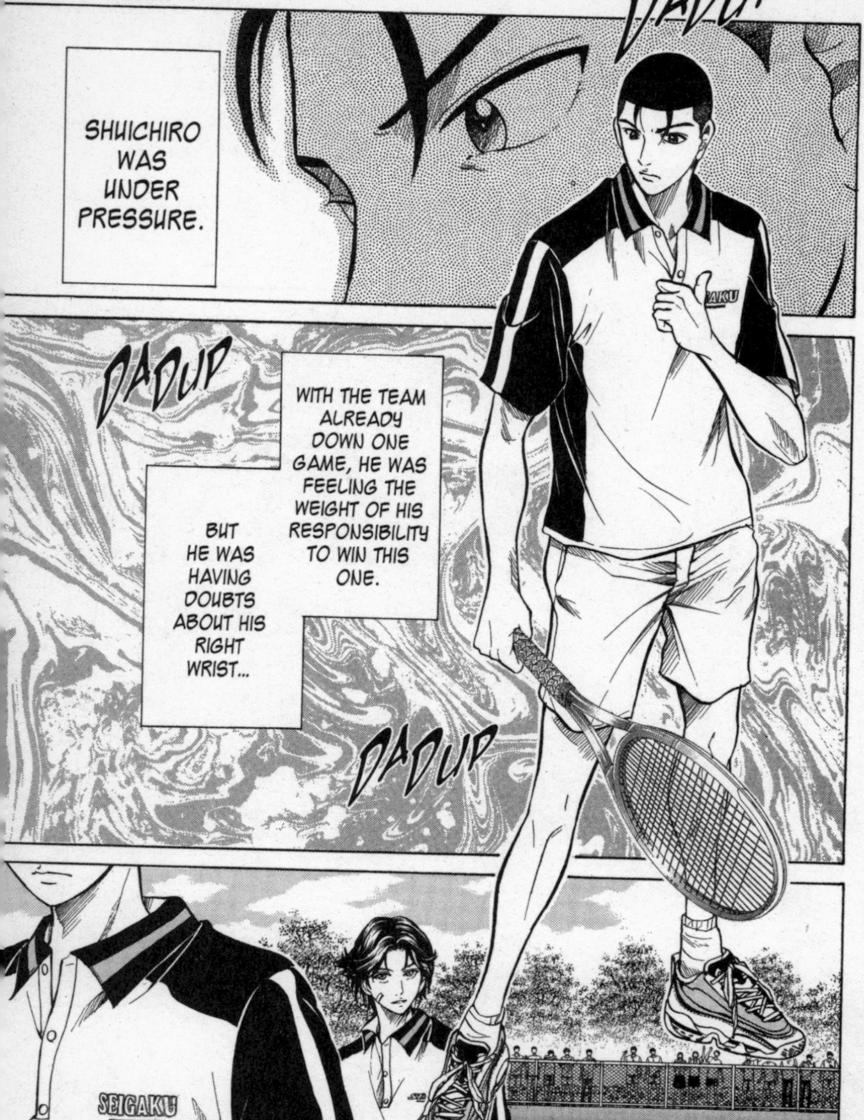
DADUP
SHUICHIRO WAS UNDER PRESSURE.
DADUP
WITH THE TEAM ALREADY DOWN ONE GAME, HE WAS FEELING THE WEIGHT OF HIS RESPONSIBILITY TO WIN THIS ONE.
BUT HE WAS HAVING DOUBTS ABOUT HIS RIGHT WRIST...
DADUP
SEIGAKU

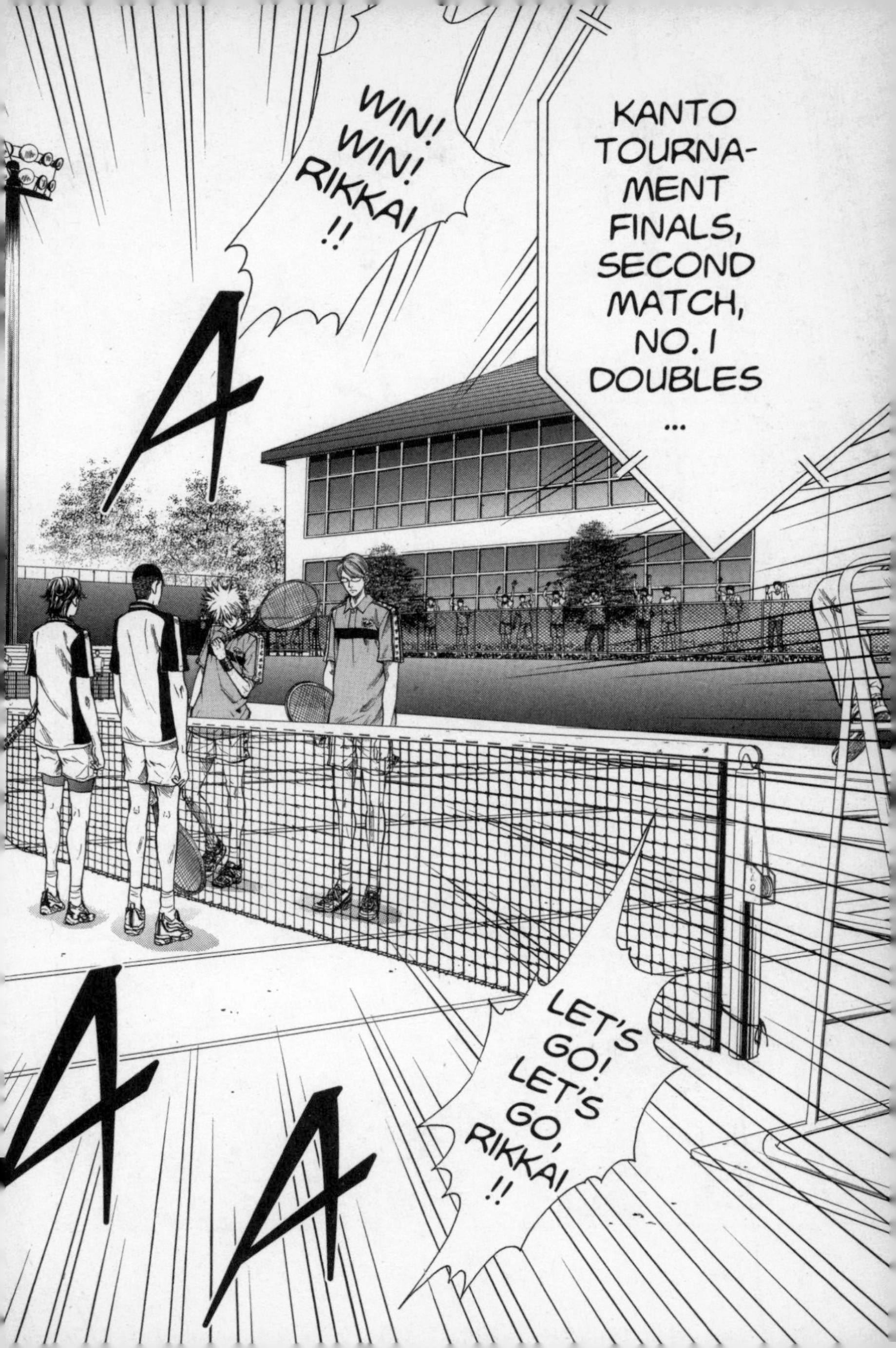
KANTO TOURNAMENT FINALS, SECOND MATCH, NO. 1 DOUBLES ...
WIN! WIN! RIKKAI !!
LET'S GO! LET'S GO, RIKKAI !!

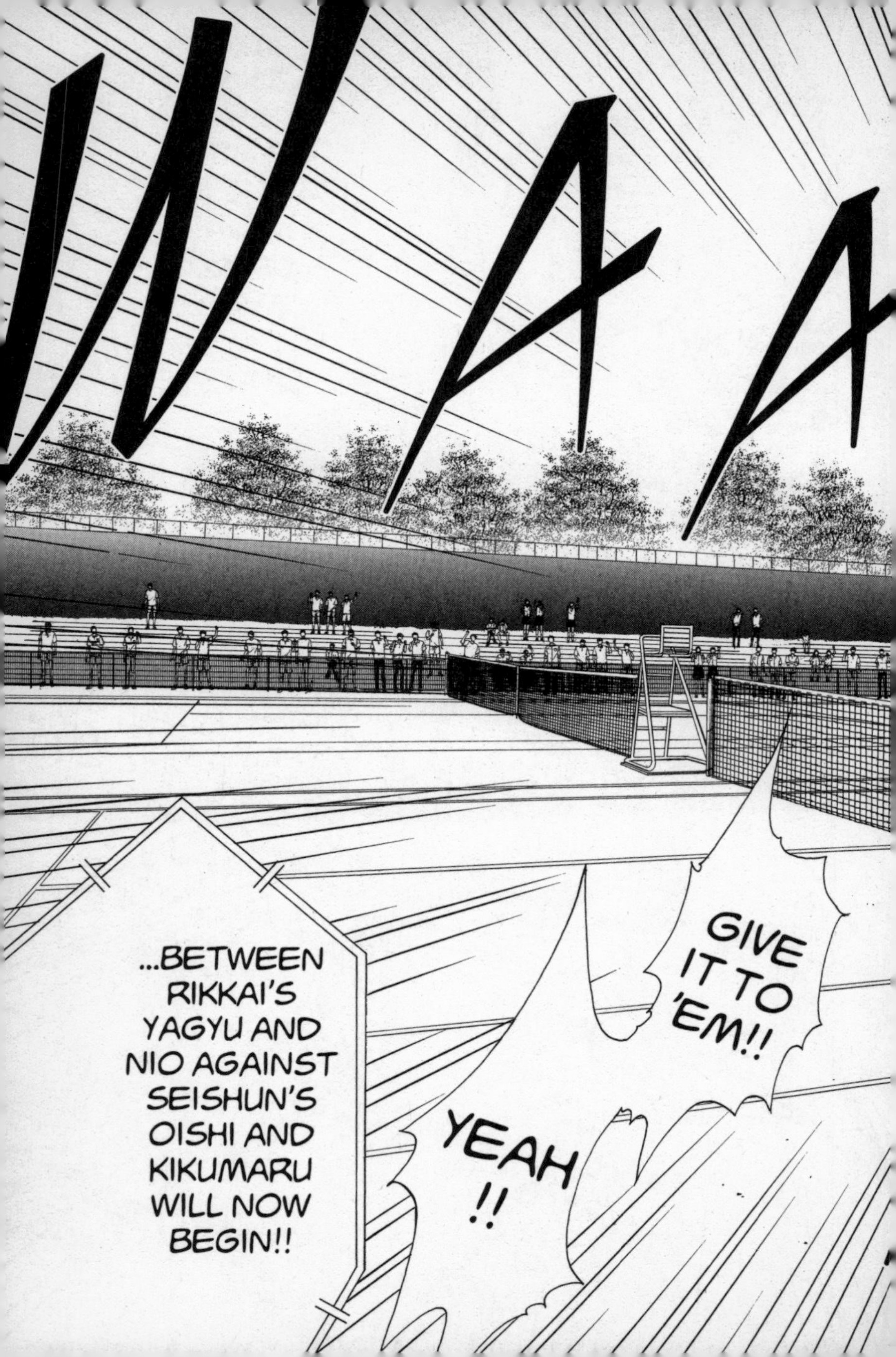
WAA
GIVE IT TO 'EM!!
YEAH !!
...BETWEEN RIKKAI'S YAGYU AND NIO AGAINST SEISHUN'S OISHI AND KIKUMARU WILL NOW BEGIN!!

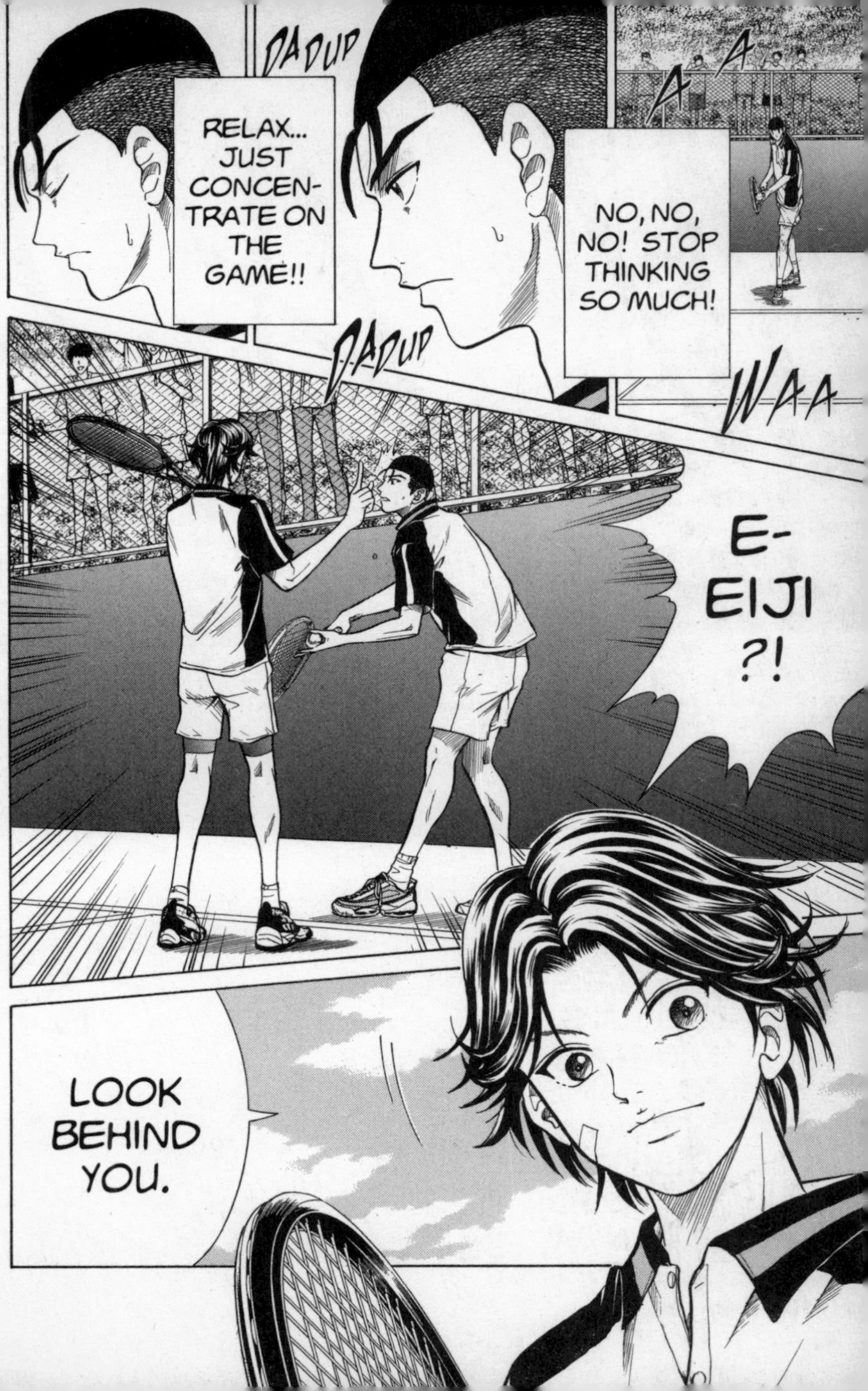
A A
NO, NO, NO! STOP THINKING SO MUCH!
DADUP
RELAX... JUST CONCENTRATE ON THE GAME!!
DADUP
WAA
E-EIJI?!
LOOK BEHIND YOU.

READ THIS WAY

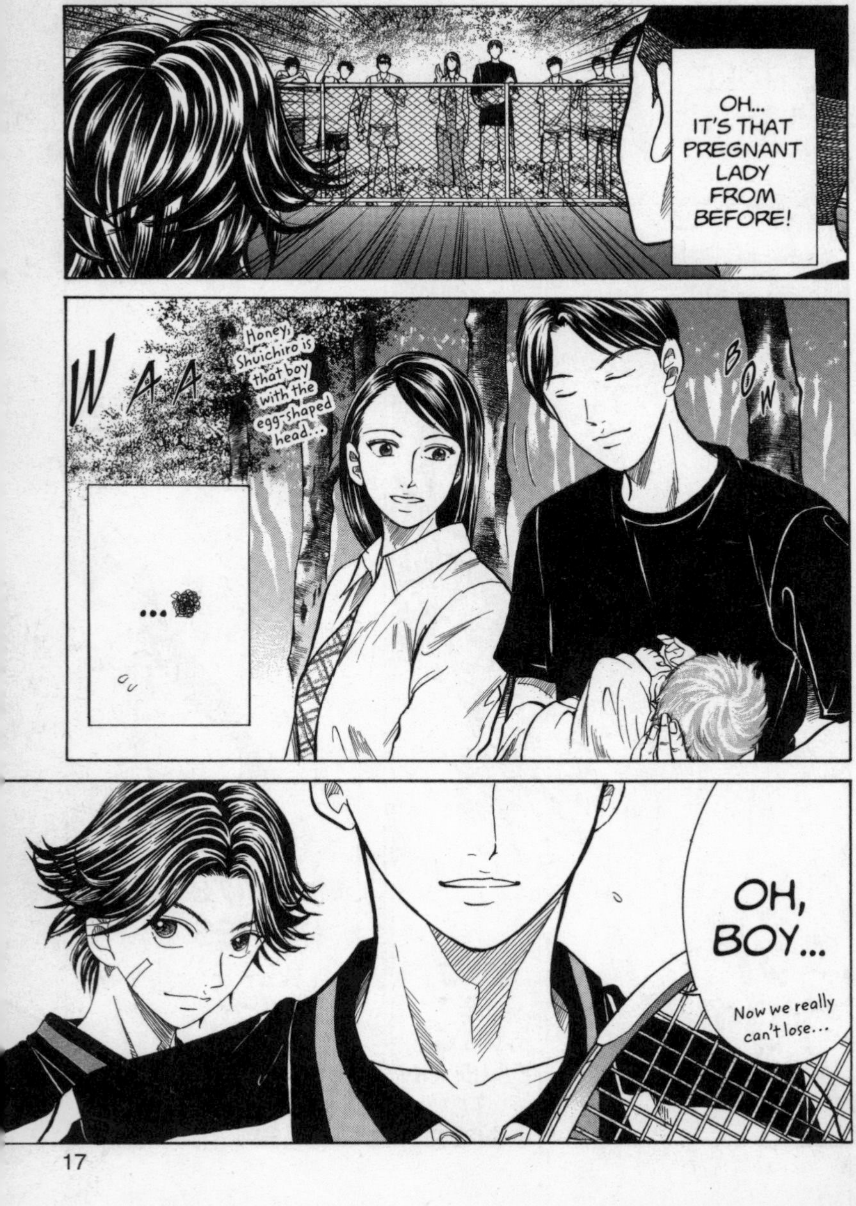
OH... IT'S THAT PREGNANT LADY FROM BEFORE!
BOW
Honey, Shuichiro is that boy with the egg-shaped head...
WAA
...
OH, BOY...
Now we really can't lose...

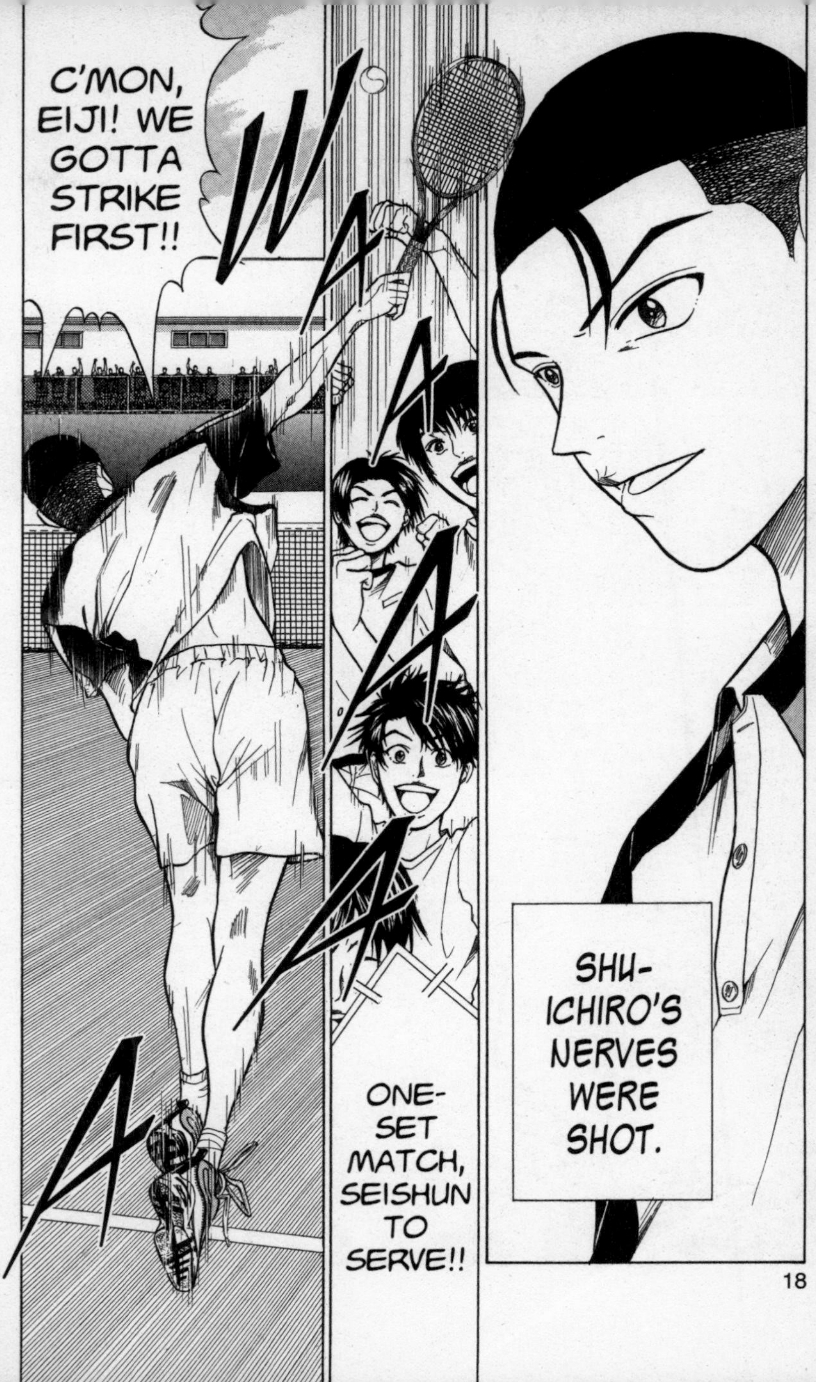
SHU-ICHIRO'S NERVES WERE SHOT.
ONE-SET MATCH, SEISHUN TO SERVE!!
WAAAAAA
C'MON, EIJI! WE GOTTA STRIKE FIRST!!

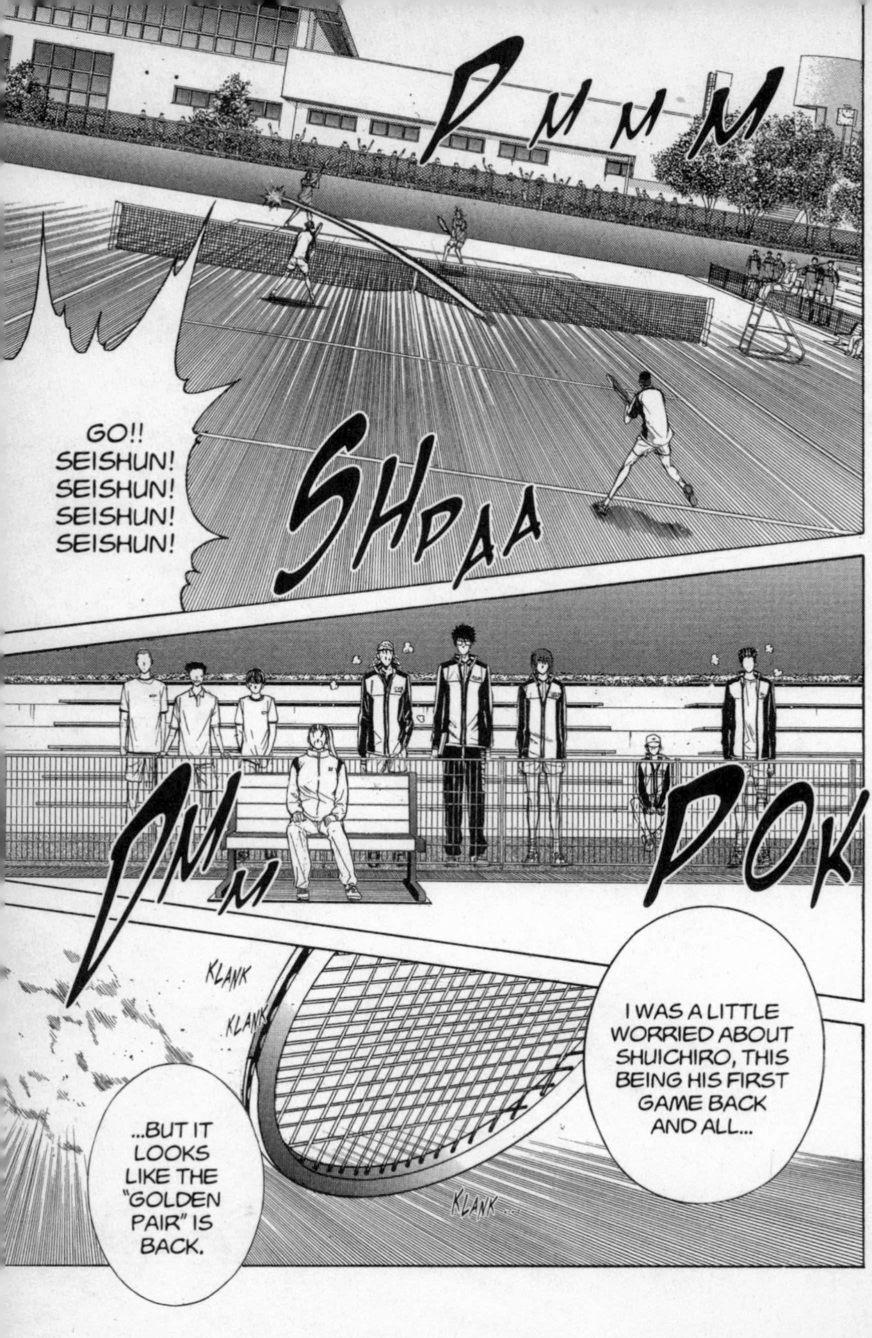
DMMM
GO!! SEISHUN! SEISHUN! SEISHUN! SEISHUN!
SHPAA
DOK
DMM
I WAS A LITTLE WORRIED ABOUT SHUICHIRO, THIS BEING HIS FIRST GAME BACK AND ALL...
KLANK
KLANK
...BUT IT LOOKS LIKE THE "GOLDEN PAIR" IS BACK.
KLANK...

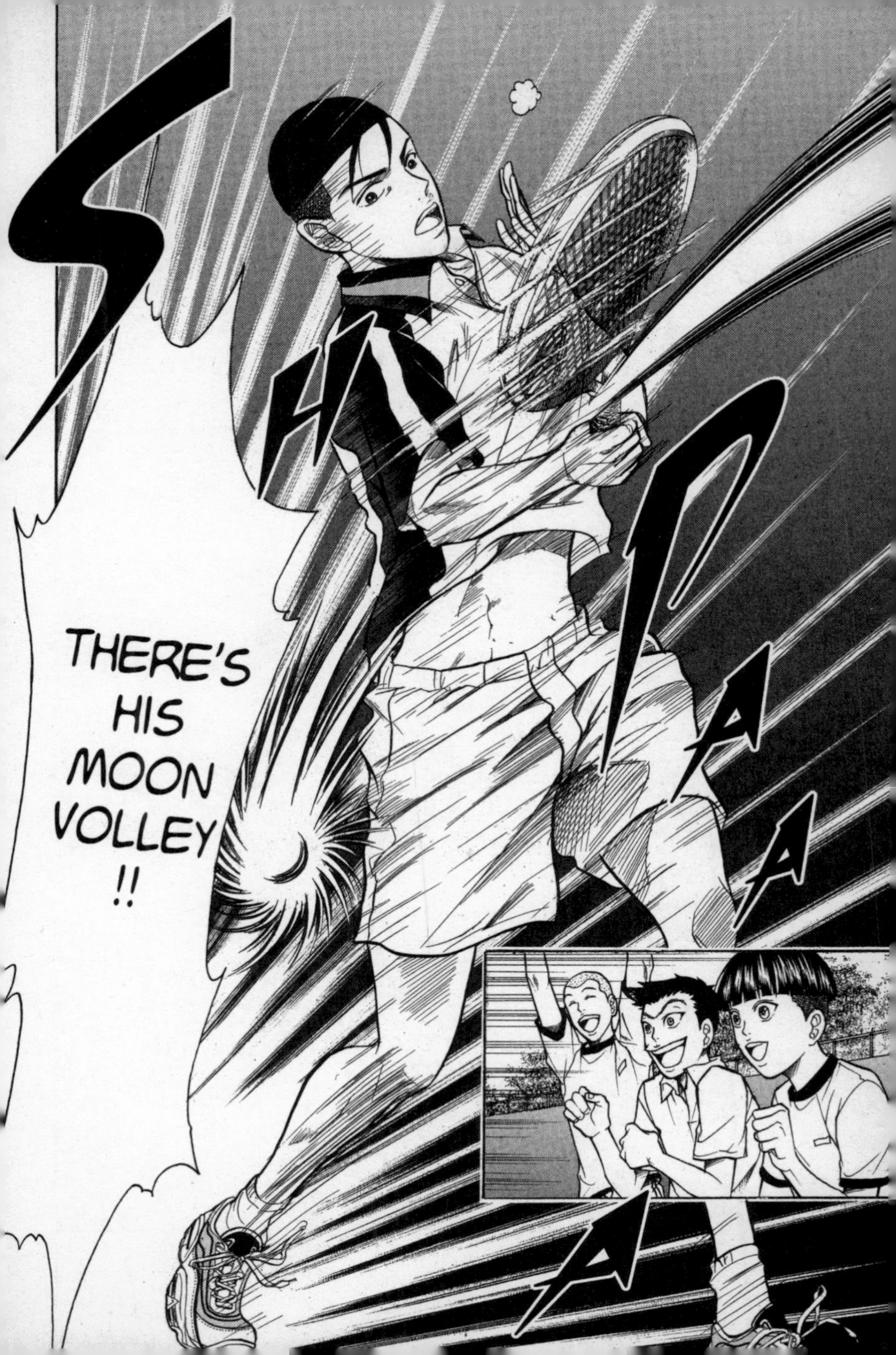
SHPAAA
THERE'S HIS MOON VOLLEY !!
A

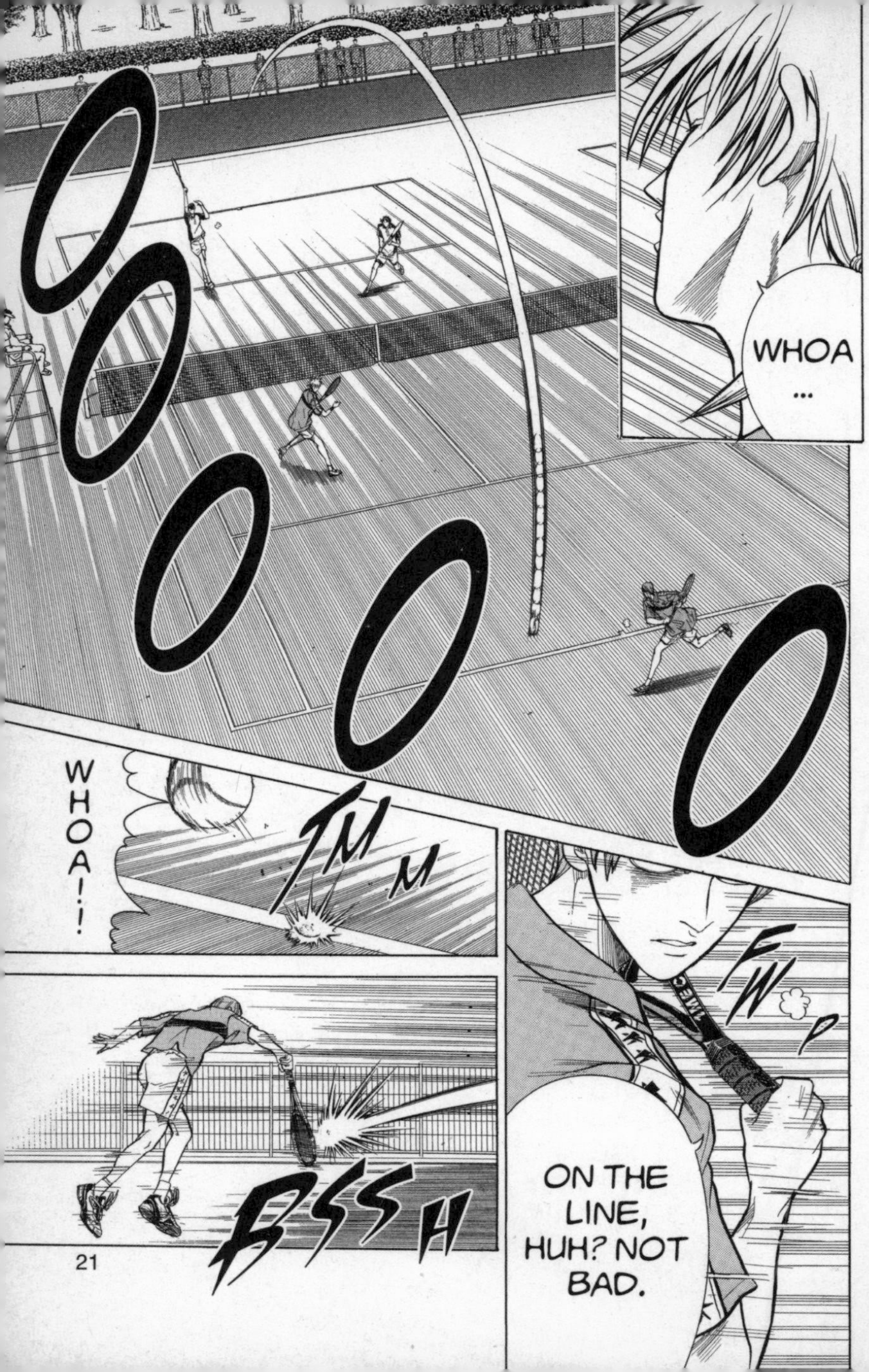
WHOA ...
OOOOOO
FWP
ON THE LINE, HUH? NOT BAD.
WHOA!!
TMMM
BSSH

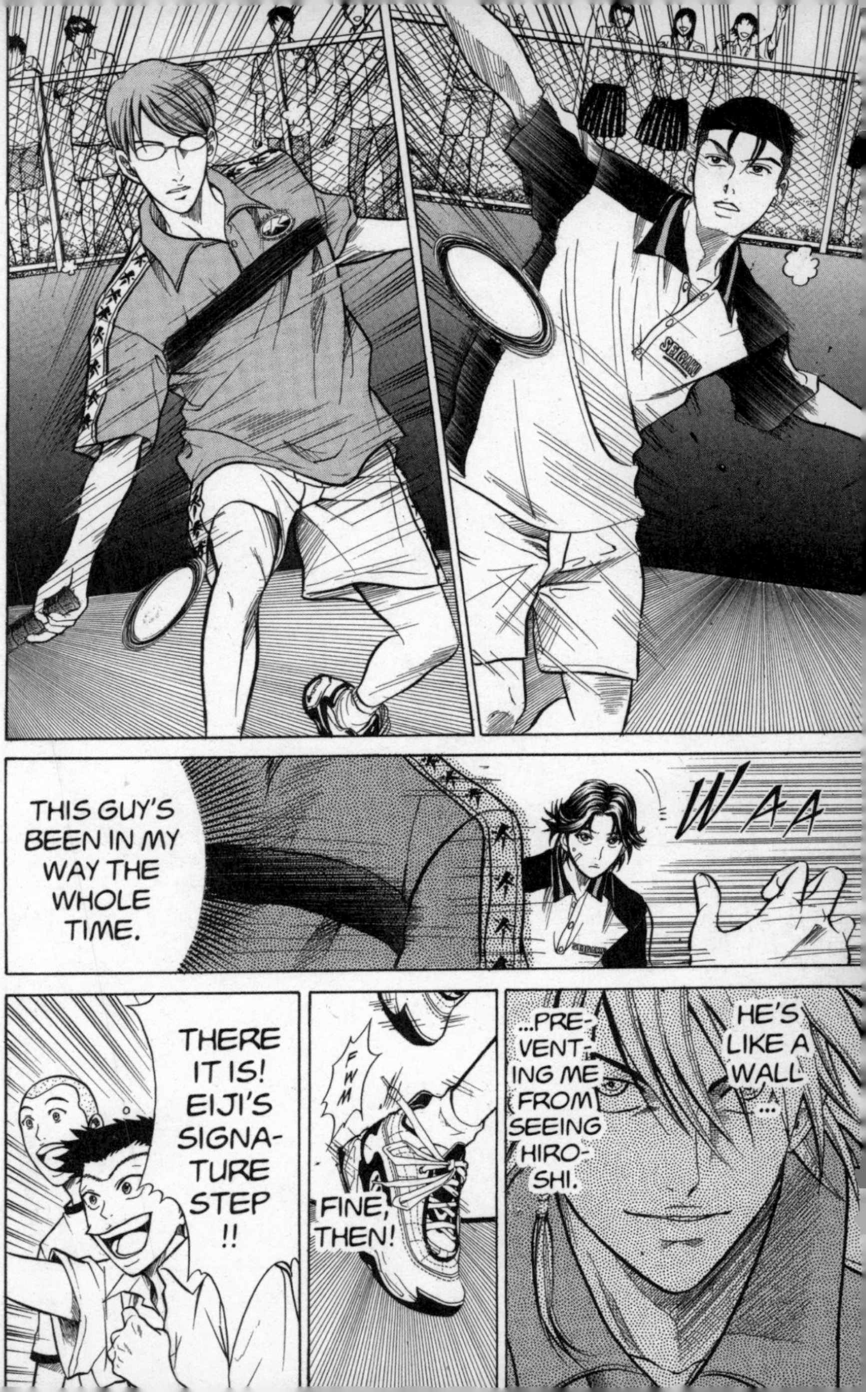
WAA
THIS GUY'S BEEN IN MY WAY THE WHOLE TIME.
HE'S LIKE A WALL...
...PREVENTING ME FROM SEEING HIROSHI.
FWM
FINE, THEN!
THERE IT IS! EIJI'S SIGNATURE STEP!!

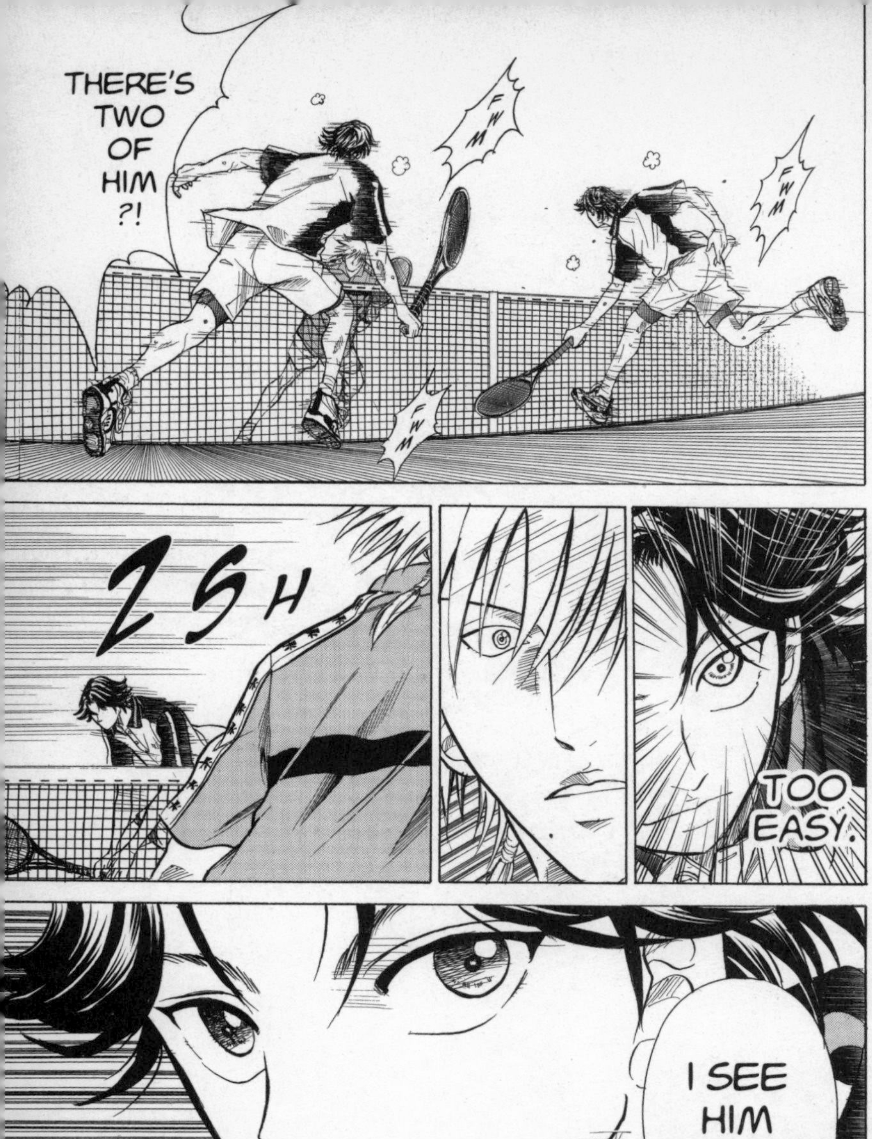
FWM
FWM
THERE'S TWO OF HIM ?!
FWM
TOO EASY.
ZSH
I SEE HIM NOW!

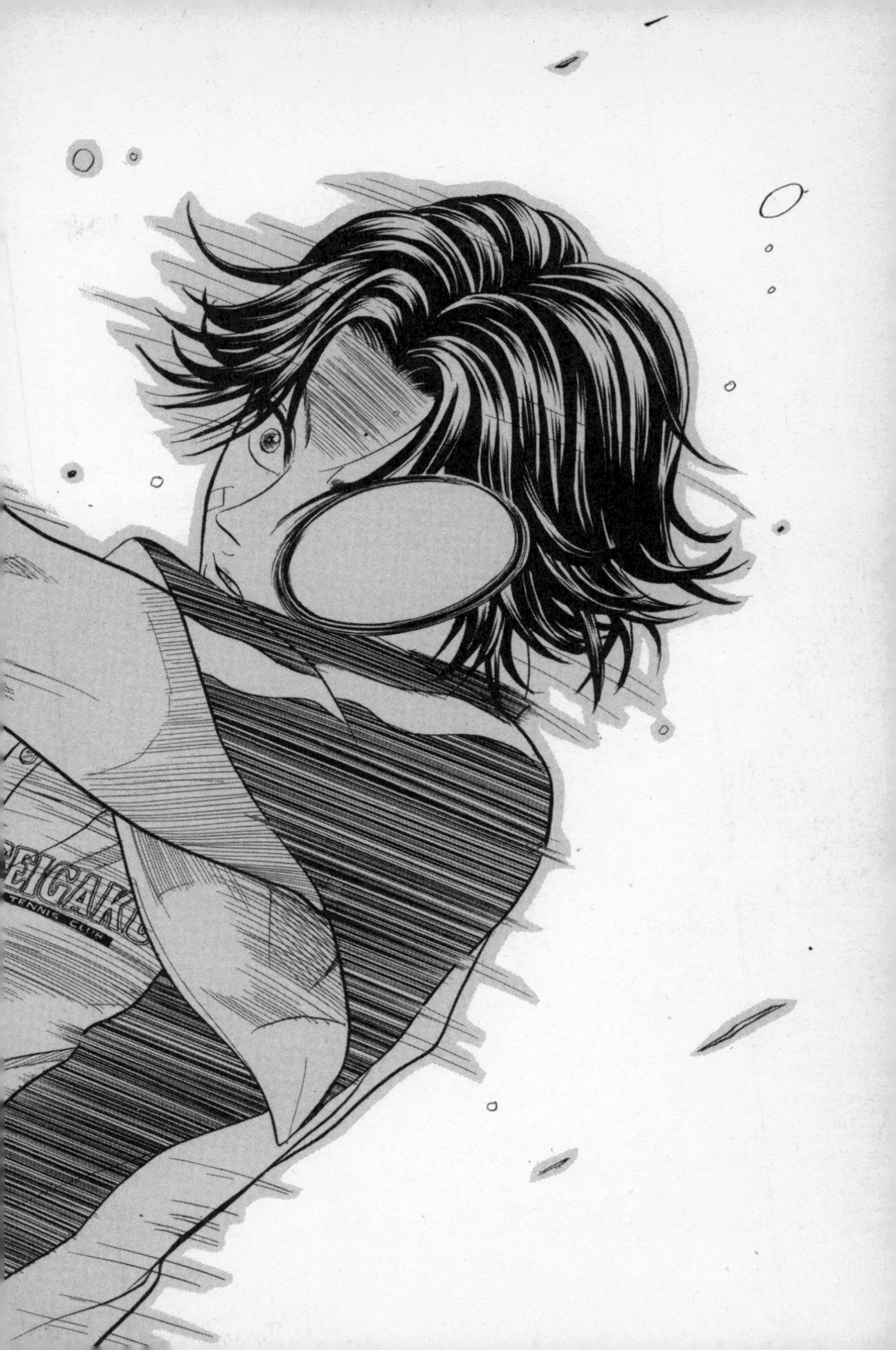
TENNIS CLUB

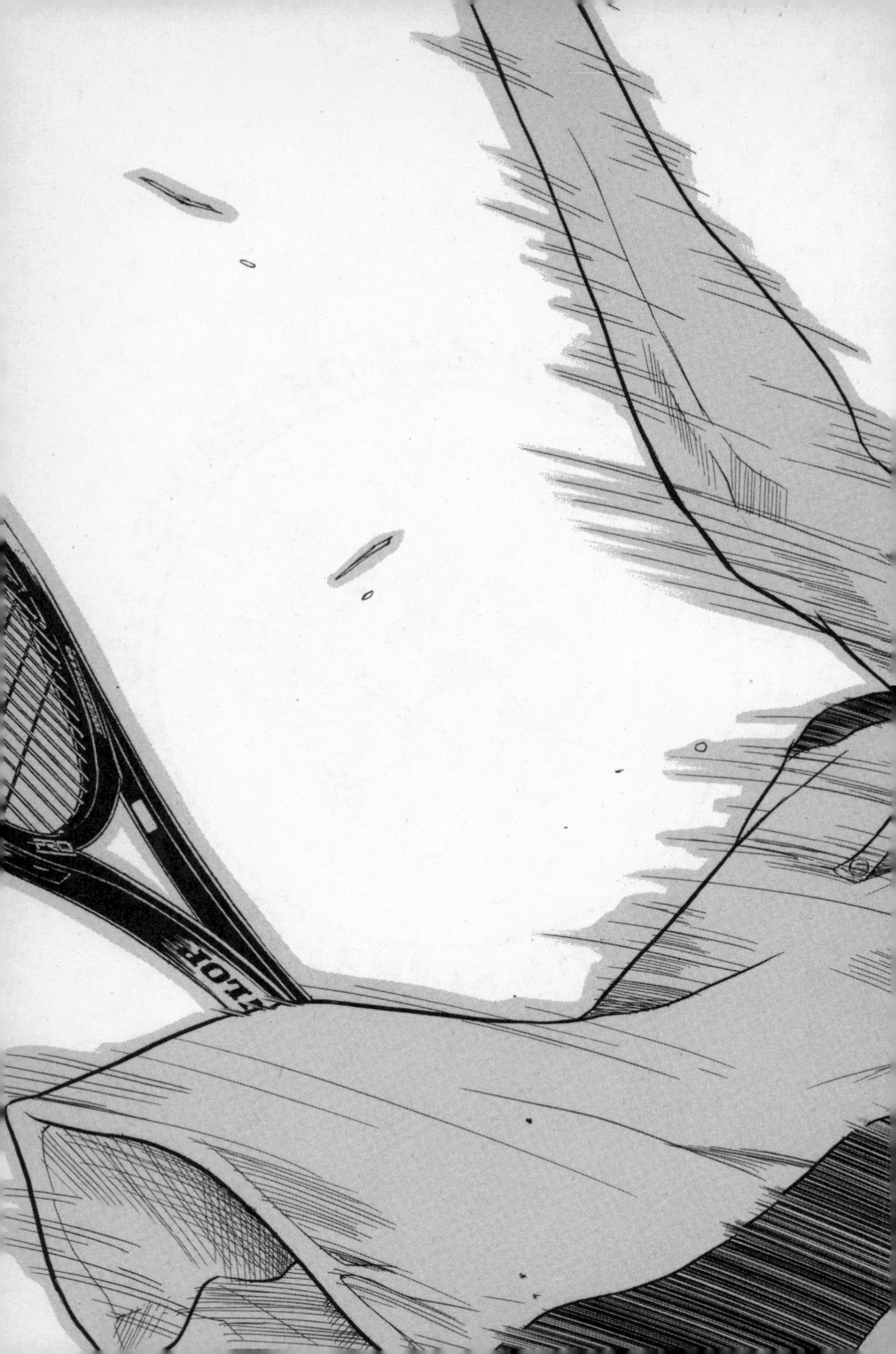

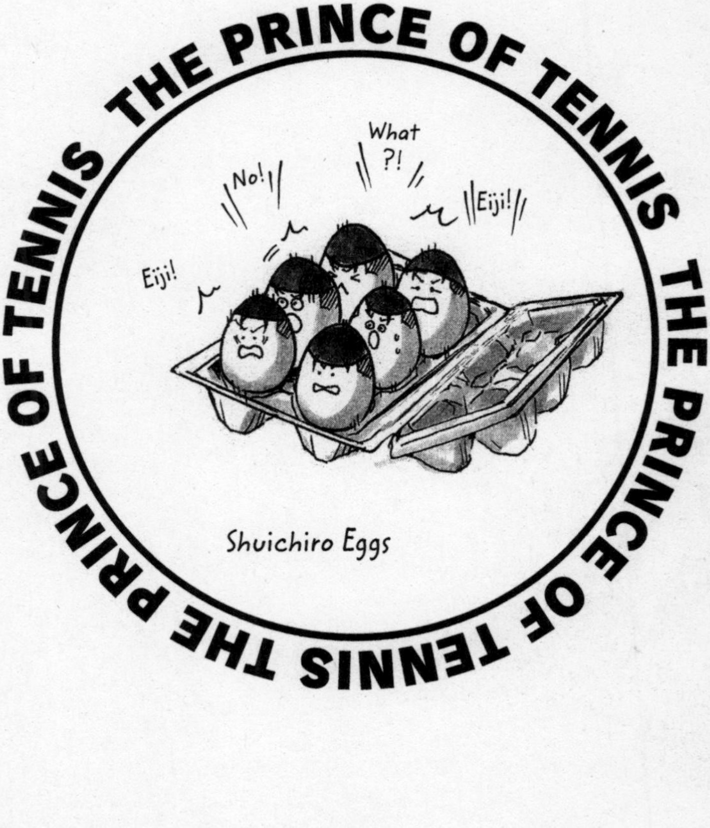
THE PRINCE OF TENNIS THE PRINCE OF TENNIS THE PRINCE OF TENNIS
What ?!
No!
Eiji!
Eiji!
Shuichiro Eggs

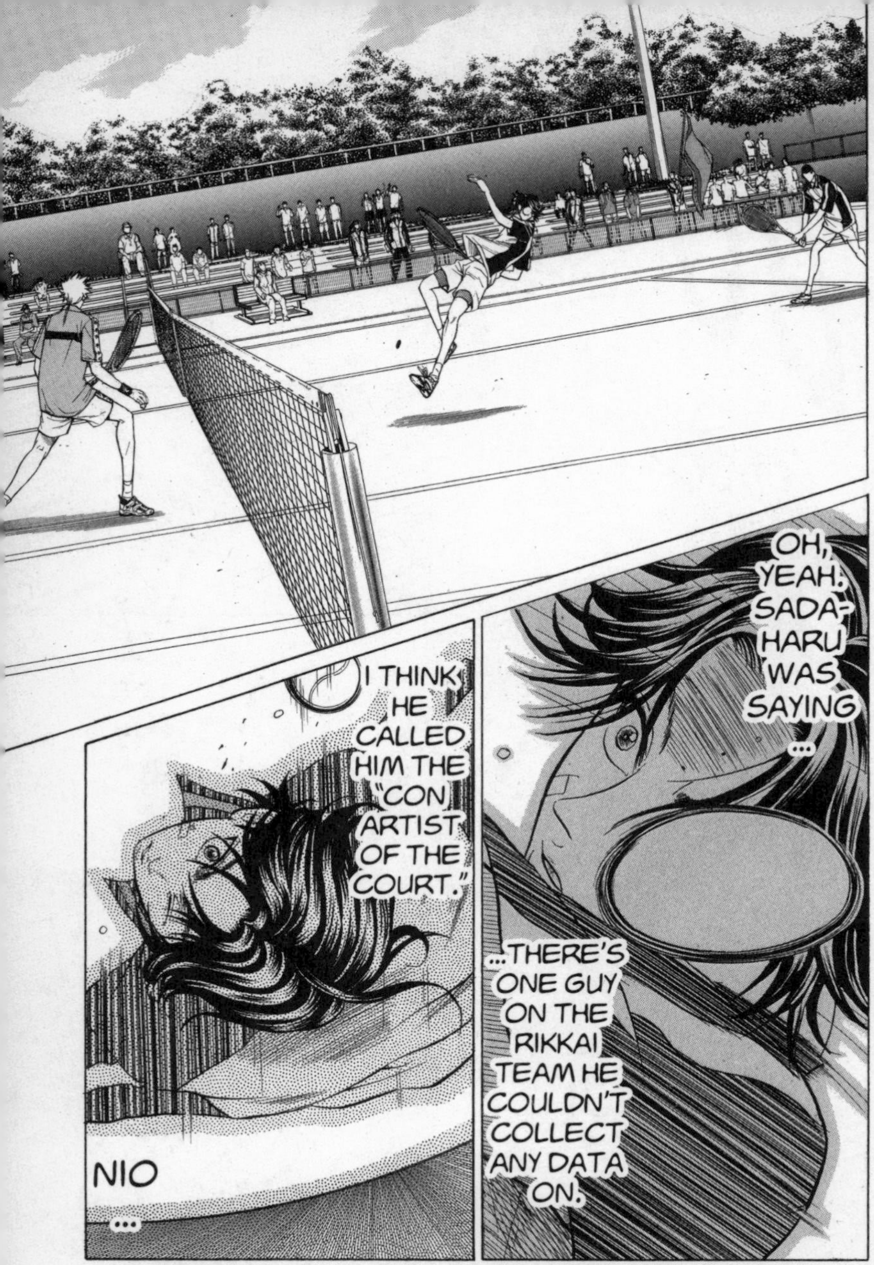
OH, YEAH. SADAHARU WAS SAYING...
...THERE'S ONE GUY ON THE RIKKAI TEAM HE COULDN'T COLLECT ANY DATA ON.
I THINK HE CALLED HIM THE "CON ARTIST OF THE COURT."
NIO...

GENIUS 203: EIJI'S PROMISE

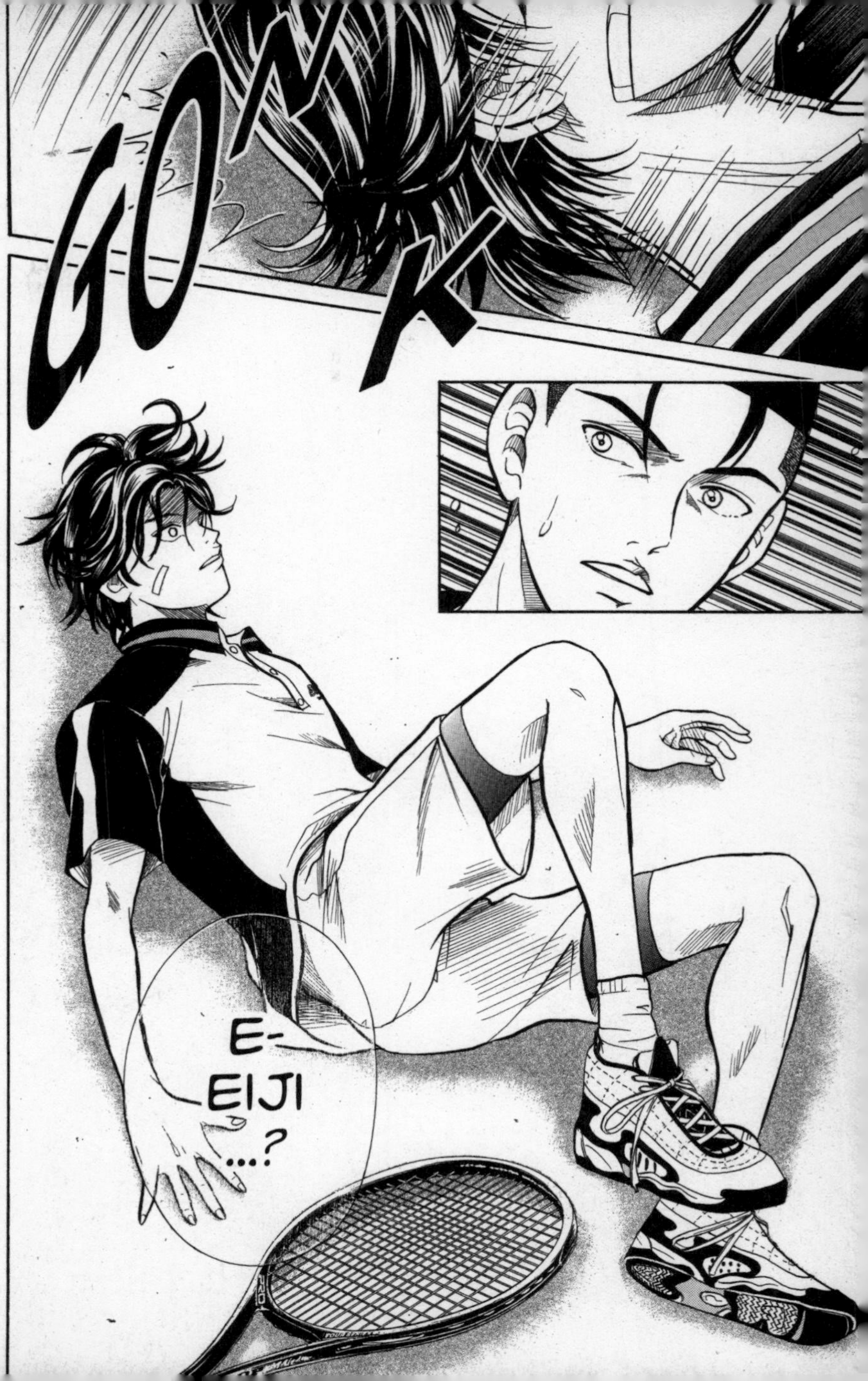
GONK
E-
EIJI
...?

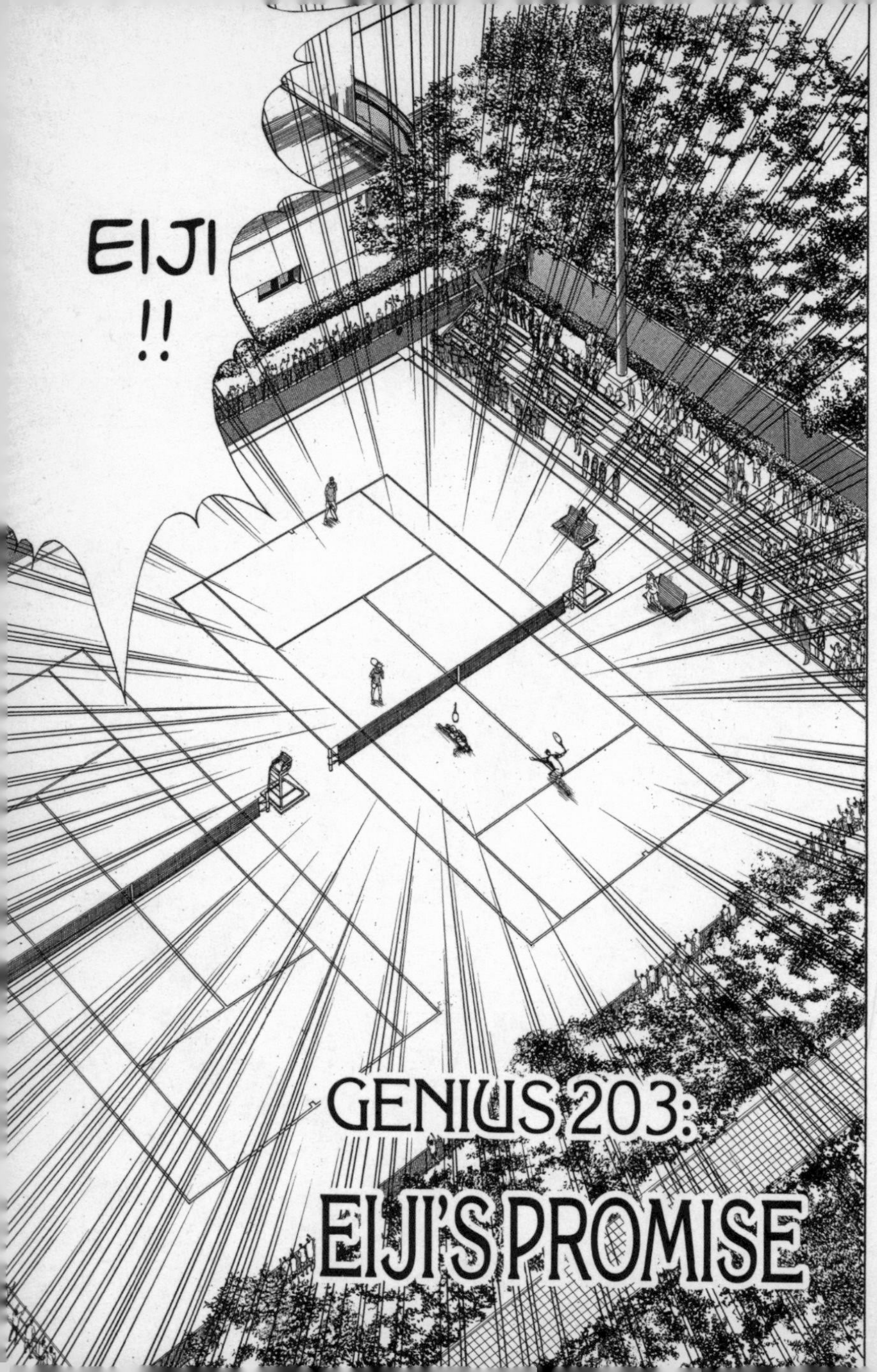
EIJI !!
GENIUS 203:
EIJI'S PROMISE

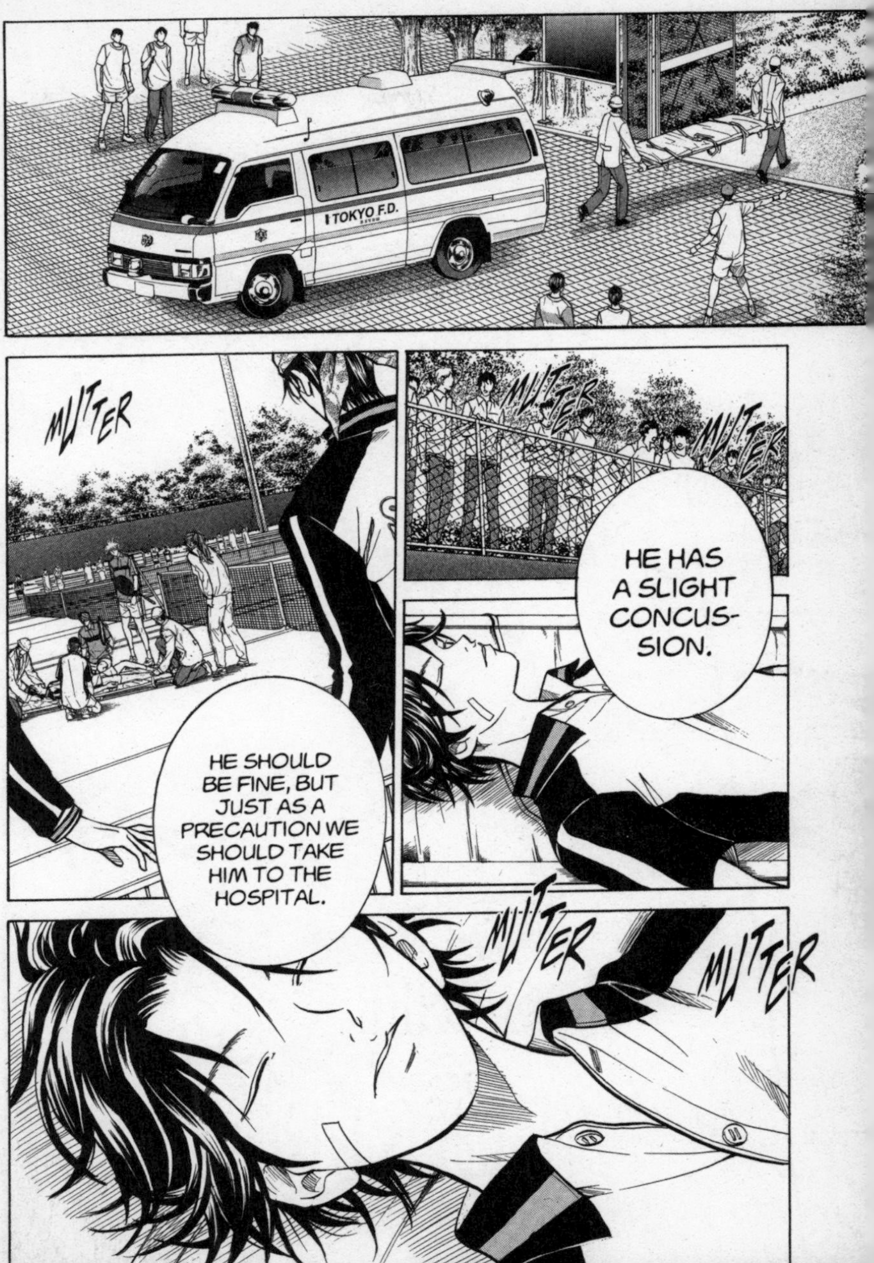
MUTTER
MUTTER
HE HAS A SLIGHT CONCUSSION.
MUTTER
HE SHOULD BE FINE, BUT JUST AS A PRECAUTION WE SHOULD TAKE HIM TO THE HOSPITAL.
MUTTER
MUTTER

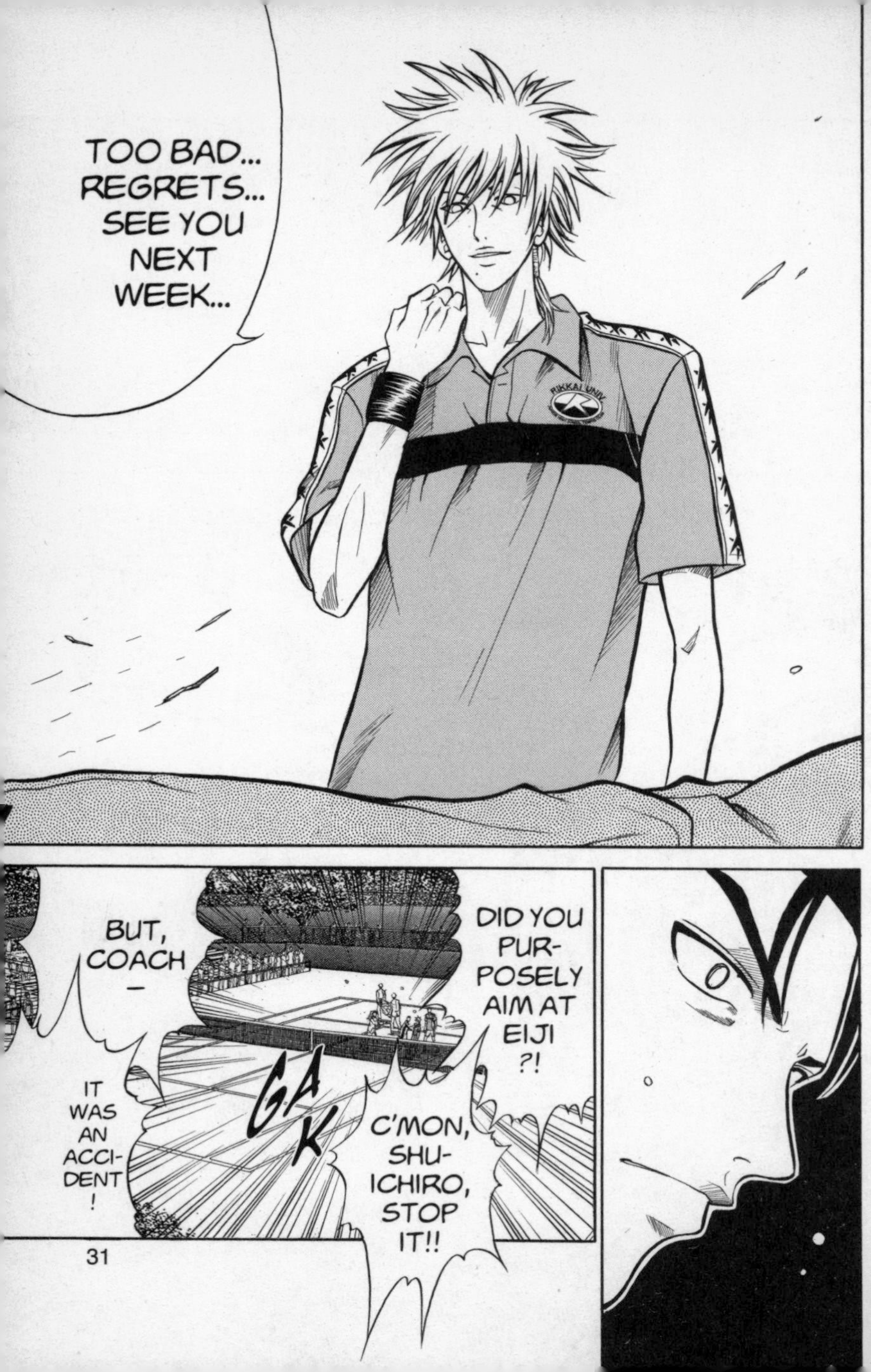
TOO BAD... REGRETS... SEE YOU NEXT WEEK...
DID YOU PURPOSELY AIM AT EIJI?!
BUT, COACH—
IT WAS AN ACCIDENT!
GAK
C'MON, SHUICHIRO, STOP IT!!

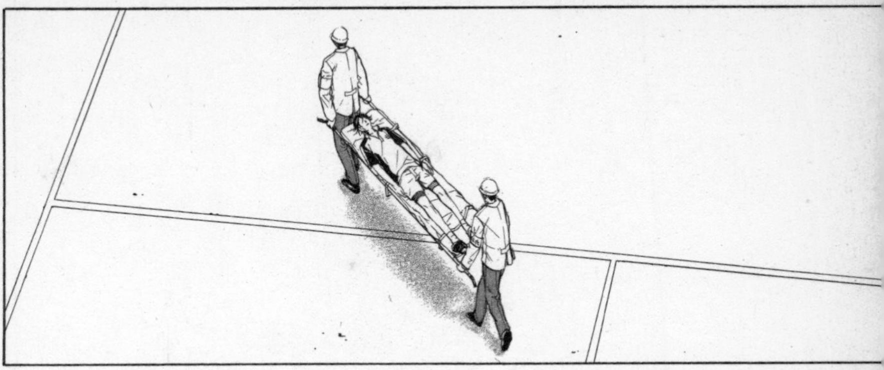

HEY, WAIT! WHERE ARE YOU TAKING ME...? I CAN STILL PLAY!!

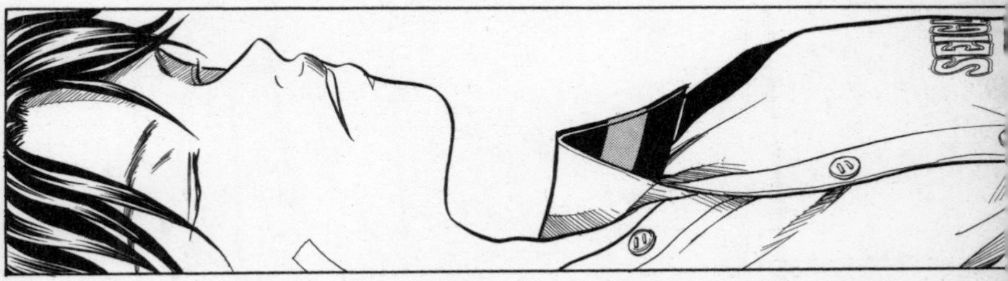

DON'T LET 'EM TAKE ME, SHUICHIRO...

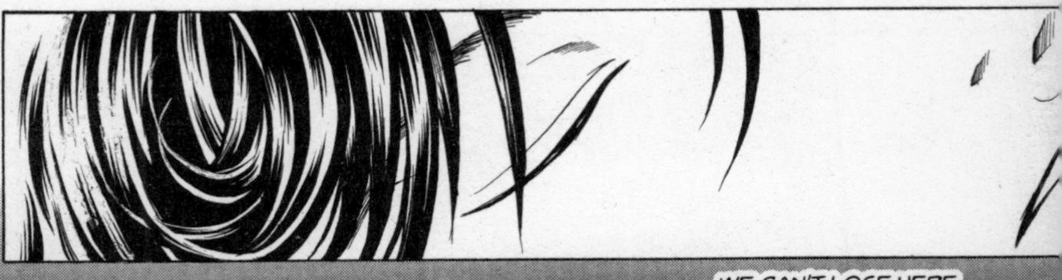

WE CAN'T LOSE HERE...

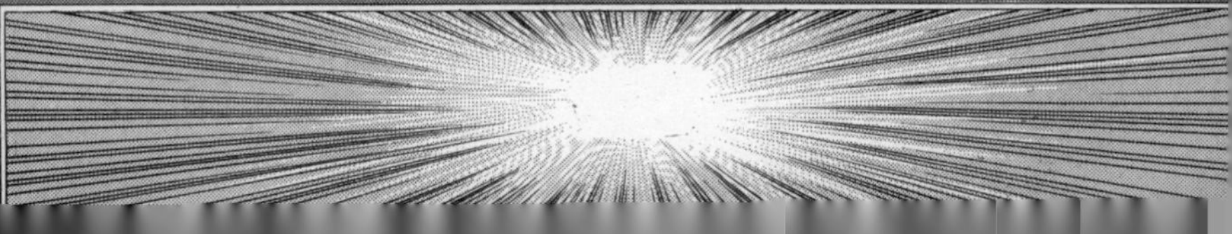

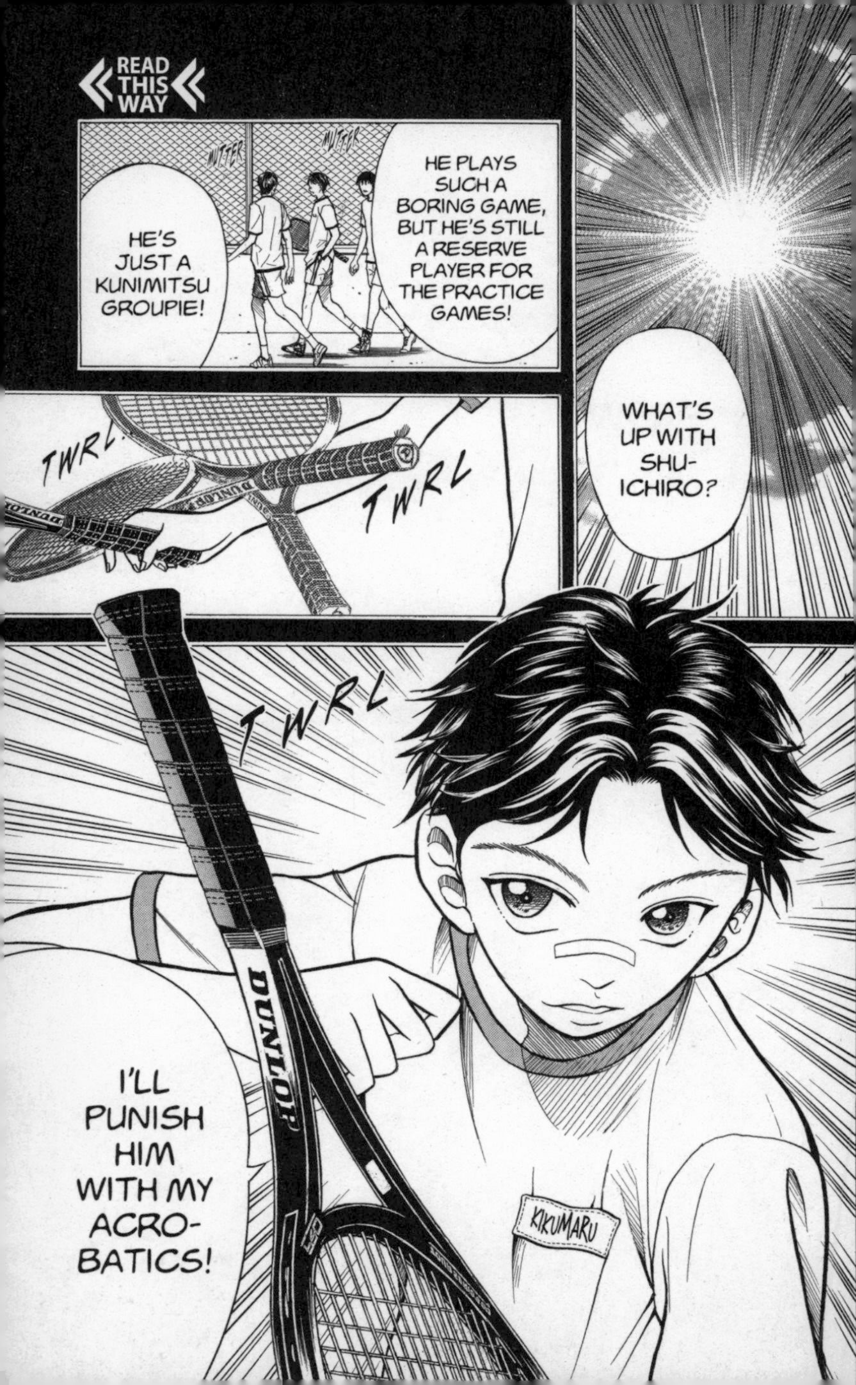
READ THIS WAY
WHAT'S UP WITH SHU-ICHIRO?
MUTTER
MUTTER
HE PLAYS SUCH A BORING GAME, BUT HE'S STILL A RESERVE PLAYER FOR THE PRACTICE GAMES!
HE'S JUST A KUNIMITSU GROUPIE!
TWRL
TWRL
TWRL
I'LL PUNISH HIM WITH MY ACRO-BATICS!
KIKUMARU

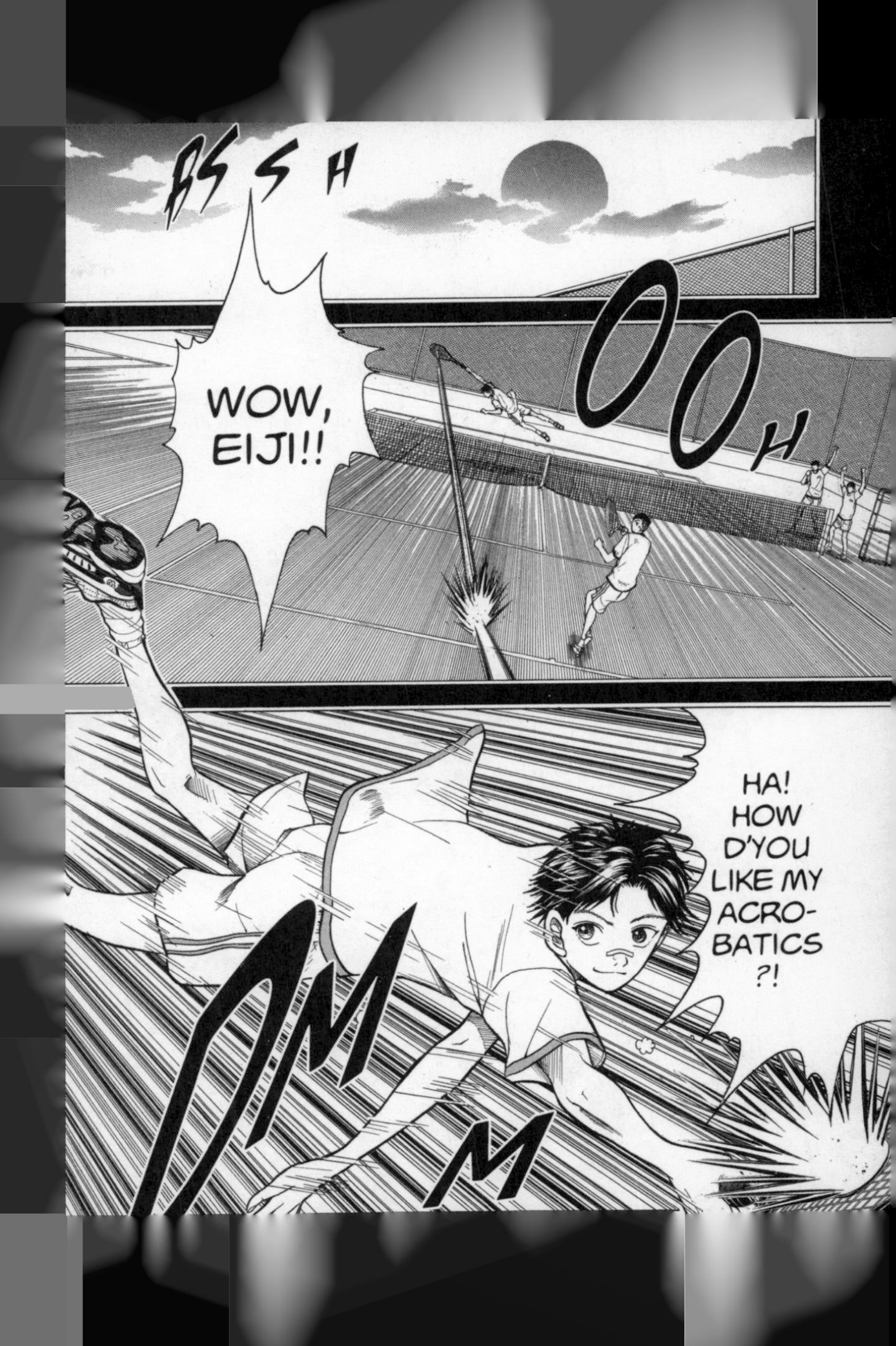
WOW, EIJI!!
OOOH
HA! HOW D'YOU LIKE MY ACRO-BATICS?!

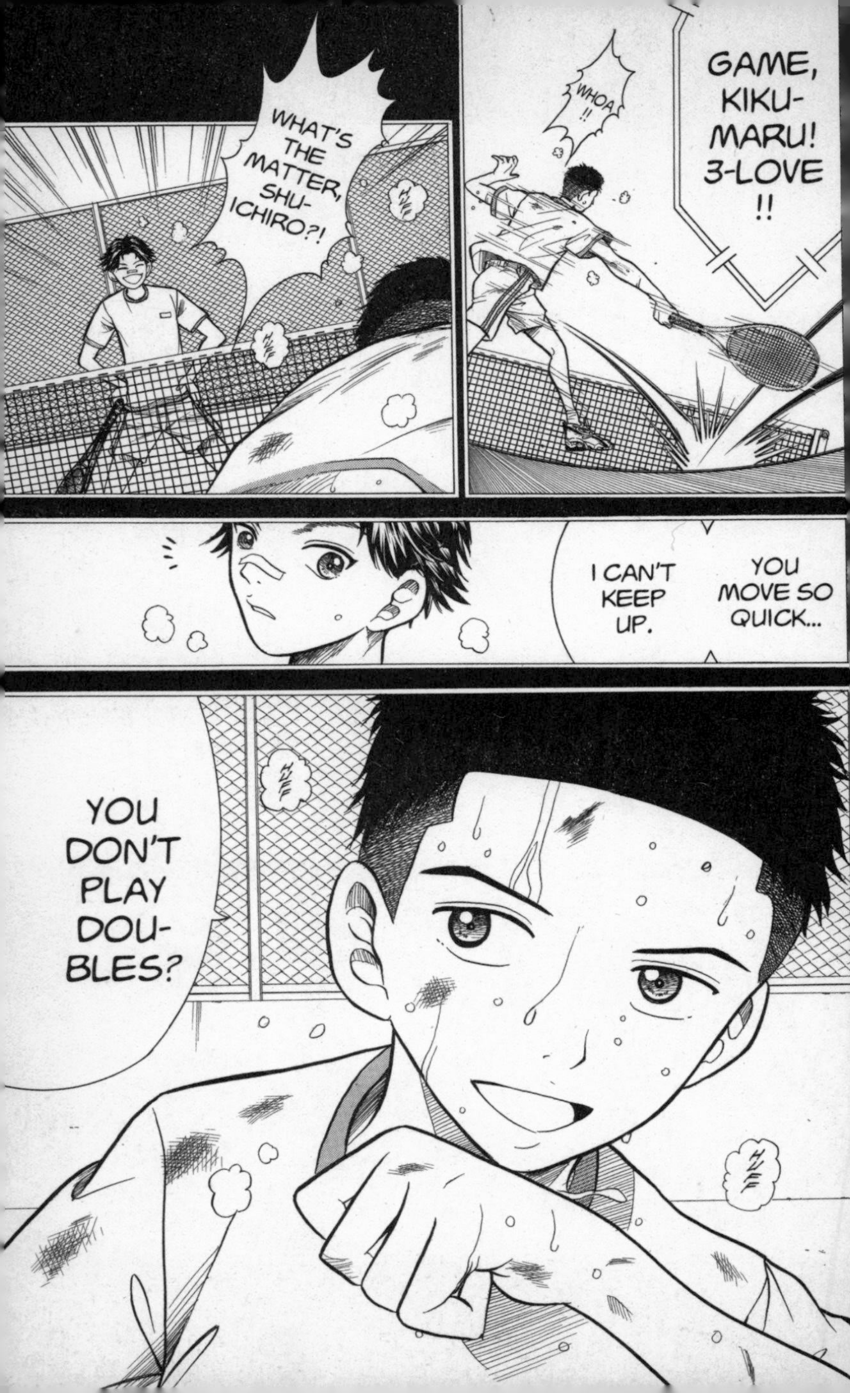
GAME, KIKU-MARU! 3-LOVE !!
WHOA !!
WHAT'S THE MATTER, SHU-ICHIRO?!
HUFF
HUFF
YOU MOVE SO QUICK...
I CAN'T KEEP UP.
YOU DON'T PLAY DOU-BLES?
HUFF
HUFF

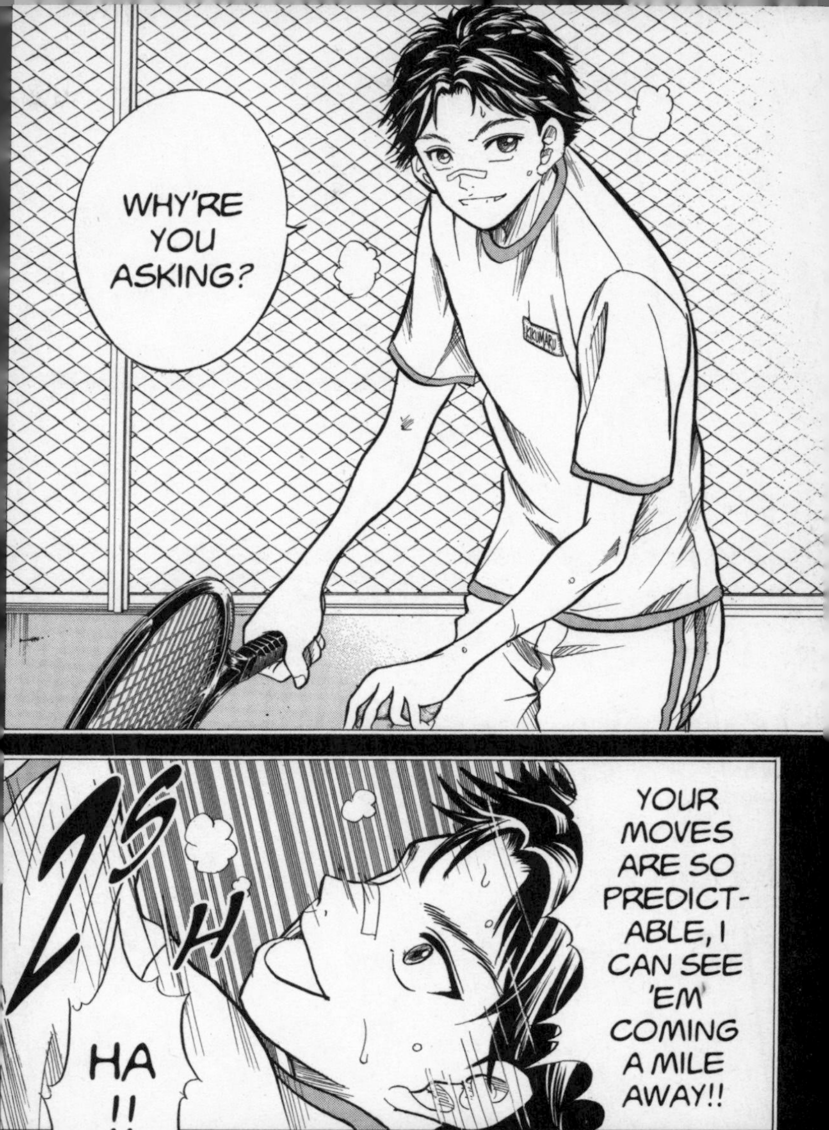
WHY'RE YOU ASKING?
KIKUMARU
ZSH
HA !!
YOUR MOVES ARE SO PREDICT-ABLE, I CAN SEE 'EM COMING A MILE AWAY!!

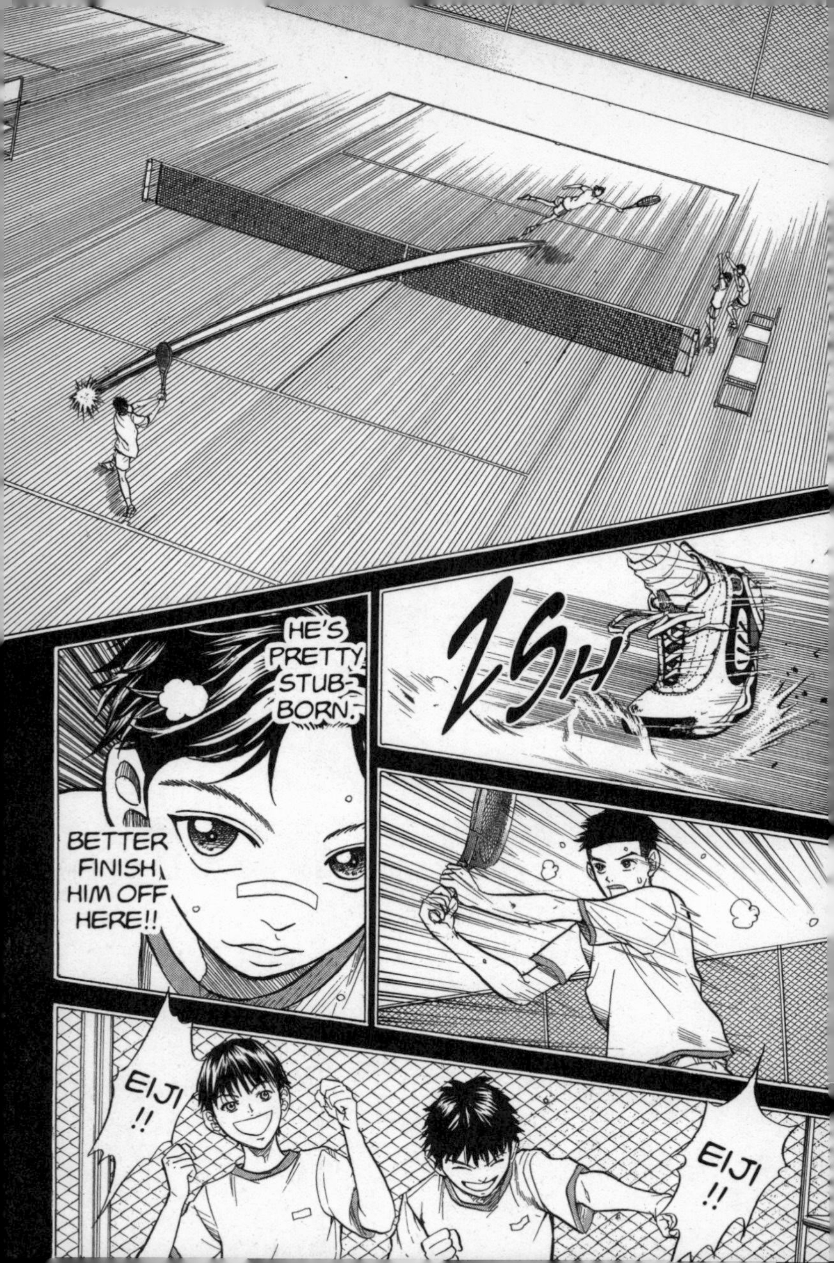
ZSH
HE'S PRETTY STUBBORN.
BETTER FINISH HIM OFF HERE!!
EIJI!!
EIJI!!

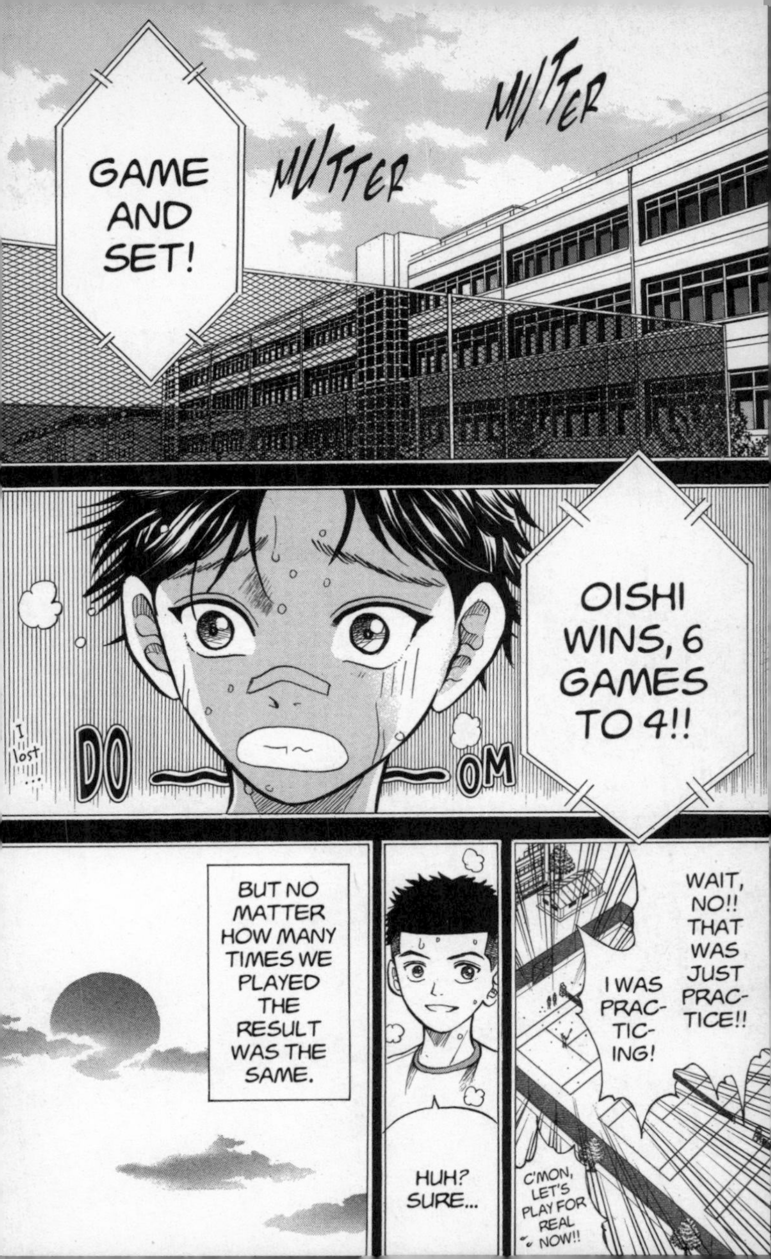
GAME AND SET!
MUTTER
MUTTER
OISHI WINS, 6 GAMES TO 4!!
DO—OM
I lost...
WAIT, NO!! THAT WAS JUST PRAC-TICE!!
I WAS PRAC-TIC-ING!
C'MON, LET'S PLAY FOR REAL NOW!!
HUH? SURE...
BUT NO MATTER HOW MANY TIMES WE PLAYED THE RESULT WAS THE SAME.

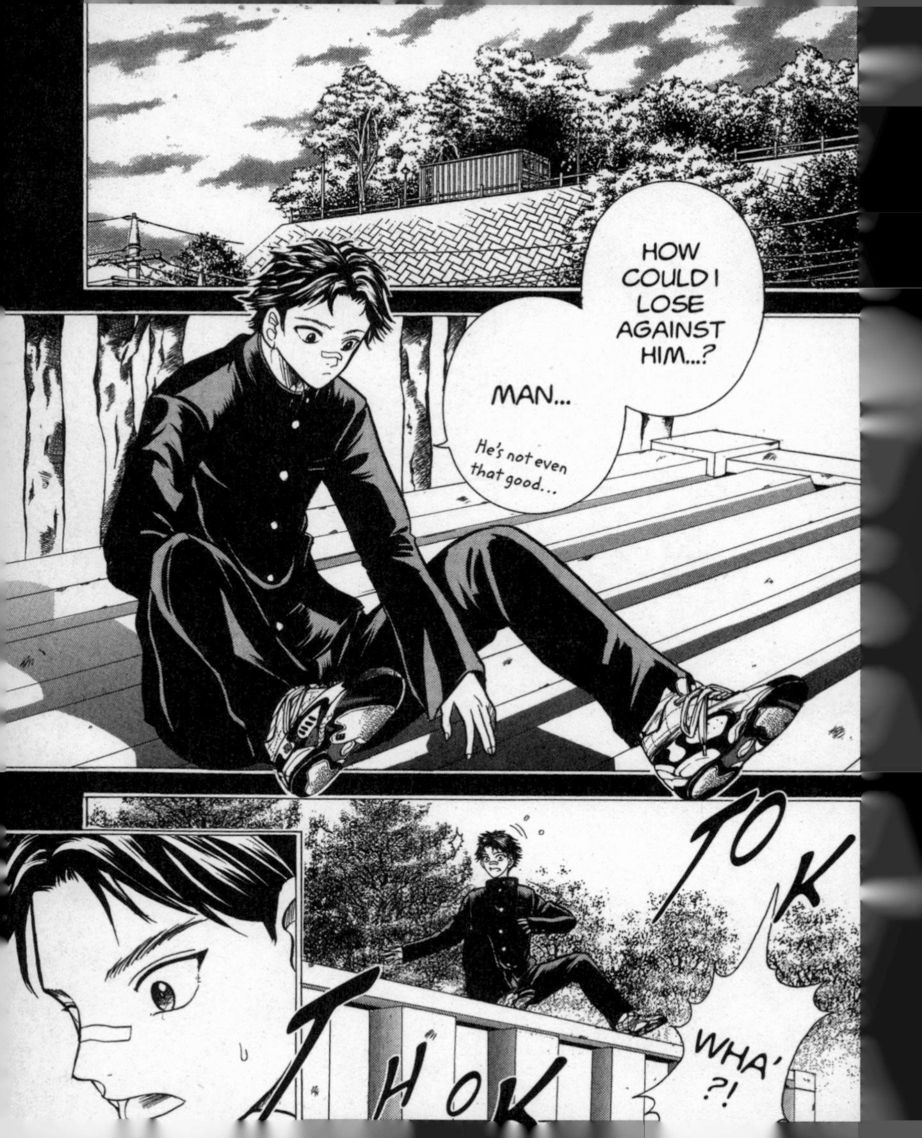
HOW COULD I LOSE AGAINST HIM...?
MAN...
He's not even that good...
TOK
WHA'?!
THOK

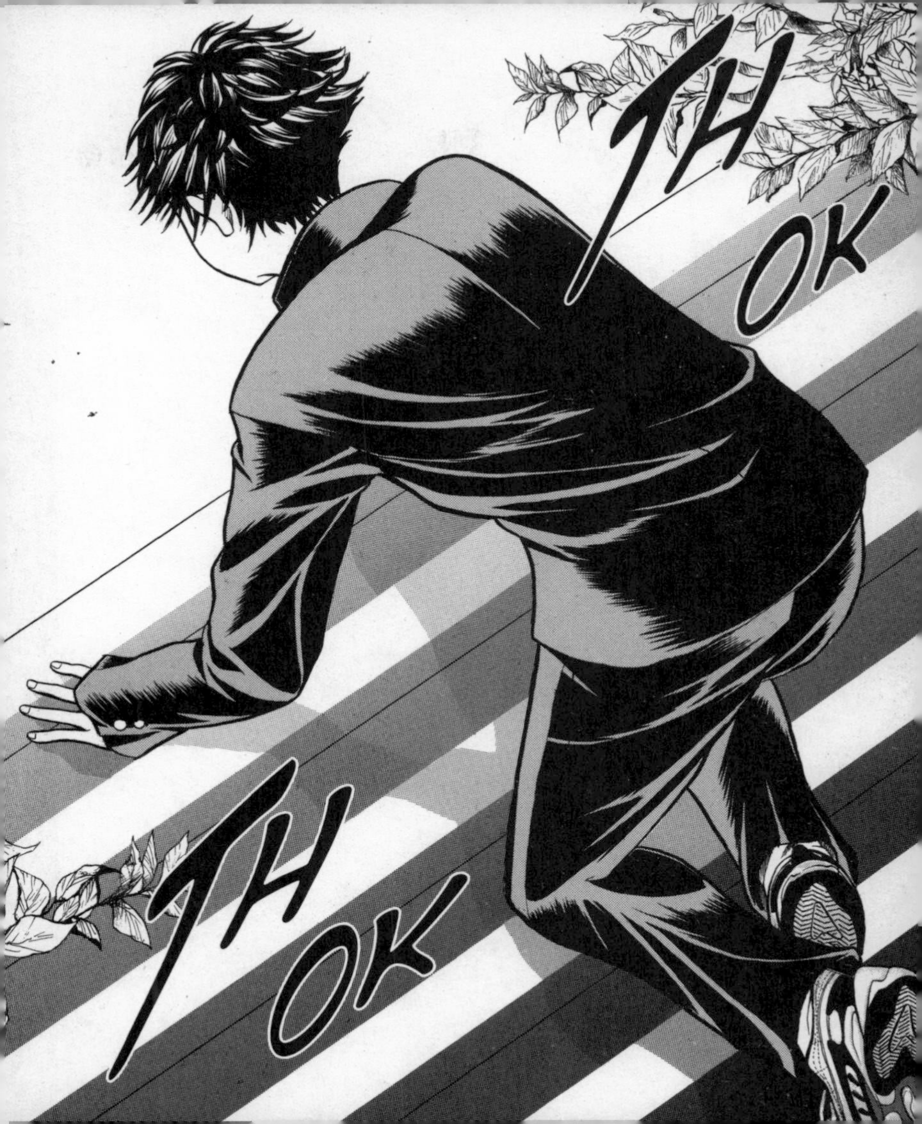
THOK
THOK

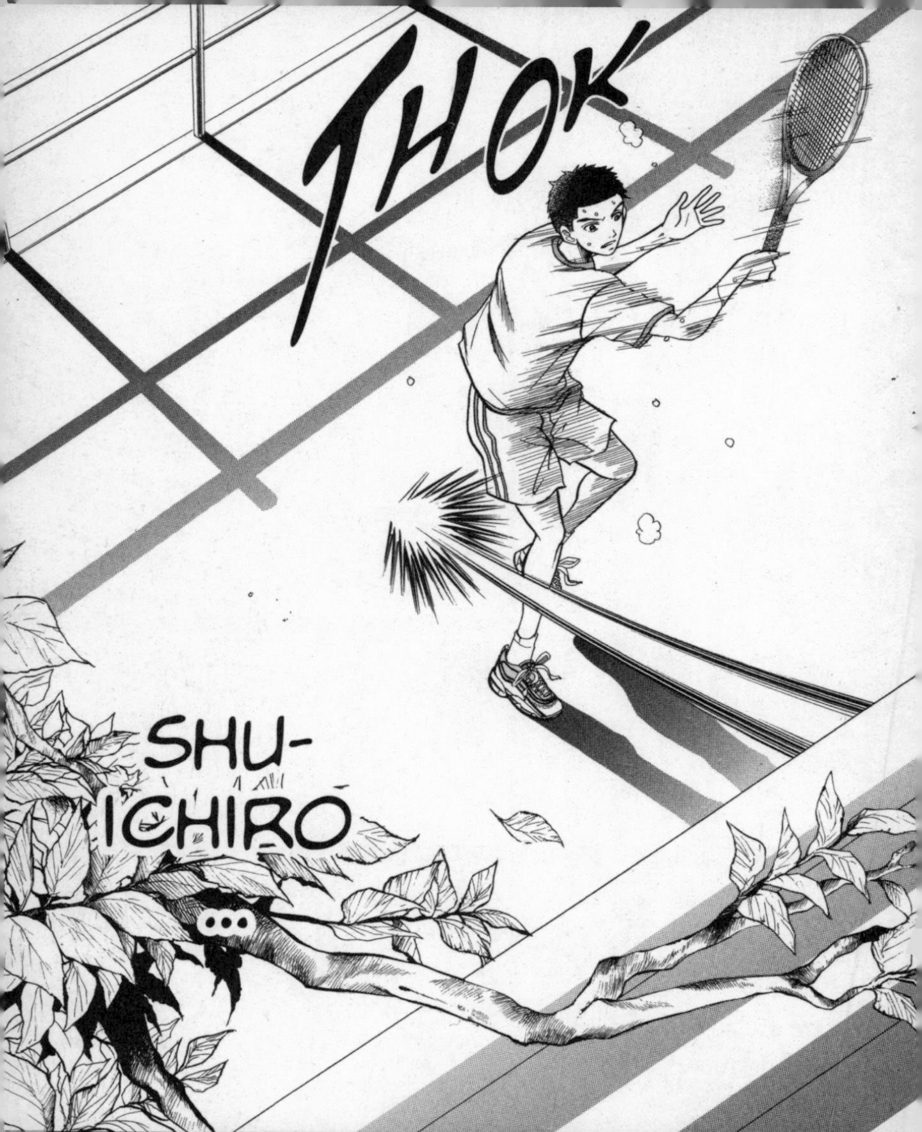
THOK
SHU-
ICHIRO
...

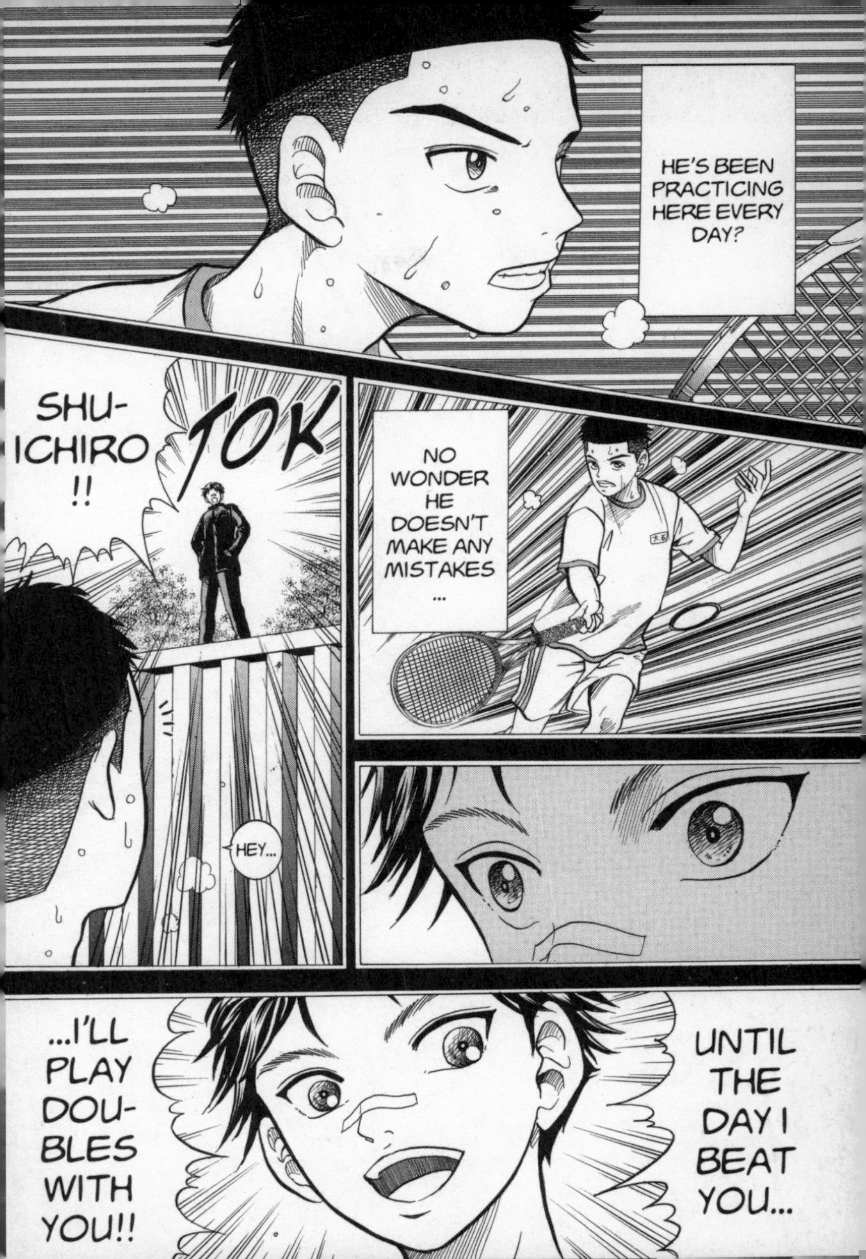
HE'S BEEN PRACTICING HERE EVERY DAY?
NO WONDER HE DOESN'T MAKE ANY MISTAKES ...
TOK
SHU-ICHIRO !!
HEY...
UNTIL THE DAY I BEAT YOU...
...I'LL PLAY DOU-BLES WITH YOU!!

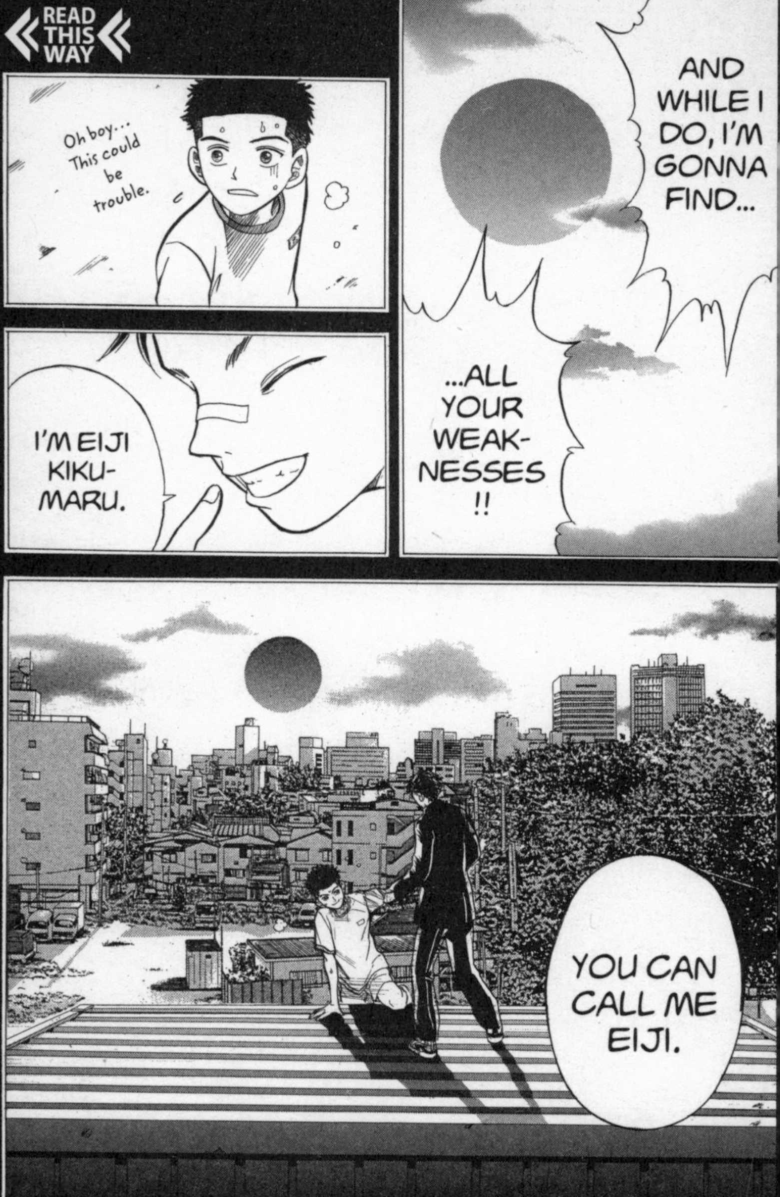
READ THIS WAY
AND WHILE I DO, I'M GONNA FIND...
...ALL YOUR WEAKNESSES !!
Oh boy... This could be trouble.
I'M EIJI KIKUMARU.
YOU CAN CALL ME EIJI.

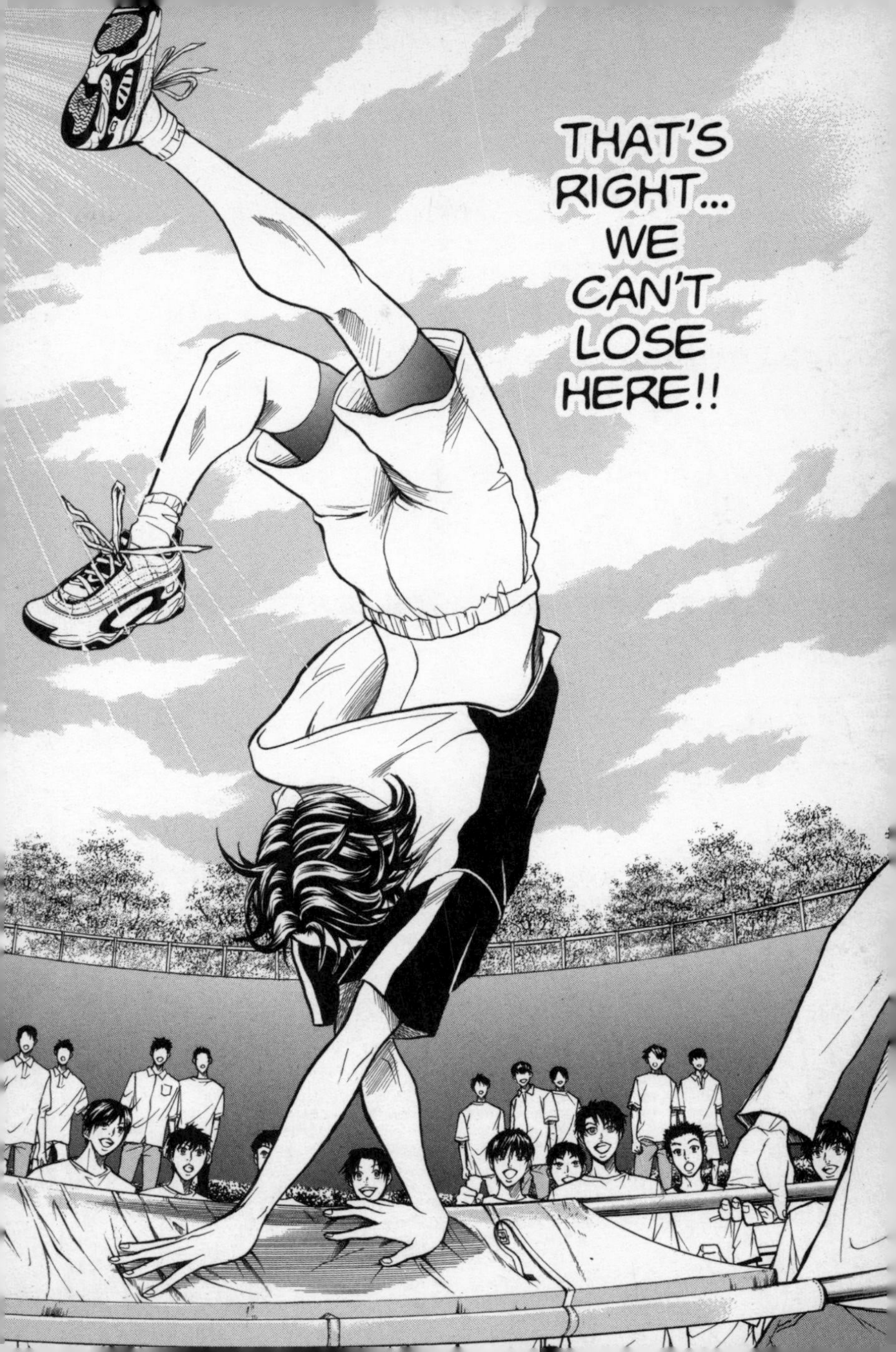
THAT'S RIGHT... WE CAN'T LOSE HERE!!

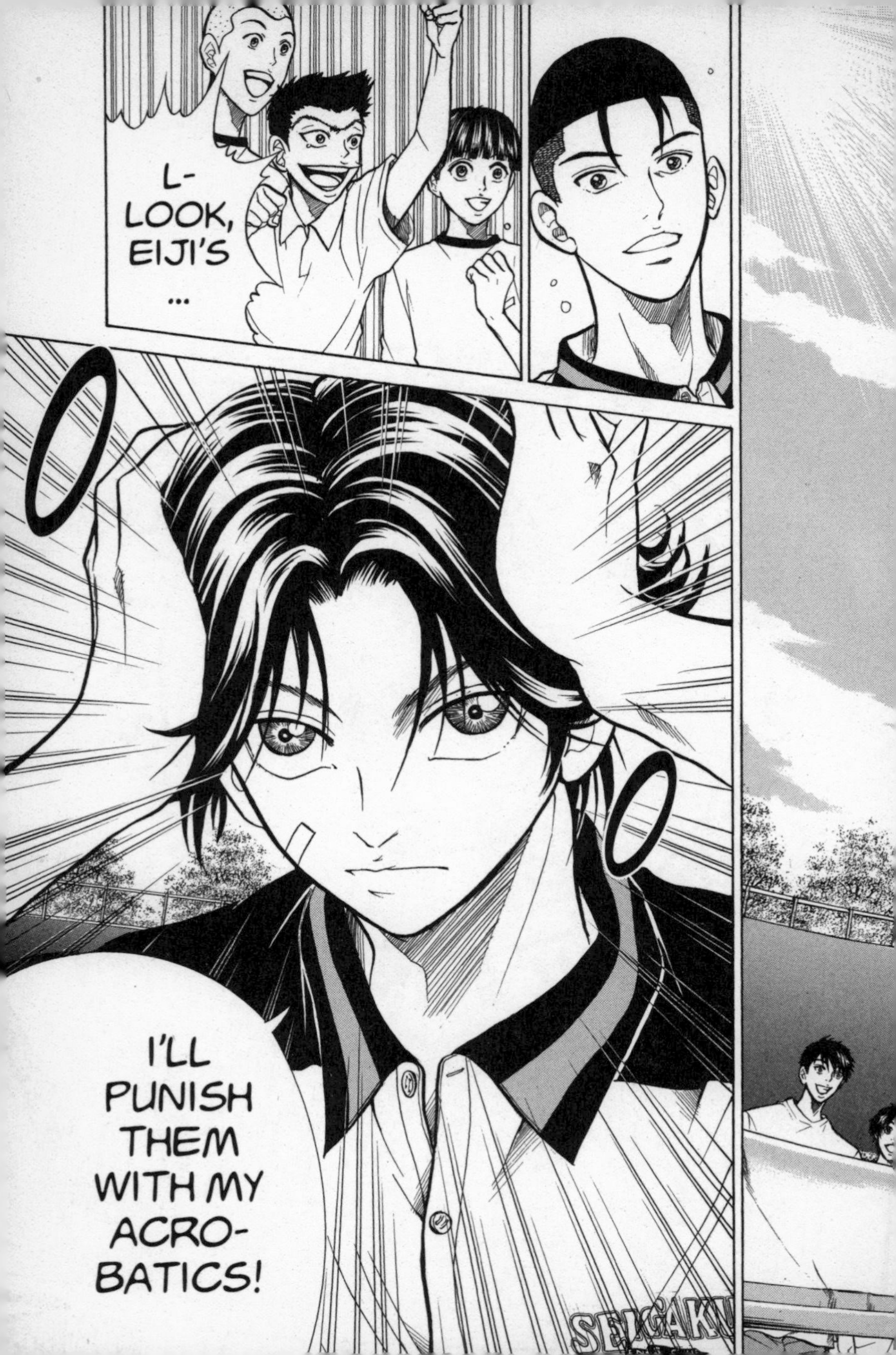
L-LOOK, EIJI'S ...
I'LL PUNISH THEM WITH MY ACRO-BATICS!
SEIGAKU

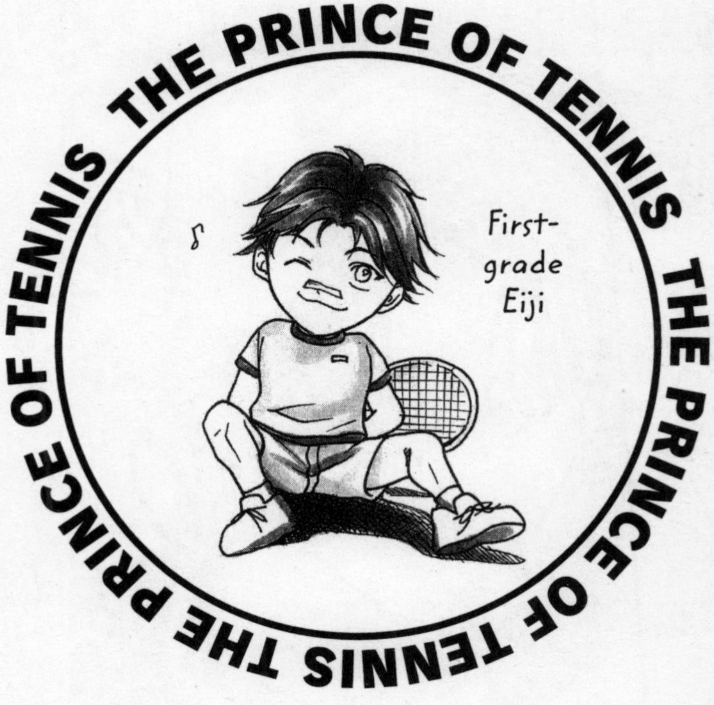
THE PRINCE OF TENNIS THE PRINCE OF TENNIS THE PRINCE OF TENNIS
First-grade Eiji

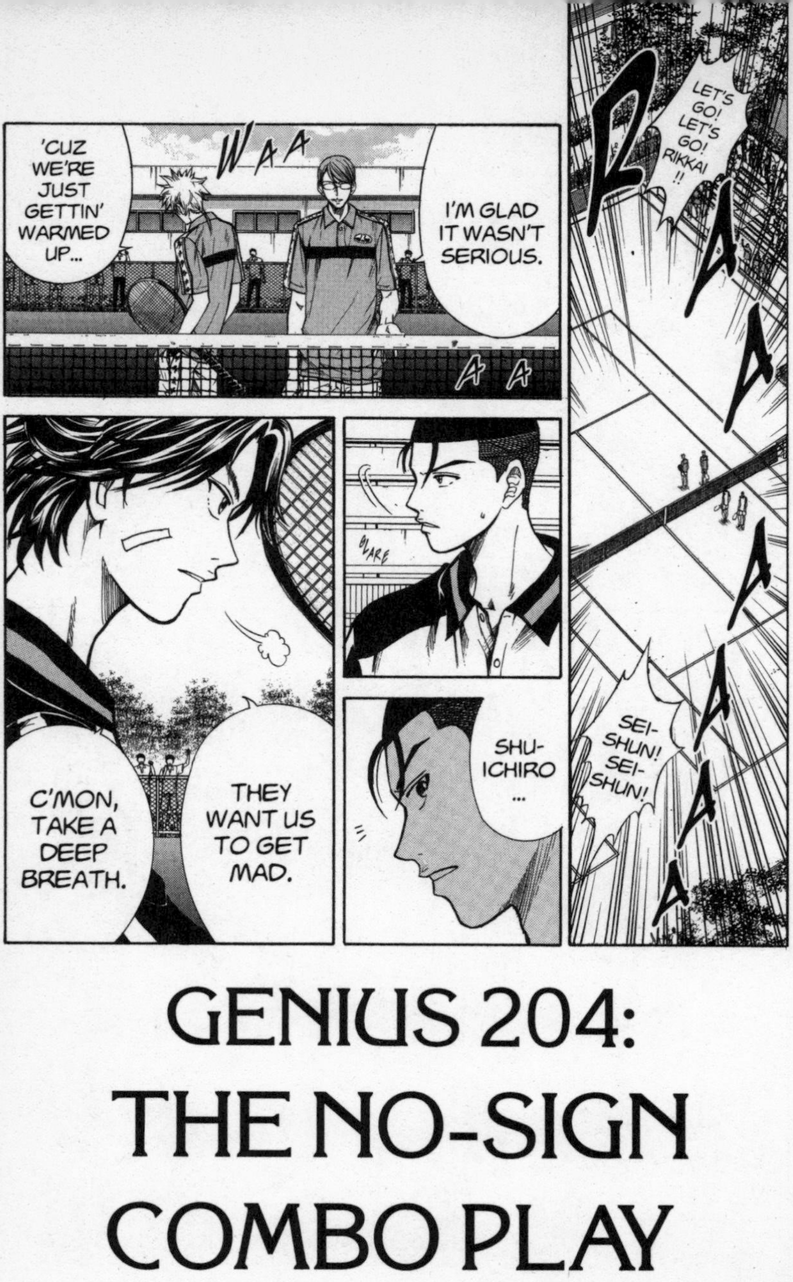
LET'S GO! LET'S GO! RIKKAI !!
SEI-SHUN! SEI-SHUN!
I'M GLAD IT WASN'T SERIOUS.
'CUZ WE'RE JUST GETTIN' WARMED UP...
WAA
AA
GLARE
SHU-ICHIRO ...
THEY WANT US TO GET MAD.
C'MON, TAKE A DEEP BREATH.

GENIUS 204: THE NO-SIGN COMBO PLAY

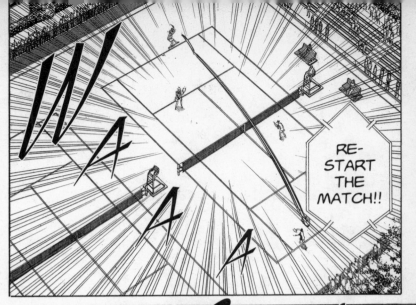

RE-START THE MATCH!!

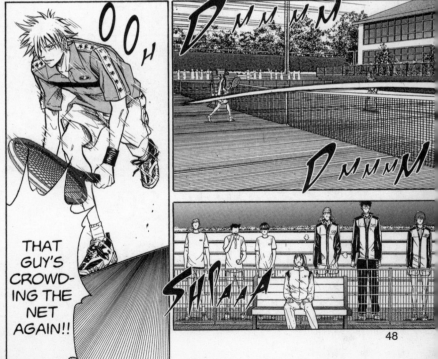

OOH

THAT GUY'S CROWDING THE NET AGAIN!!

DMMMM

DMMMM

SHAAA

48

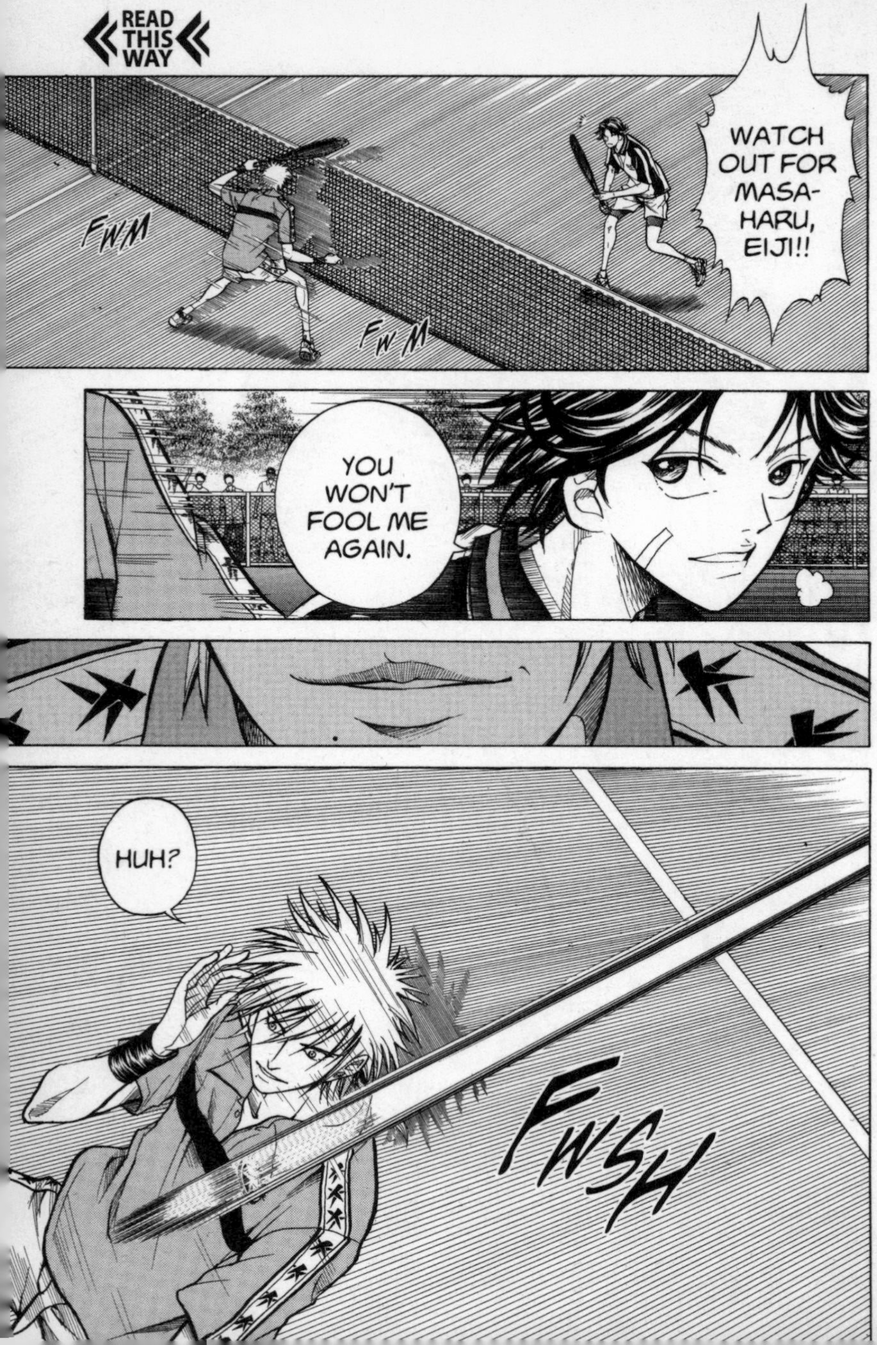
READ THIS WAY
WATCH OUT FOR MASA-HARU, EIJI!!
FWM
FWM
YOU WON'T FOOL ME AGAIN.
HUH?
FWSH

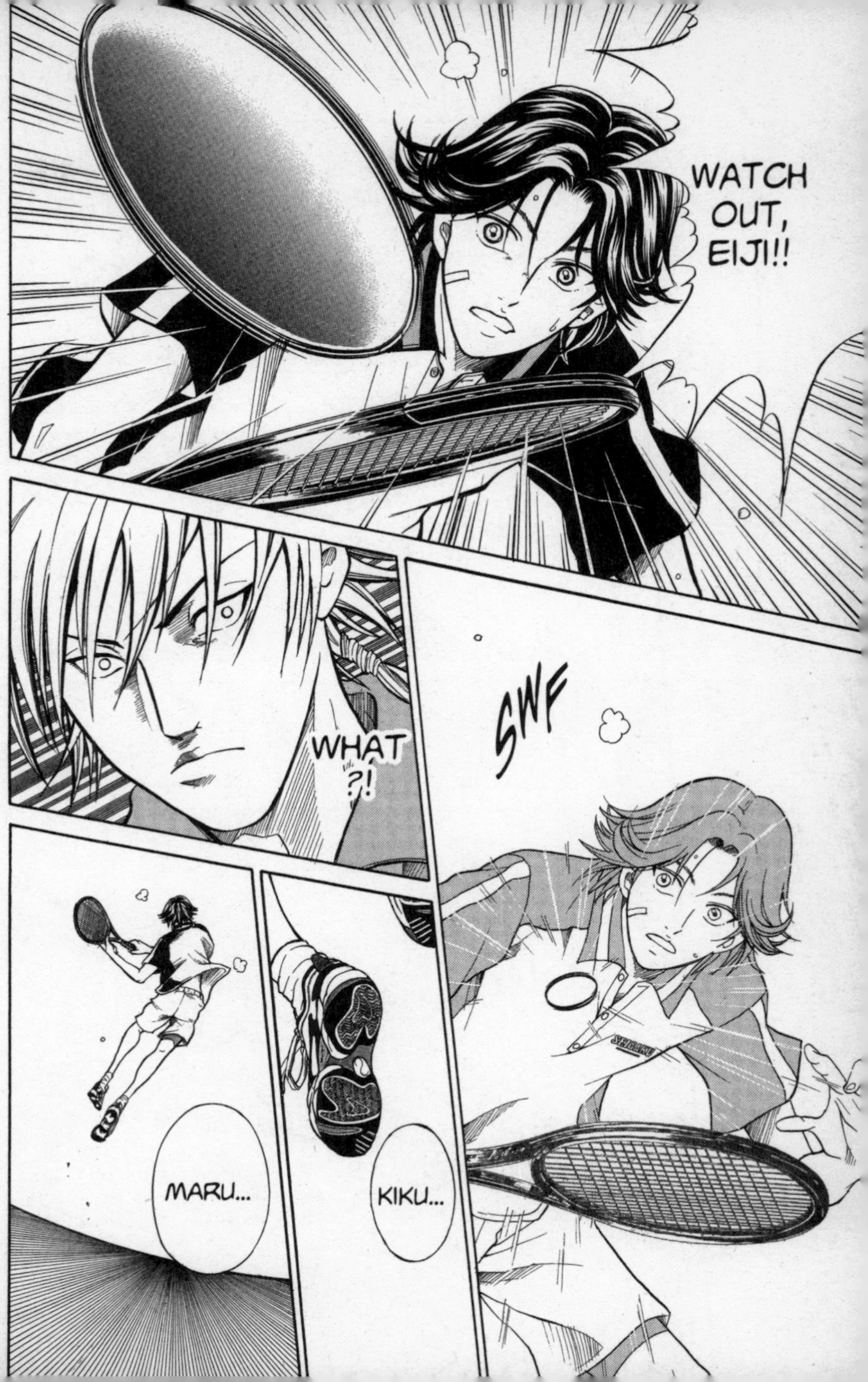
WATCH OUT, EIJI!!
SWF
WHAT ?!
KIKU...
MARU...

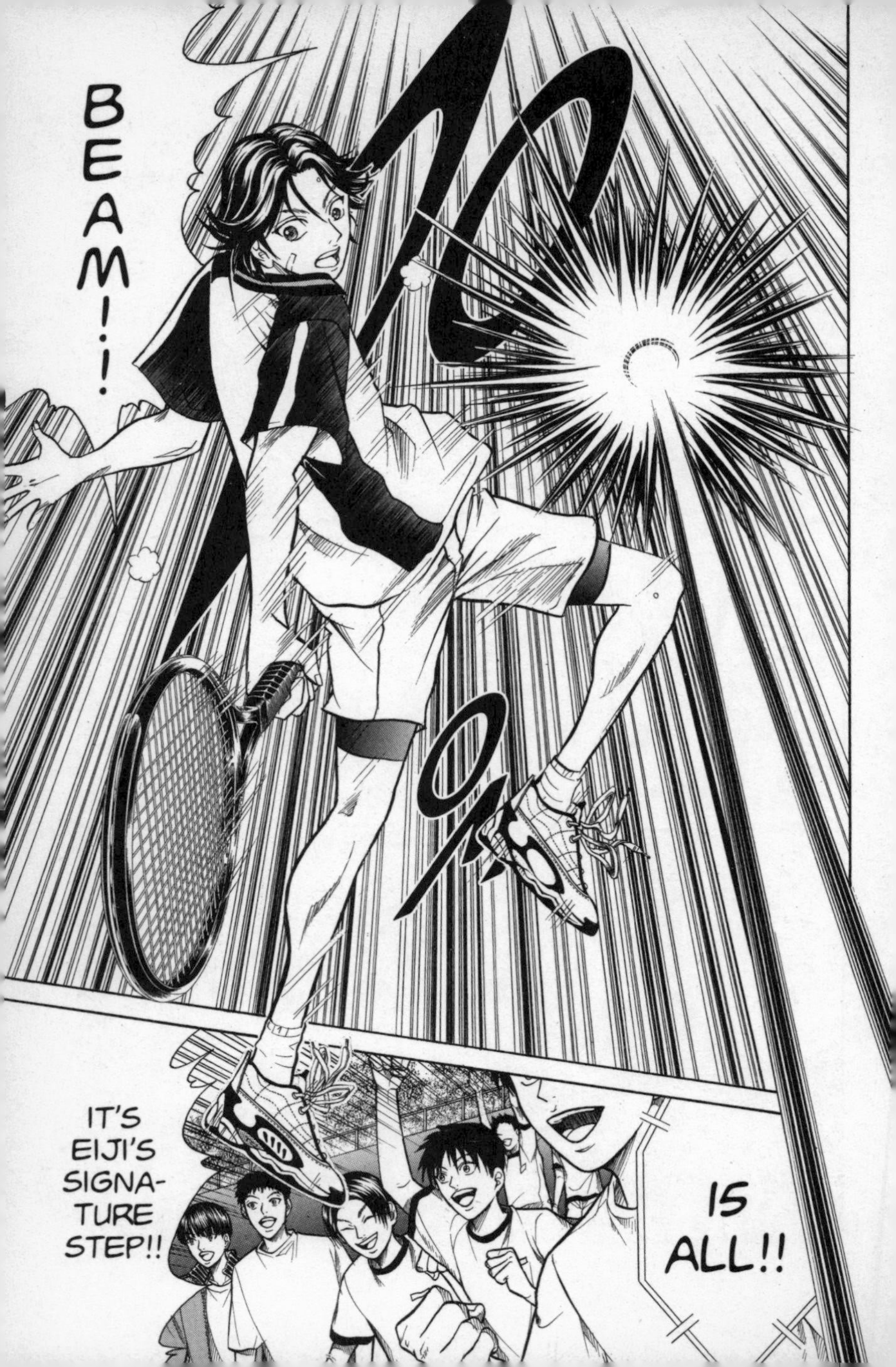
BEAM!!
15 ALL!!
IT'S EIJI'S SIGNATURE STEP!!

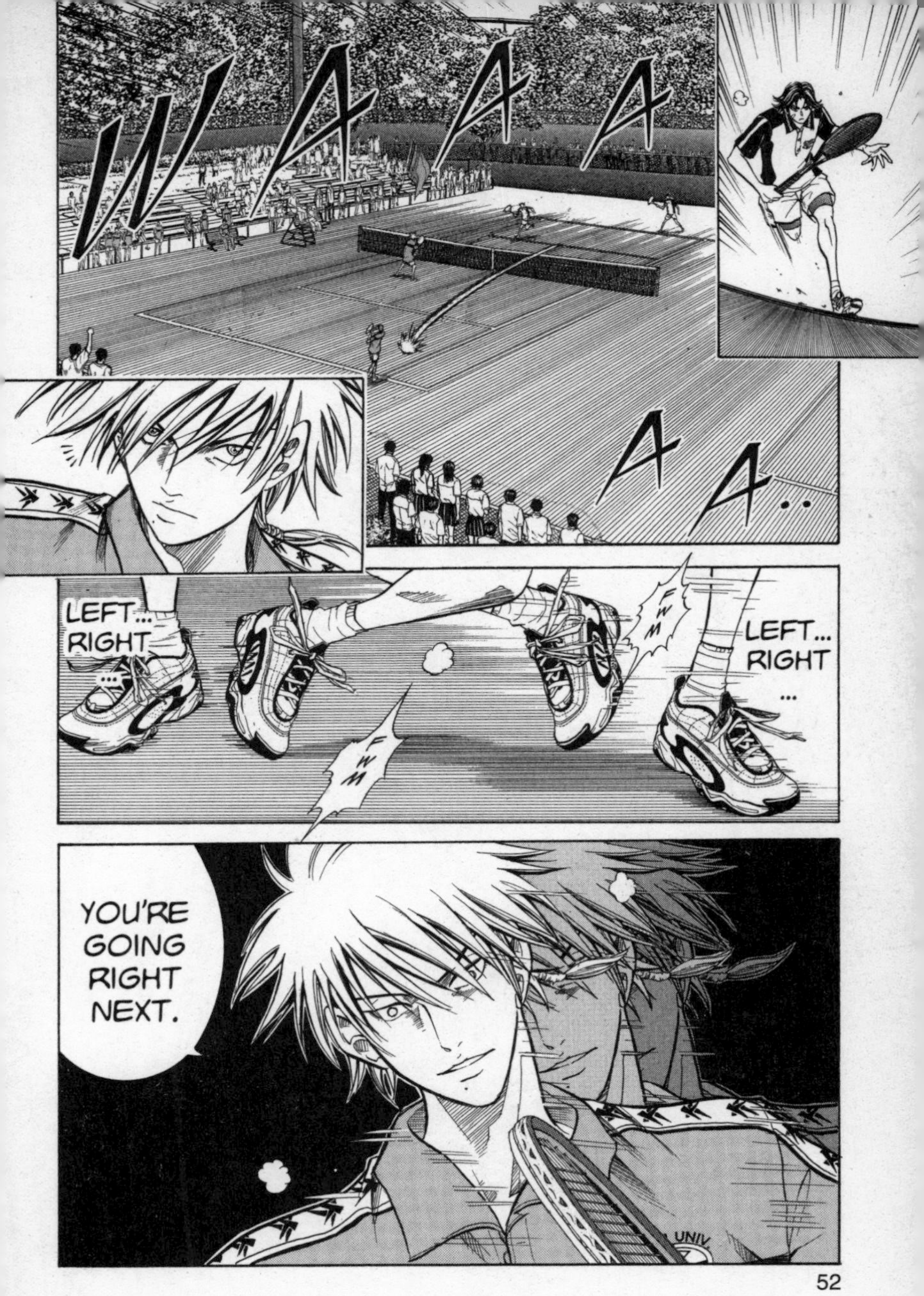
WAAA
AA..
LEFT... RIGHT ...
FWM
FWM
LEFT... RIGHT ...
YOU'RE GOING RIGHT NEXT.

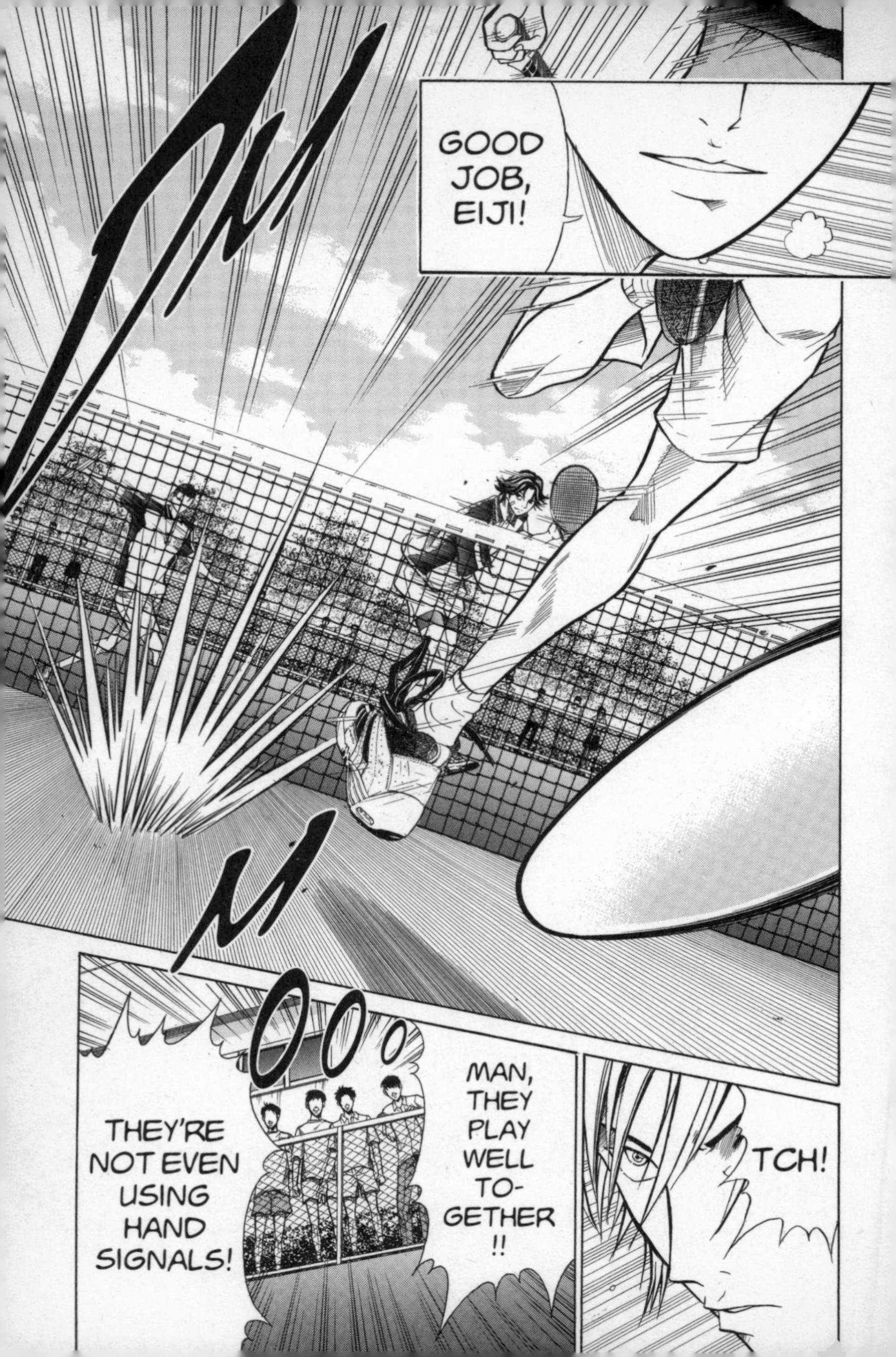
GOOD JOB, EIJI!
TCH!
MAN, THEY PLAY WELL TO-GETHER!!
THEY'RE NOT EVEN USING HAND SIGNALS!

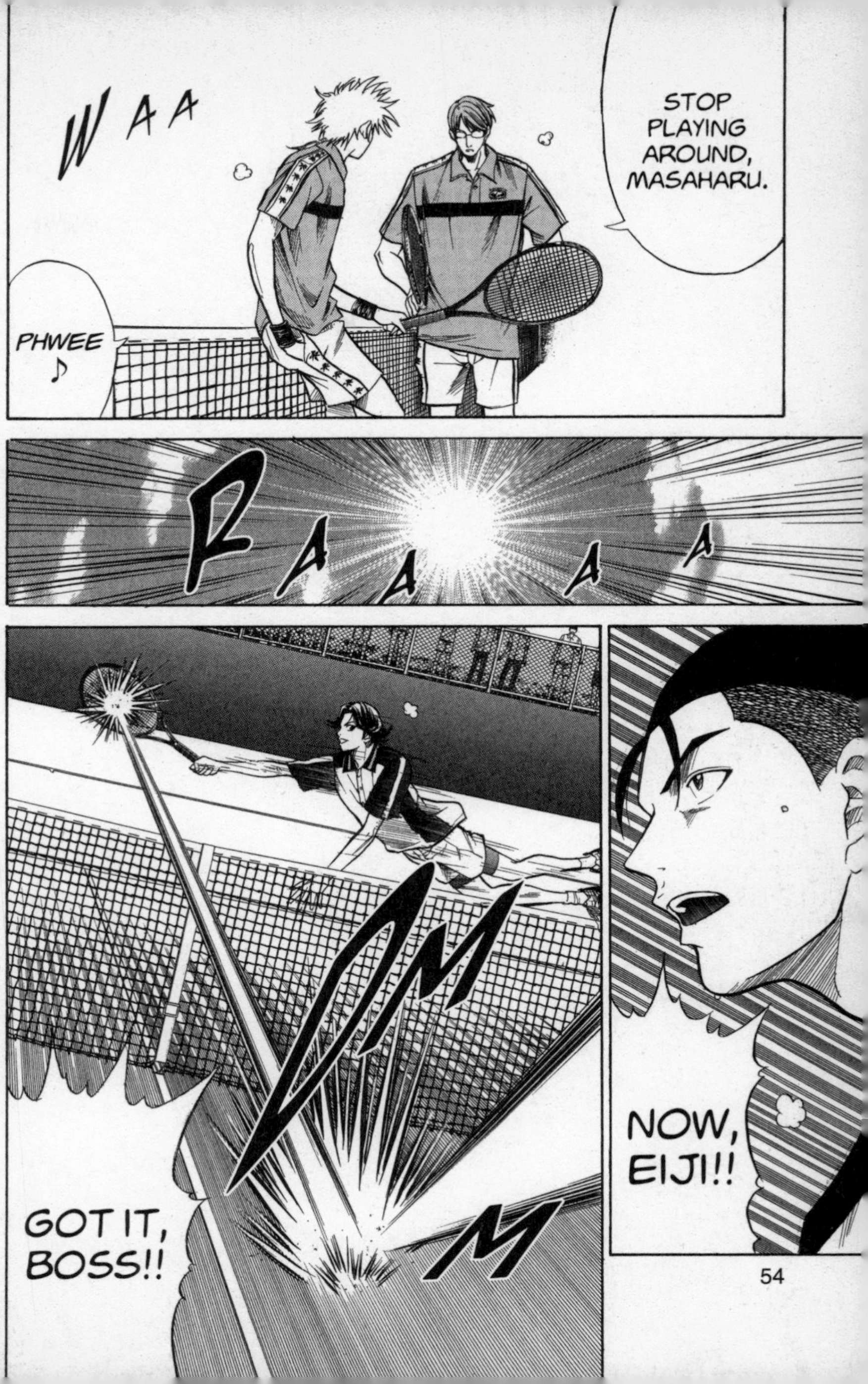
STOP PLAYING AROUND, MASAHARU.
WAA
PHWEE ♪
PAAAAA
NOW, EIJI!!
GOT IT, BOSS!!
WMM

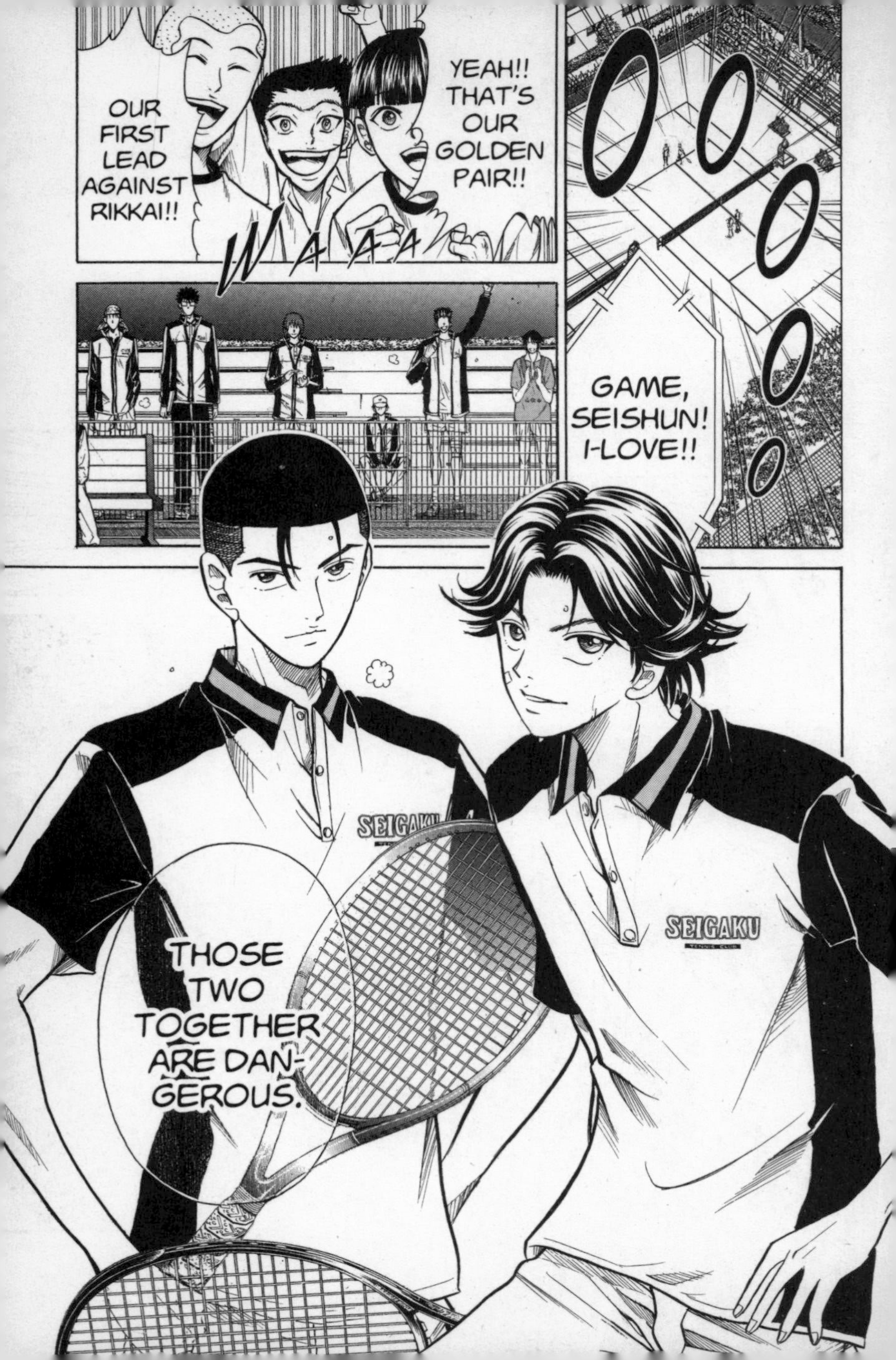
GAME, SEISHUN! I-LOVE!!
OUR FIRST LEAD AGAINST RIKKAI!!
YEAH!! THAT'S OUR GOLDEN PAIR!!
WAAA
THOSE TWO TOGETHER ARE DAN-GEROUS.
SEIGAKU
SEIGAKU

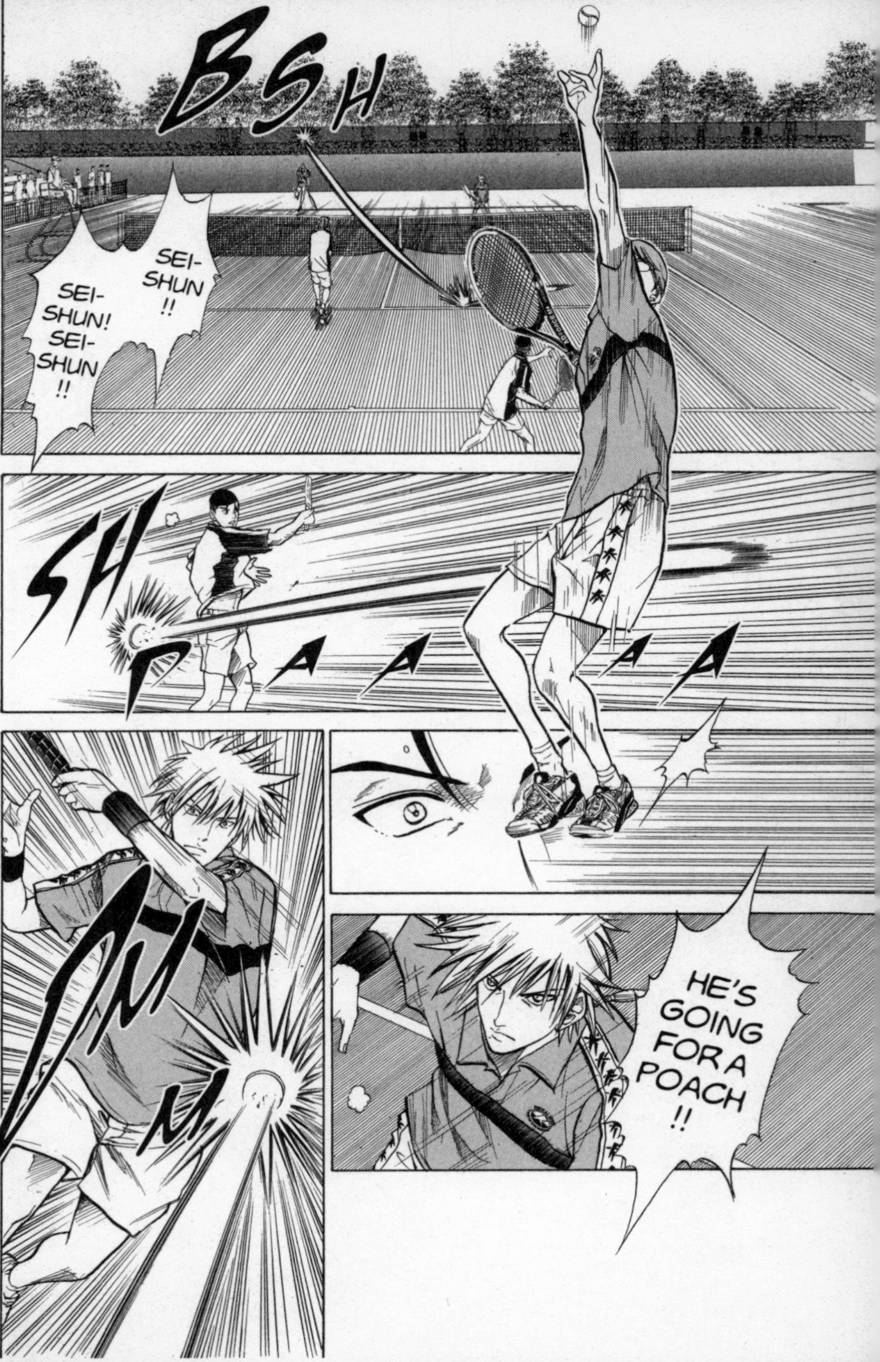
BSH
SEI-SHUN!!
SEI-SHUN! SEI-SHUN!!
SHPAAAA
HE'S GOING FOR A POACH!!

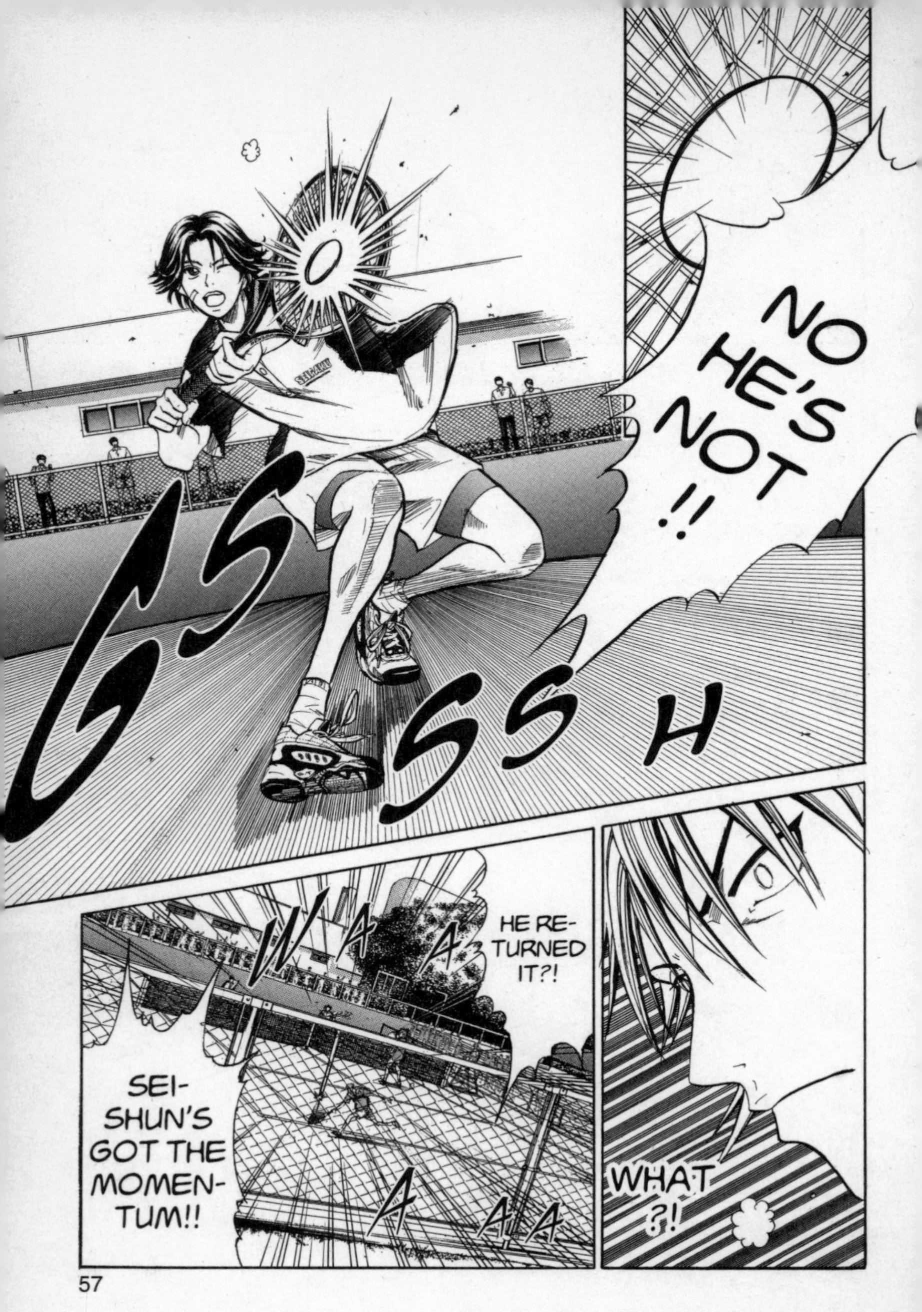
NO HE'S NOT!!
GSSSSH
WHAT?!
WAA
HE RE-TURNED IT?!
SEI-SHUN'S GOT THE MOMEN-TUM!!
AAA

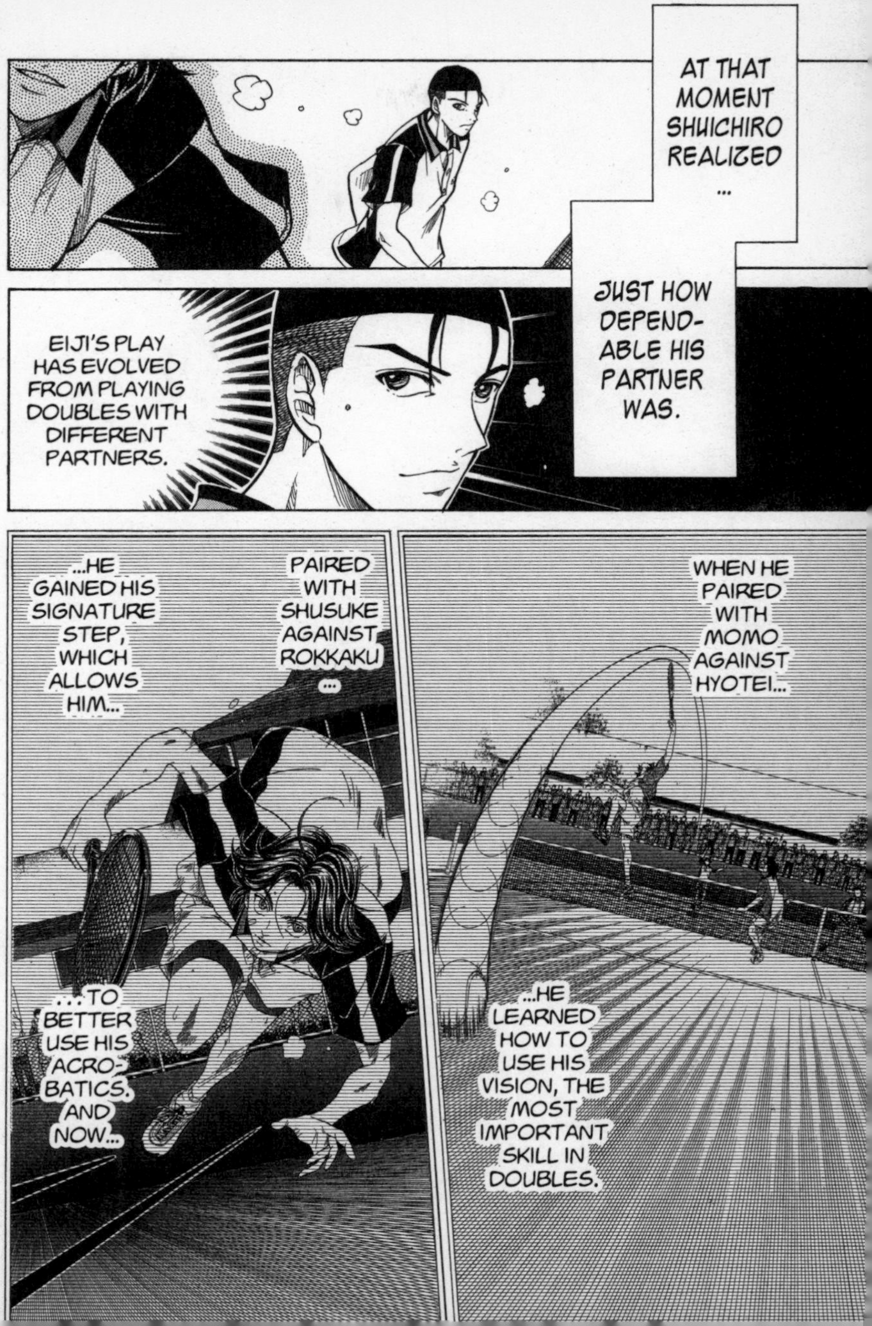
AT THAT MOMENT SHUICHIRO REALIZED ...
JUST HOW DEPEND-ABLE HIS PARTNER WAS.
EIJI'S PLAY HAS EVOLVED FROM PLAYING DOUBLES WITH DIFFERENT PARTNERS.
WHEN HE PAIRED WITH MOMO AGAINST HYOTEI...
...HE LEARNED HOW TO USE HIS VISION, THE MOST IMPORTANT SKILL IN DOUBLES.
PAIRED WITH SHUSUKE AGAINST ROKKAKU ...
...HE GAINED HIS SIGNATURE STEP, WHICH ALLOWS HIM...
...TO BETTER USE HIS ACRO-BATICS.
AND NOW...

READ THIS WAY

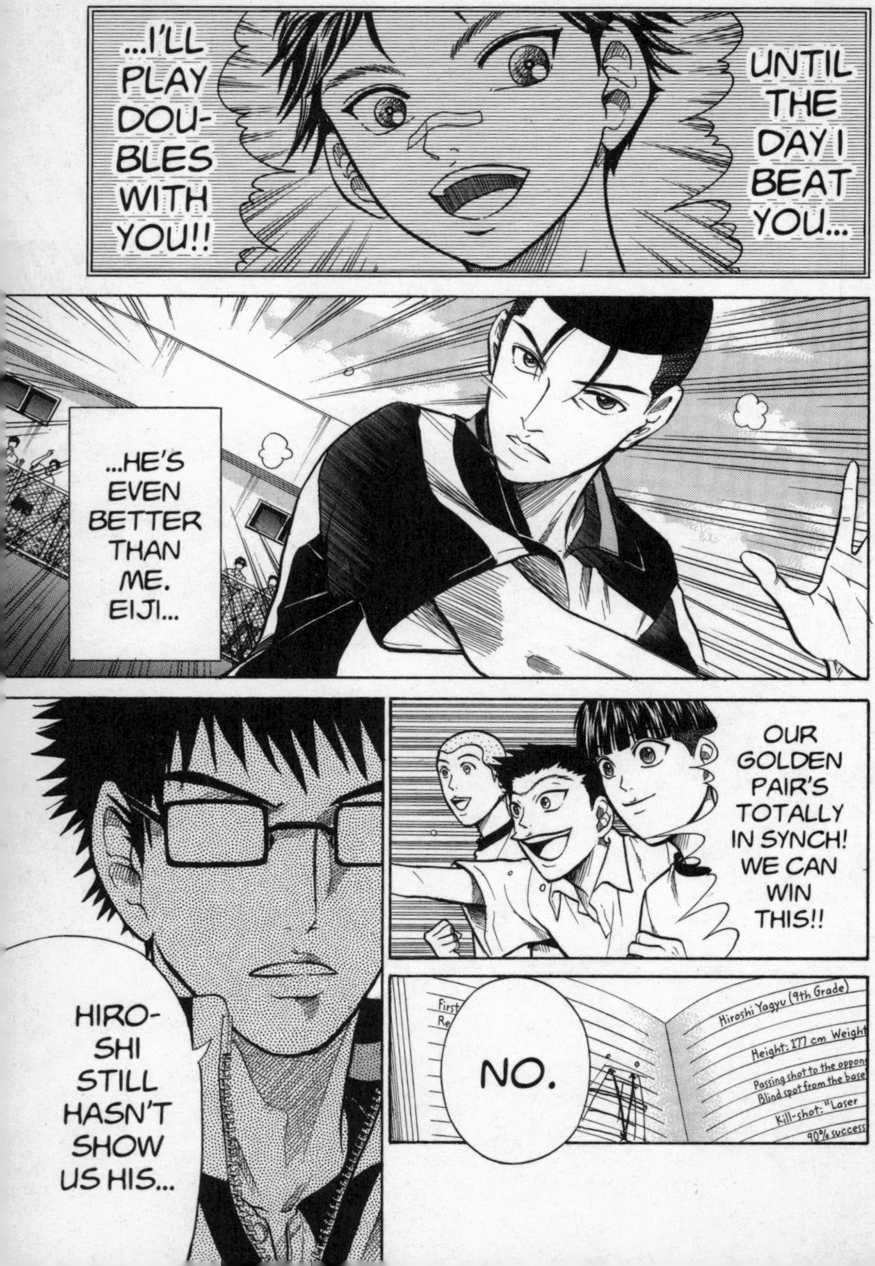
UNTIL THE DAY I BEAT YOU...
...I'LL PLAY DOU-BLES WITH YOU!!
...HE'S EVEN BETTER THAN ME. EIJI...
OUR GOLDEN PAIR'S TOTALLY IN SYNCH! WE CAN WIN THIS!!
NO.
Hiroshi Yagyu (9th Grade)
Height: 177 cm Weight
Passing shot to the oppon
Blind spot from the base
Kill-shot: "Laser
90% success
HIRO-SHI STILL HASN'T SHOW US HIS...

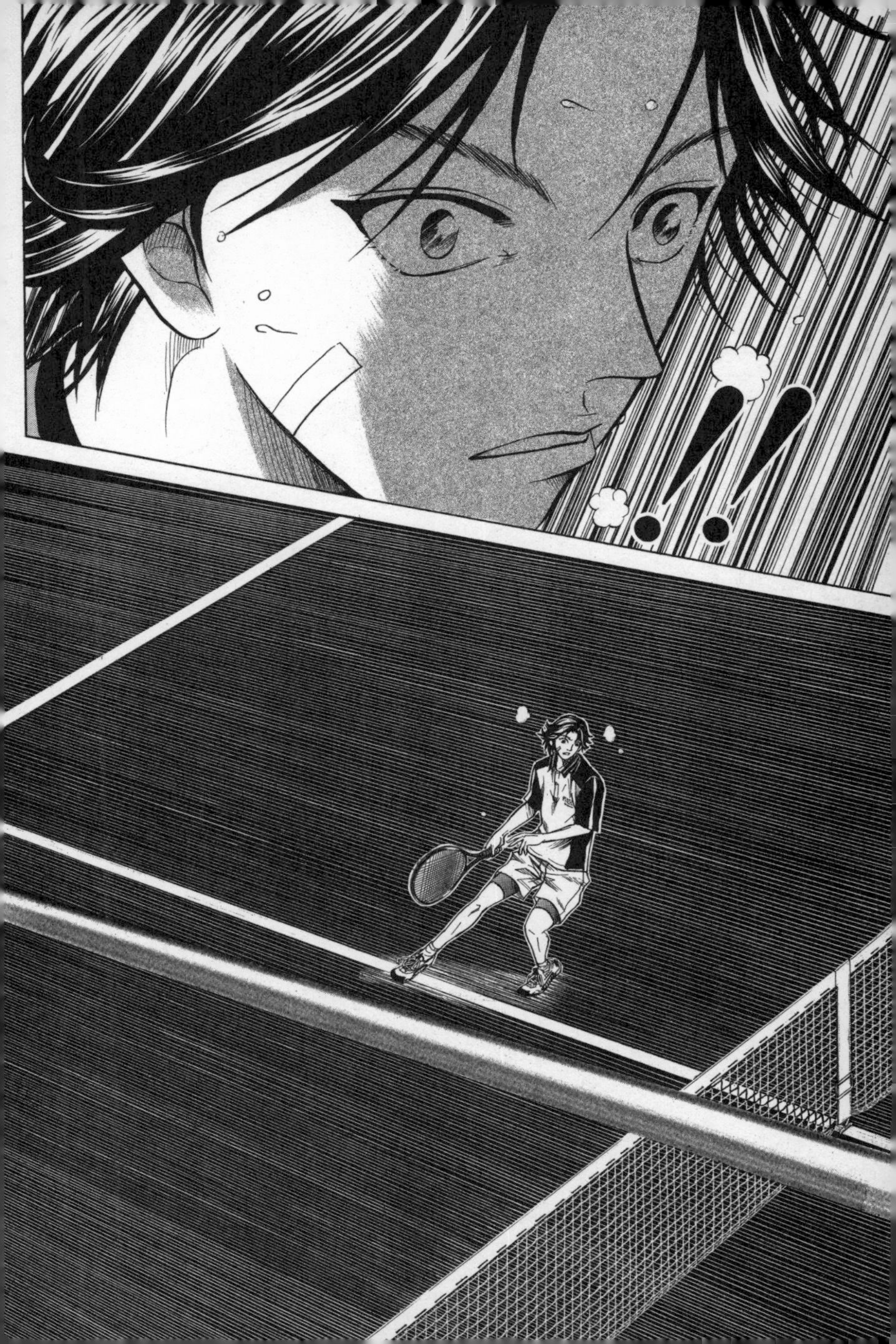
!!

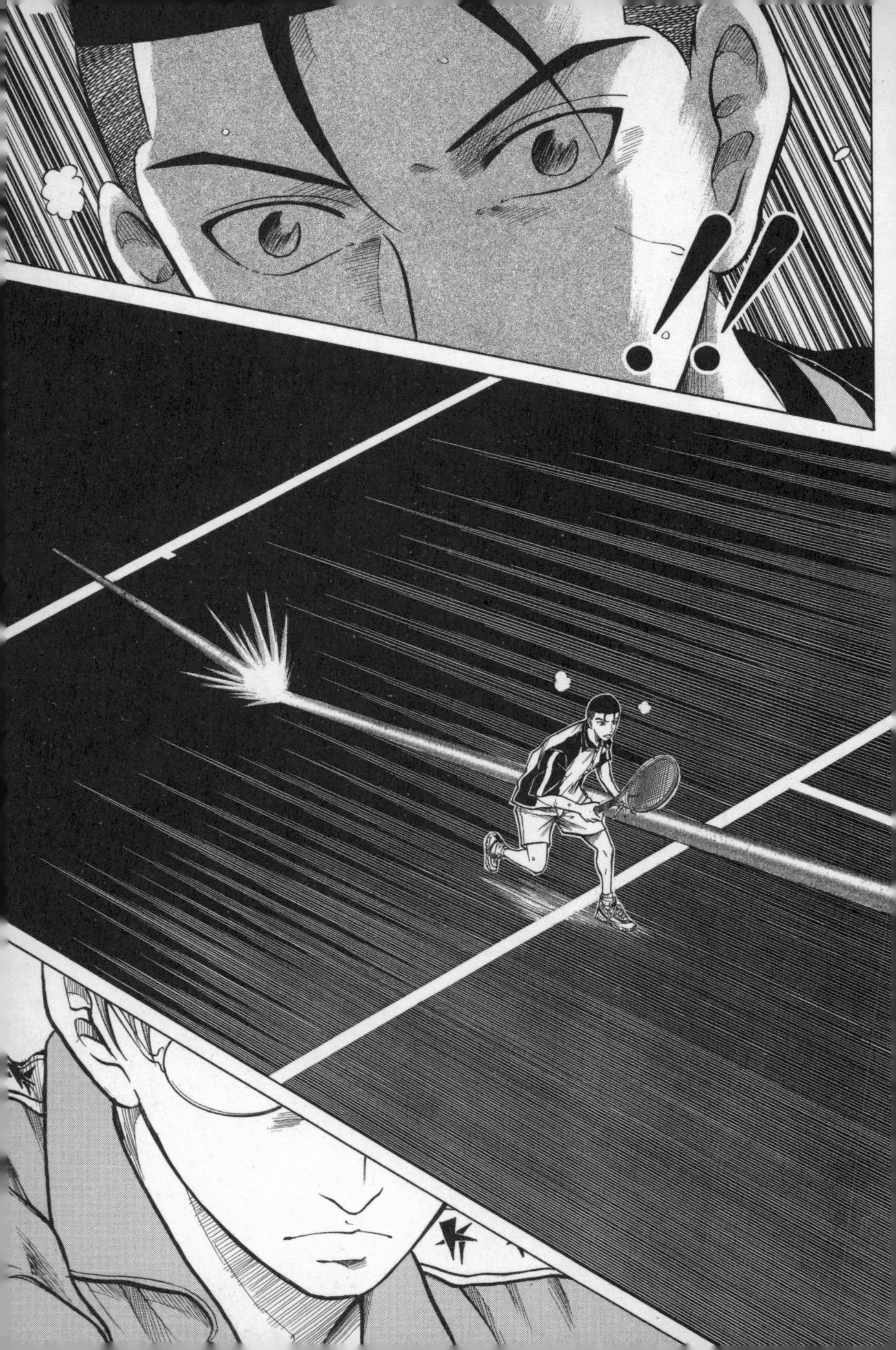
!!

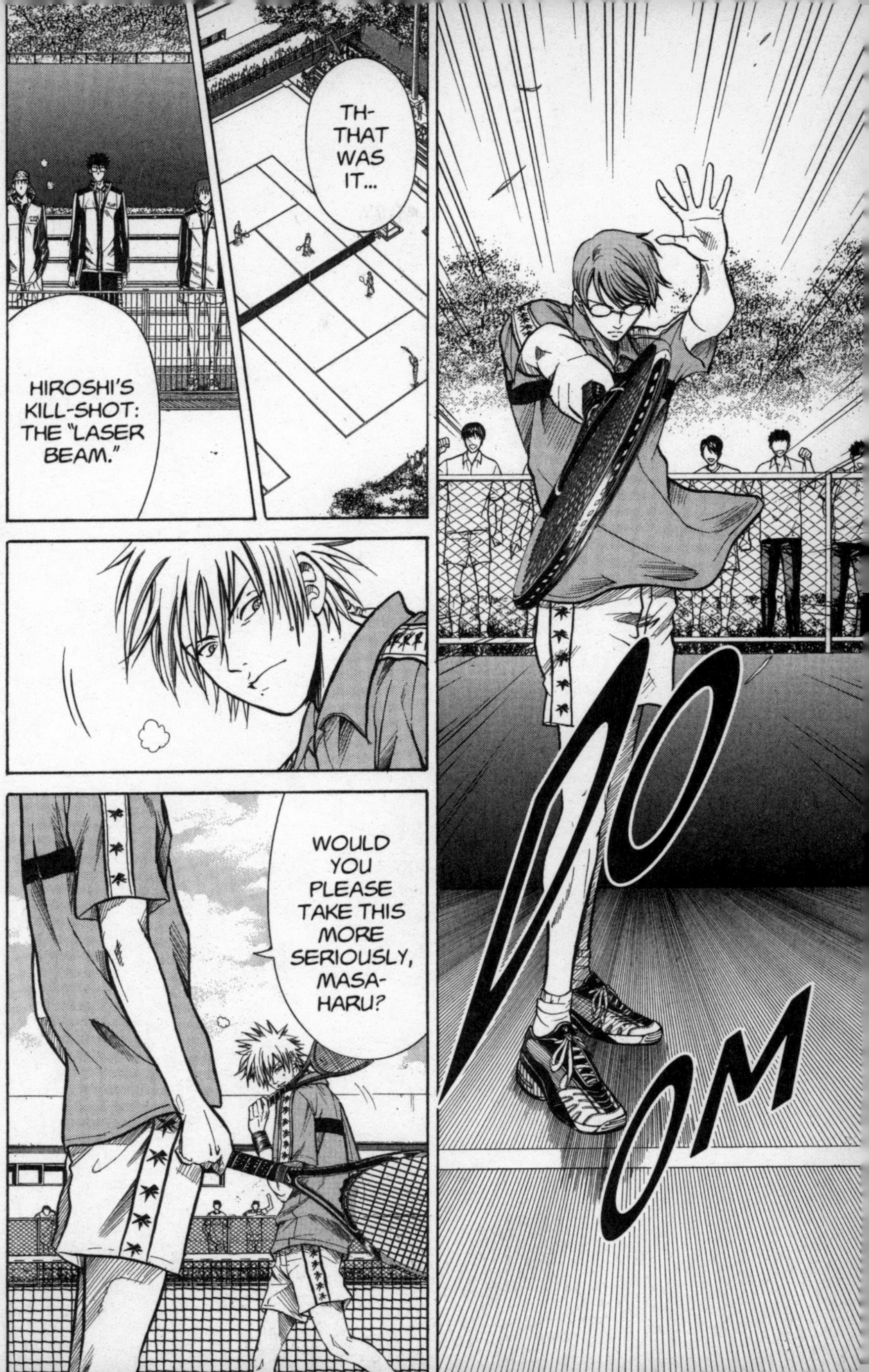
DOOM
TH- THAT WAS IT...
HIROSHI'S KILL-SHOT: THE "LASER BEAM."
WOULD YOU PLEASE TAKE THIS MORE SERIOUSLY, MASA-HARU?

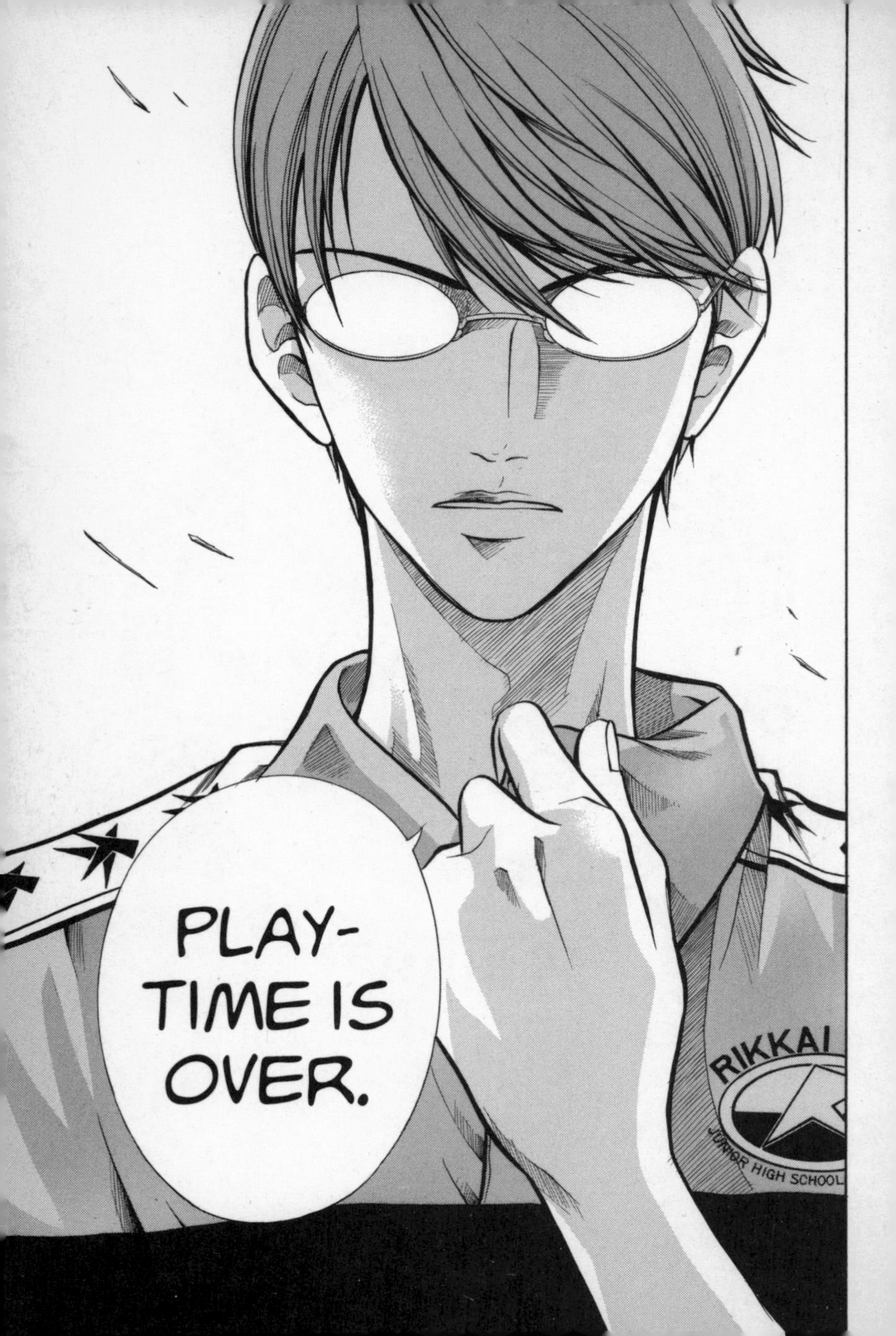
PLAY-TIME IS OVER.
RIKKAI JUNIOR HIGH SCHOOL

THE PRINCE OF TENNIS THE PRINCE OF TENNIS THE PRINCE OF TENNIS THE PRINCE OF TENNIS
Yagyu Beam !!
Whoa ...

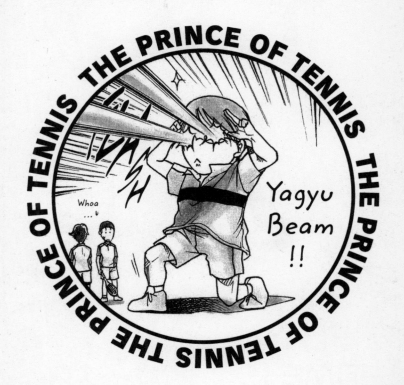

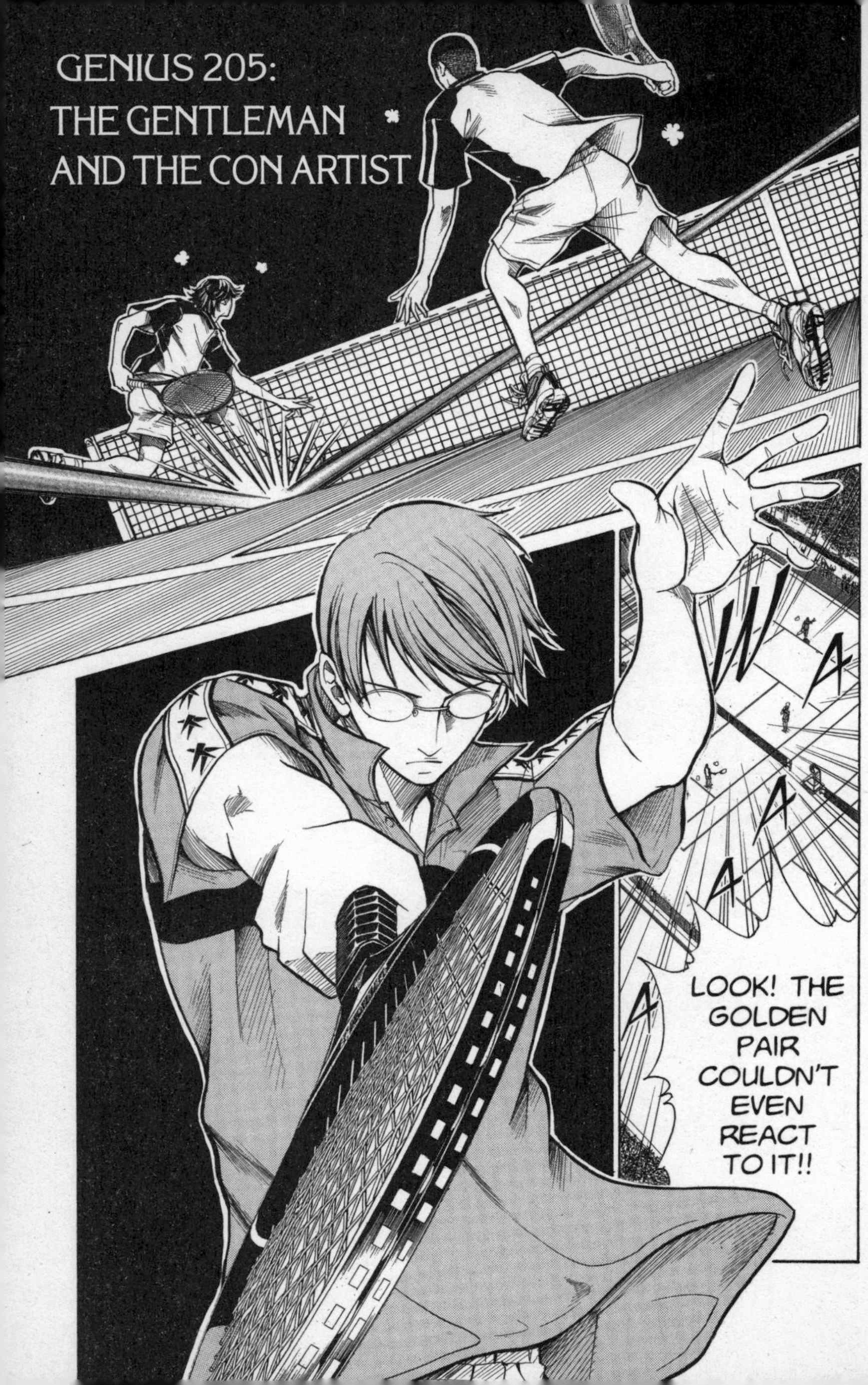
GENIUS 205:
THE GENTLEMAN AND THE CON ARTIST
WAAAA
LOOK! THE GOLDEN PAIR COULDN'T EVEN REACT TO IT!!

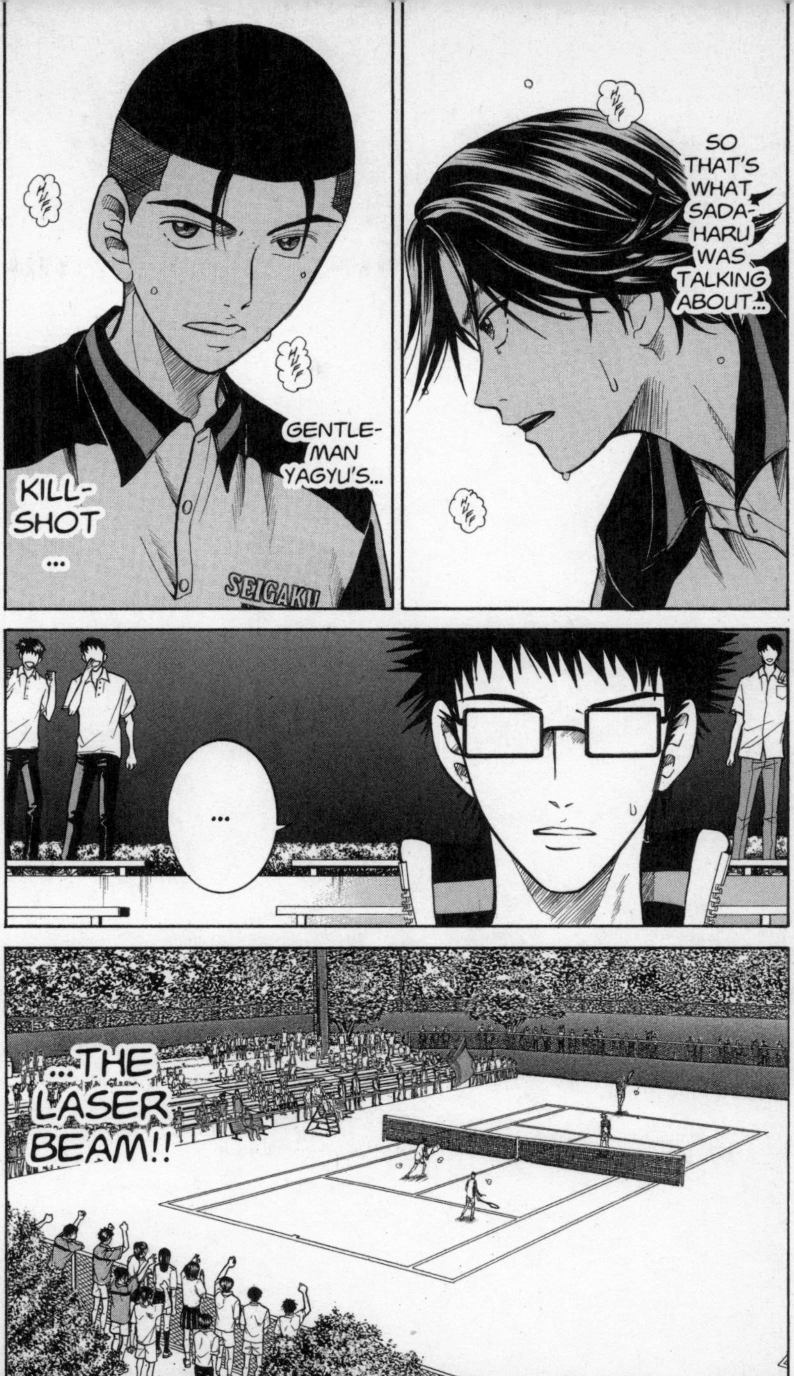
SO THAT'S WHAT SADA-HARU WAS TALKING ABOUT...
GENTLE-MAN YAGYU'S...
KILL-SHOT ...
...
...THE LASER BEAM!!

GENIUS 205: THE GENTLEMAN AND THE CON ARTIST

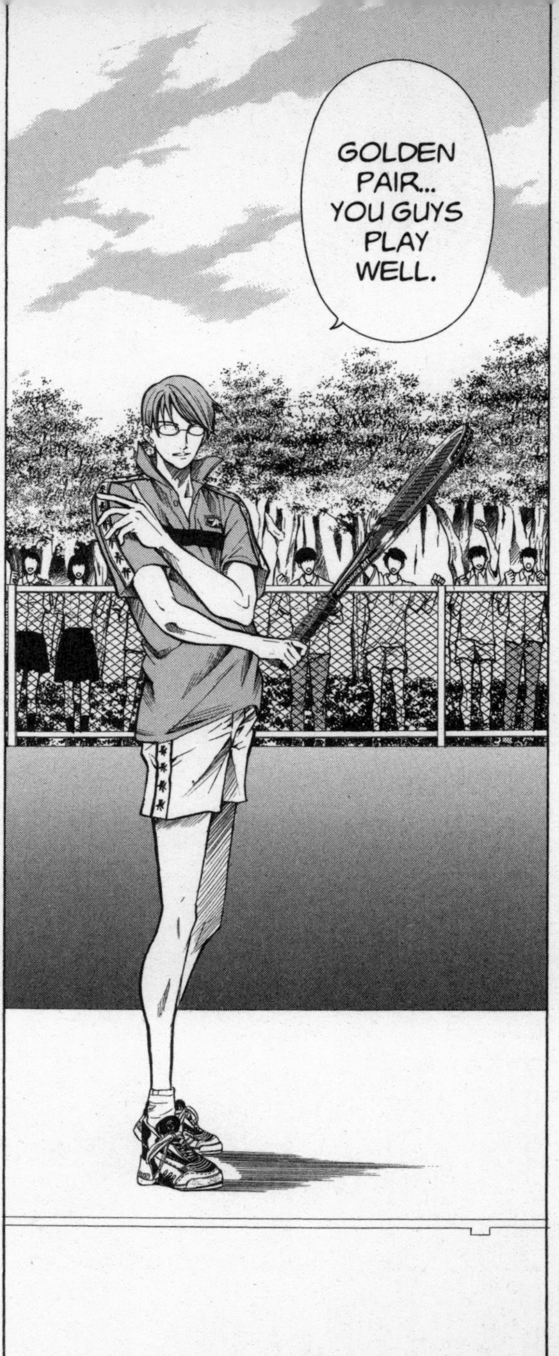
GOLDEN PAIR... YOU GUYS PLAY WELL.

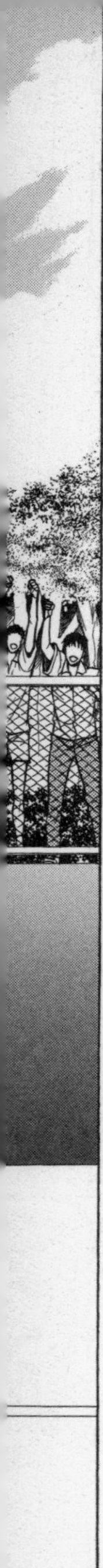

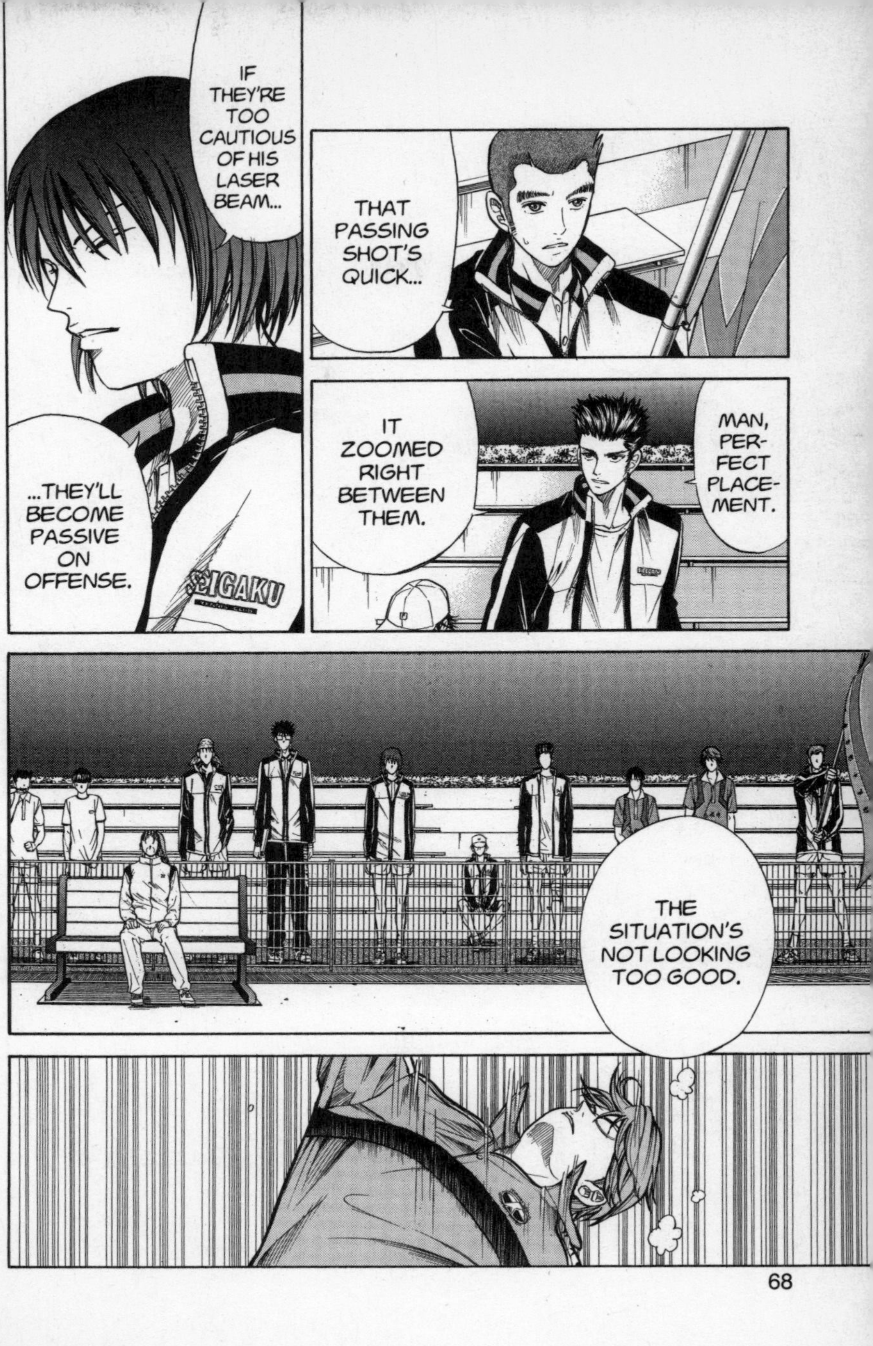
THAT PASSING SHOT'S QUICK...
MAN, PERFECT PLACEMENT.
IT ZOOMED RIGHT BETWEEN THEM.
IF THEY'RE TOO CAUTIOUS OF HIS LASER BEAM...
...THEY'LL BECOME PASSIVE ON OFFENSE.
SEIGAKU
THE SITUATION'S NOT LOOKING TOO GOOD.

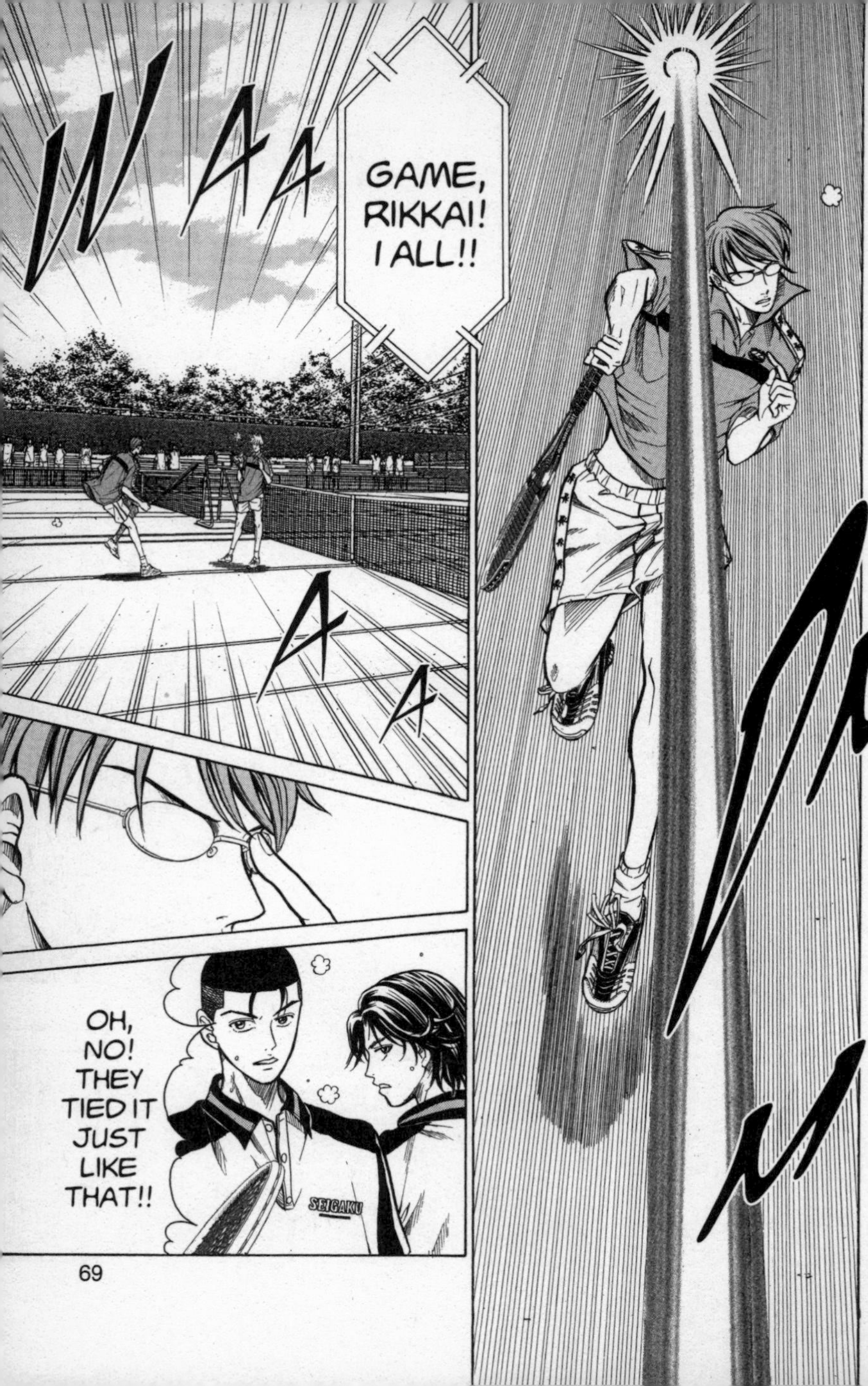
WAAAA
GAME, RIKKAI! I ALL!!
OH, NO! THEY TIED IT JUST LIKE THAT!!
SEIGAKU

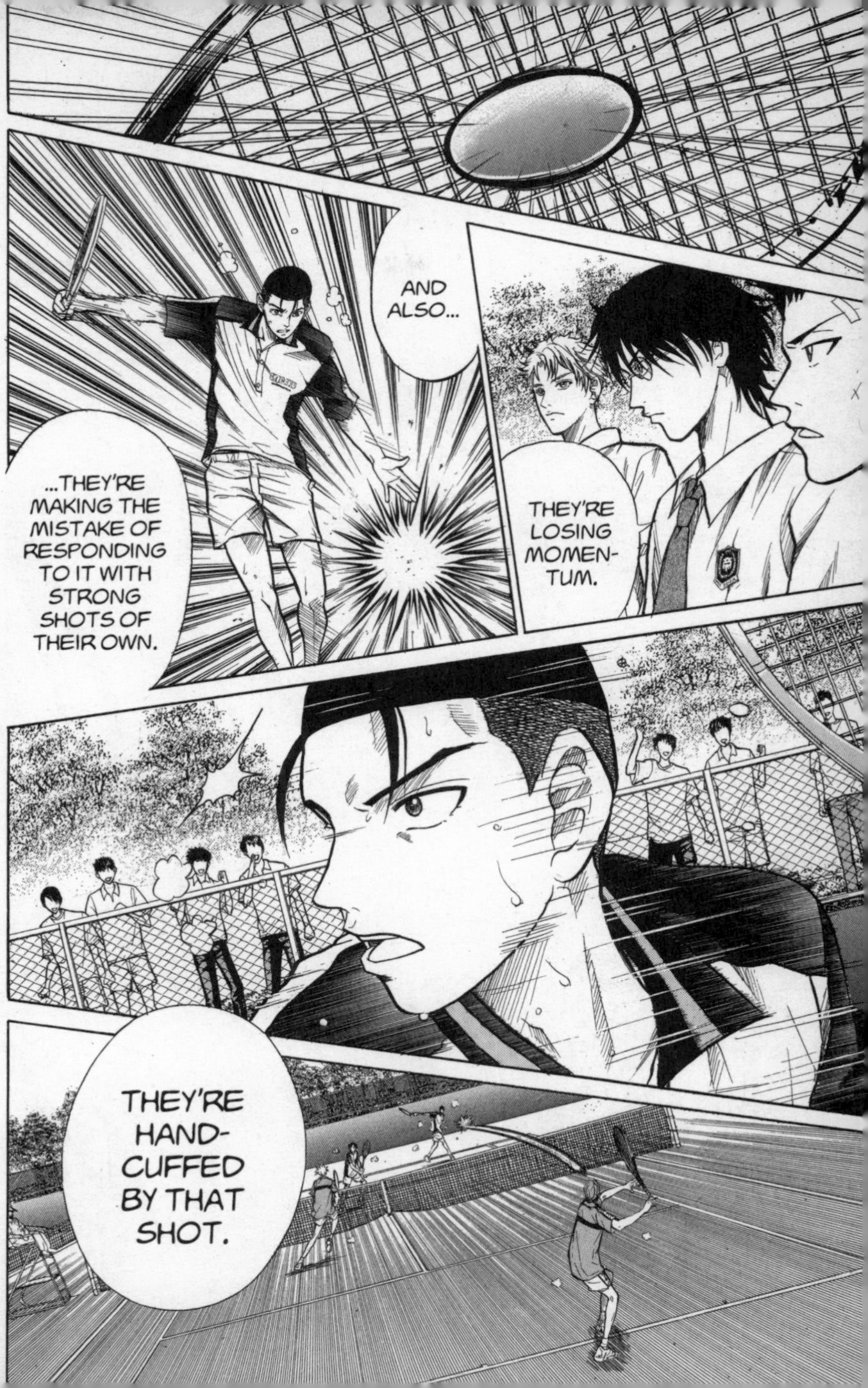
THEY'RE LOSING MOMEN-TUM.
AND ALSO...
...THEY'RE MAKING THE MISTAKE OF RESPONDING TO IT WITH STRONG SHOTS OF THEIR OWN.
THEY'RE HAND-CUFFED BY THAT SHOT.

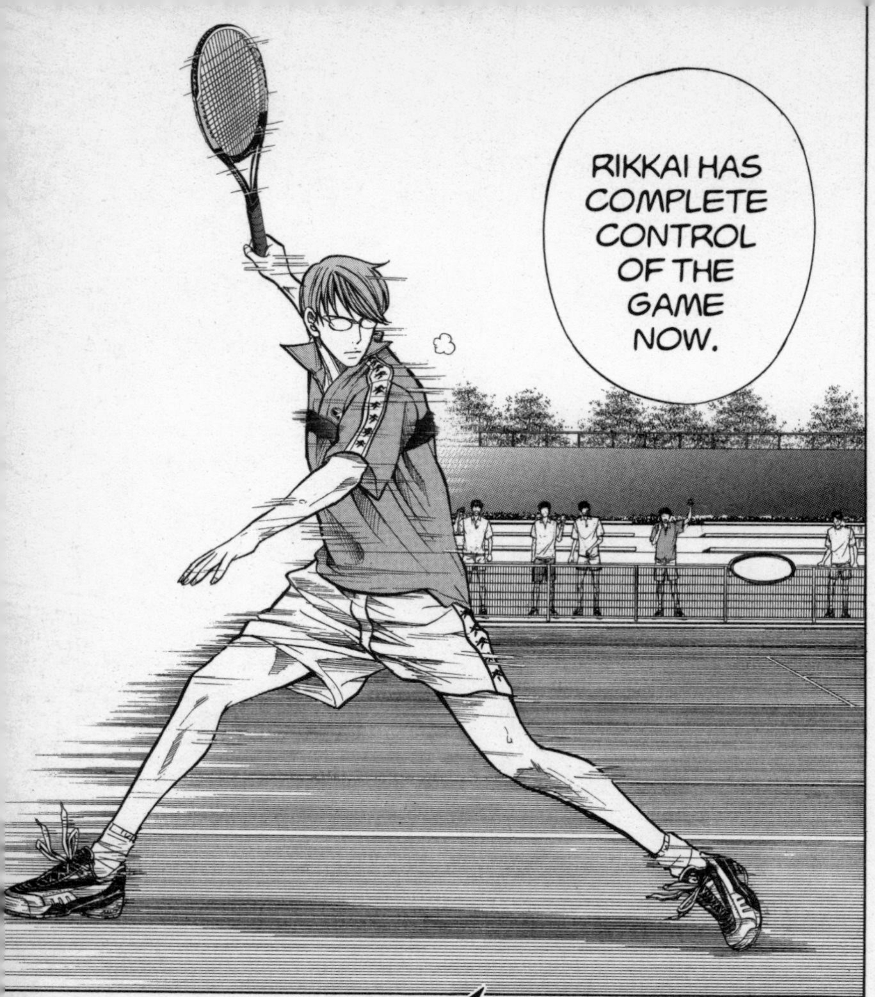
RIKKAI HAS COMPLETE CONTROL OF THE GAME NOW.

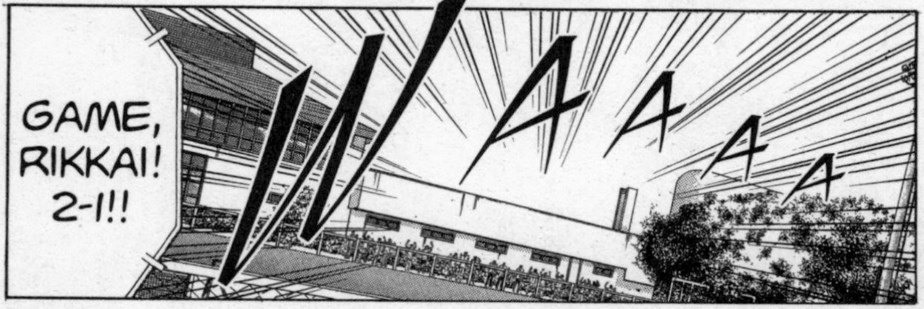
GAME, RIKKAI! 2-1!!
WAAAA

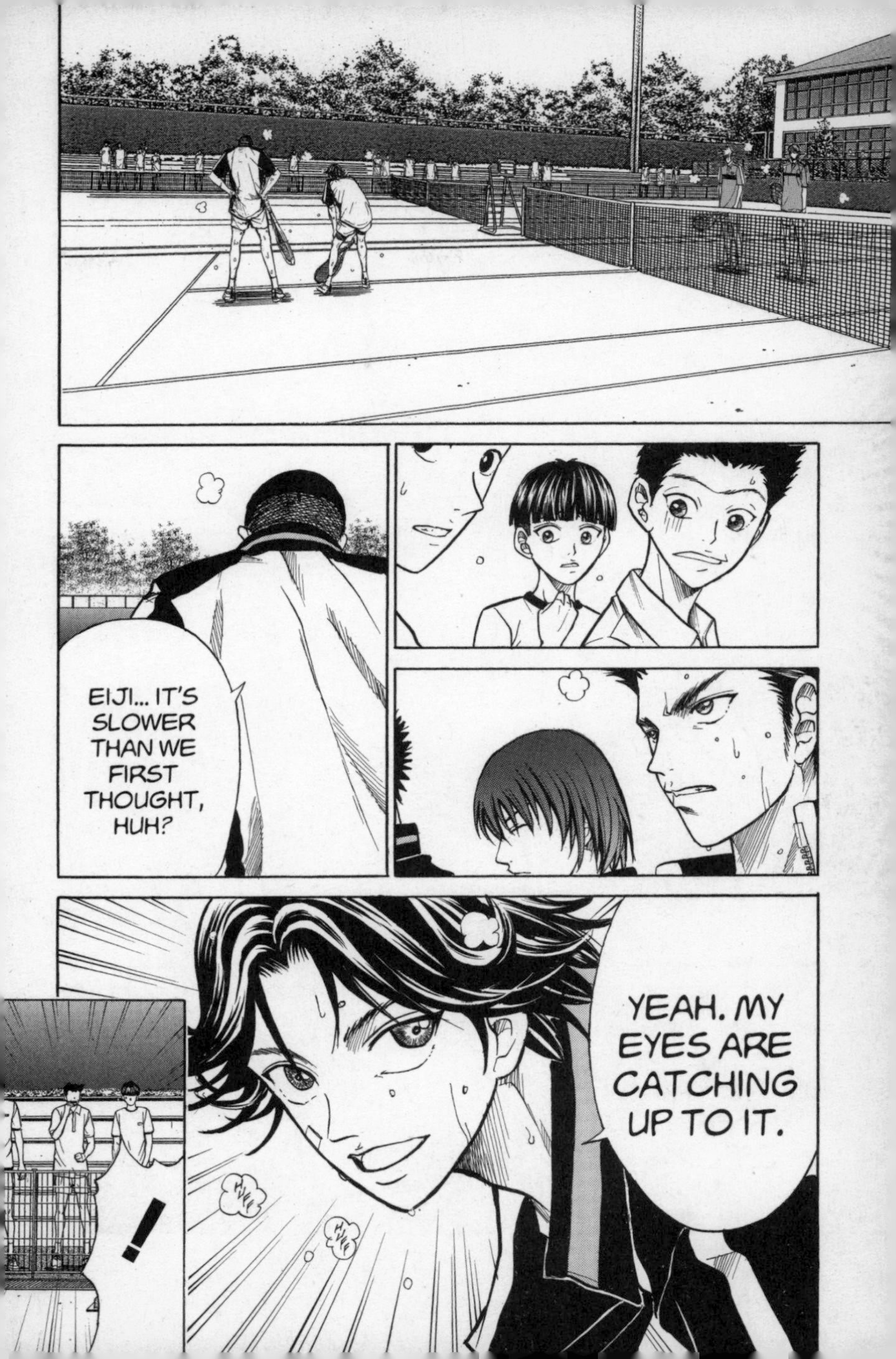
EIJI... IT'S SLOWER THAN WE FIRST THOUGHT, HUH?
YEAH. MY EYES ARE CATCHING UP TO IT.
!

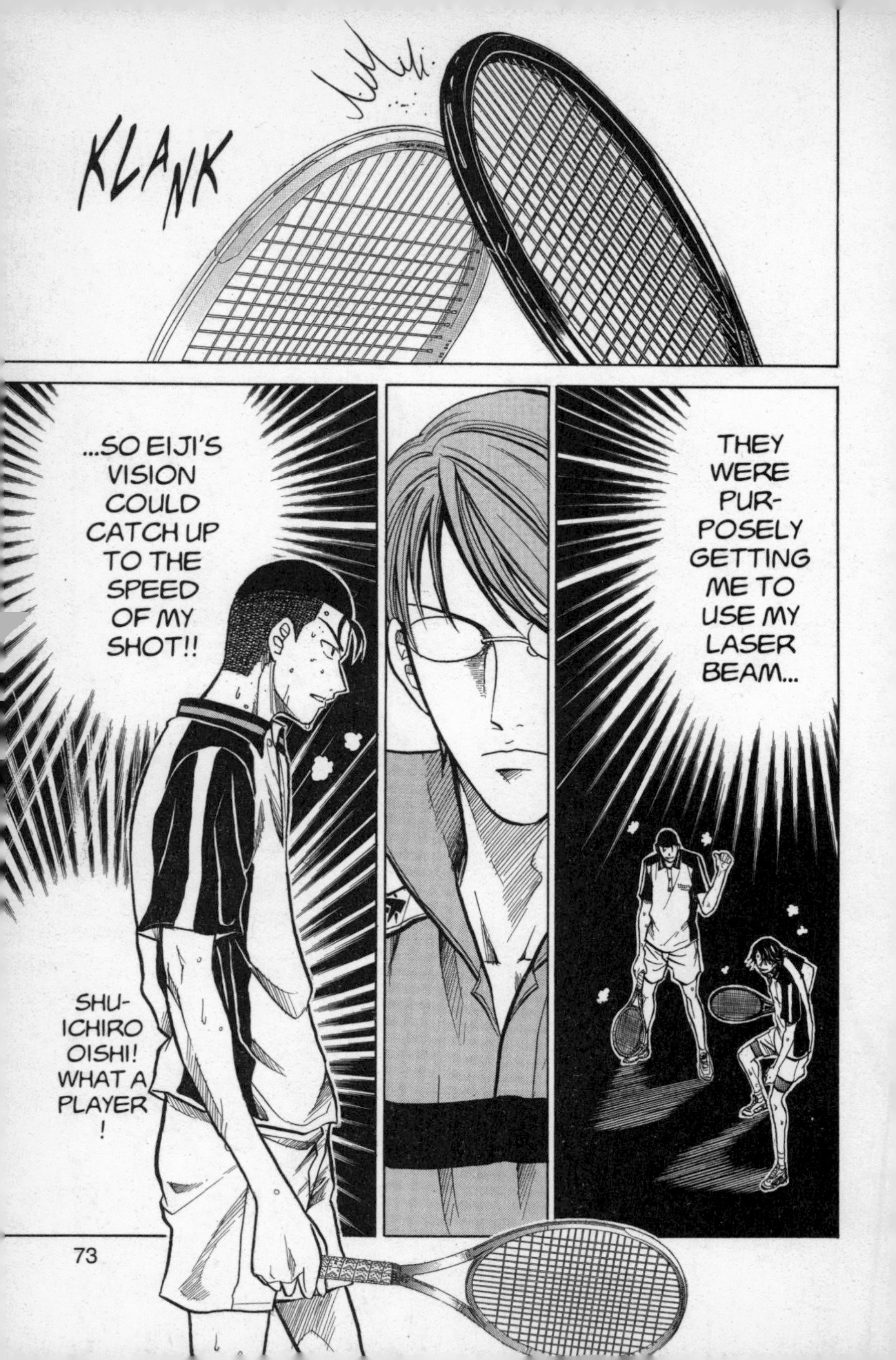
KLANK
THEY WERE PURPOSELY GETTING ME TO USE MY LASER BEAM...
...SO EIJI'S VISION COULD CATCH UP TO THE SPEED OF MY SHOT!!
SHUICHIRO OISHI! WHAT A PLAYER!

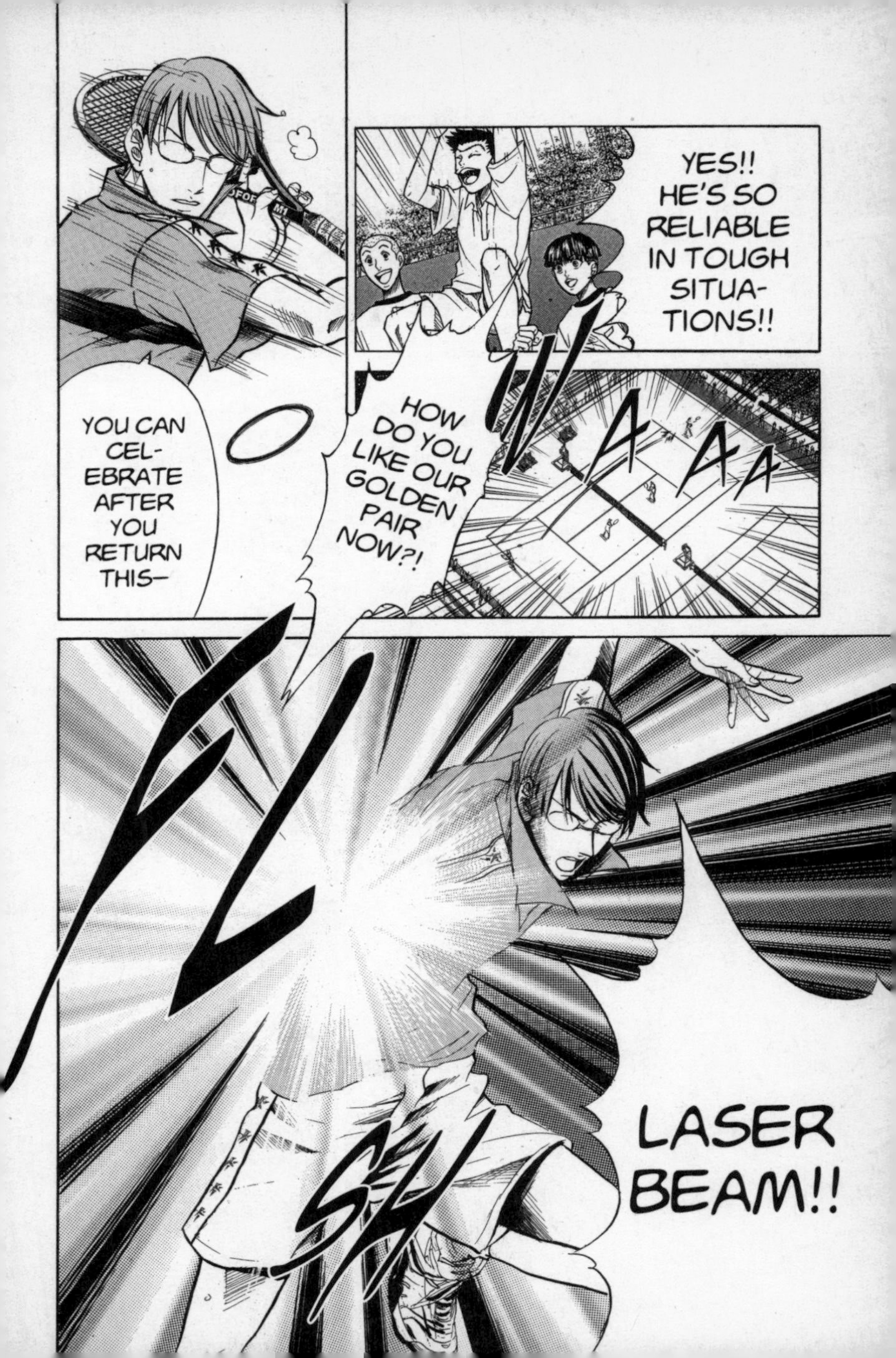
YES!! HE'S SO RELIABLE IN TOUGH SITUA- TIONS!!
WAAA
HOW DO YOU LIKE OUR GOLDEN PAIR NOW?!
YOU CAN CEL- EBRATE AFTER YOU RETURN THIS—
LASER BEAM!!
SH

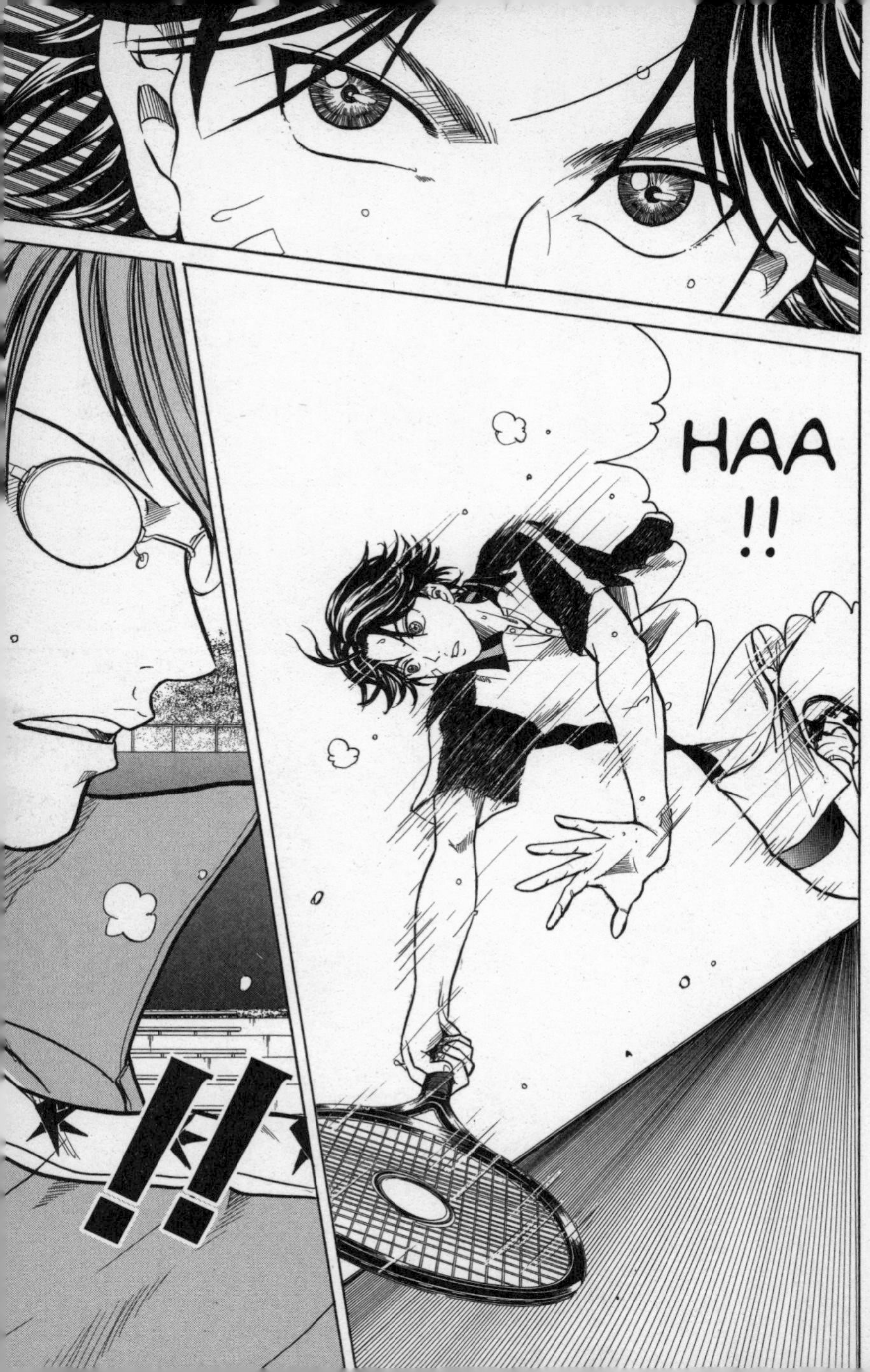
HAA
!!
!!

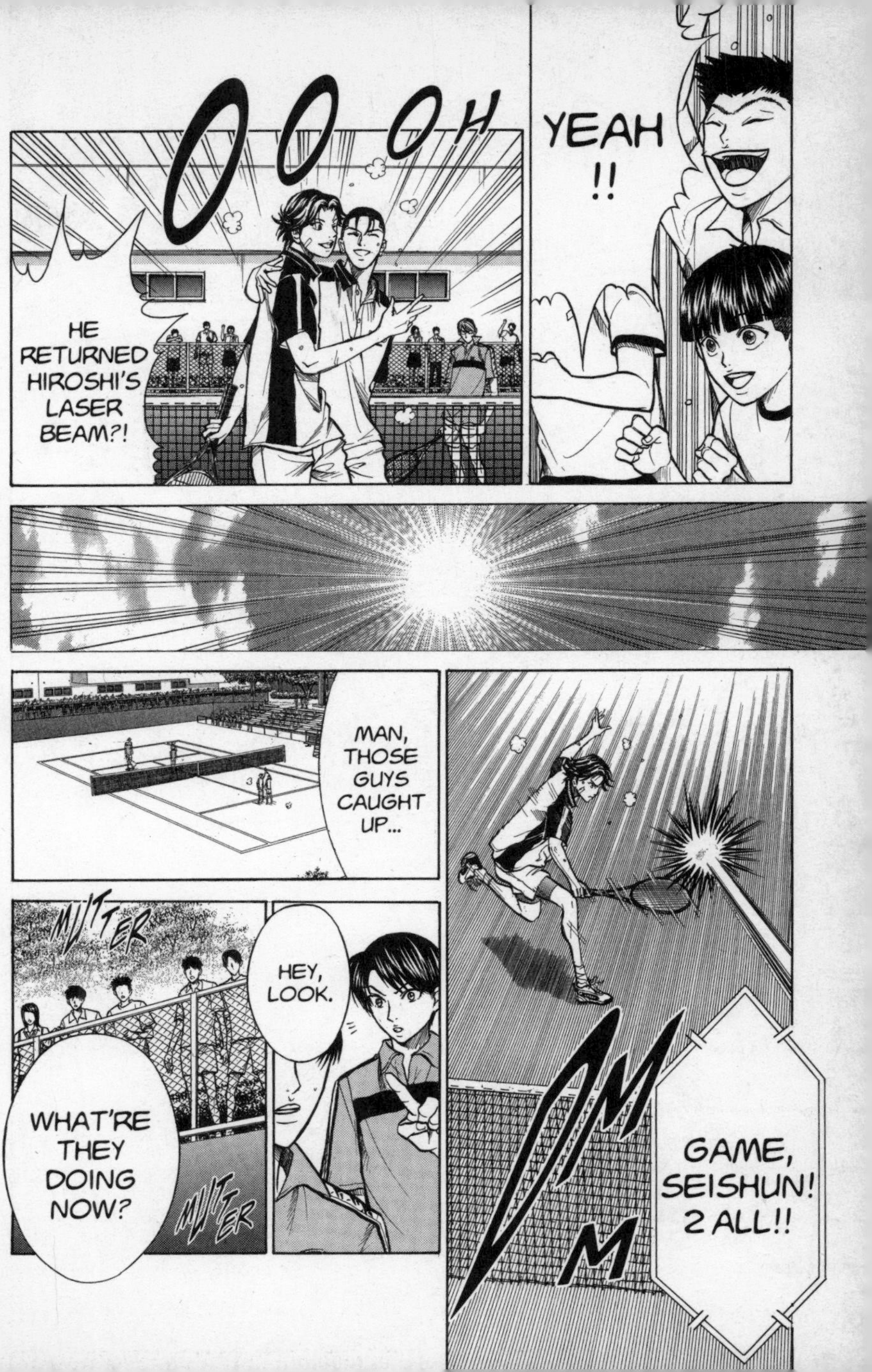
YEAH !!
OOOH
HE RETURNED HIROSHI'S LASER BEAM?!
GAME, SEISHUN! 2 ALL!!
MAN, THOSE GUYS CAUGHT UP...
HEY, LOOK.
WHAT'RE THEY DOING NOW?
MUTTER
MUTTER

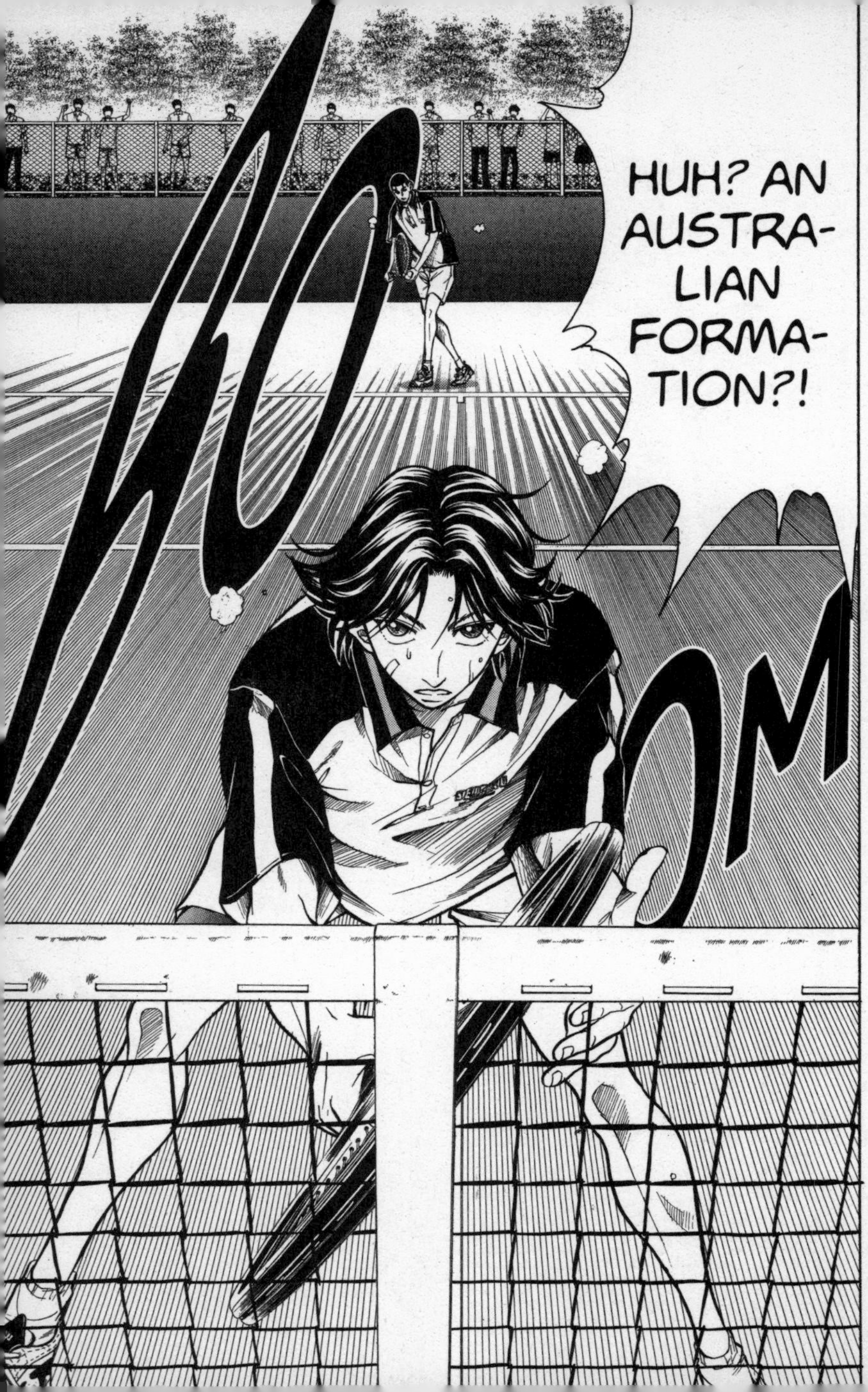
HUH? AN AUSTRA-LIAN FORMA-TION?!
SWOOM

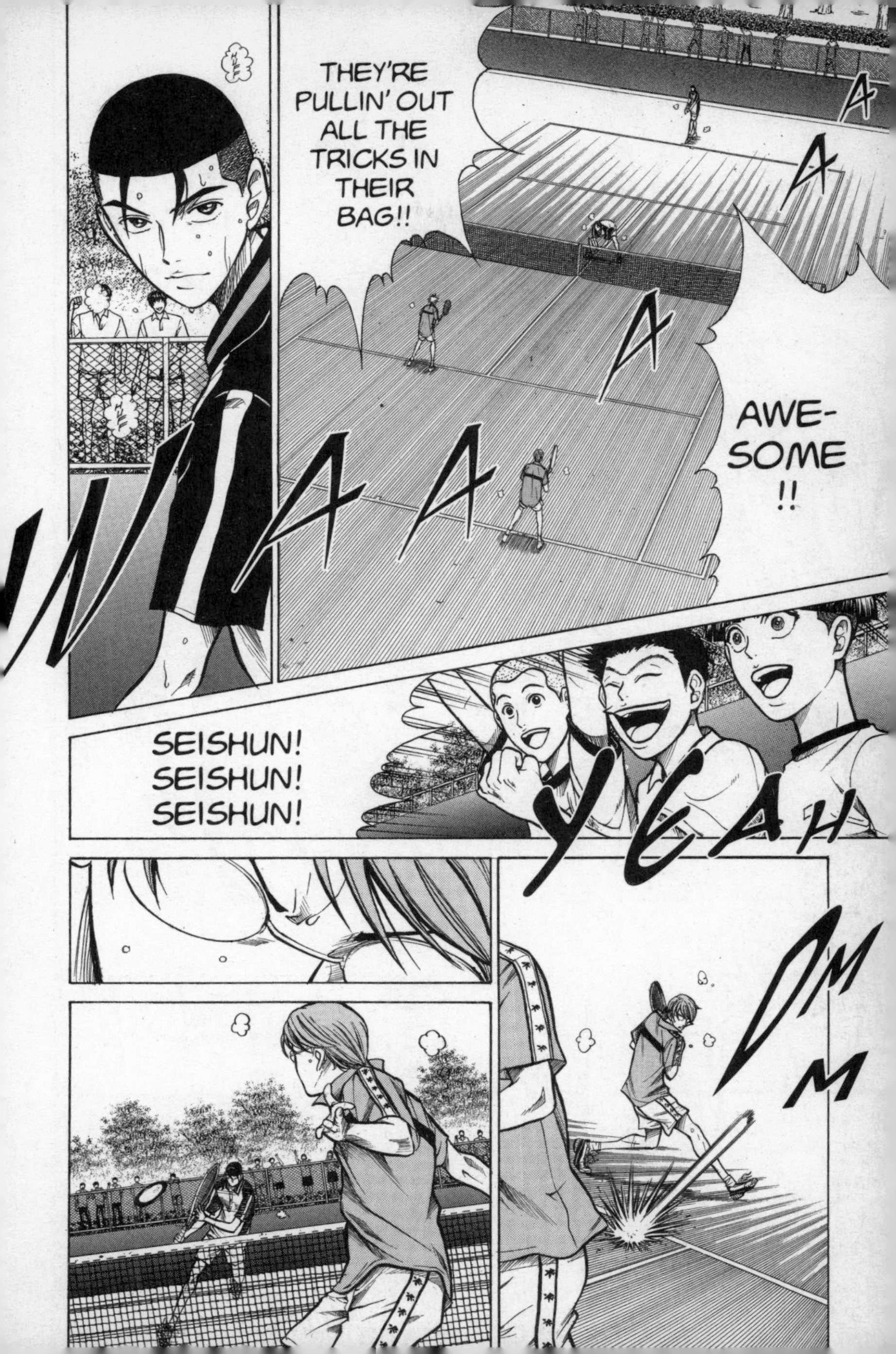
THEY'RE PULLIN' OUT ALL THE TRICKS IN THEIR BAG!!
AWE-SOME!!
WAAAAAA
SEISHUN! SEISHUN! SEISHUN!
YEAH

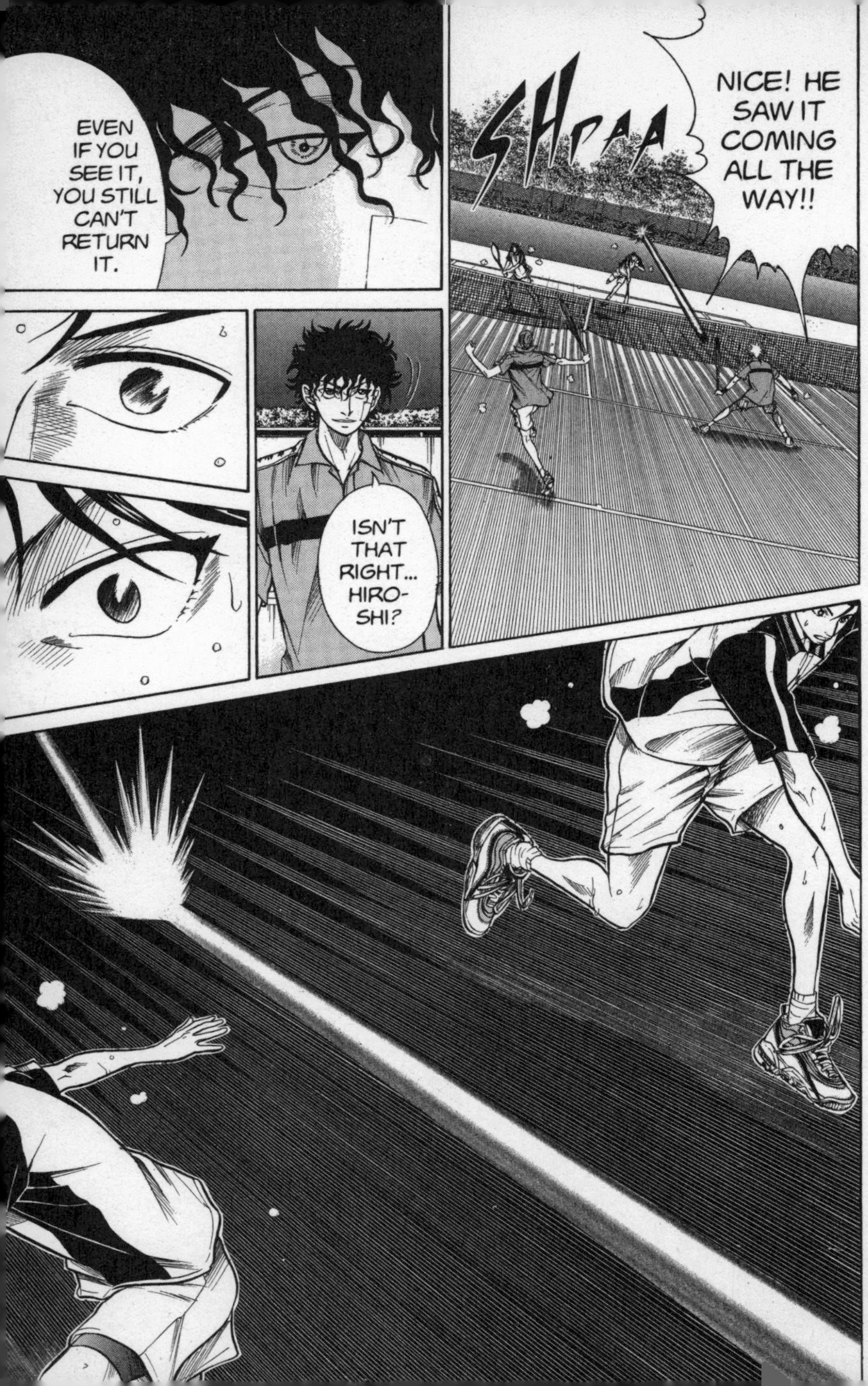
SHRAA
NICE! HE SAW IT COMING ALL THE WAY!!
EVEN IF YOU SEE IT, YOU STILL CAN'T RETURN IT.
ISN'T THAT RIGHT... HIRO-SHI?

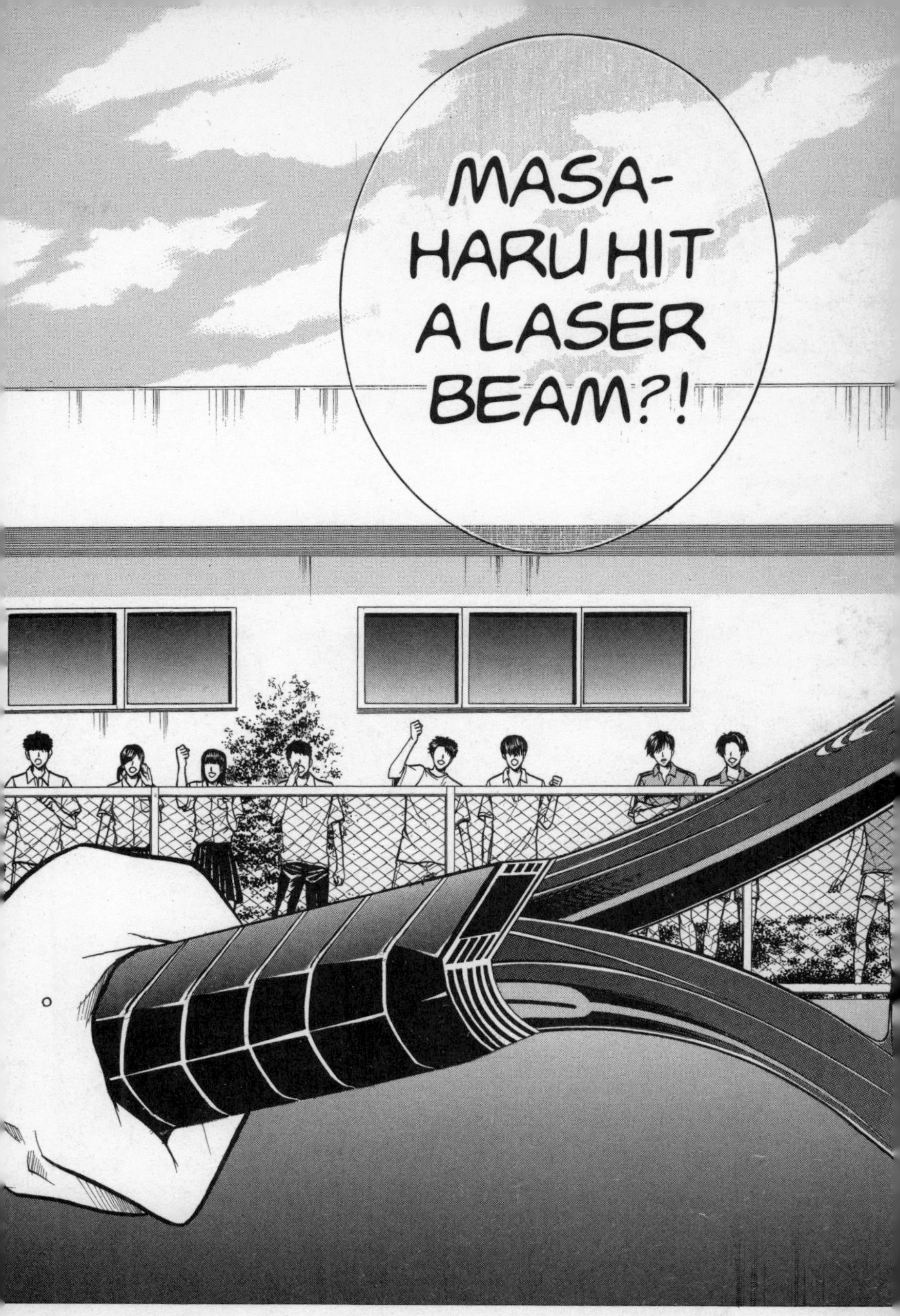
MASA-HARU HIT A LASER BEAM?!

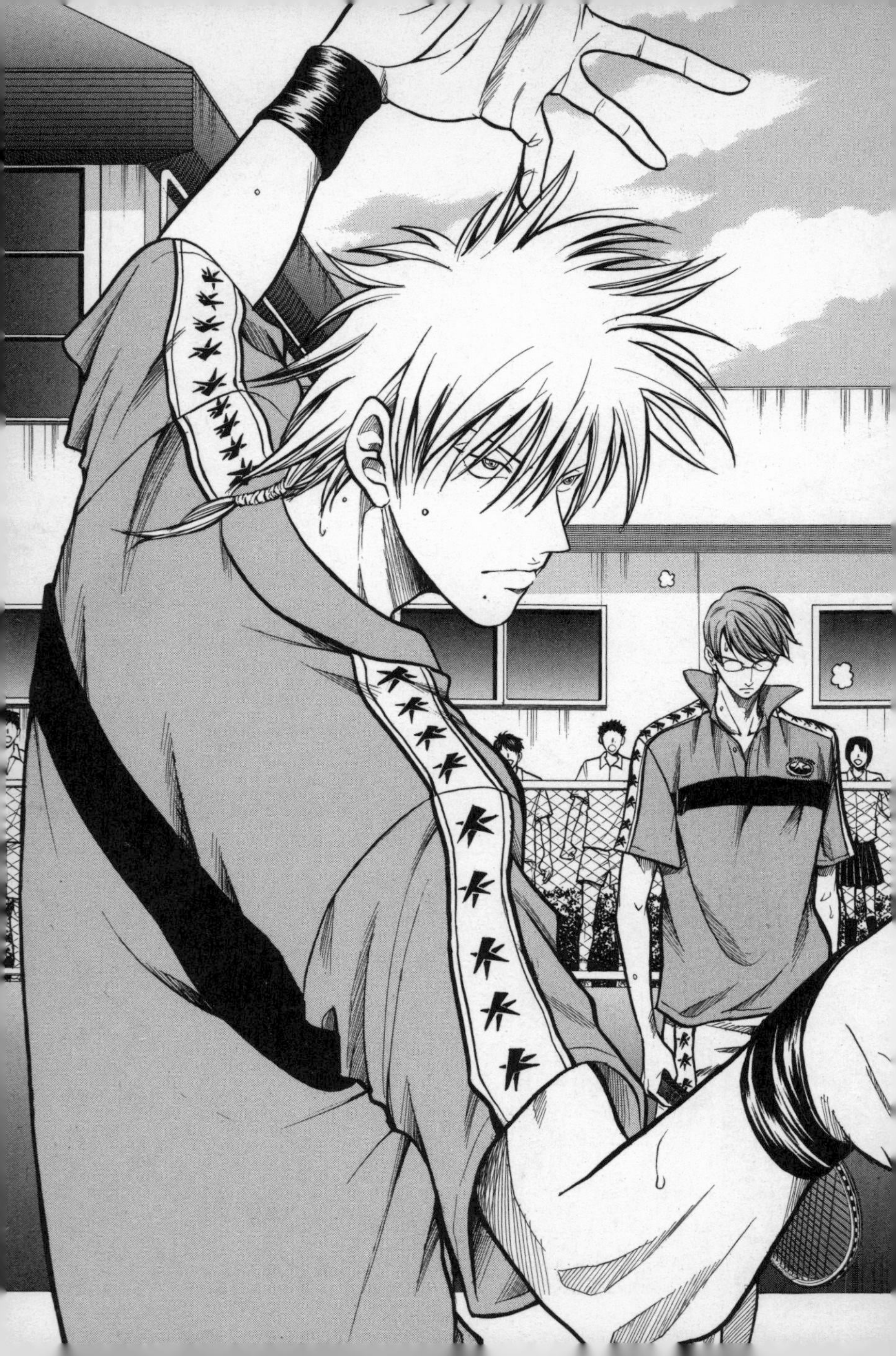

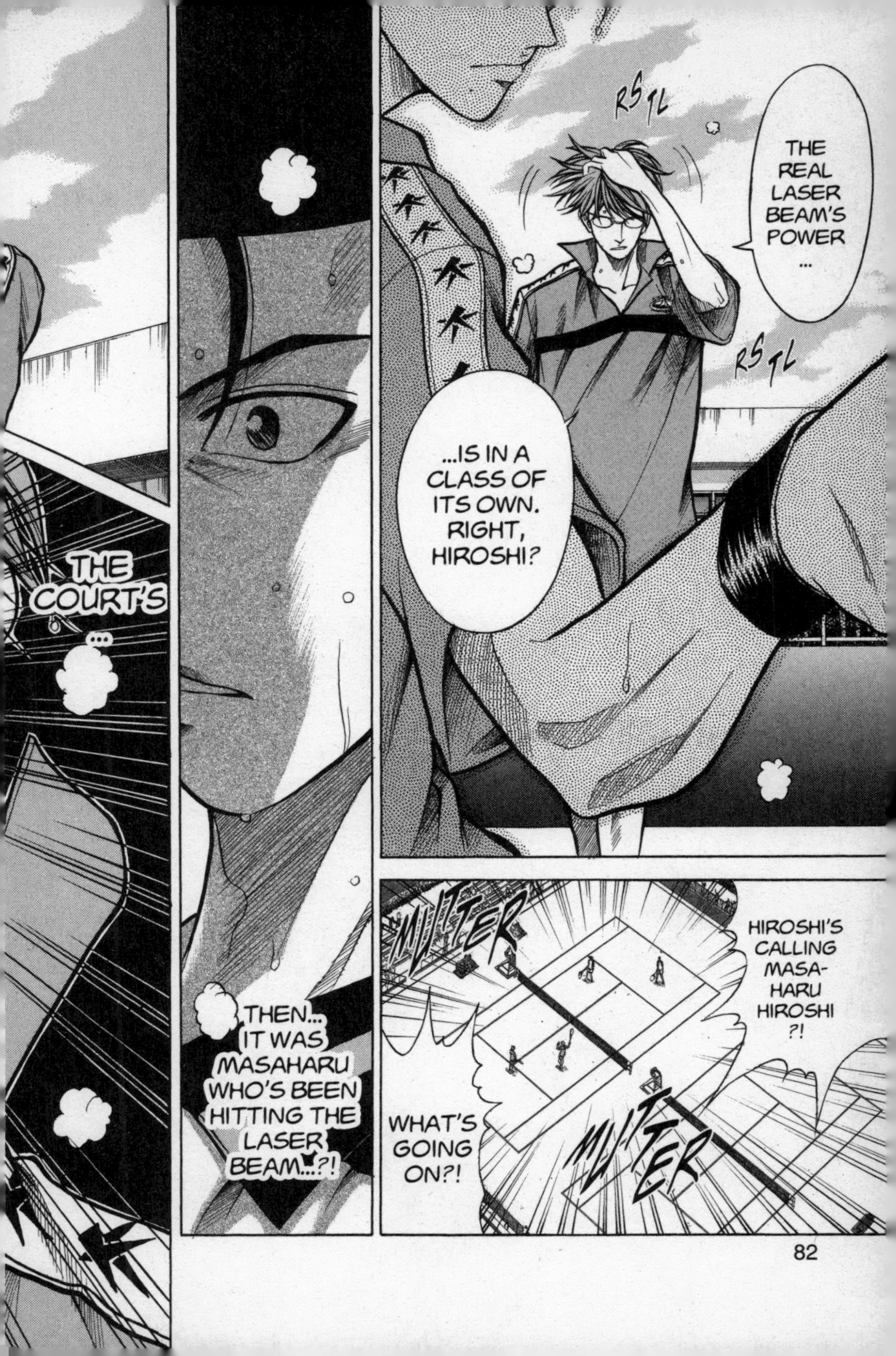
RSTL
THE REAL LASER BEAM'S POWER ...
RSTL
...IS IN A CLASS OF ITS OWN. RIGHT, HIROSHI?
HIROSHI'S CALLING MASA-HARU HIROSHI ?!
MUTTER
WHAT'S GOING ON?!
MUTTER
THEN... IT WAS MASAHARU WHO'S BEEN HITTING THE LASER BEAM...?!
THE COURT'S ...

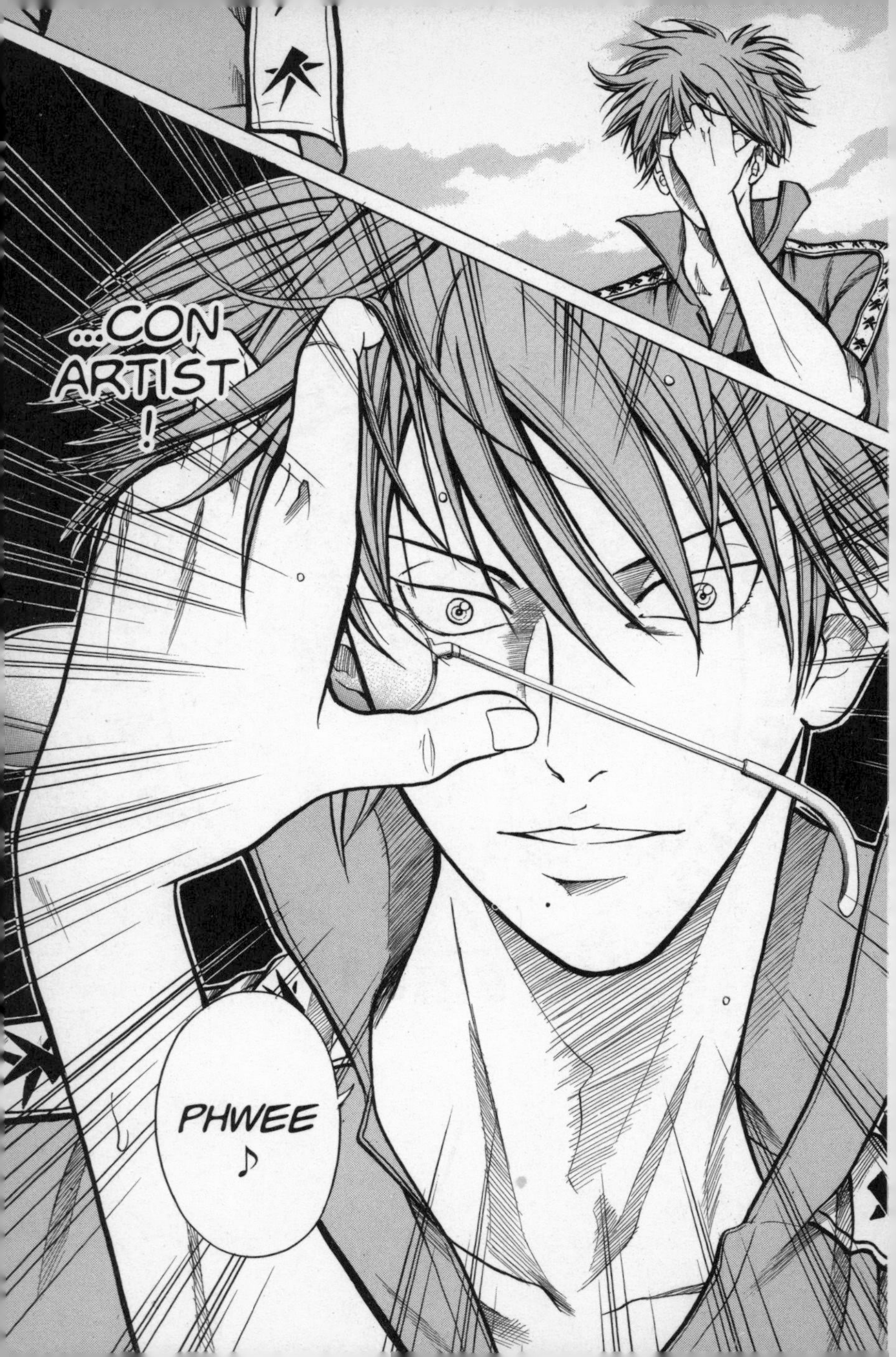
...CON ARTIST !
PHWEE ♪

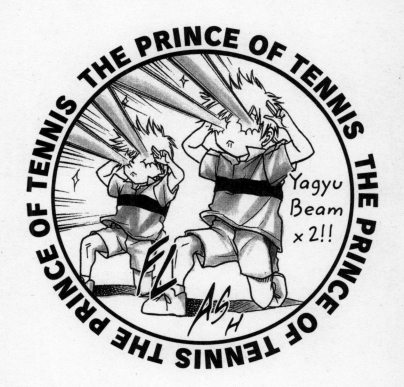

THE PRINCE OF TENNIS THE PRINCE OF TENNIS THE PRINCE OF TENNIS THE PRINCE OF TENNIS

Yagyu
Beam
x 2!!

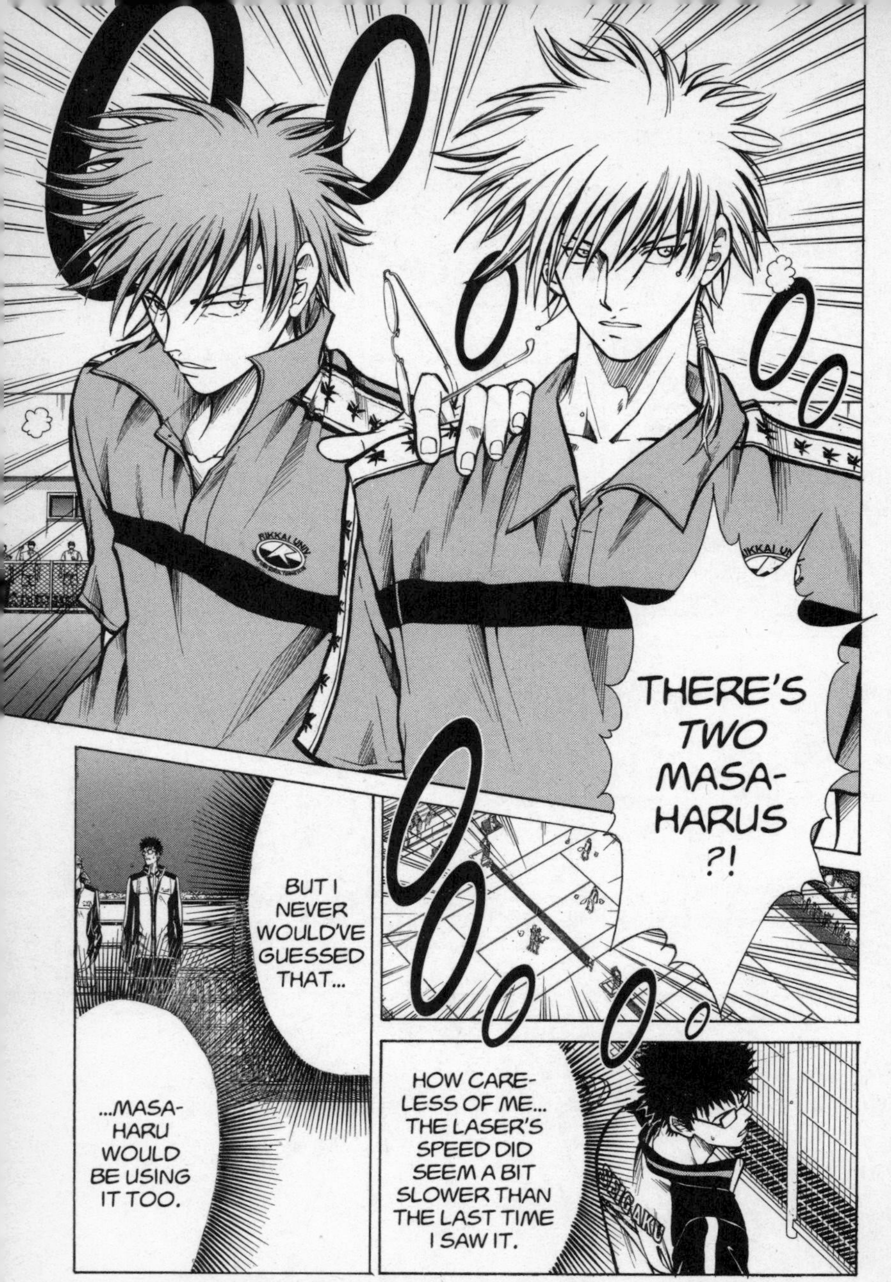
THERE'S TWO MASA-HARUS ?!
HOW CARE-LESS OF ME... THE LASER'S SPEED DID SEEM A BIT SLOWER THAN THE LAST TIME I SAW IT.
BUT I NEVER WOULD'VE GUESSED THAT...
...MASA-HARU WOULD BE USING IT TOO.

GENIUS 206: TWO LASERS

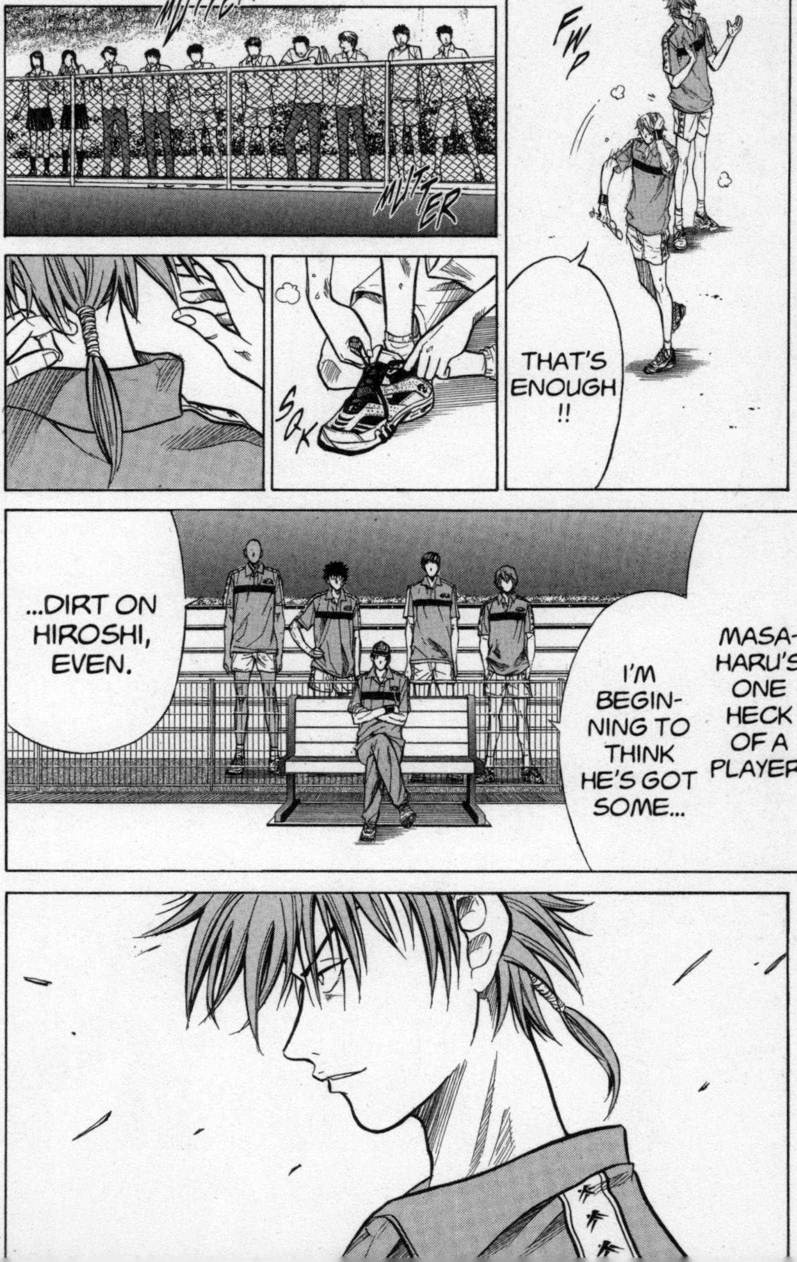
FWP
THAT'S ENOUGH !!
MUTTER
MUTTER
SQK
MASA-HARU'S ONE HECK OF A PLAYER.
I'M BEGIN-NING TO THINK HE'S GOT SOME...
...DIRT ON HIROSHI, EVEN.

READ THIS WAY

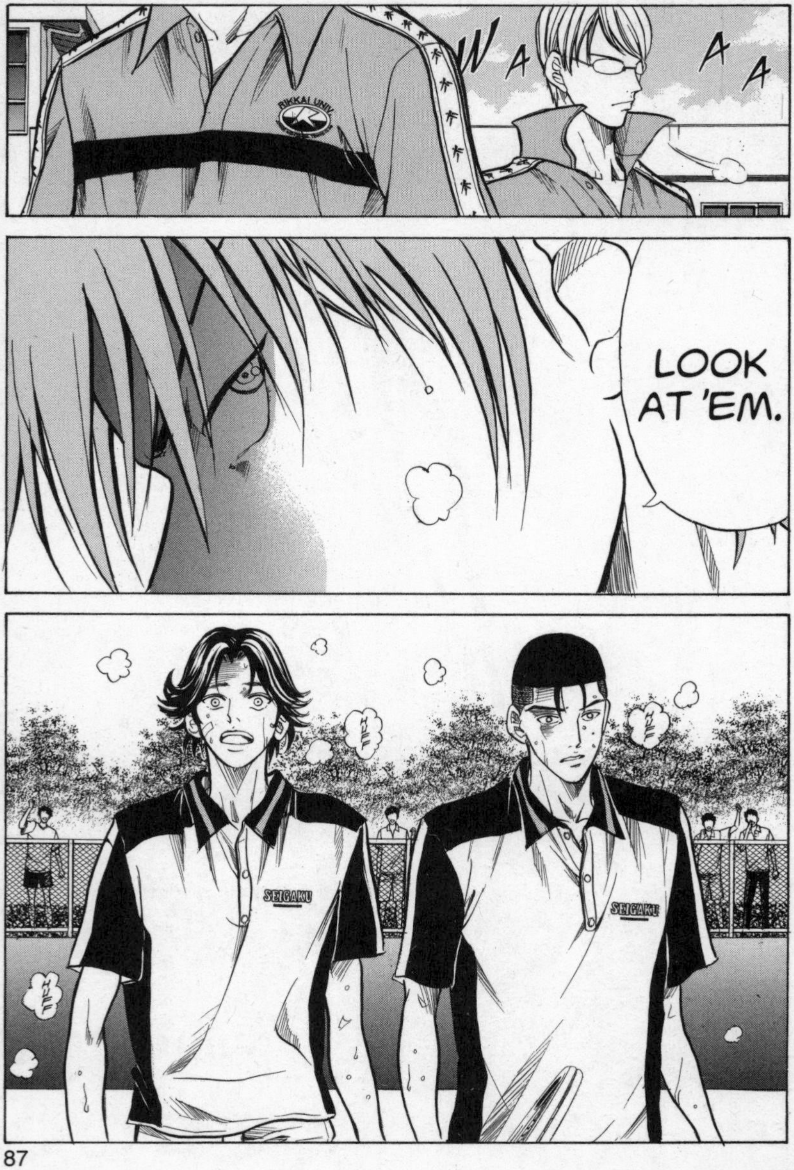
WAAAA
LOOK AT 'EM.
HUFF

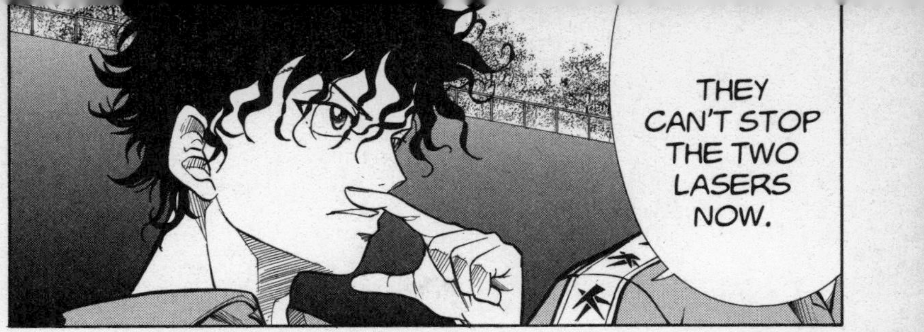
THEY CAN'T STOP THE TWO LASERS NOW.
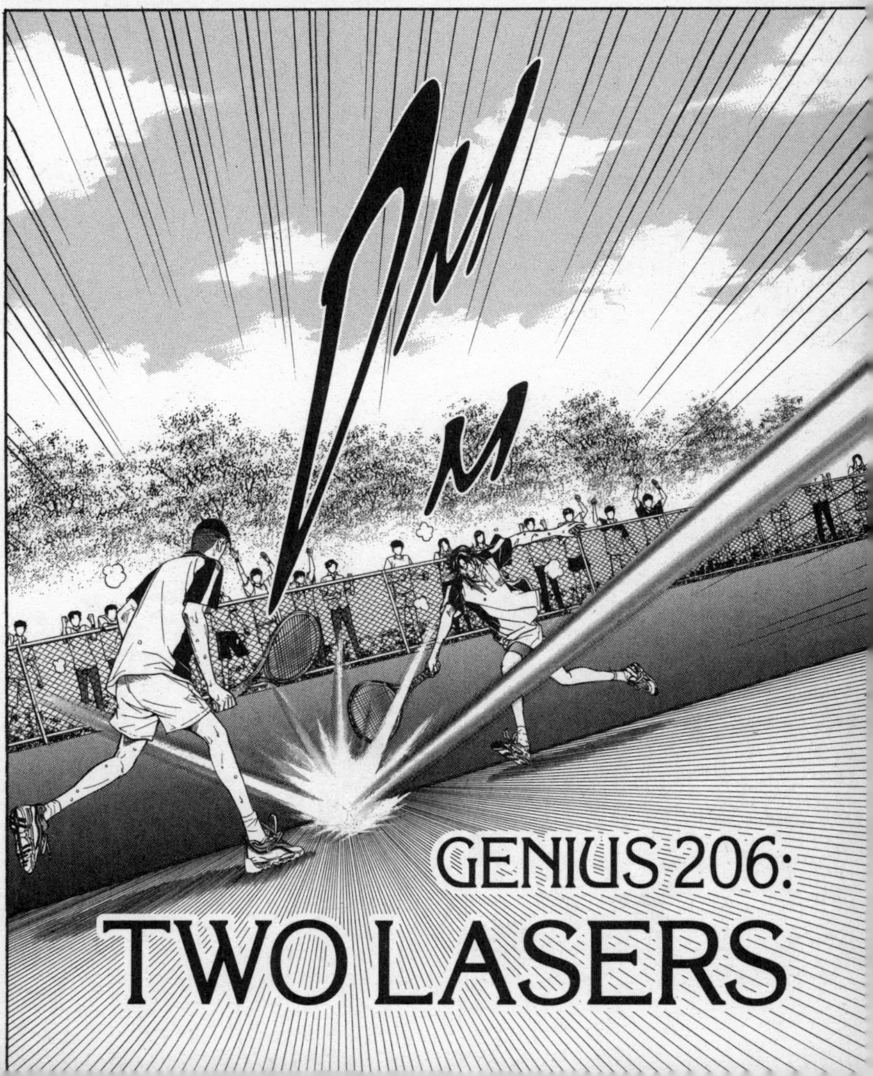
GENIUS 206:
TWO LASERS

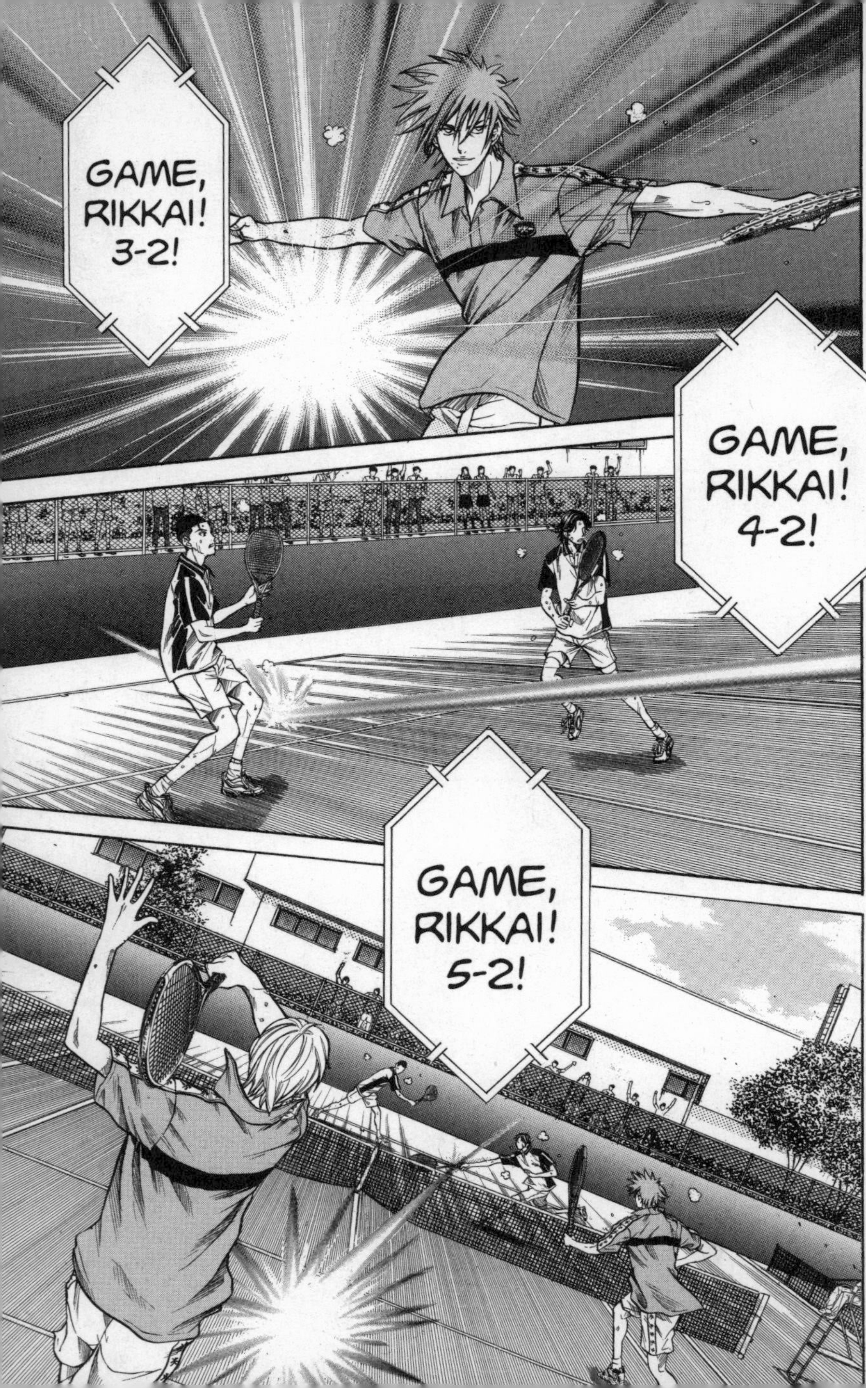
GAME, RIKKAI! 3-2!
GAME, RIKKAI! 4-2!
GAME, RIKKAI! 5-2!

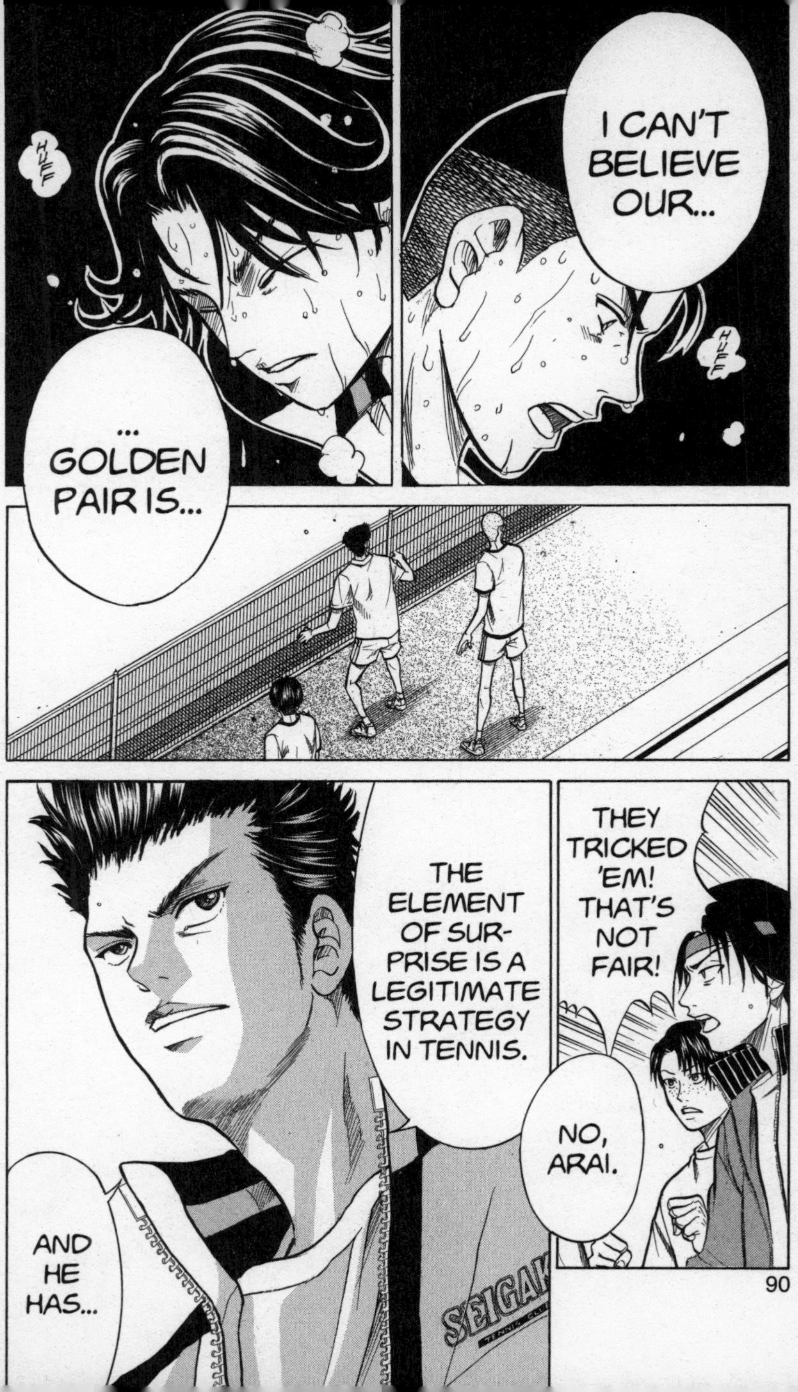
I CAN'T BELIEVE OUR...
HUFF
HUFF
... GOLDEN PAIR IS...
THEY TRICKED 'EM! THAT'S NOT FAIR!
NO, ARAI.
THE ELEMENT OF SURPRISE IS A LEGITIMATE STRATEGY IN TENNIS.
AND HE HAS...

READ THIS WAY

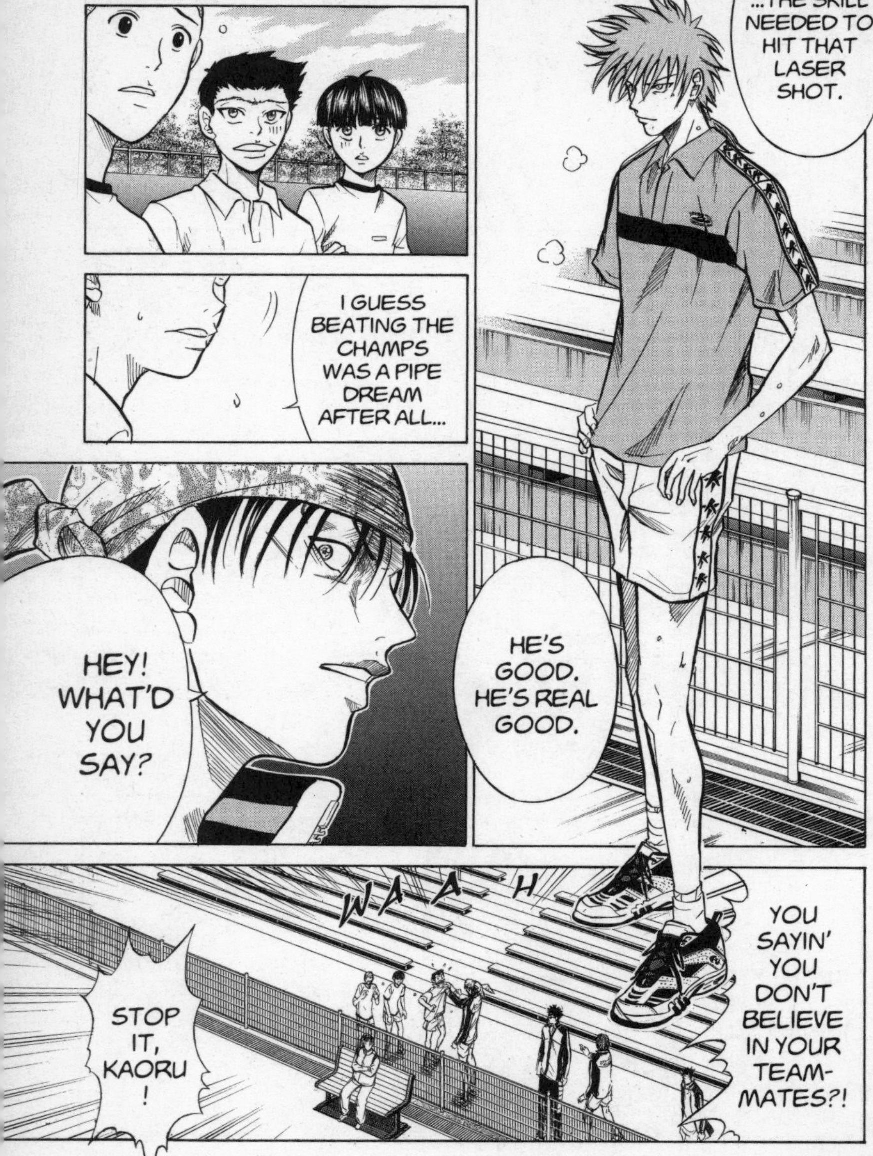
...THE SKILL NEEDED TO HIT THAT LASER SHOT.
HE'S GOOD. HE'S REAL GOOD.
I GUESS BEATING THE CHAMPS WAS A PIPE DREAM AFTER ALL...
HEY! WHAT'D YOU SAY?
YOU SAYIN' YOU DON'T BELIEVE IN YOUR TEAM-MATES?!
WAAH
STOP IT, KAORU!

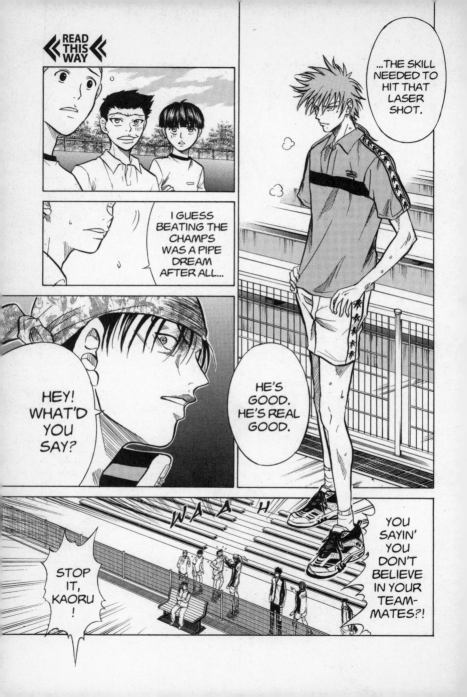

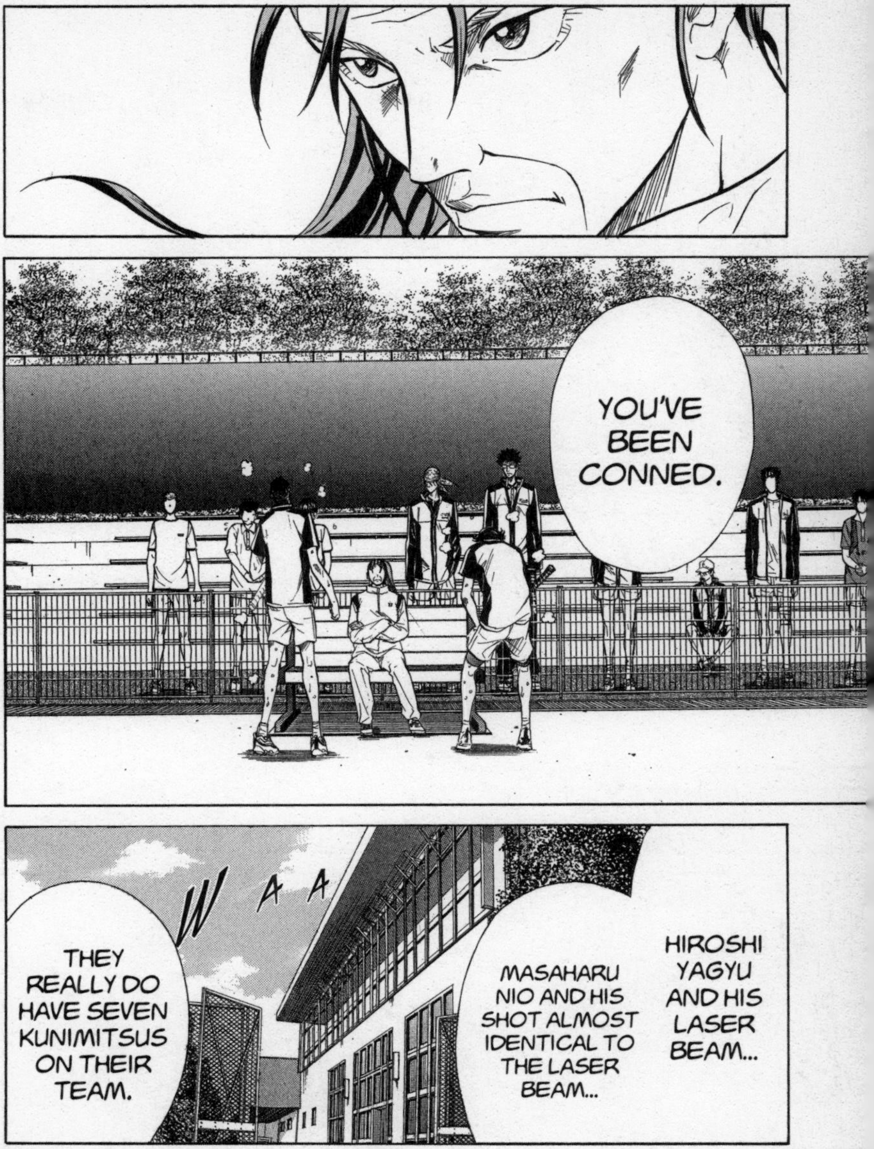
YOU'VE BEEN CONNED.
HIROSHI YAGYU AND HIS LASER BEAM...
MASAHARU NIO AND HIS SHOT ALMOST IDENTICAL TO THE LASER BEAM...
WAA
THEY REALLY DO HAVE SEVEN KUNIMITSUS ON THEIR TEAM.

READ THIS WAY

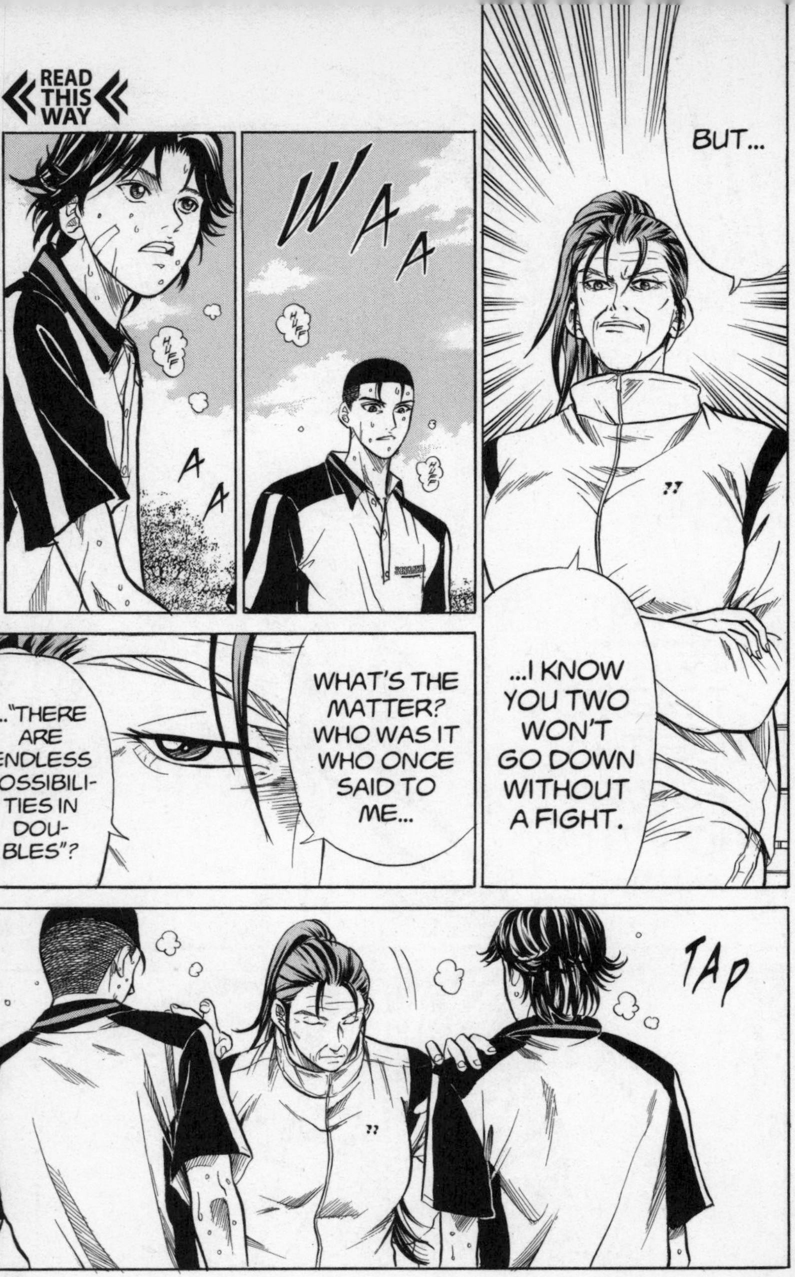

WAA
HUFF
HUFF
HUFF
AA
BUT...
...I KNOW YOU TWO WON'T GO DOWN WITHOUT A FIGHT.
WHAT'S THE MATTER? WHO WAS IT WHO ONCE SAID TO ME...
..."THERE ARE ENDLESS POSSIBILI-TIES IN DOU-BLES"?
TAP

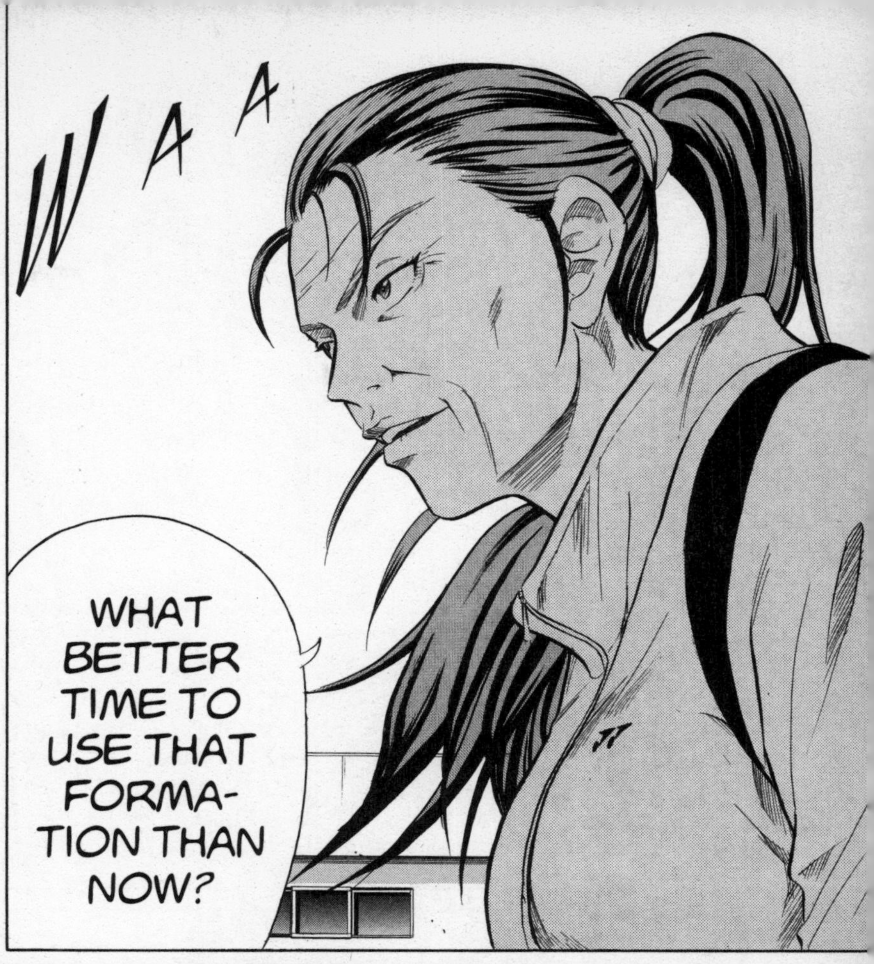
WAA
WHAT BETTER TIME TO USE THAT FORMATION THAN NOW?

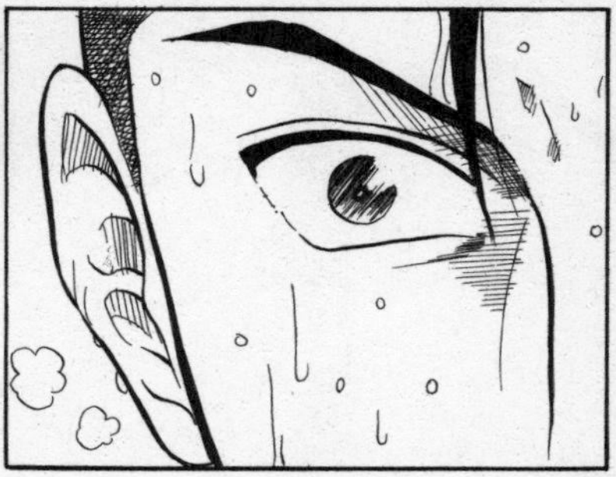

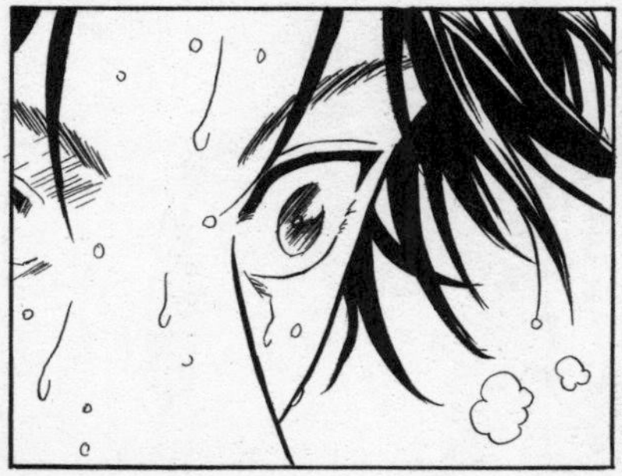

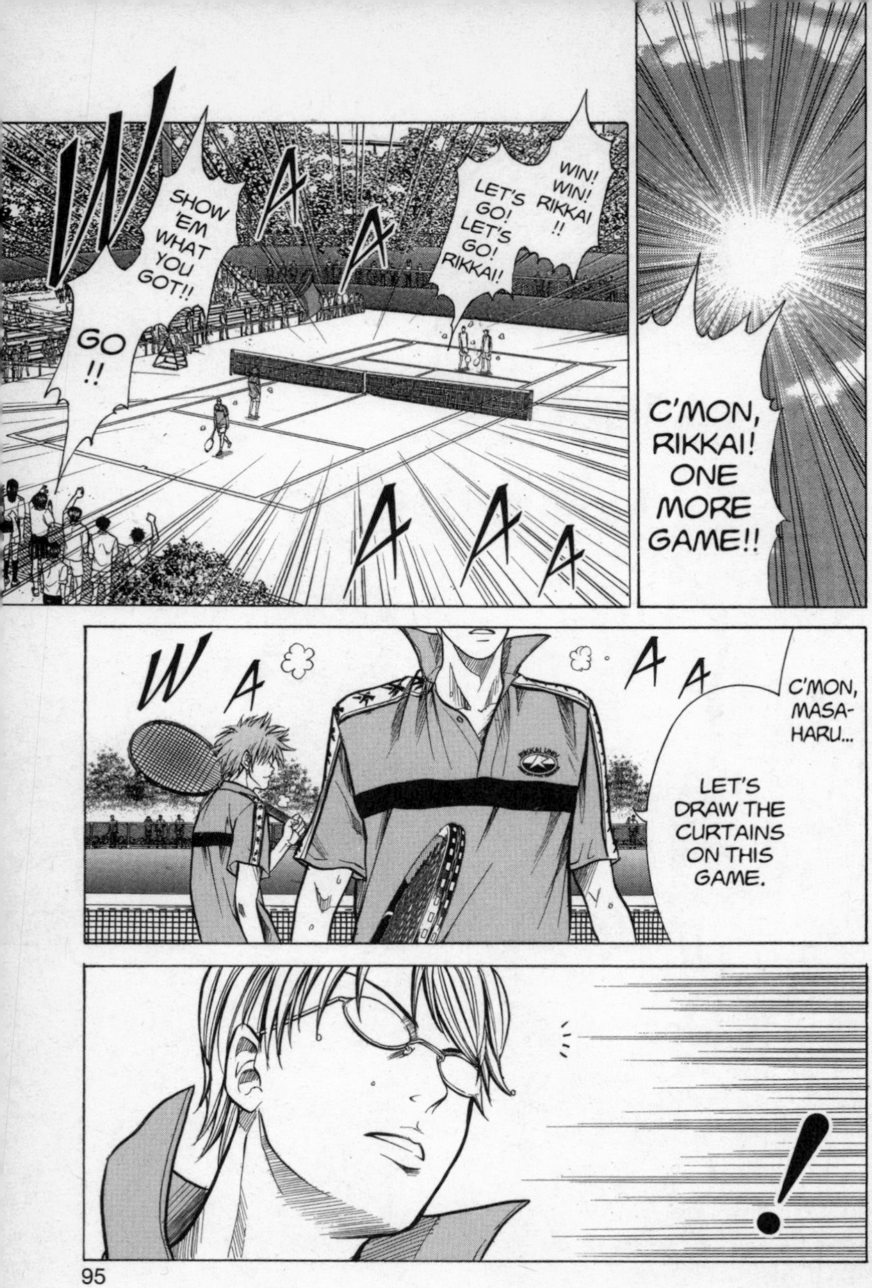
C'MON, RIKKAI! ONE MORE GAME!!
WIN! WIN! RIKKAI!!
LET'S GO! LET'S GO! RIKKAI!
SHOW 'EM WHAT YOU GOT!!
WAA
GO!!
AAA
AA
C'MON, MASA-HARU...
LET'S DRAW THE CURTAINS ON THIS GAME.
WA
!

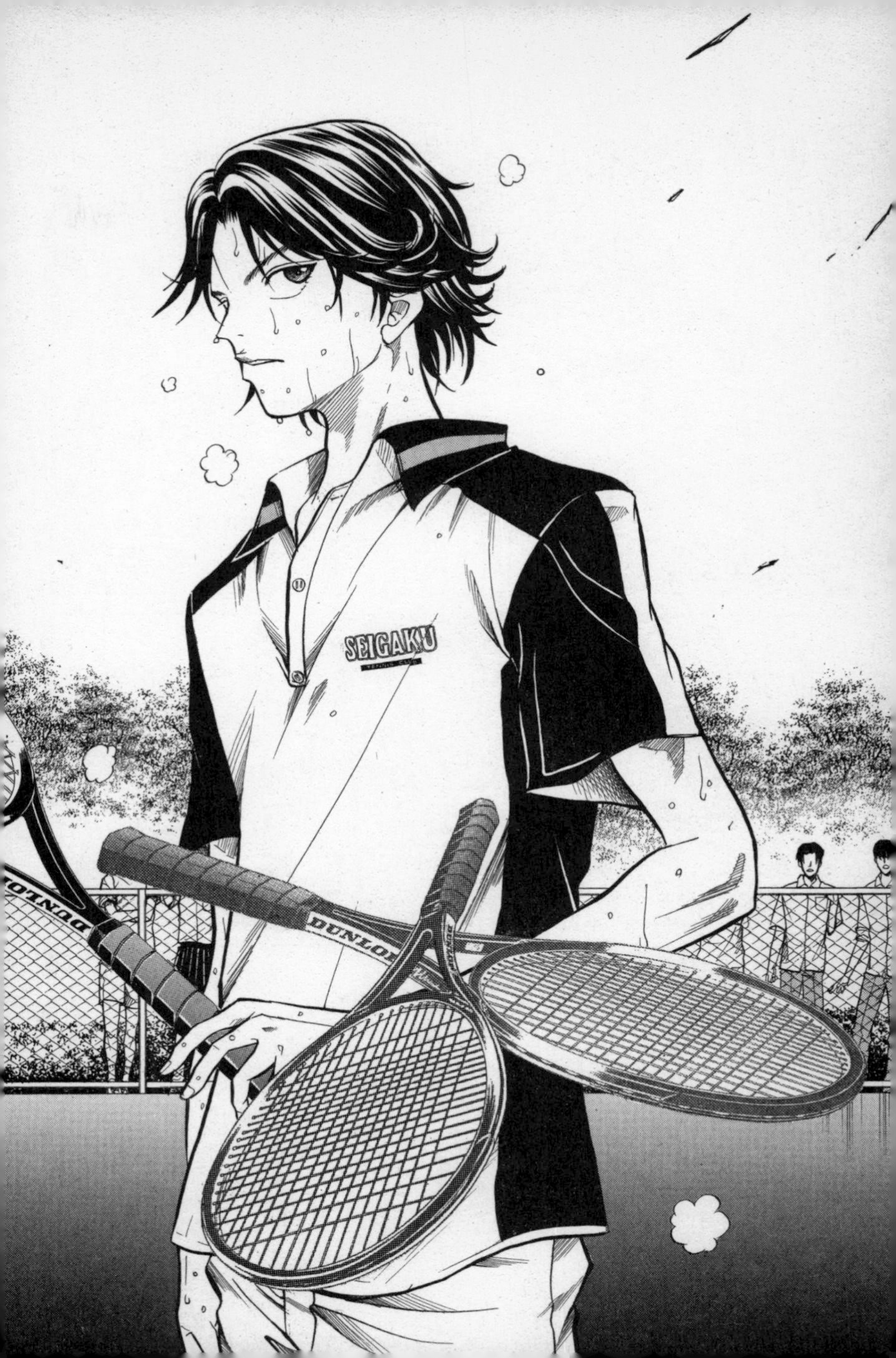
SEIGAKU

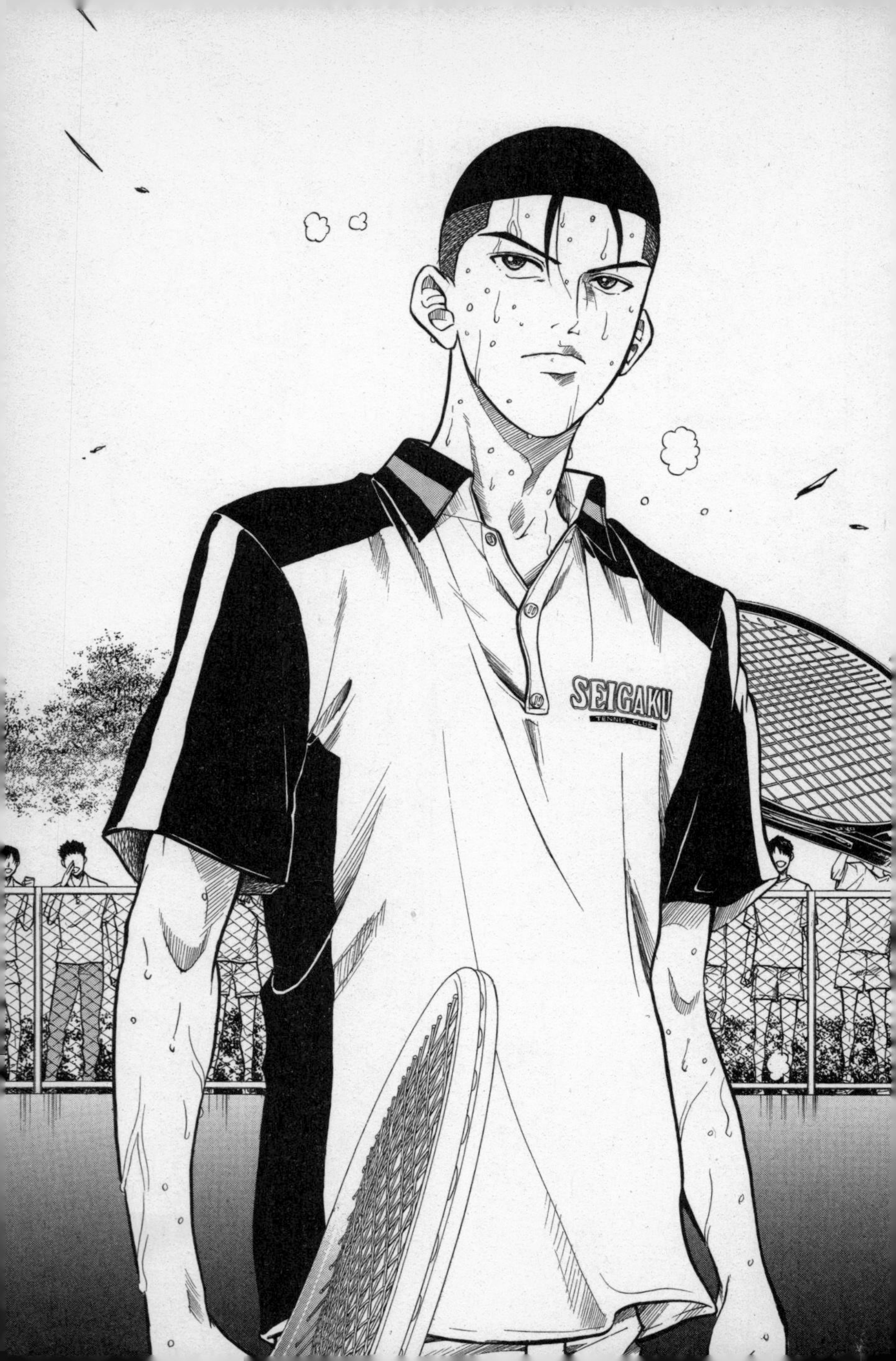
SEIGAKU
TENNIS CLUB

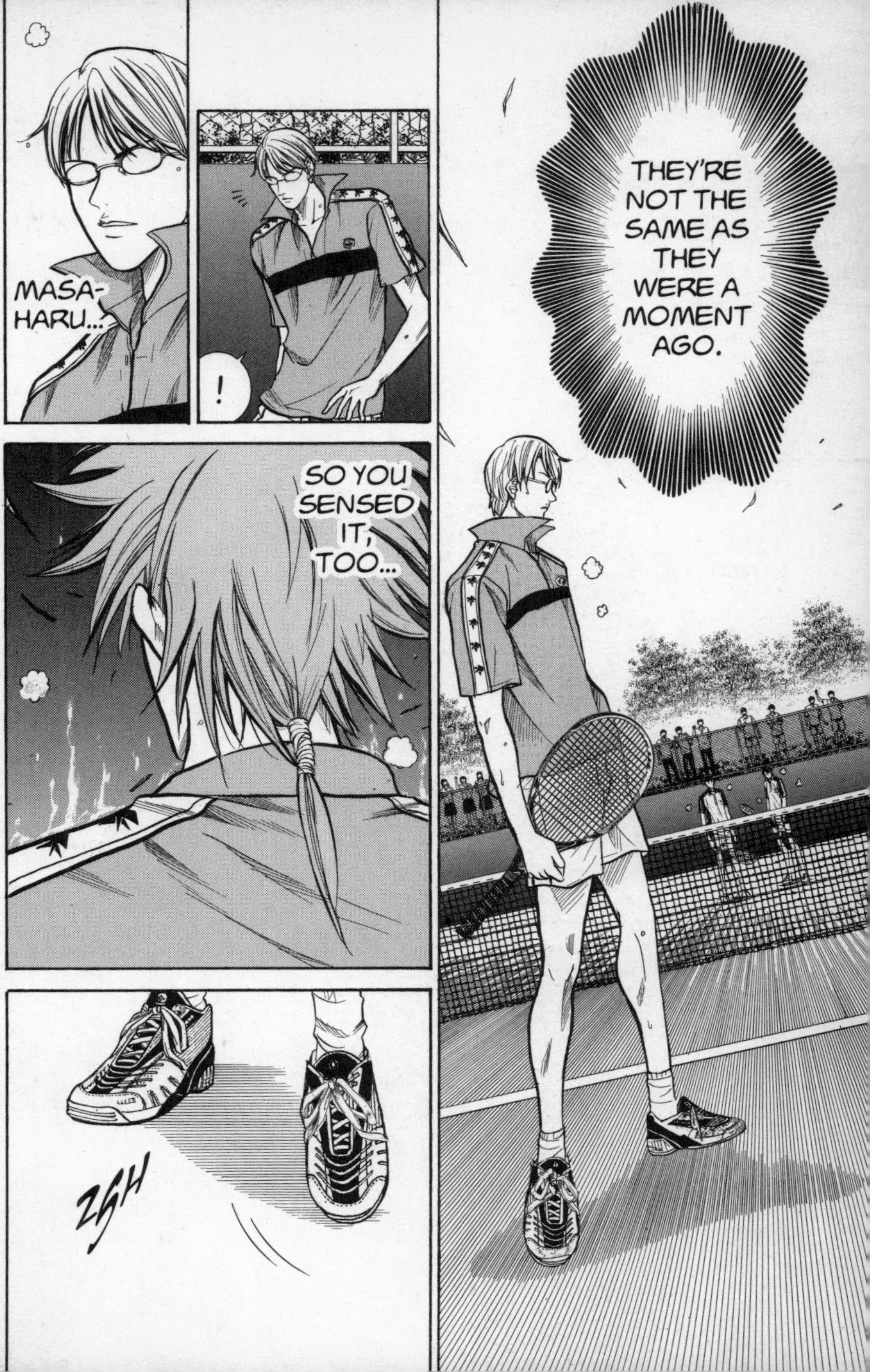
THEY'RE NOT THE SAME AS THEY WERE A MOMENT AGO.
!
MASA-HARU...
SO YOU SENSED IT, TOO...
ZSH

READ THIS WAY

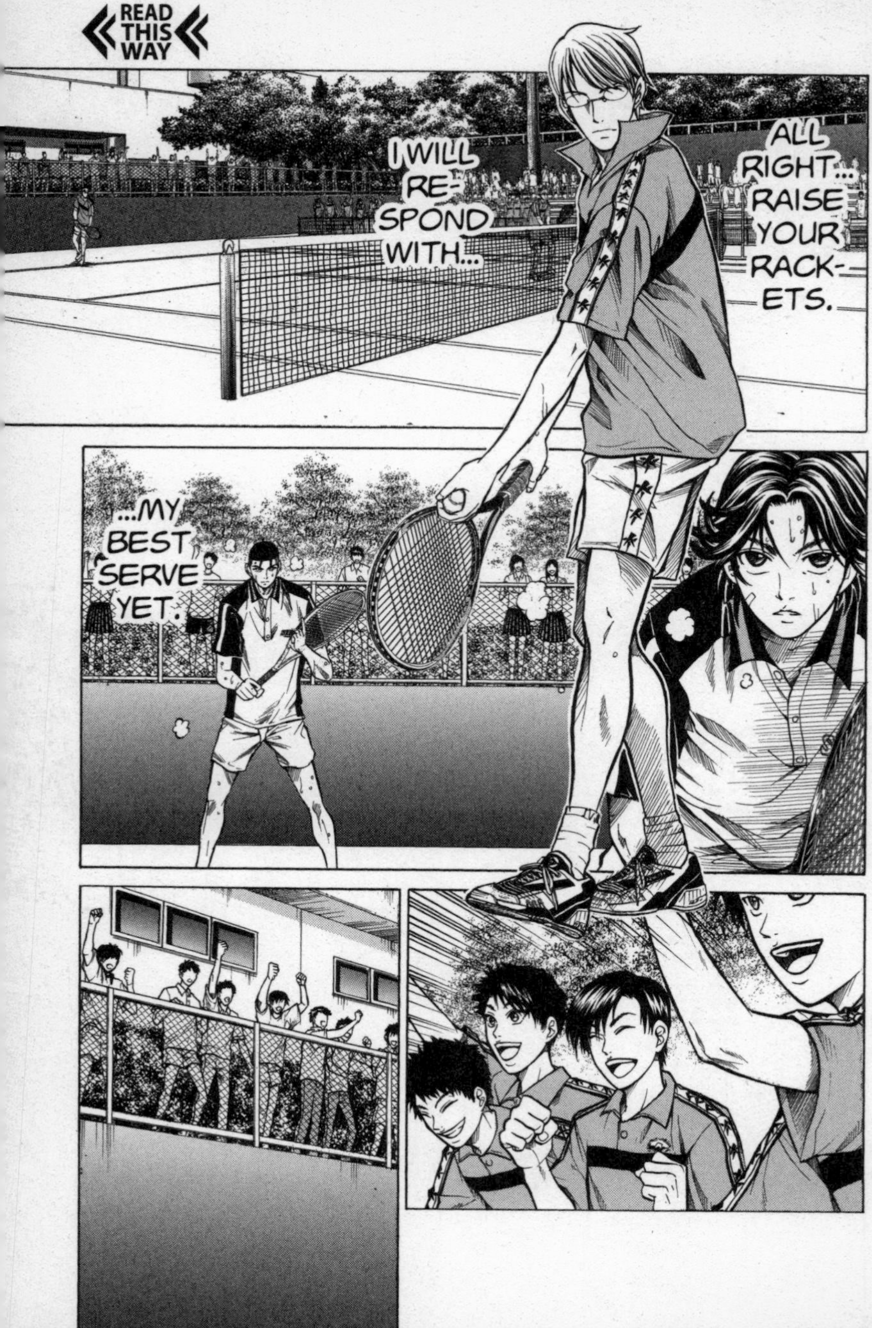
ALL RIGHT... RAISE YOUR RACK-ETS.
I WILL RE-SPOND WITH...
...MY BEST SERVE YET.

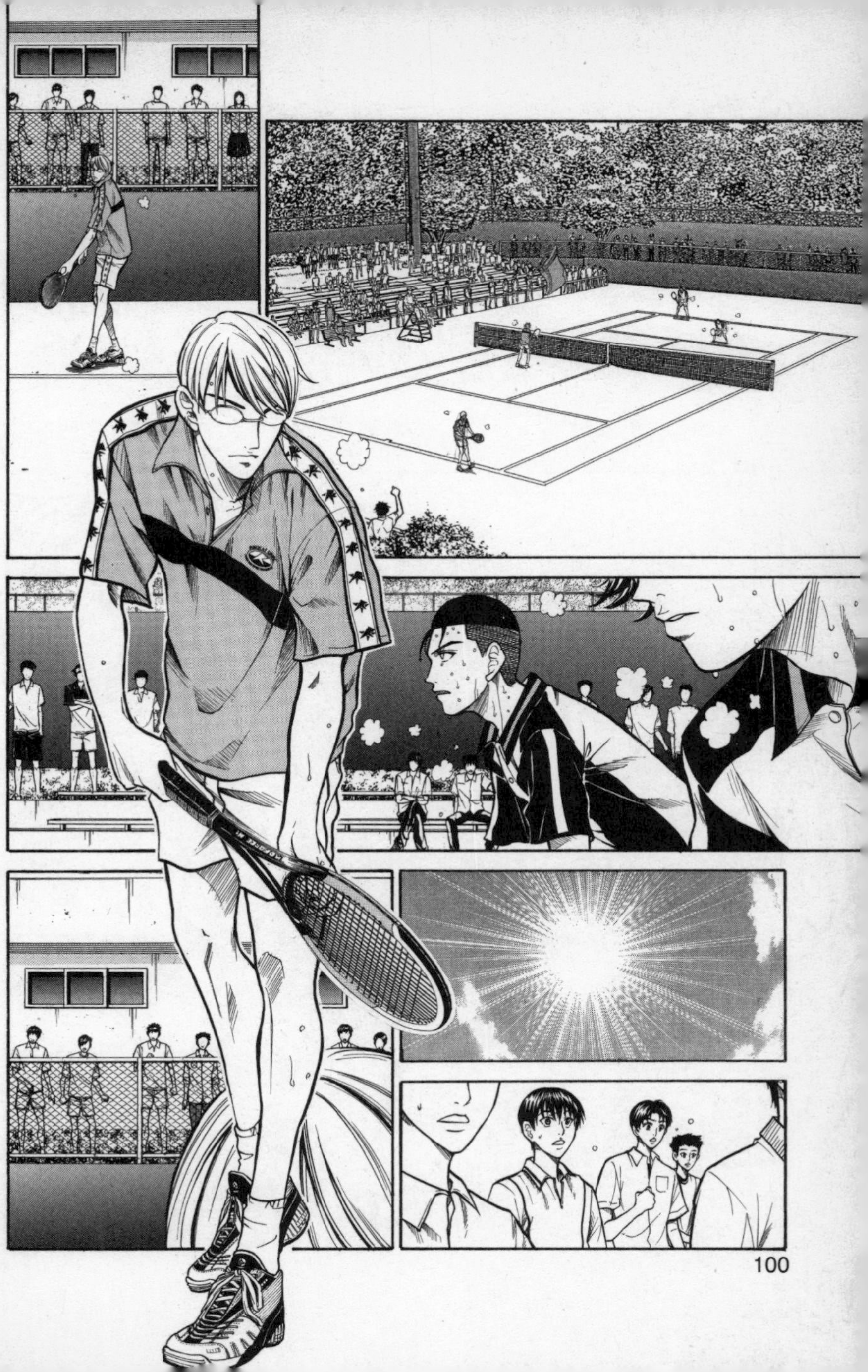

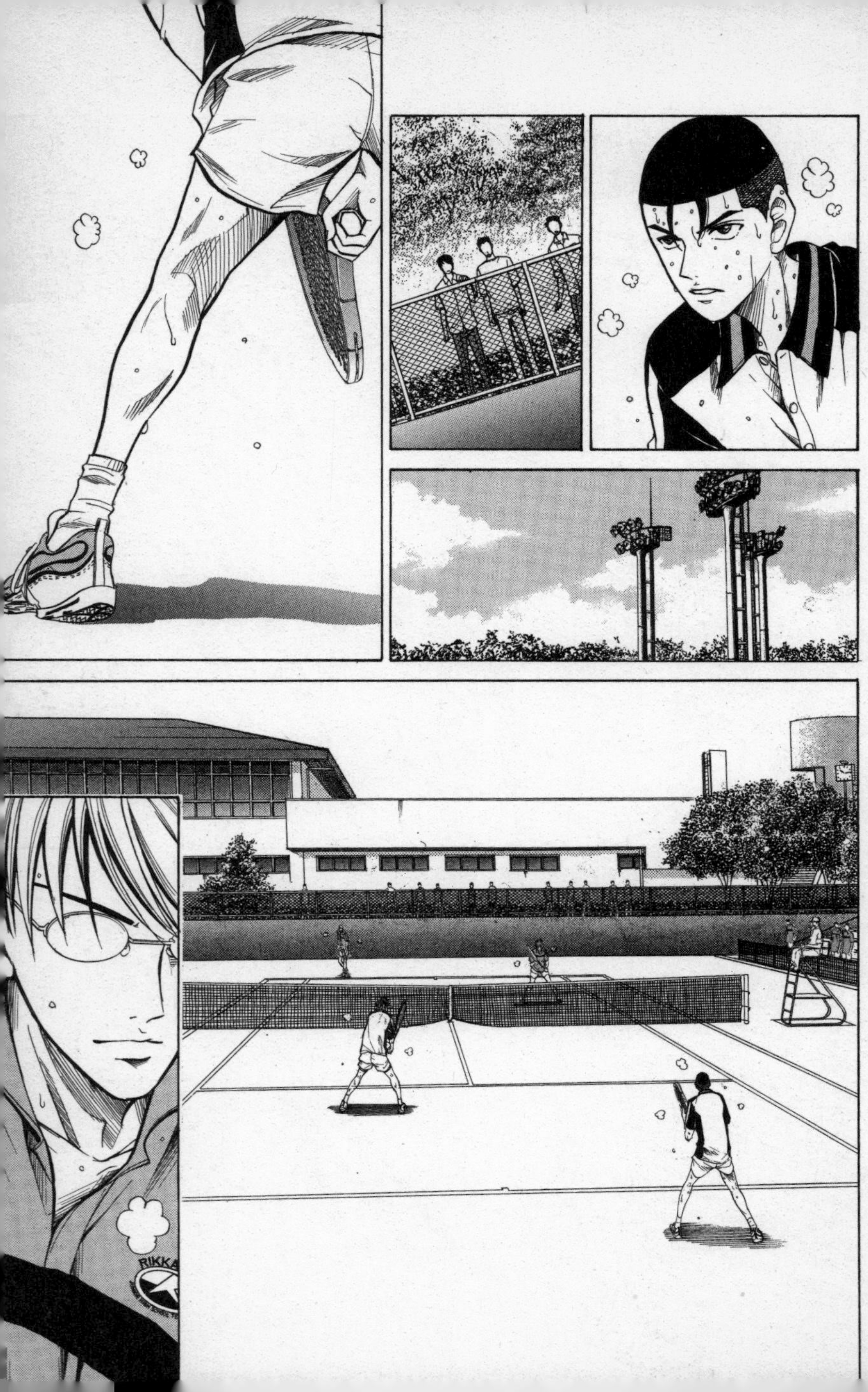
RIKKA

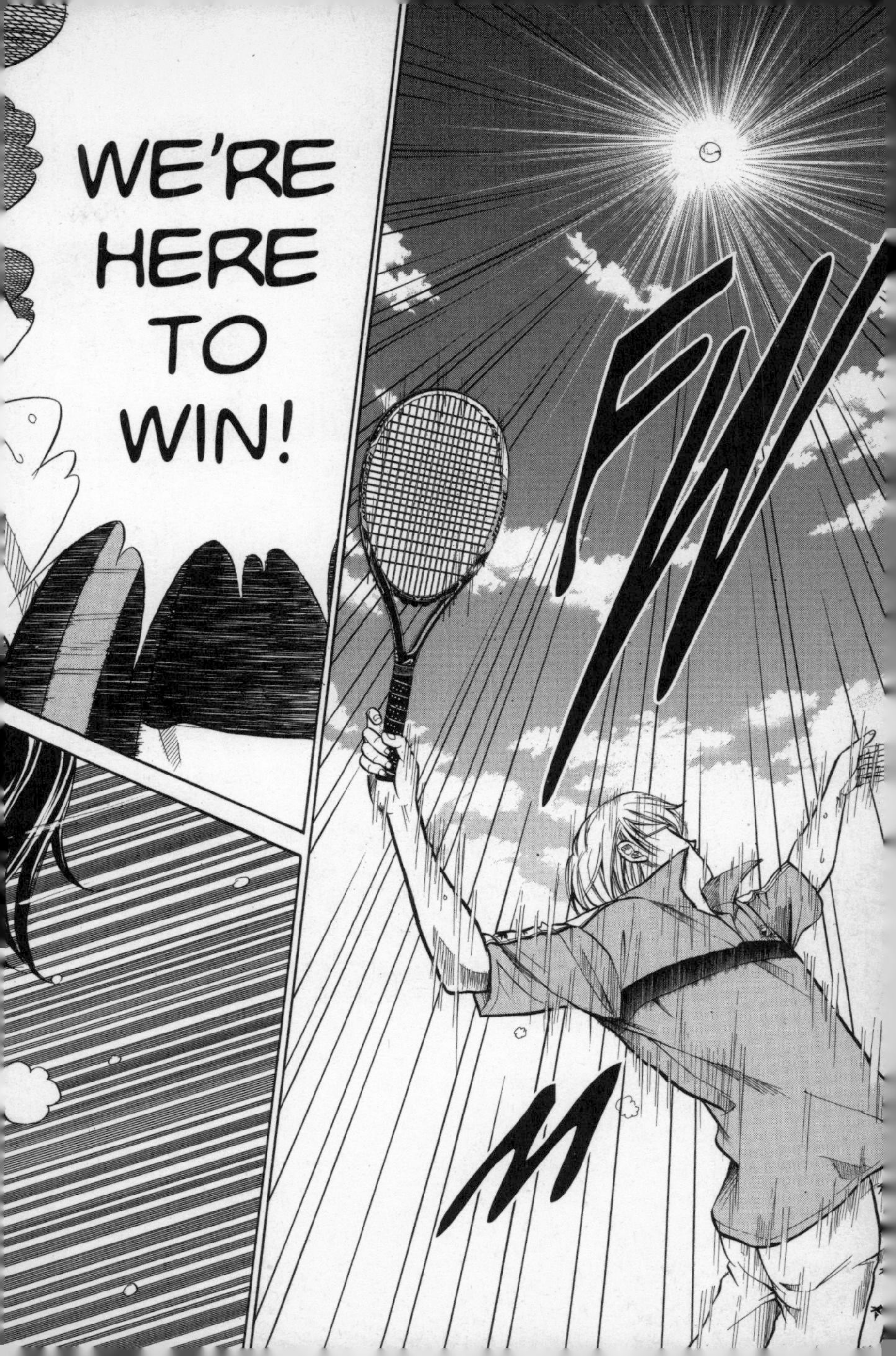
WE'RE HERE TO WIN!

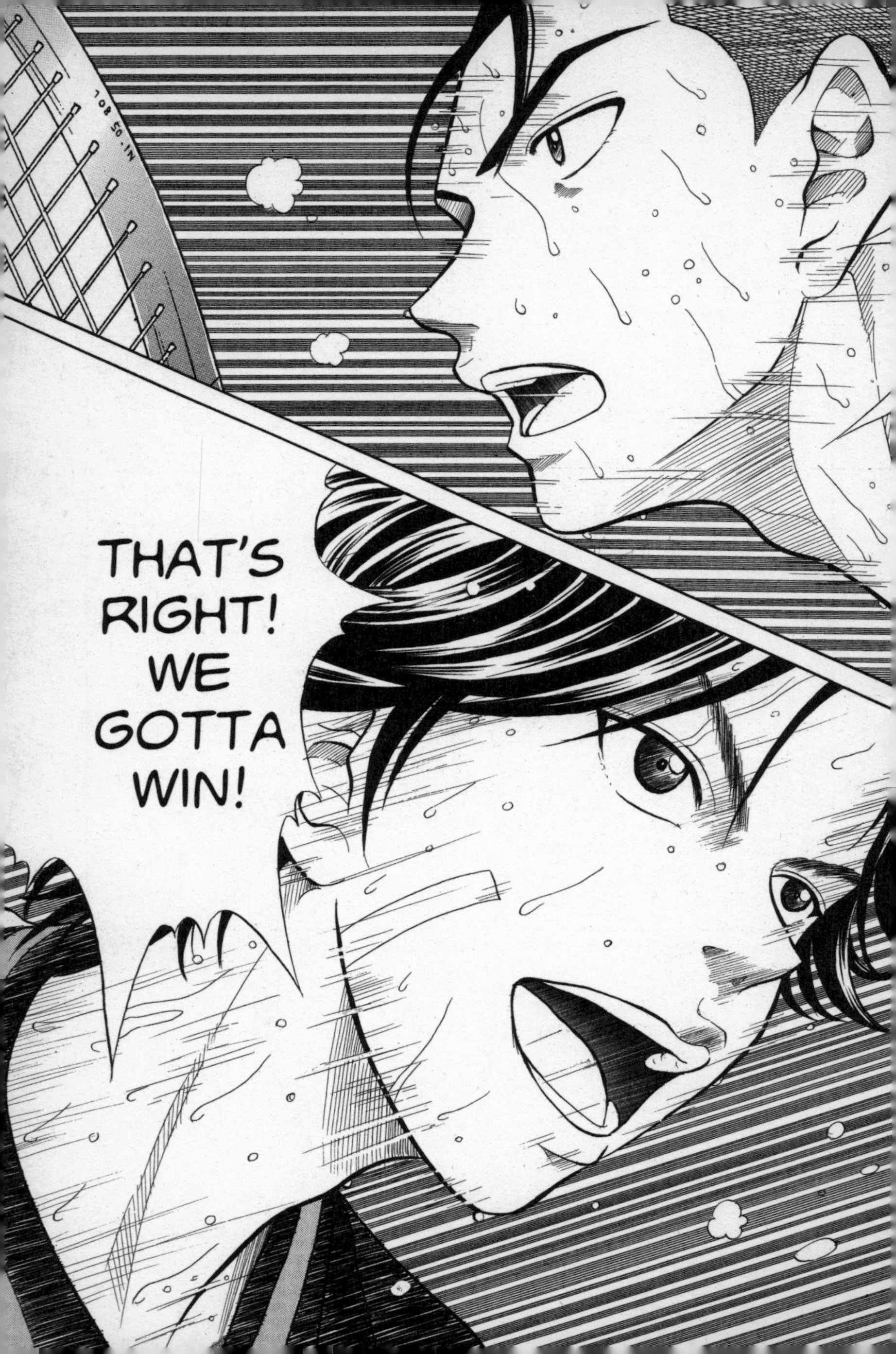
THAT'S RIGHT! WE GOTTA WIN!

テニスの王子様 THE PRINCE OF TENNIS

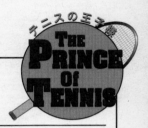

Thank you for reading *The Prince of Tennis*, volume 24.

It's our fifth-year anniversary!! We're now entering our sixth year. I am really grateful to all the fans and to everybody who's involved with the comic. Come October, the anime will be in its third year. (I watch every episode!). The musical's in its third installment (St. Rudolph—I highly recommend it), and a movie will be released next January! We're currently working on a movie that'll blow your minds. If you're a *Prince of Tennis* fan, you'll regret it if you don't watch it!

I'm in a serious pinch with a deadline coming up, so I gotta cut this short!

Zsssh—... (I'm back.)

So keep supporting *The Prince of Tennis* and Ryoma!!

I'll see you in the next volume!

テニスの王子様 T. KONOMI

Send fan letters to: *The Prince of Tennis*, Takeshi Konomi, c/o VIZ Media LLC, P.O. Box 77010, San Francisco, CA 94107

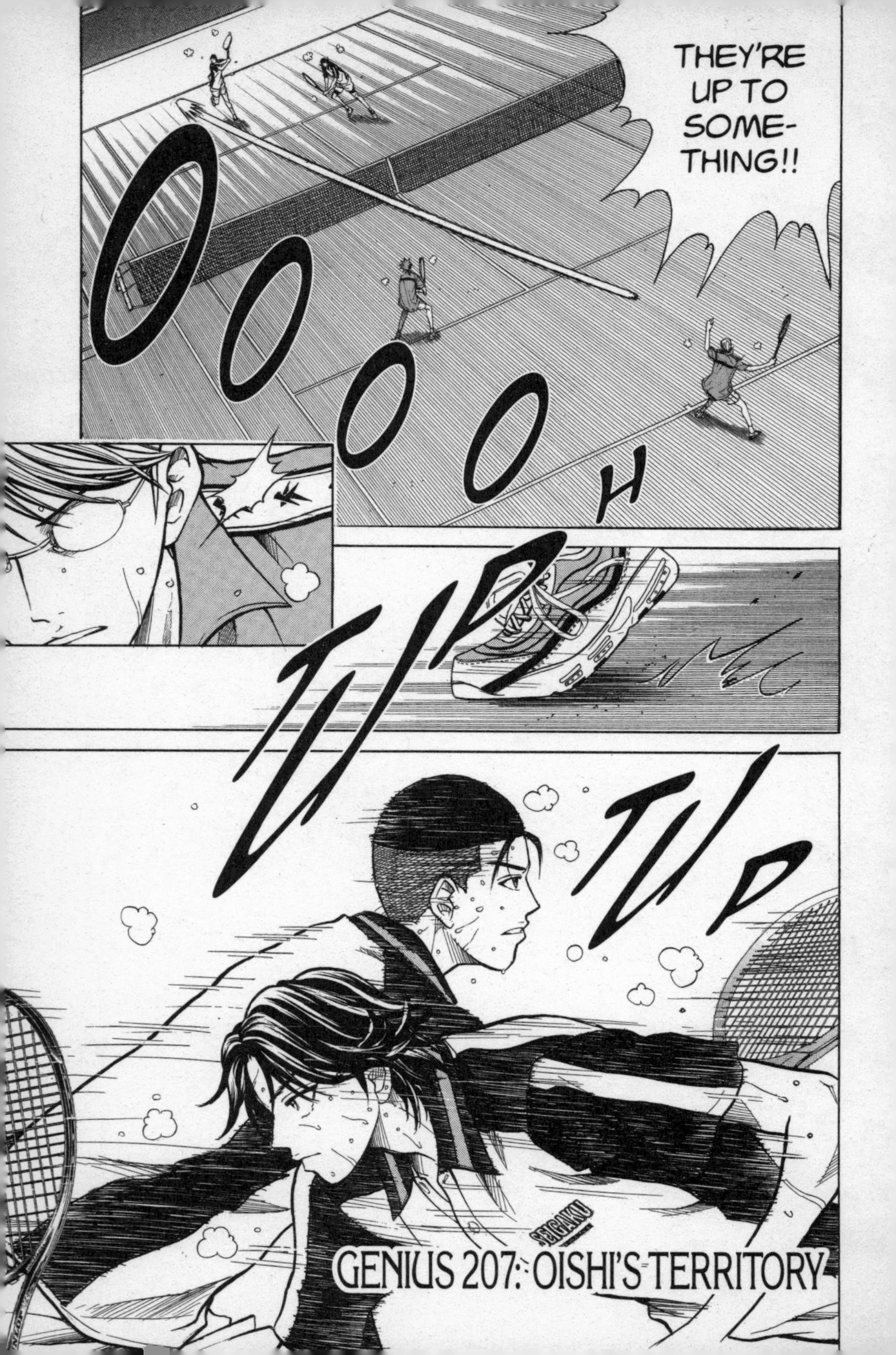
THEY'RE UP TO SOME-THING!!
OOOOOH
TUP
TUP
GENIUS 207: OISHI'S TERRITORY

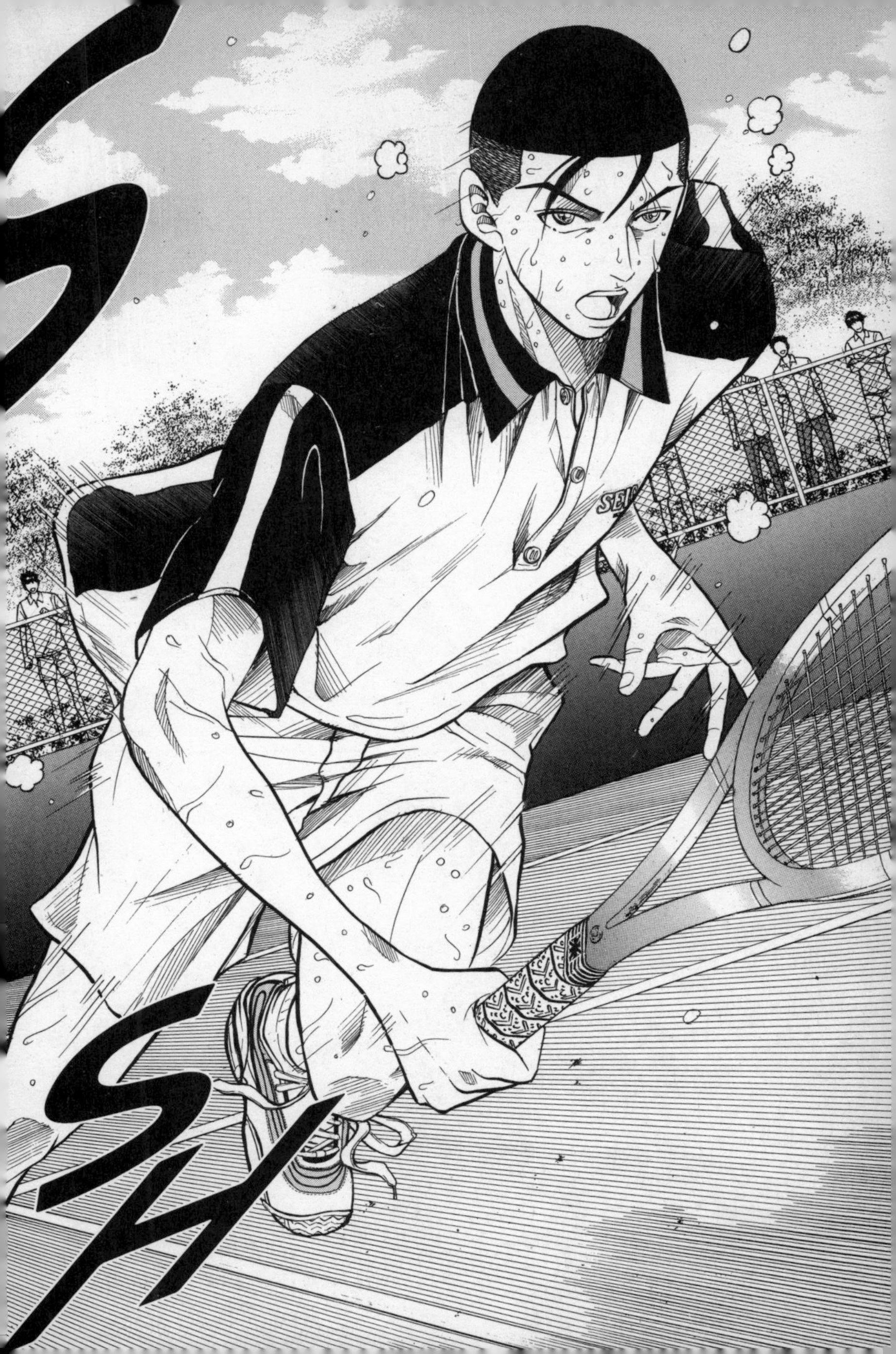
SH

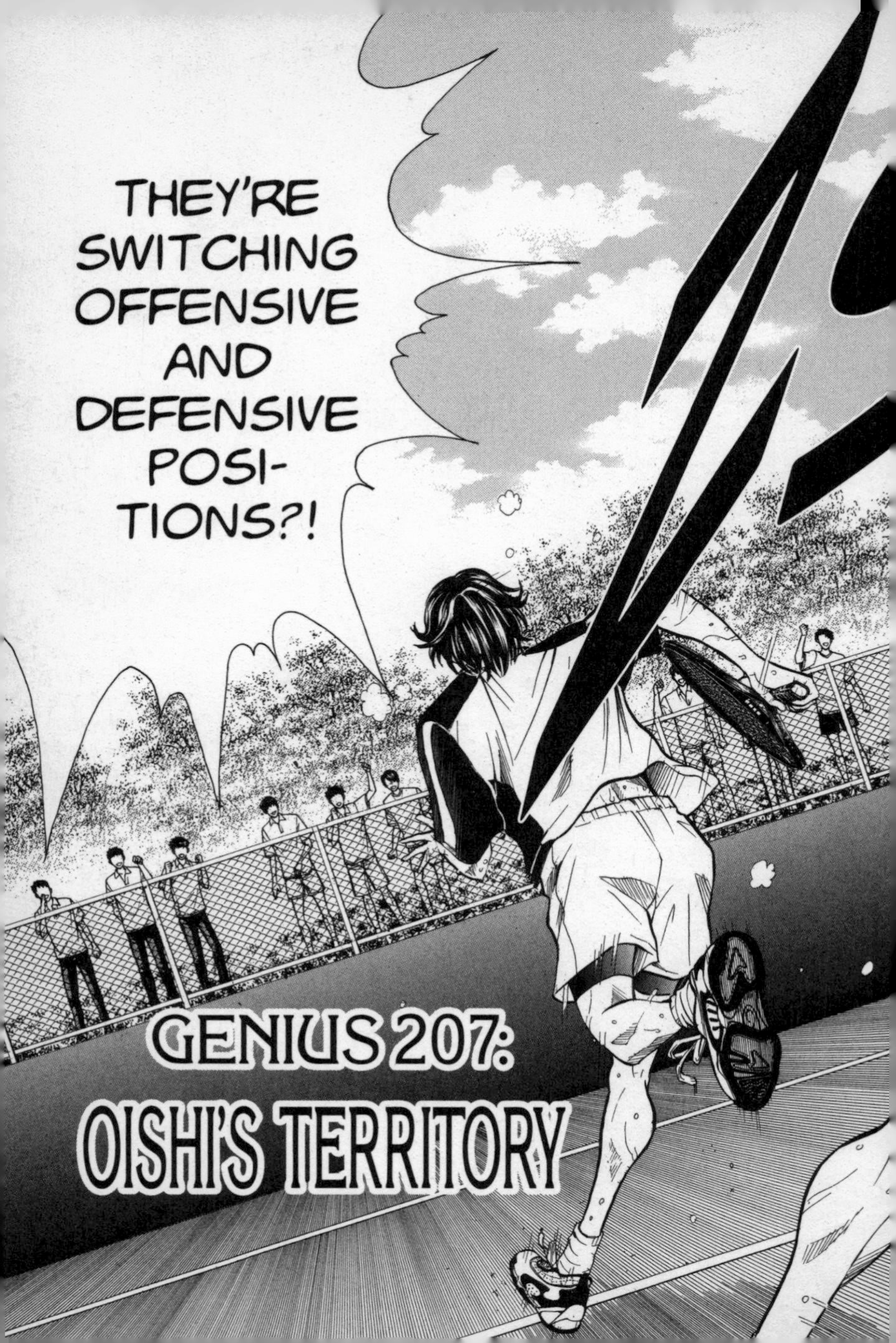
THEY'RE SWITCHING OFFENSIVE AND DEFENSIVE POSI-TIONS?!
GENIUS 207:
OISHI'S TERRITORY

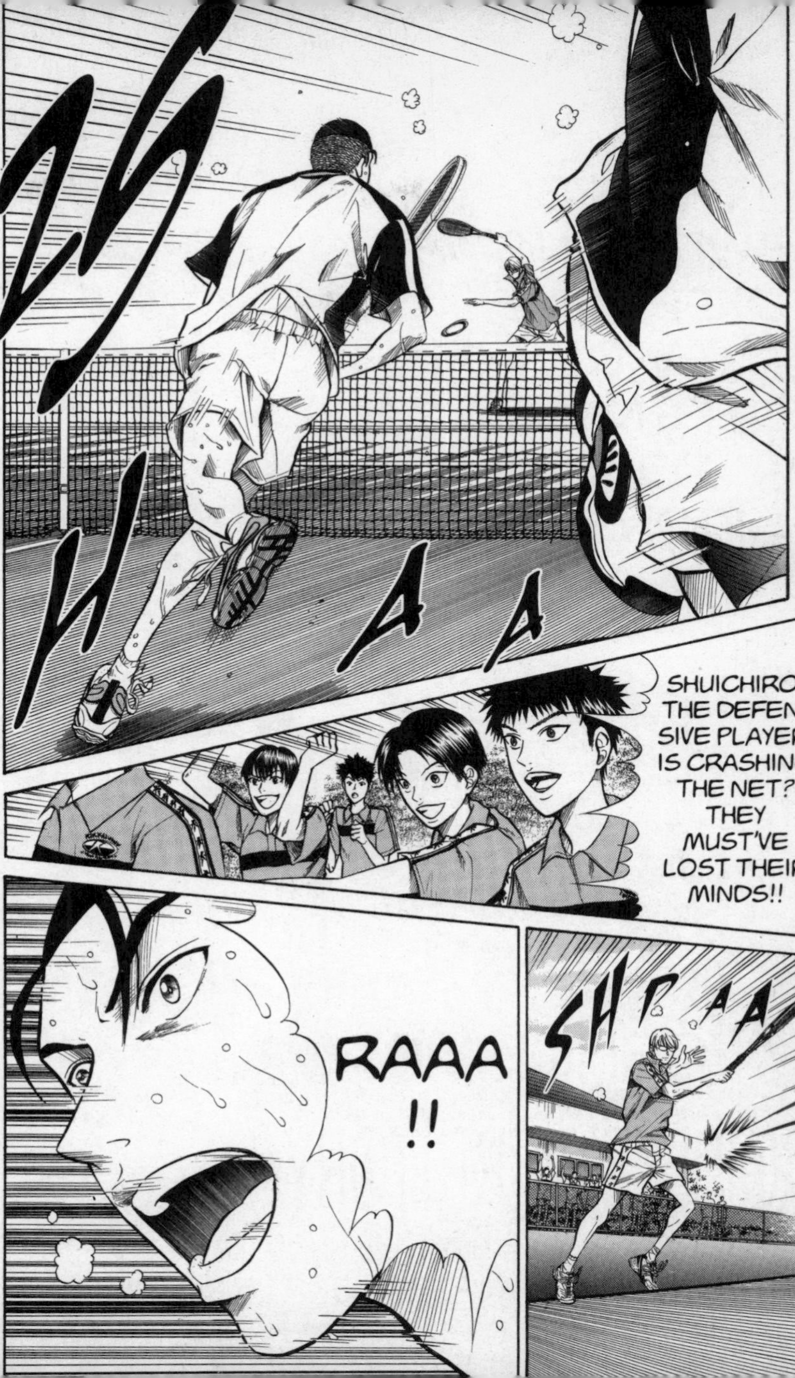
SHUICHIRO, THE DEFENSIVE PLAYER, IS CRASHING THE NET? THEY MUST'VE LOST THEIR MINDS!!
RAAA !!

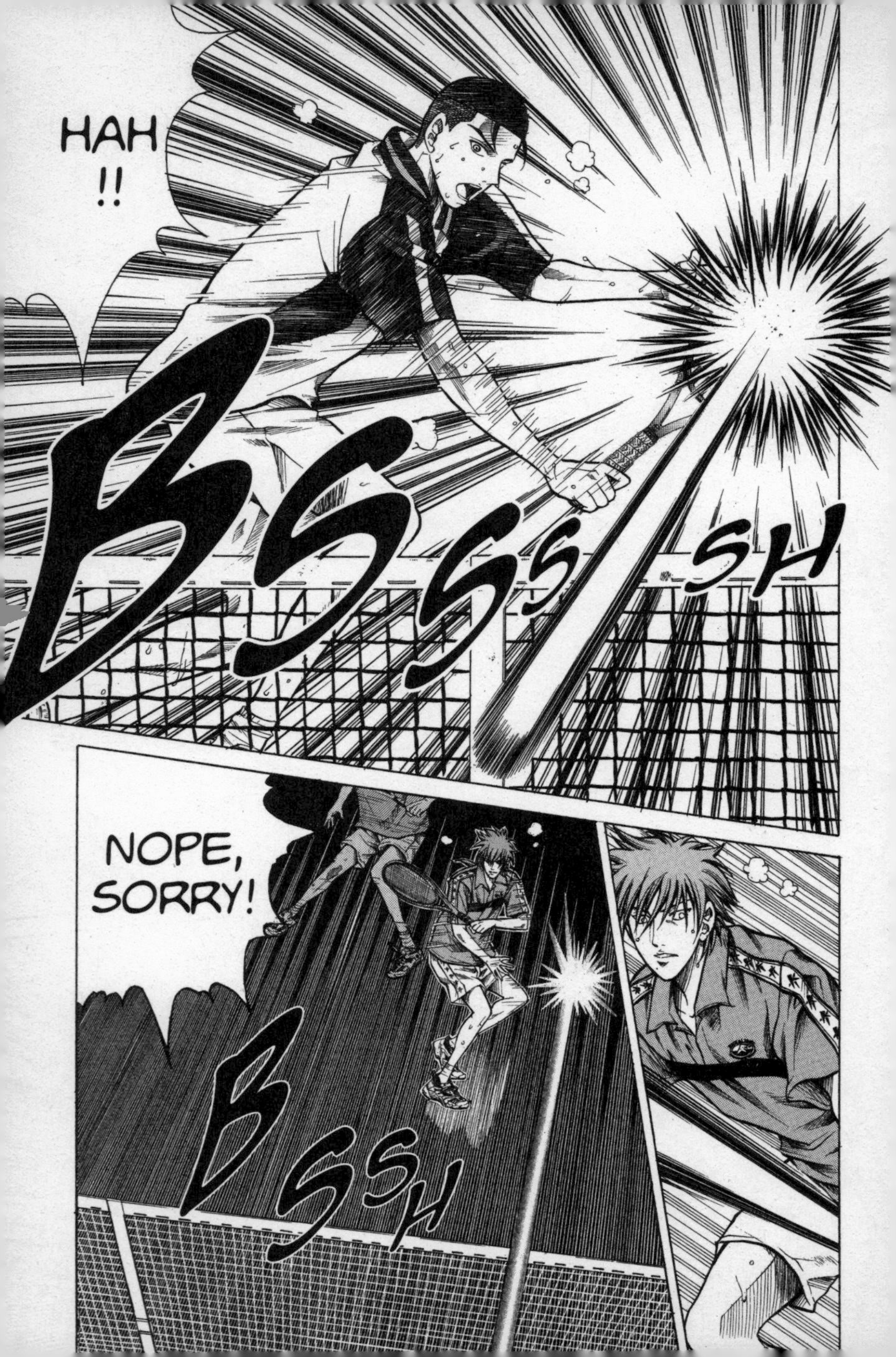
HAH !!
BSSSSH
NOPE, SORRY!
BSSSH

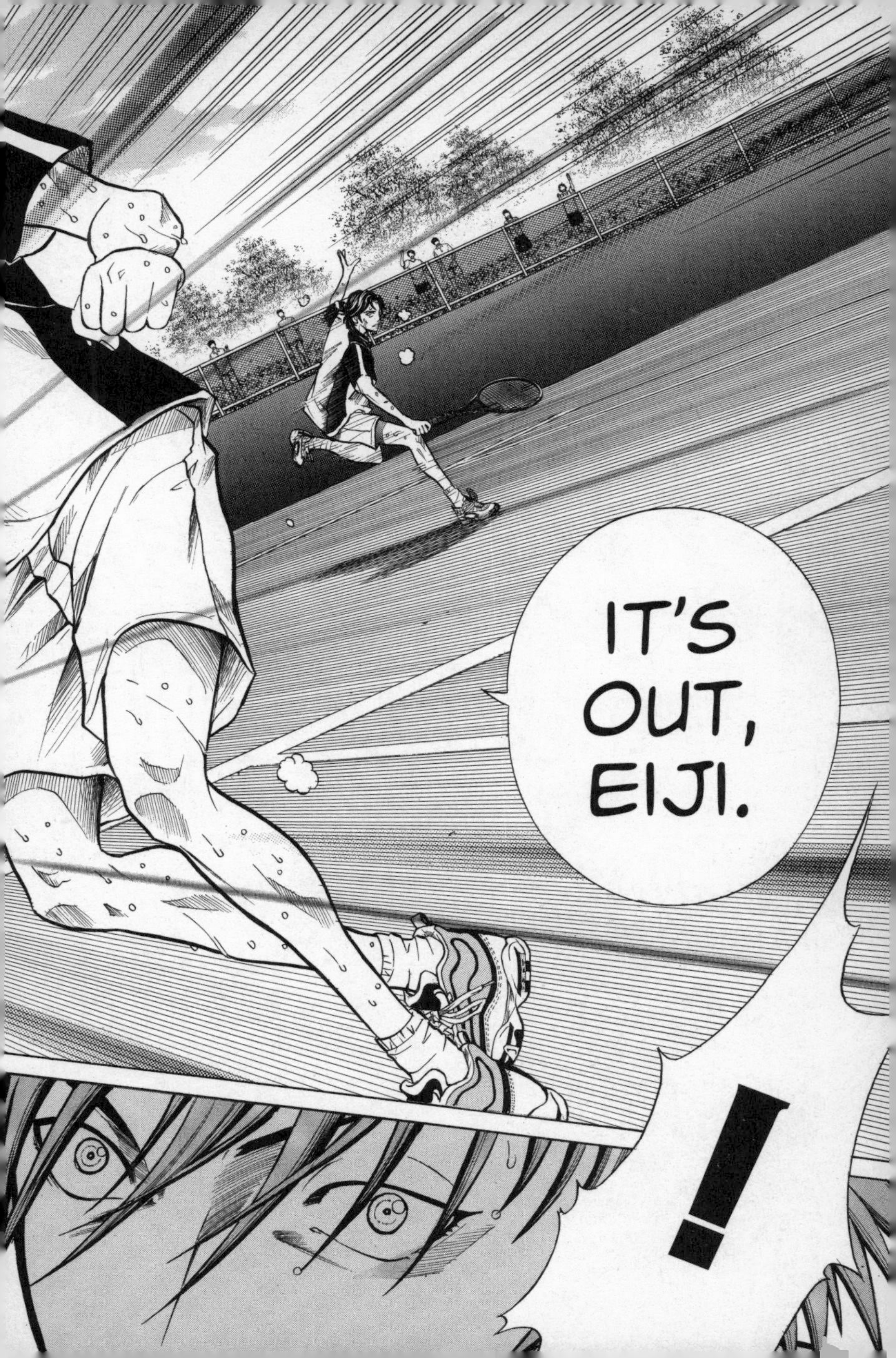
IT'S OUT, EIJI.
!

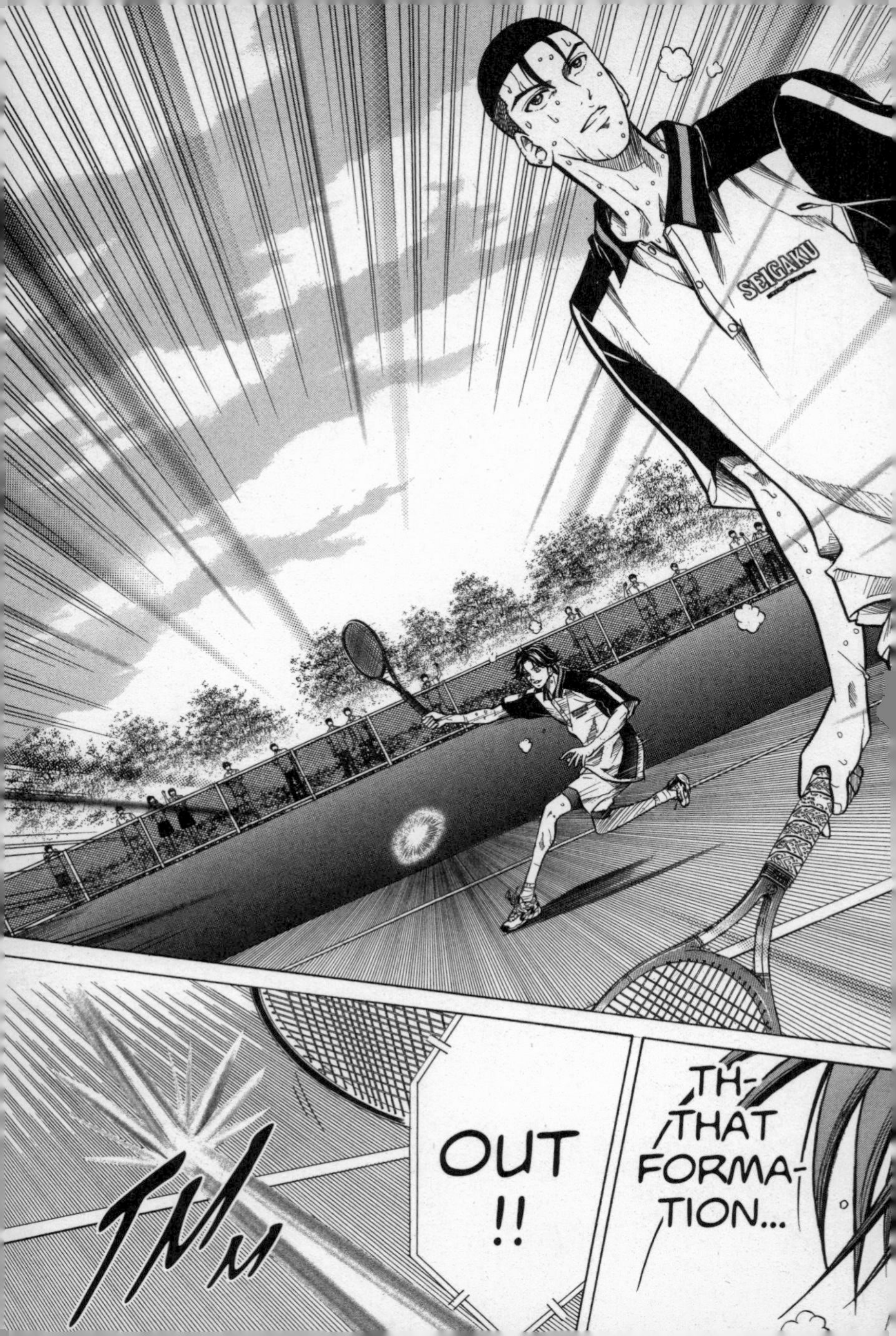
TH-THAT FORMATION...
OUT!!

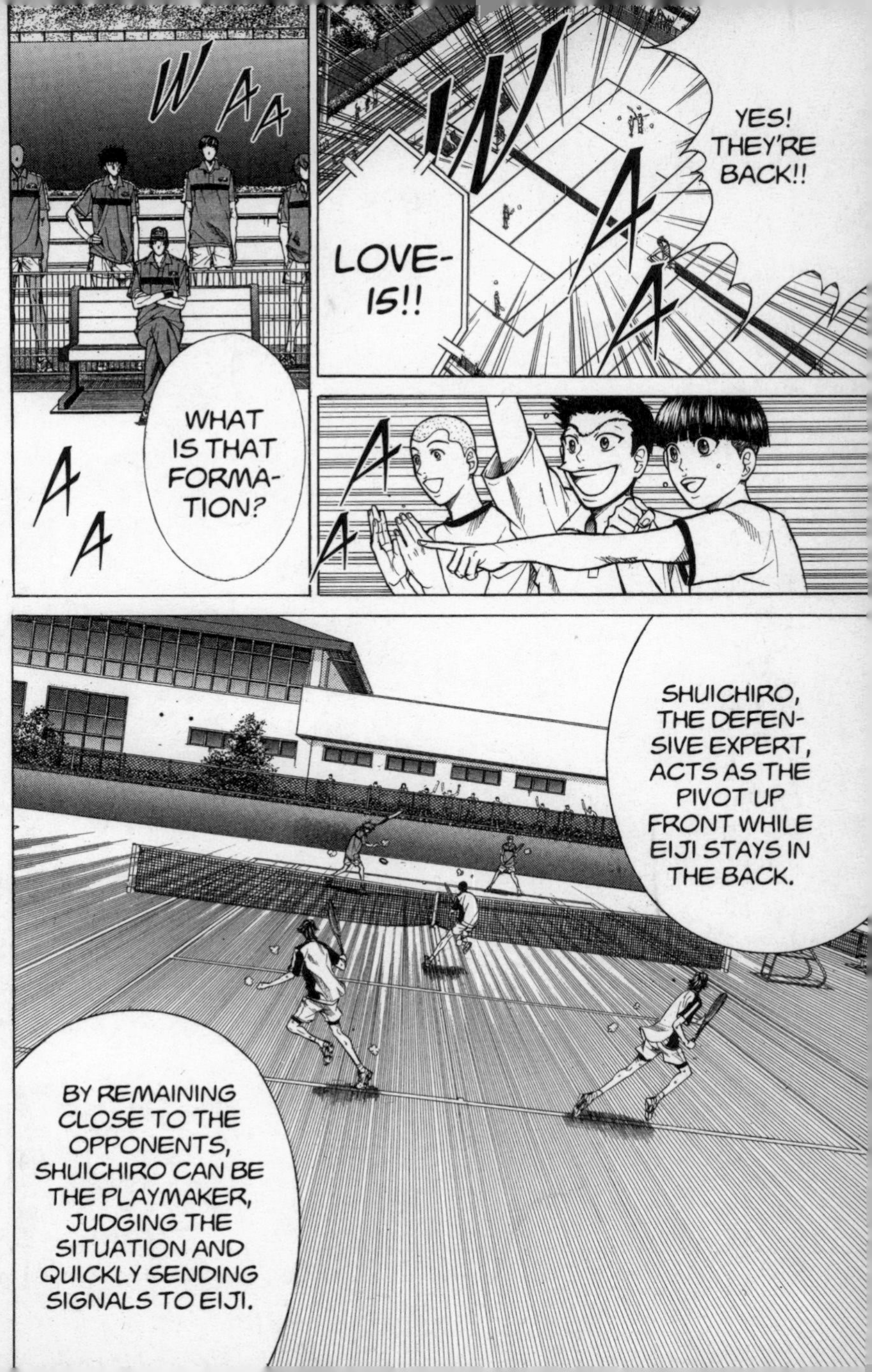

WAA
YES! THEY'RE BACK!!
LOVE-15!!
AA
WAA
WHAT IS THAT FORMATION?
AA
SHUICHIRO, THE DEFENSIVE EXPERT, ACTS AS THE PIVOT UP FRONT WHILE EIJI STAYS IN THE BACK.
BY REMAINING CLOSE TO THE OPPONENTS, SHUICHIRO CAN BE THE PLAYMAKER, JUDGING THE SITUATION AND QUICKLY SENDING SIGNALS TO EIJI.

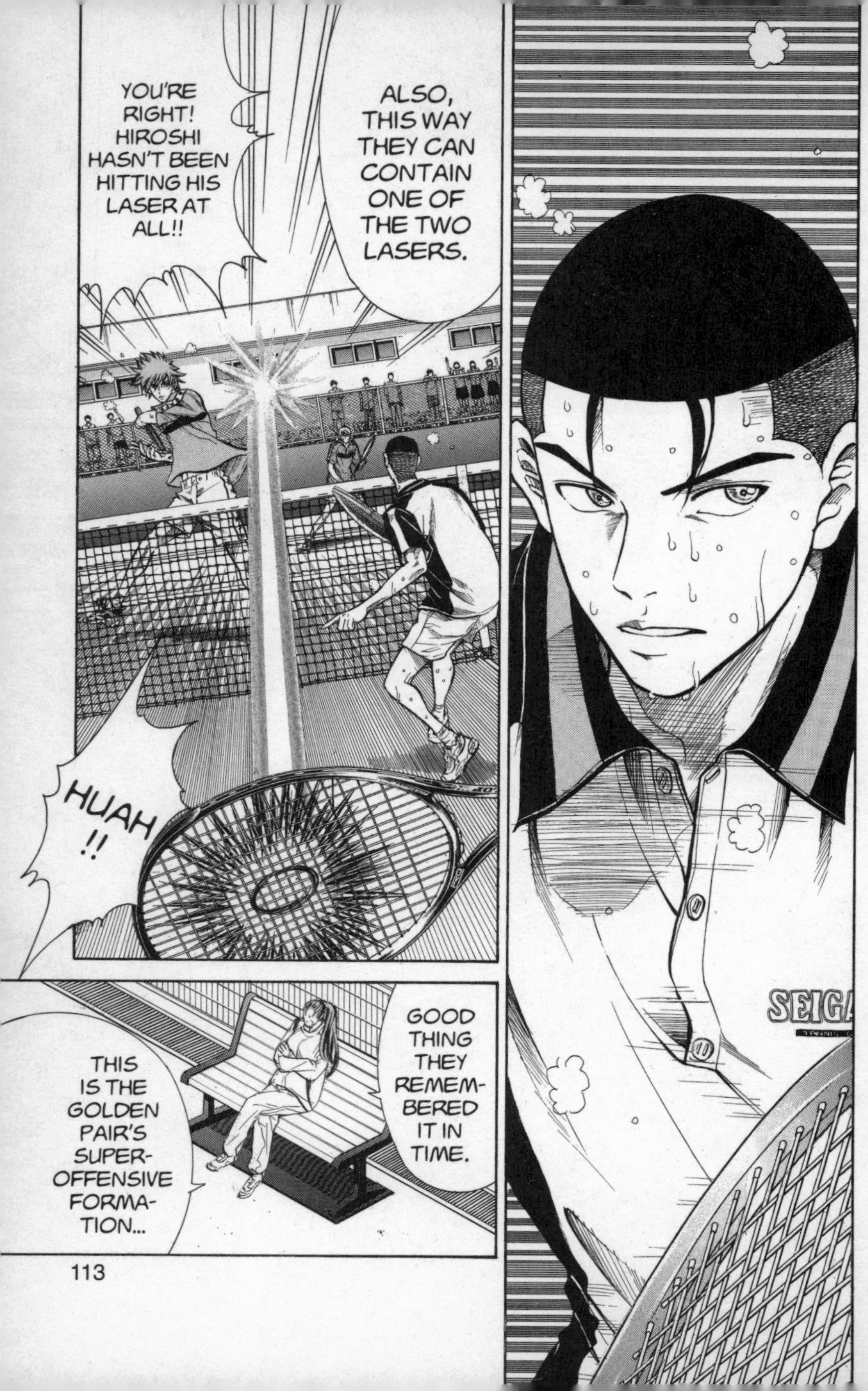
ALSO, THIS WAY THEY CAN CONTAIN ONE OF THE TWO LASERS.
YOU'RE RIGHT! HIROSHI HASN'T BEEN HITTING HIS LASER AT ALL!!
HUAH!!
GOOD THING THEY REMEMBERED IT IN TIME.
THIS IS THE GOLDEN PAIR'S SUPER-OFFENSIVE FORMATION...

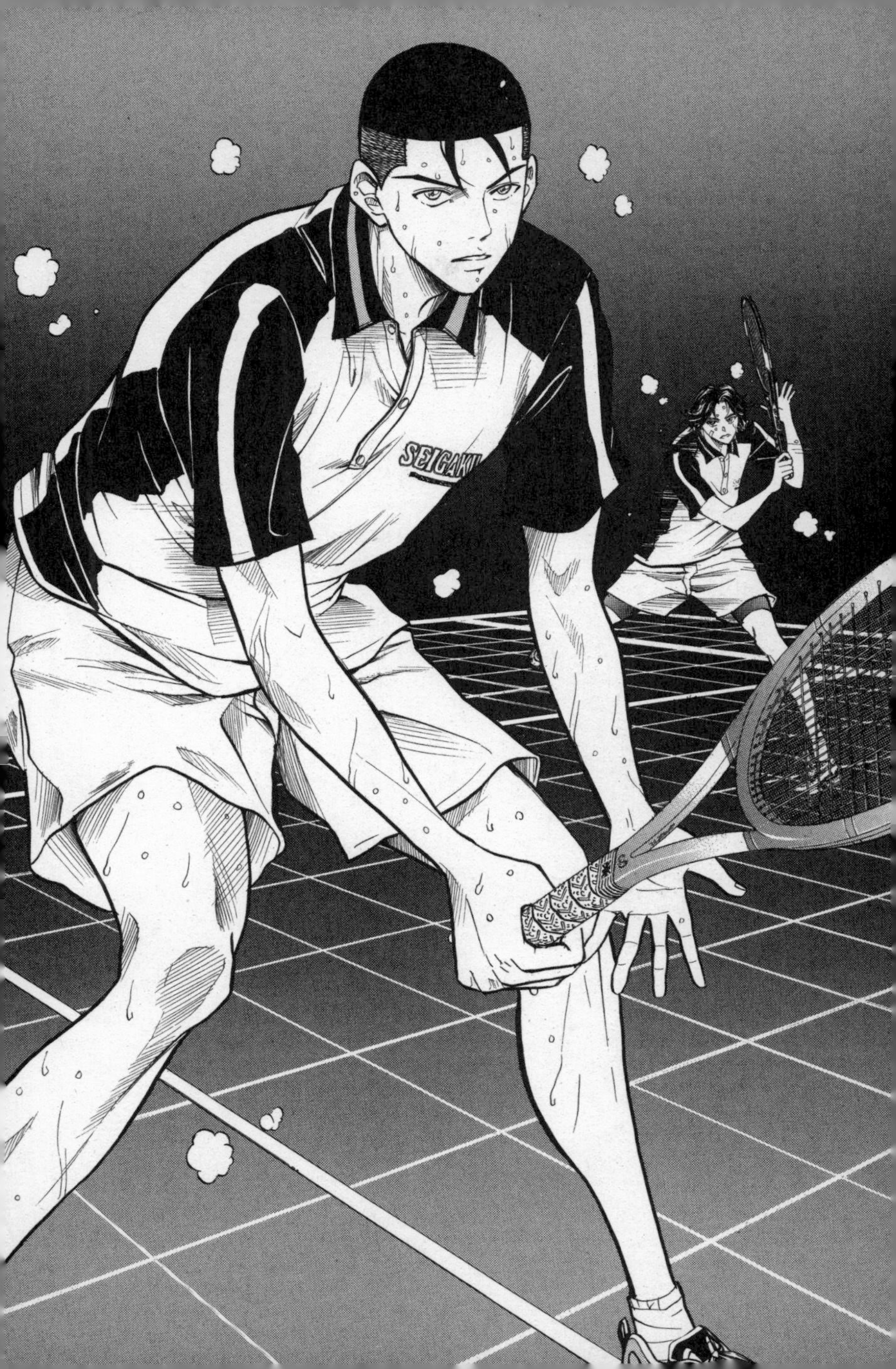
SEIGAKU

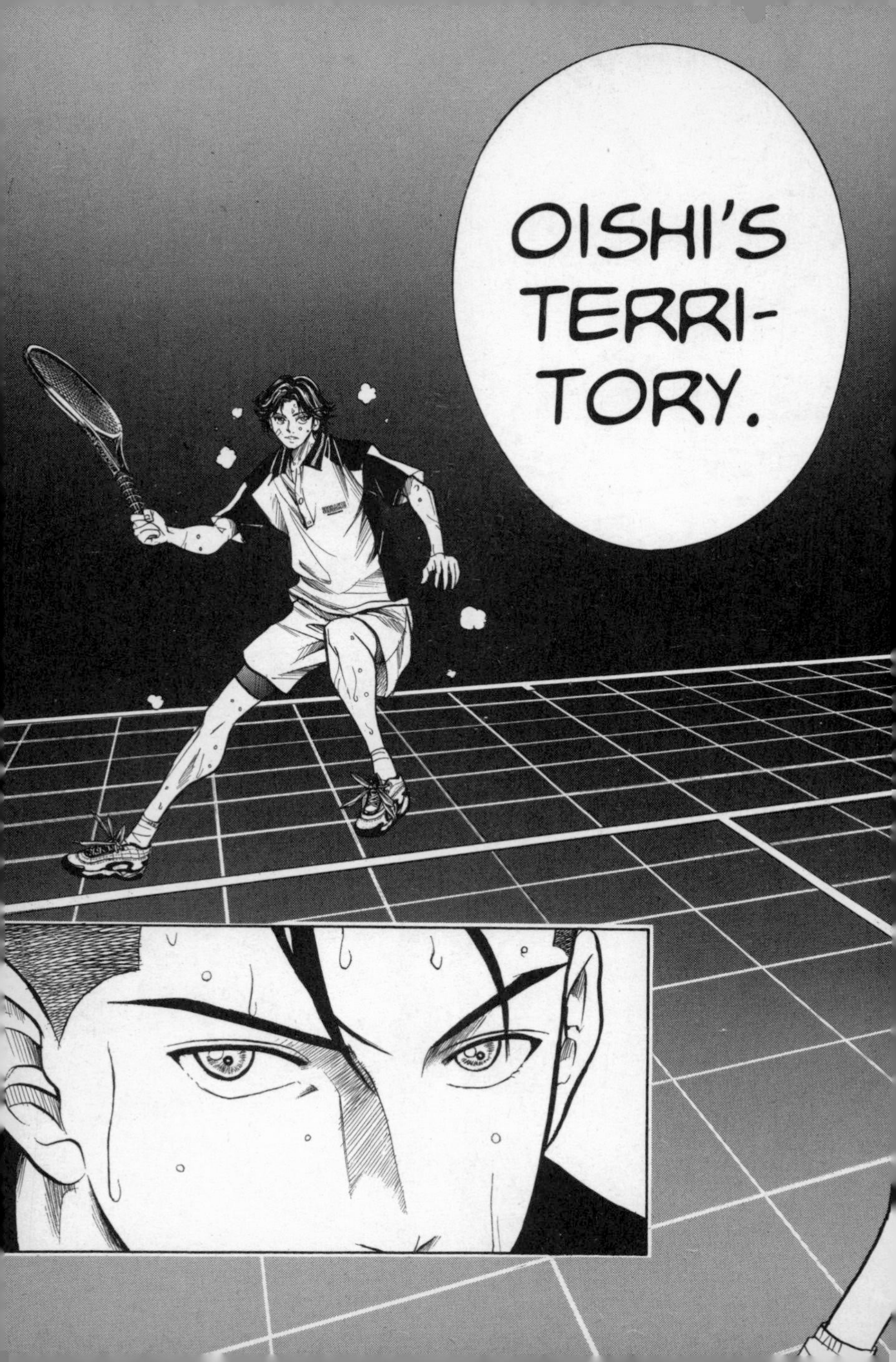
OISHI'S TERRI-TORY.

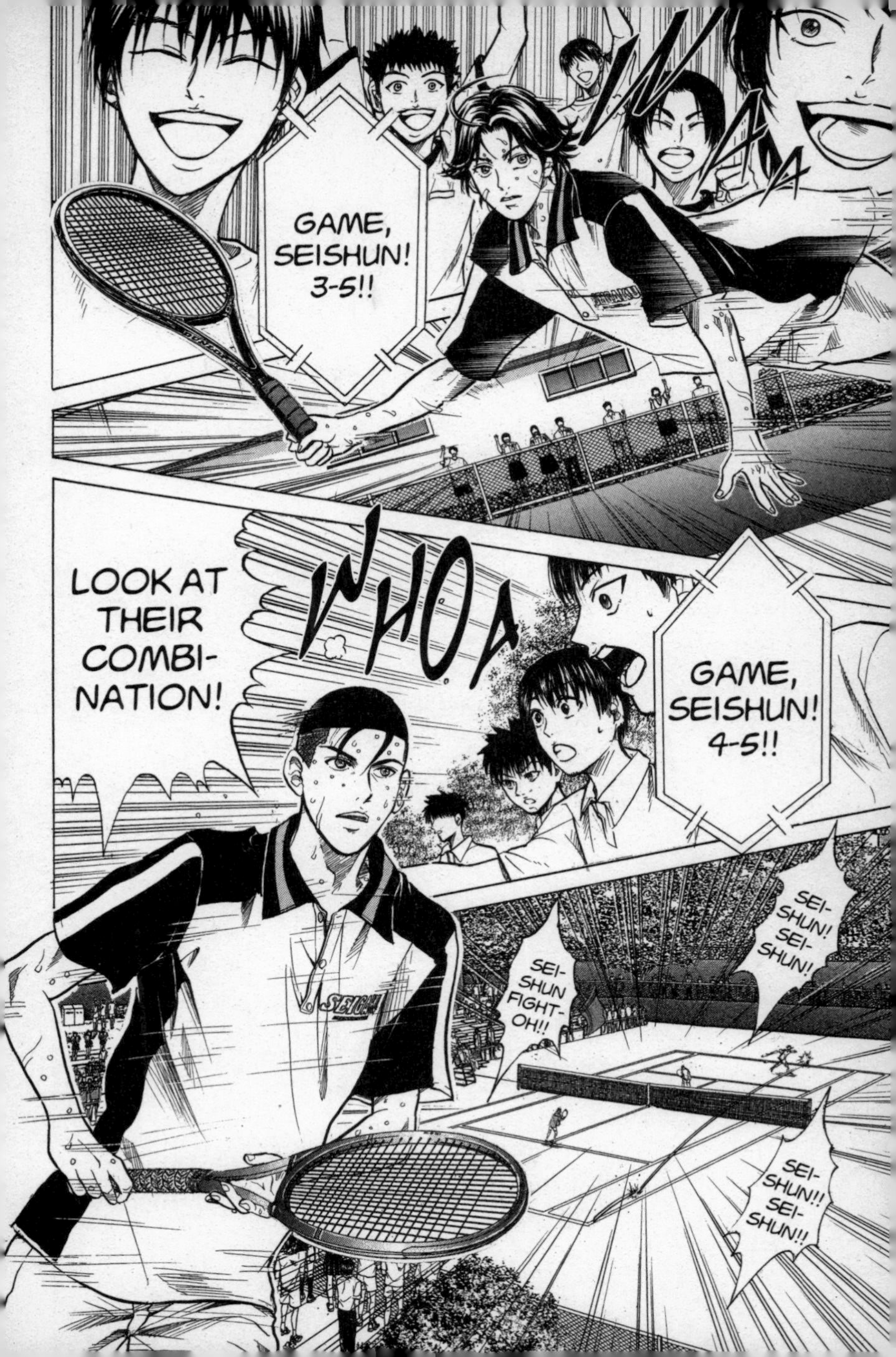
WAAA
GAME, SEISHUN! 3-5!!
GAME, SEISHUN! 4-5!!
WHOA
LOOK AT THEIR COMBINATION!
SEI-SHUN! SEI-SHUN!
SEI-SHUN FIGHT-OH!!
SEI-SHUN!! SEI-SHUN!!

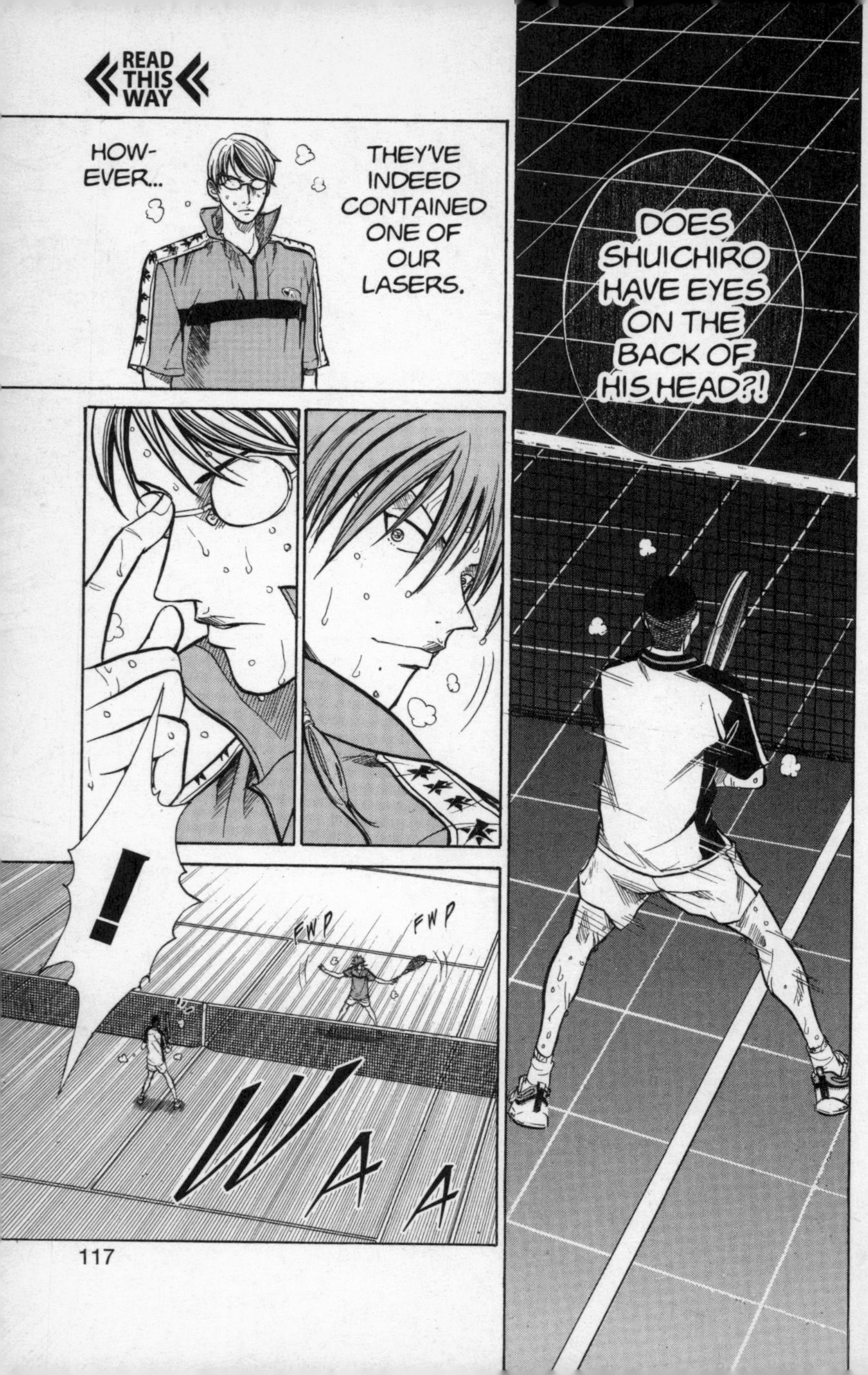
READ THIS WAY
DOES SHUICHIRO HAVE EYES ON THE BACK OF HIS HEAD?!
THEY'VE INDEED CONTAINED ONE OF OUR LASERS.
HOW-EVER...
!
FWP
FWP
WAA

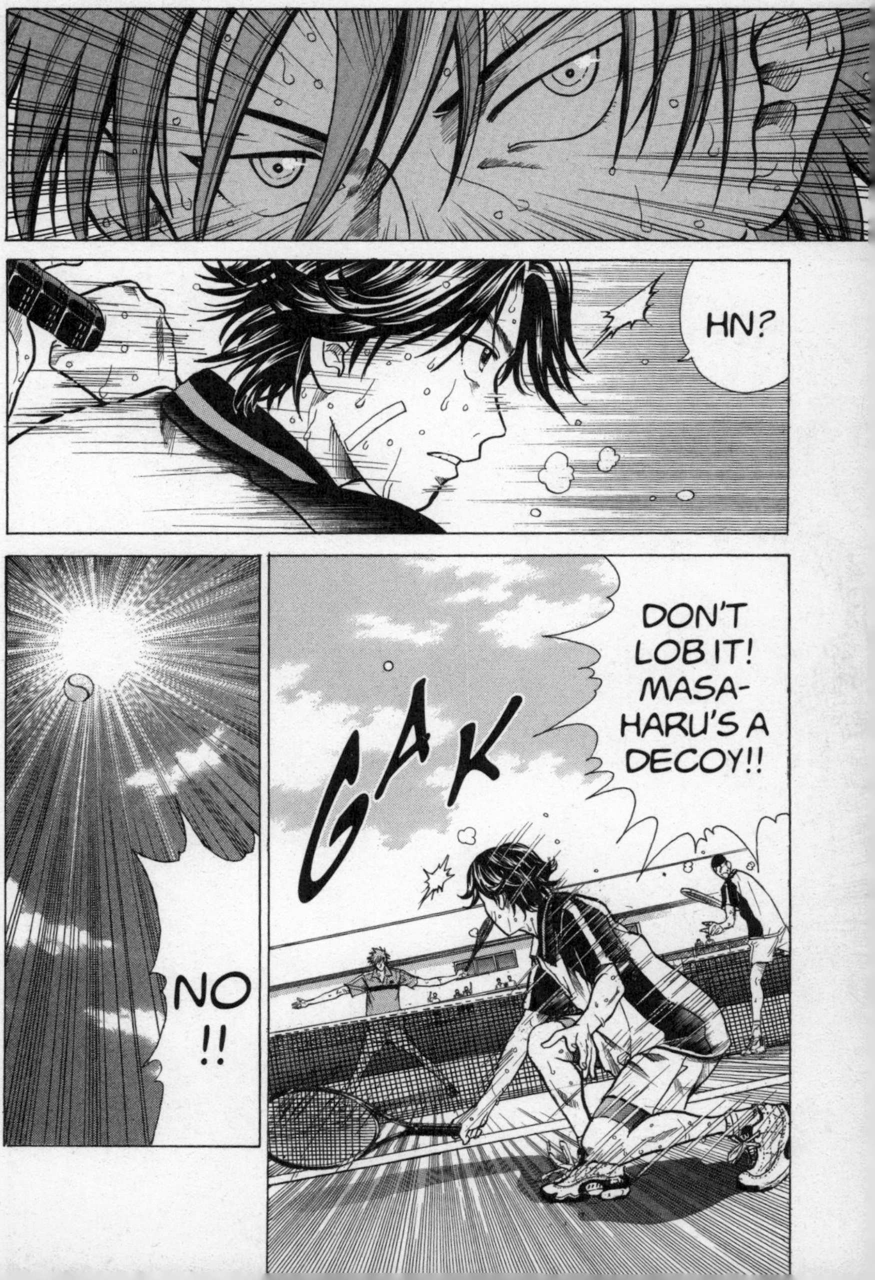
HN?
GAK
DON'T LOB IT! MASA-HARU'S A DECOY!!
NO !!

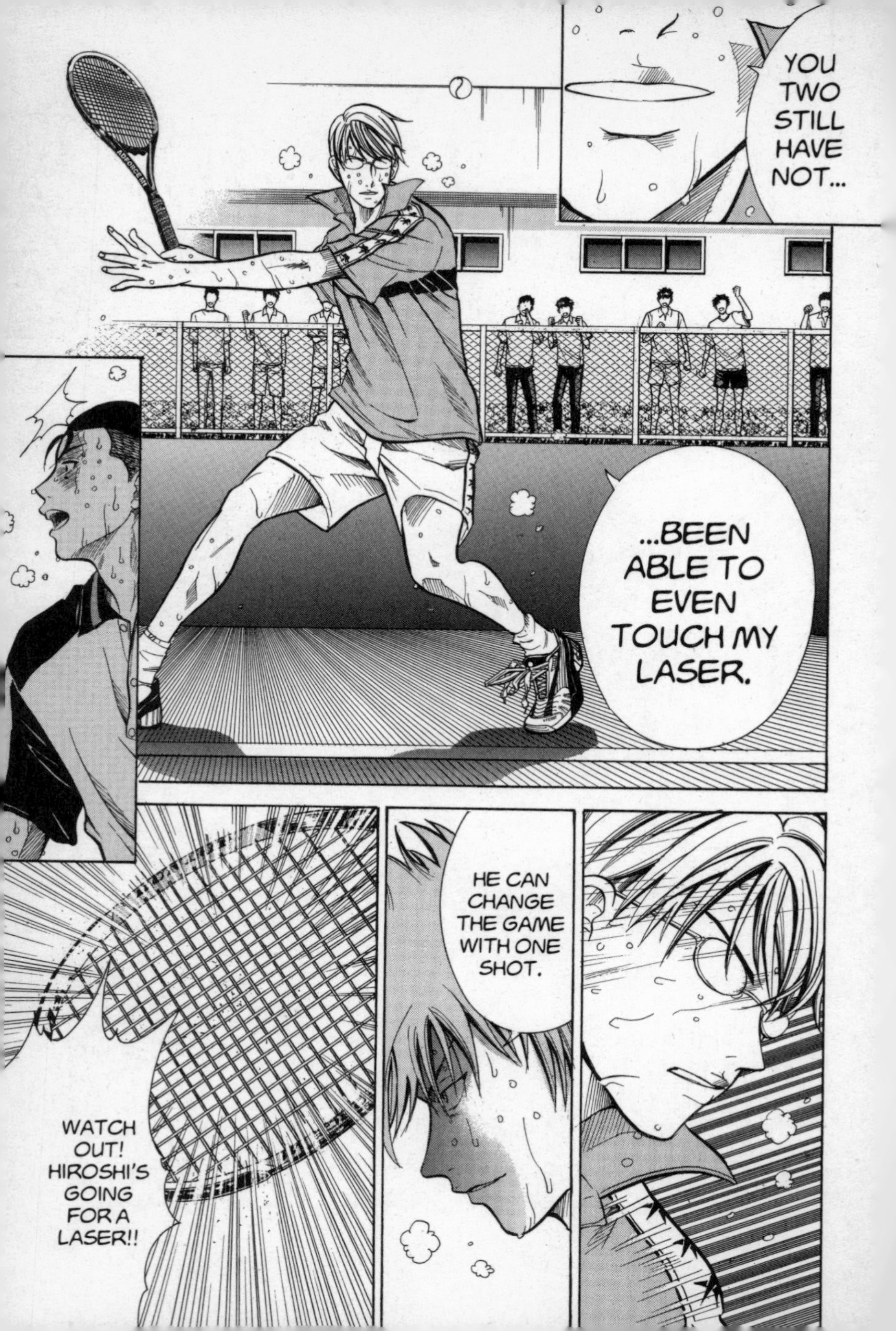
YOU TWO STILL HAVE NOT...
...BEEN ABLE TO EVEN TOUCH MY LASER.
HE CAN CHANGE THE GAME WITH ONE SHOT.
WATCH OUT! HIROSHI'S GOING FOR A LASER!!

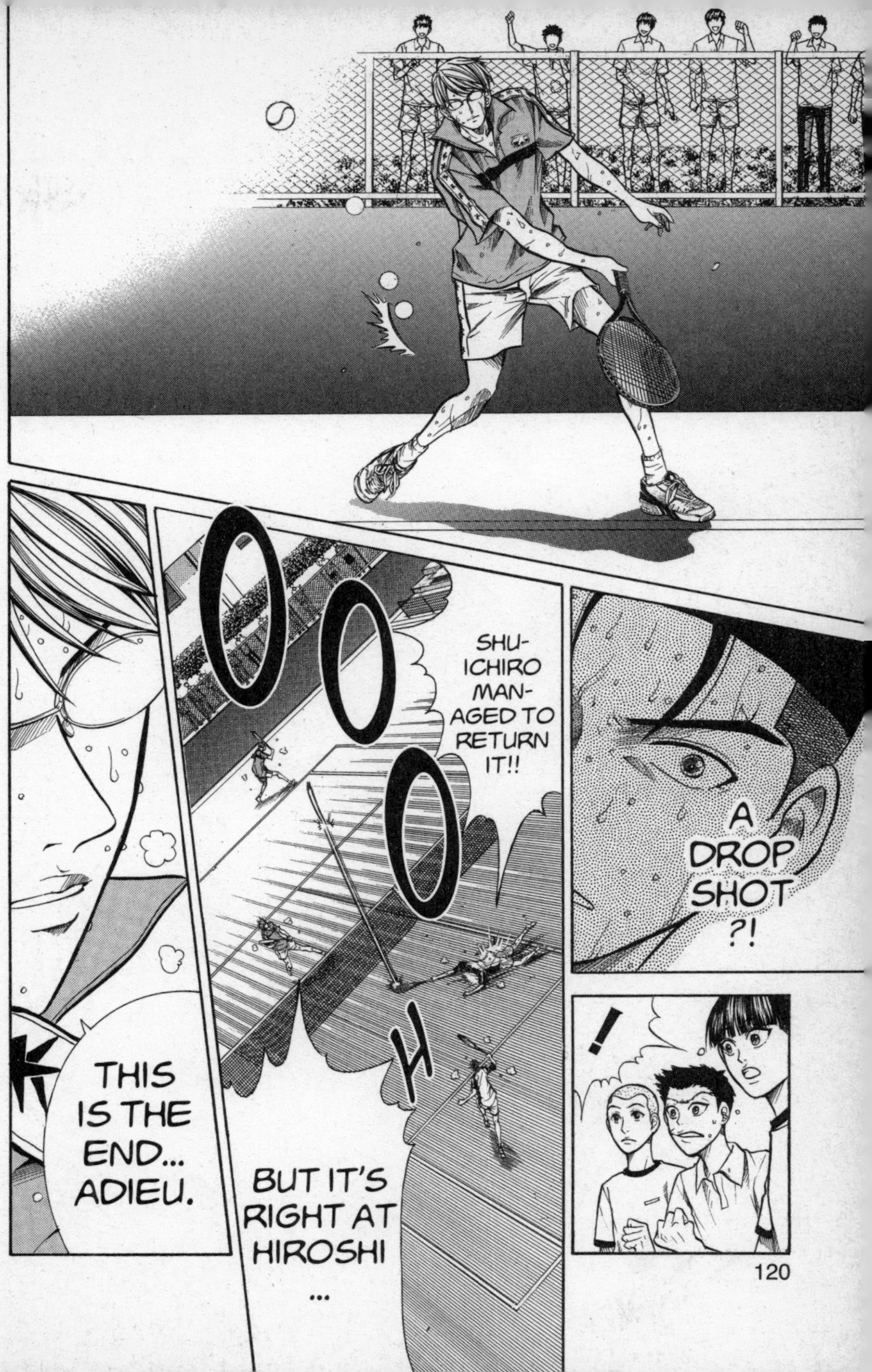
A DROP SHOT?!
!
SHUICHIRO MANAGED TO RETURN IT!!
OOOH
BUT IT'S RIGHT AT HIROSHI...
THIS IS THE END... ADIEU.

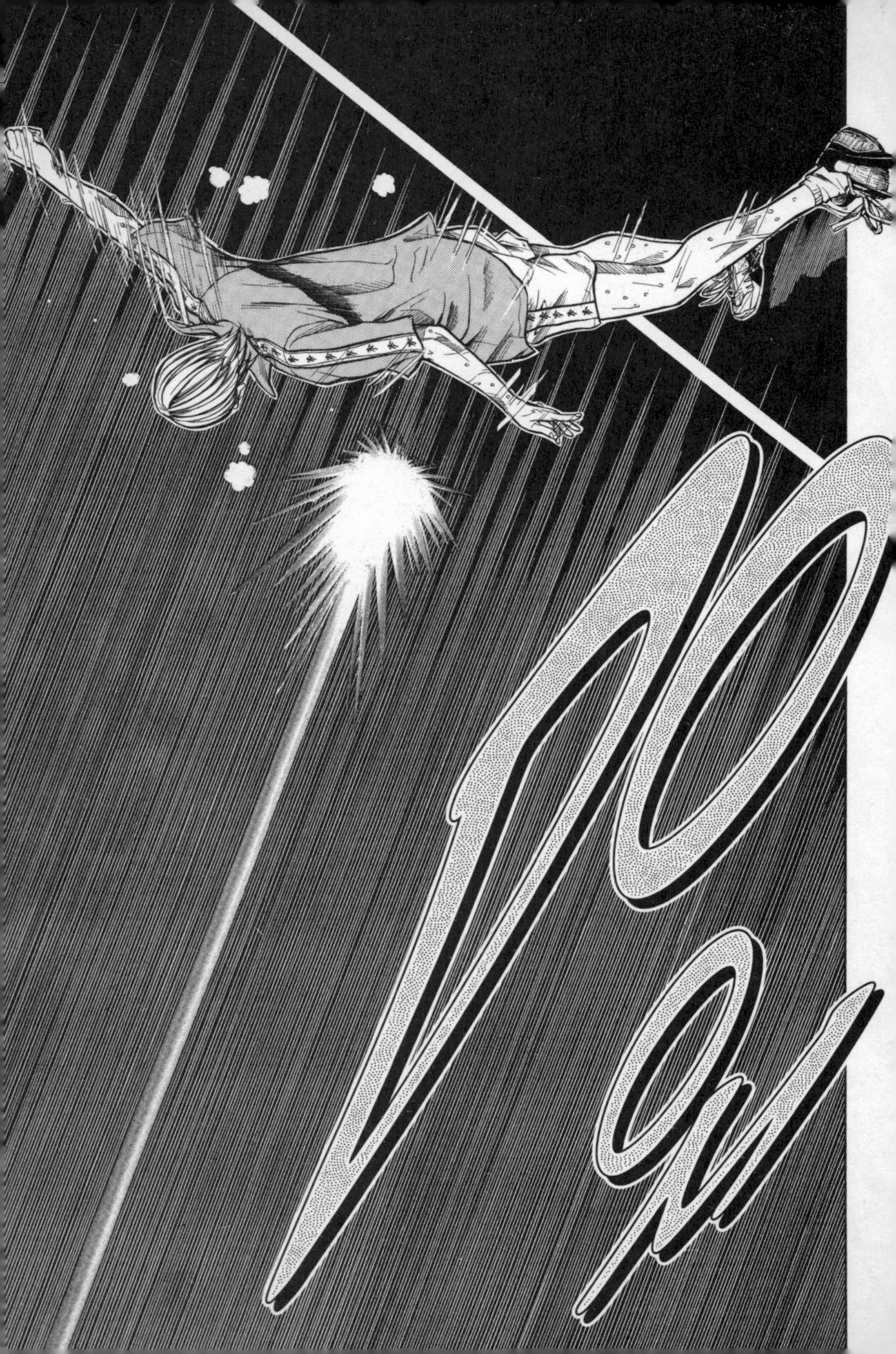

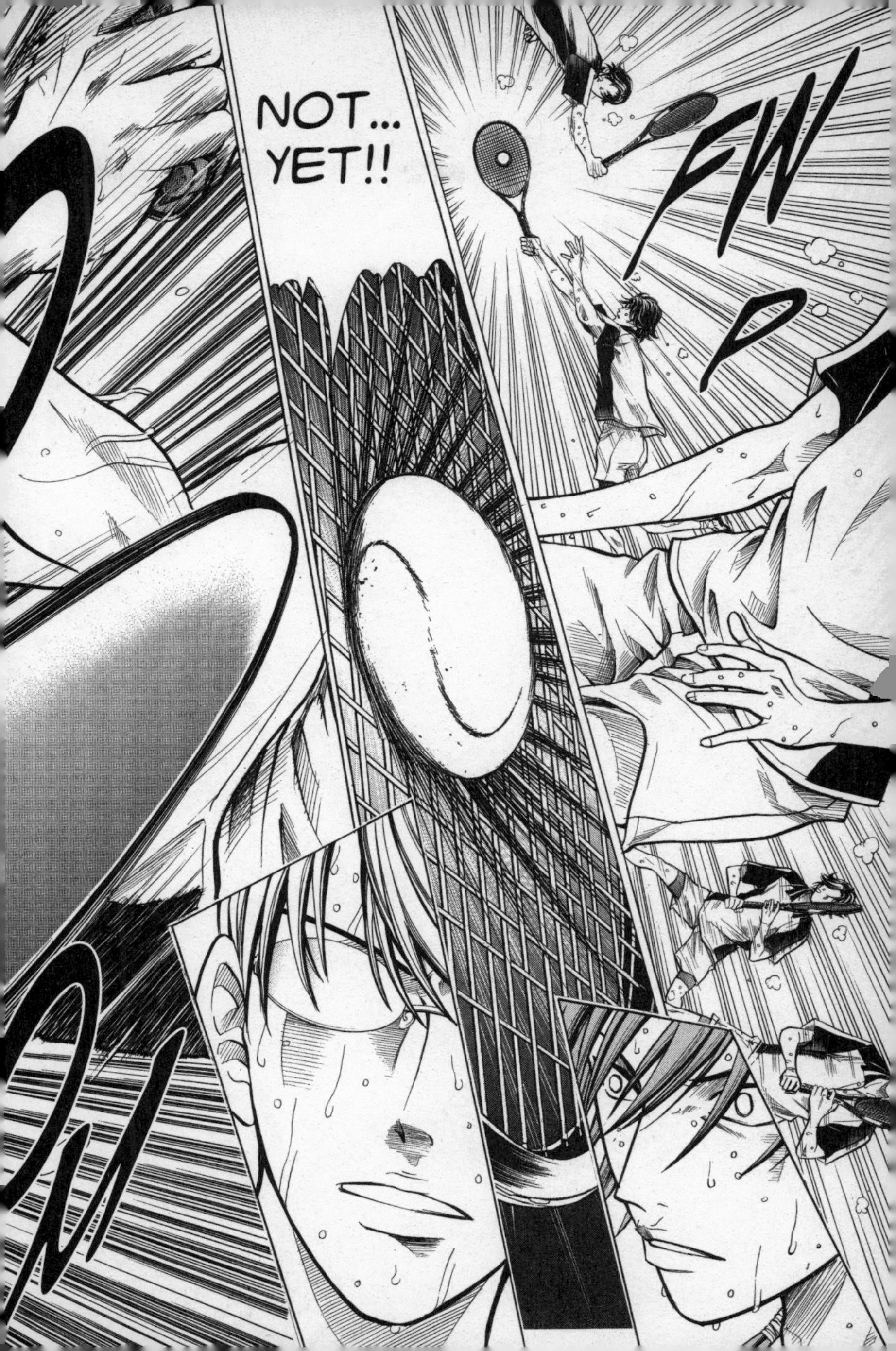
NOT... YET!!
FWP

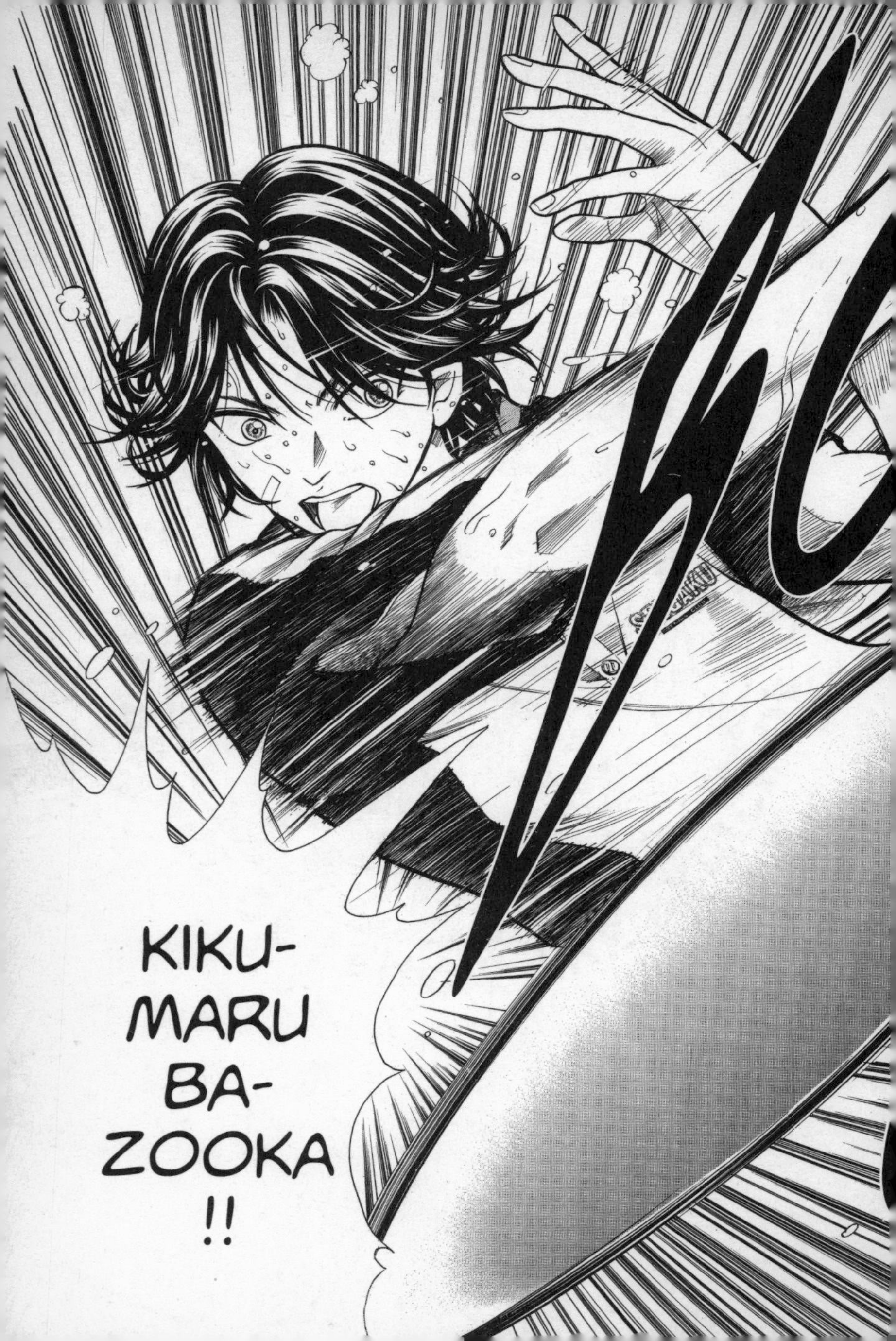
KIKU-
MARU
BA-
ZOOKA
!!

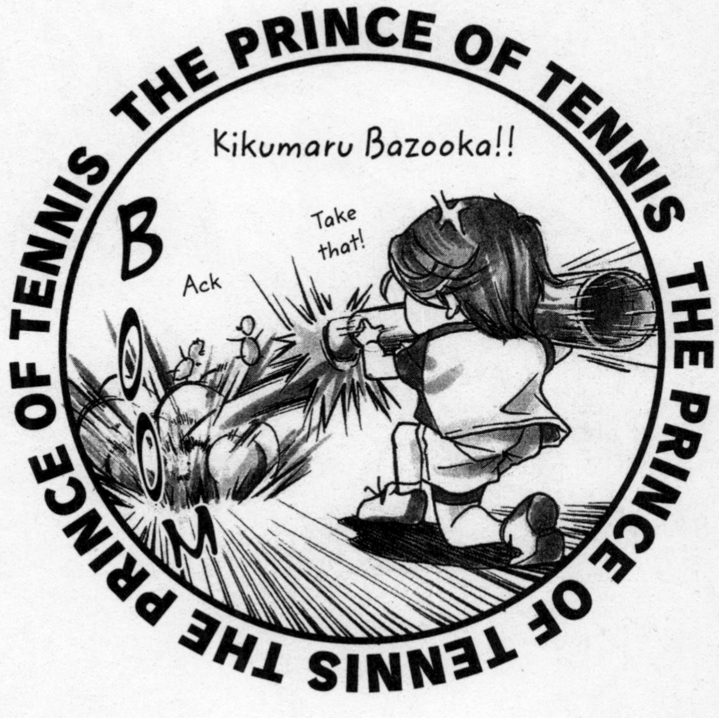
THE PRINCE OF TENNIS THE PRINCE OF TENNIS THE PRINCE OF TENNIS
Kikumaru Bazooka!!
Take that!
Ack
BOOM

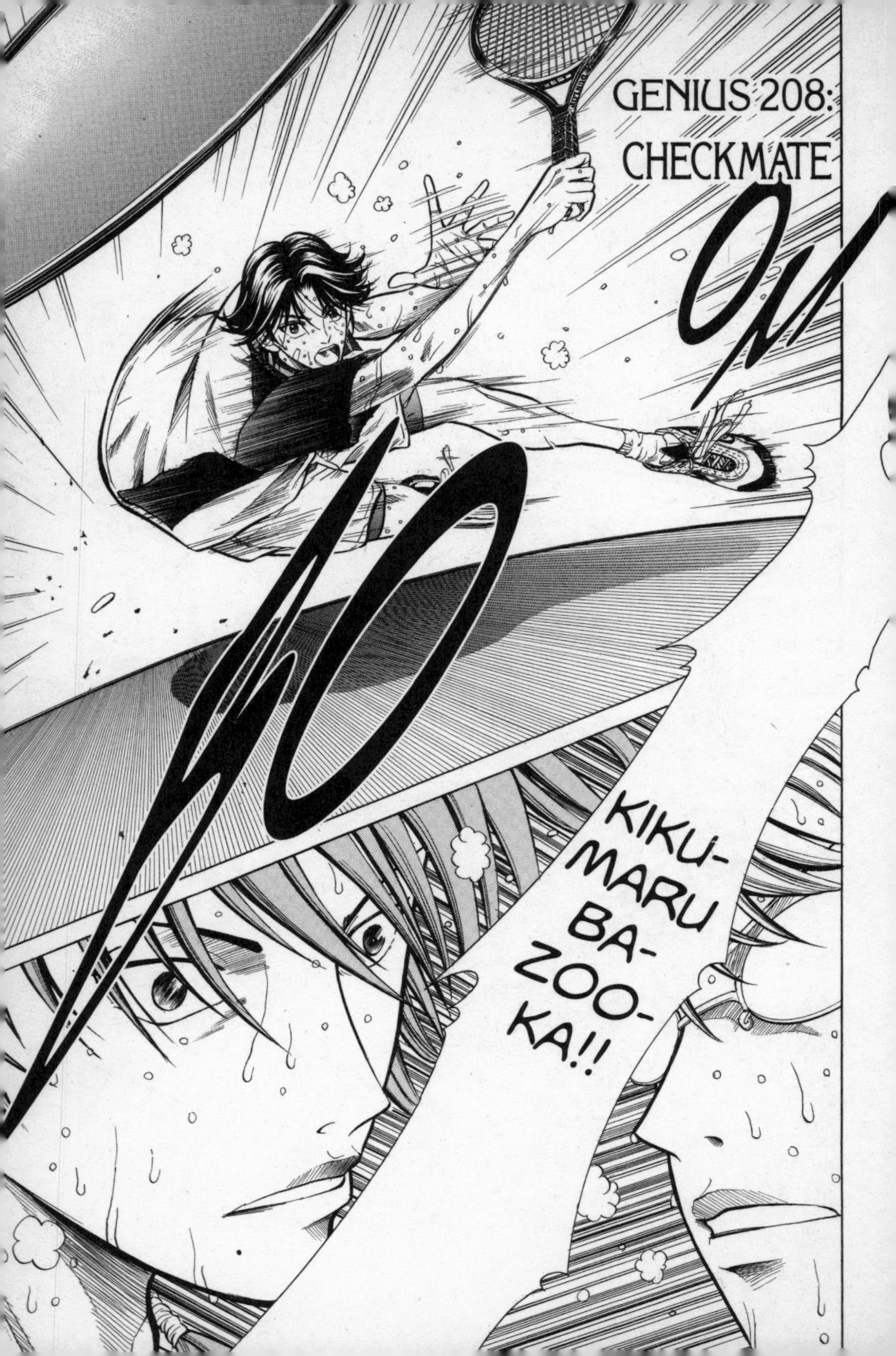
GENIUS 208: CHECKMATE
KIKU-MARU BA-ZOO-KA!!

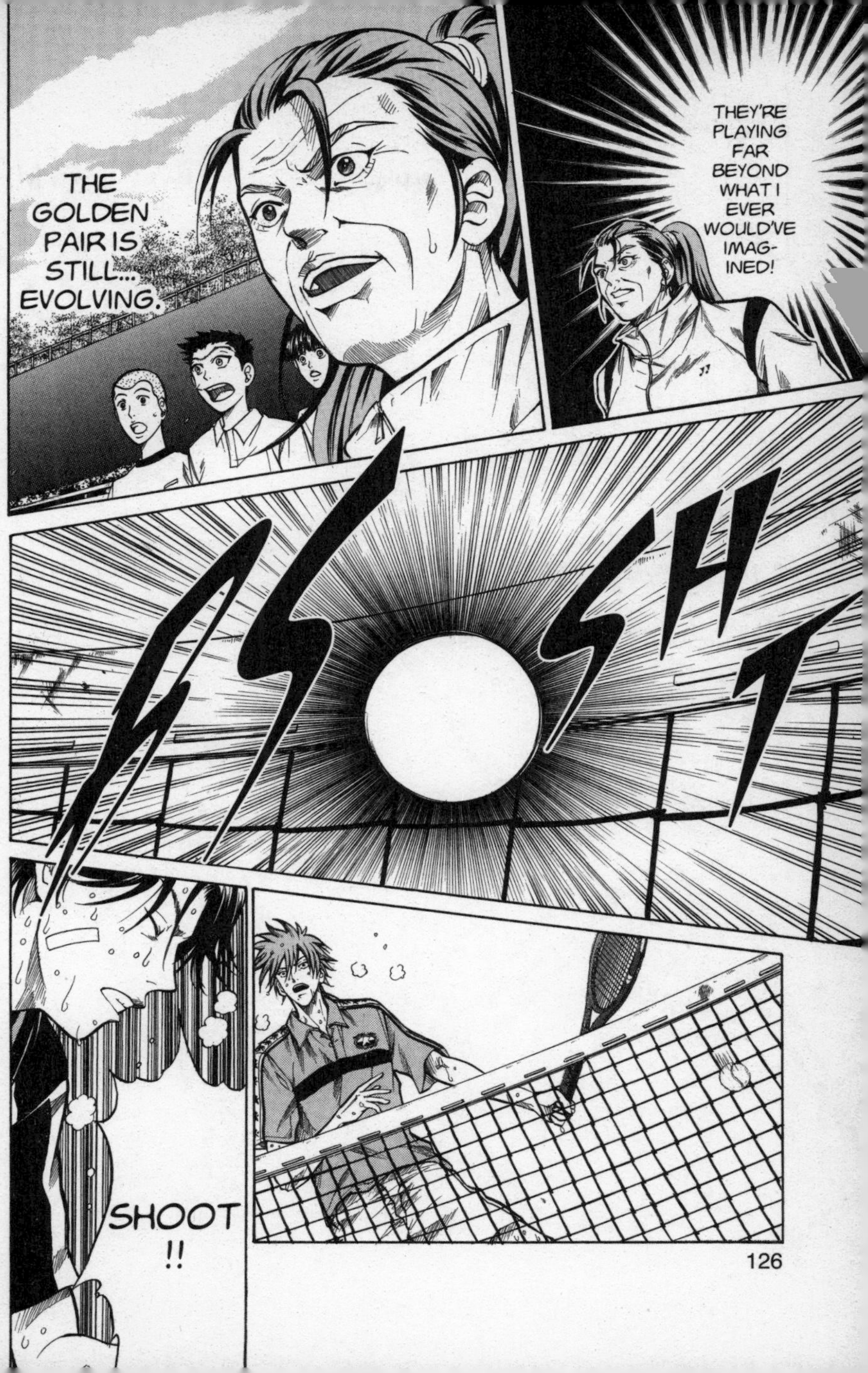
THEY'RE PLAYING FAR BEYOND WHAT I EVER WOULD'VE IMAG-INED!
THE GOLDEN PAIR IS STILL... EVOLVING.
SSSHT
SHOOT!!

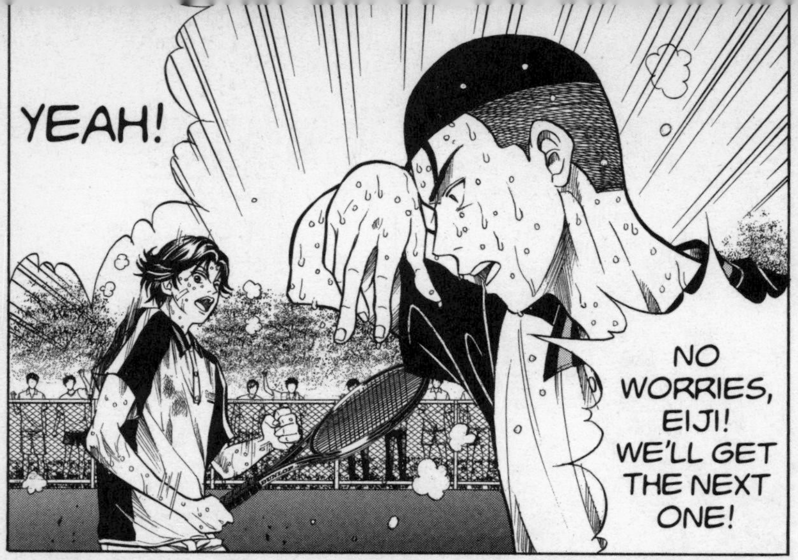
NO WORRIES, EIJI! WE'LL GET THE NEXT ONE!
YEAH!

THERE ARE ENDLESS POSSIBILITIES IN DOUBLES...

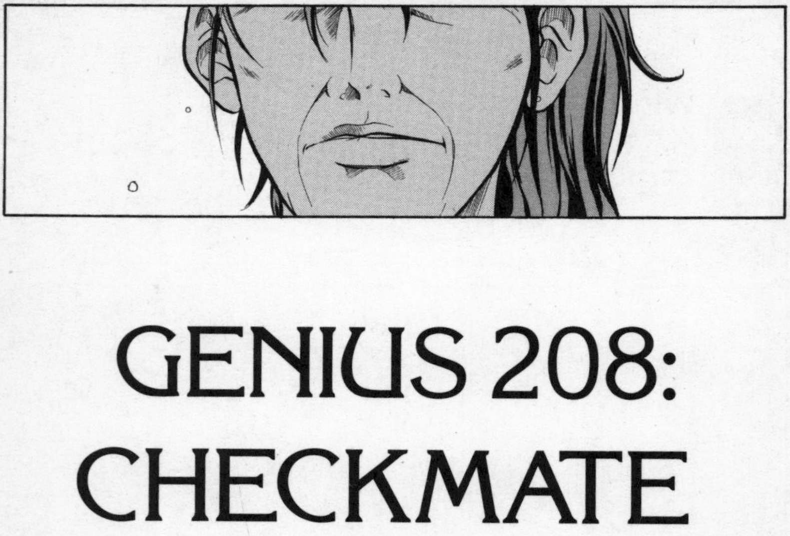

GENIUS 208: CHECKMATE

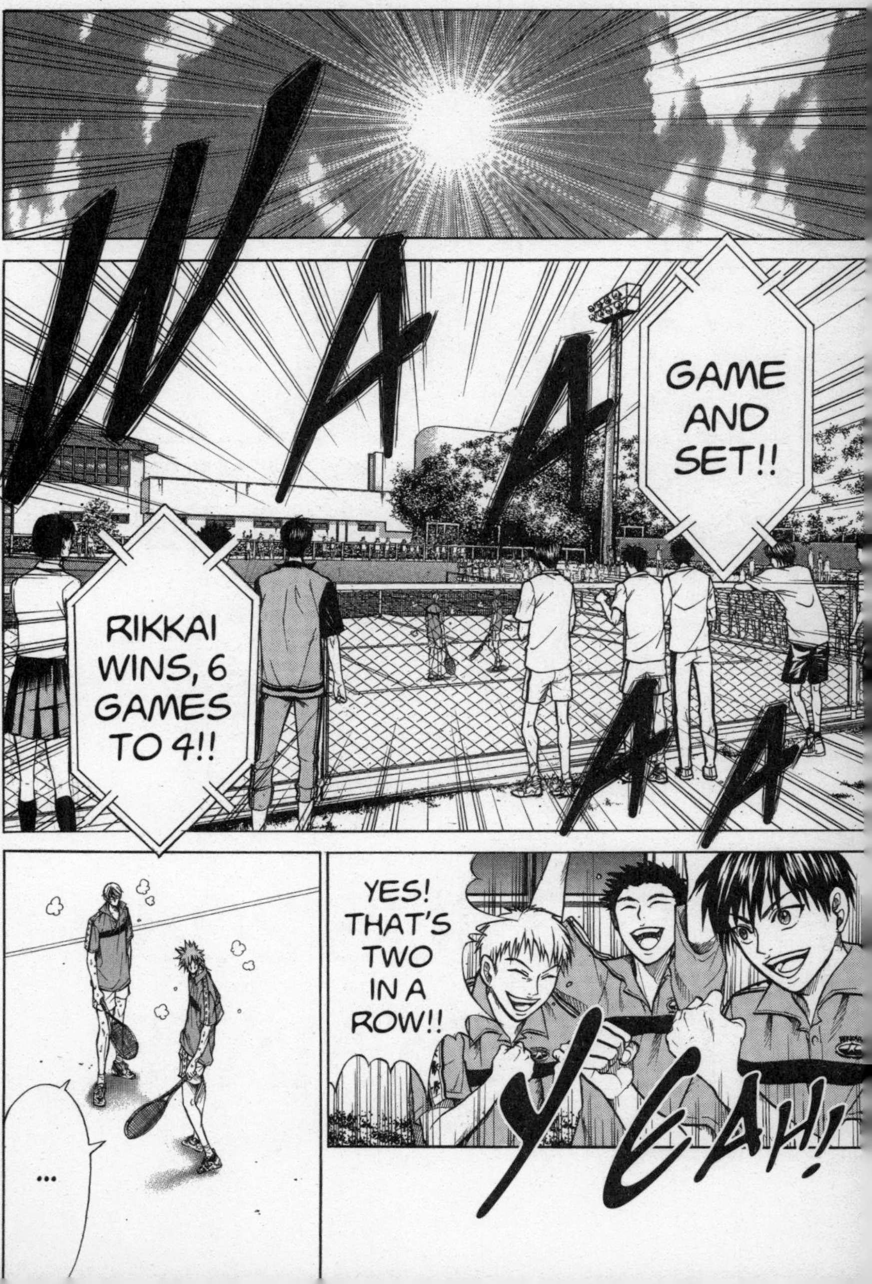
WAAAA
GAME AND SET!!
RIKKAI WINS, 6 GAMES TO 4!!
YES! THAT'S TWO IN A ROW!!
YEAH!
...

READ THIS WAY

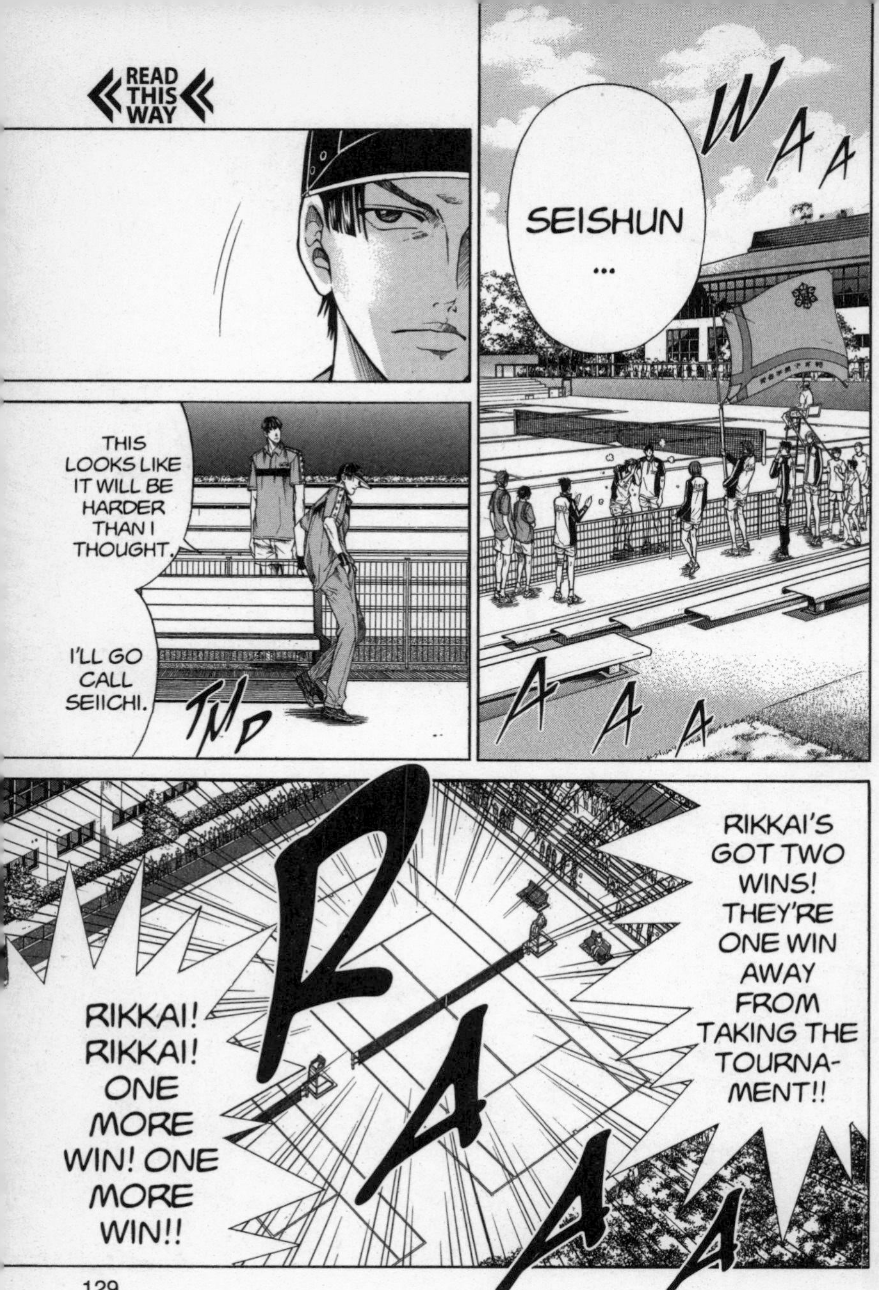

SEISHUN ...
WAAAAAA
THIS LOOKS LIKE IT WILL BE HARDER THAN I THOUGHT.
I'LL GO CALL SEIICHI.
TMP
RIKKAI'S GOT TWO WINS! THEY'RE ONE WIN AWAY FROM TAKING THE TOURNA-MENT!!
RIKKAI! RIKKAI! ONE MORE WIN! ONE MORE WIN!!
RAAAAA

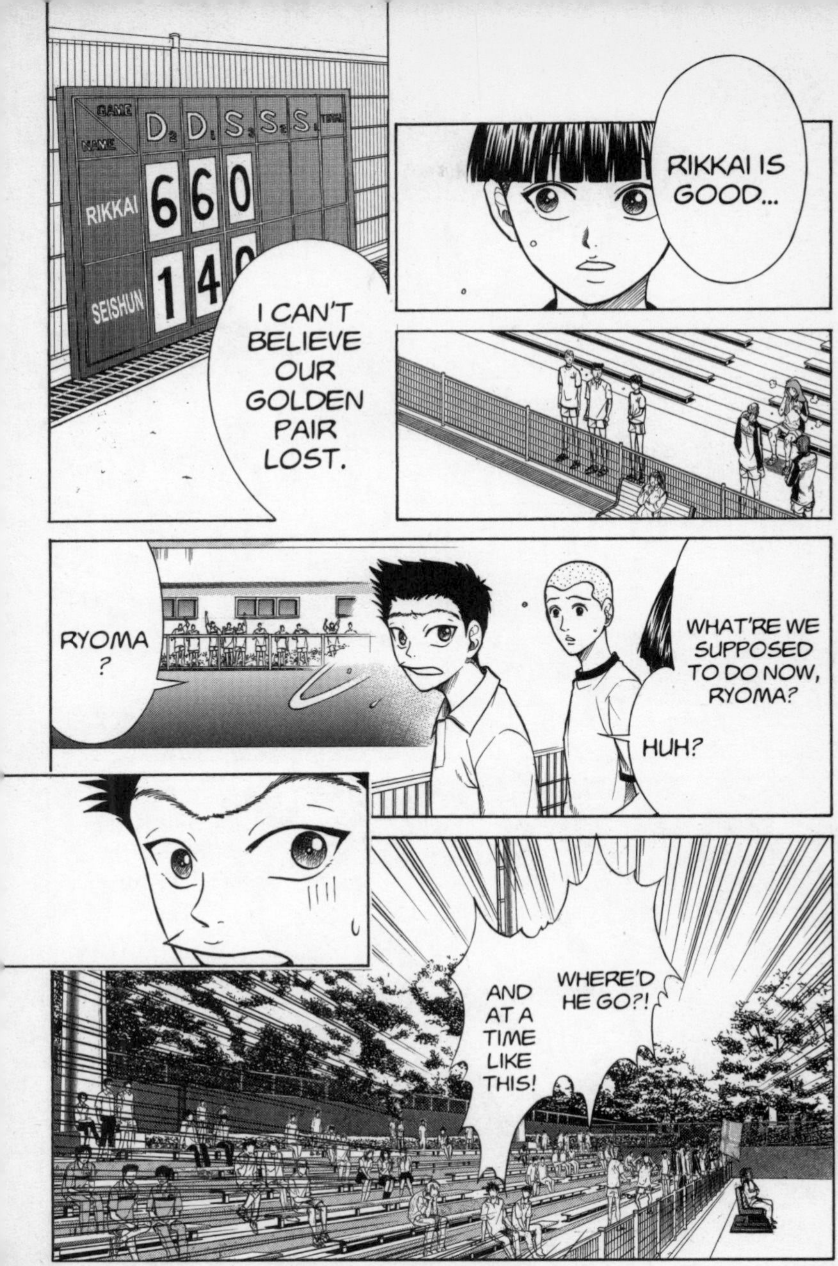
RIKKAI IS GOOD...
GAME
NAME
D2 D1 S3 S2 S1
TOTAL
RIKKAI 6 6 0
SEISHUN 1 4 0
I CAN'T BELIEVE OUR GOLDEN PAIR LOST.
WHAT'RE WE SUPPOSED TO DO NOW, RYOMA?
HUH?
RYOMA ?
WHERE'D HE GO?!
AND AT A TIME LIKE THIS!

READ THIS WAY

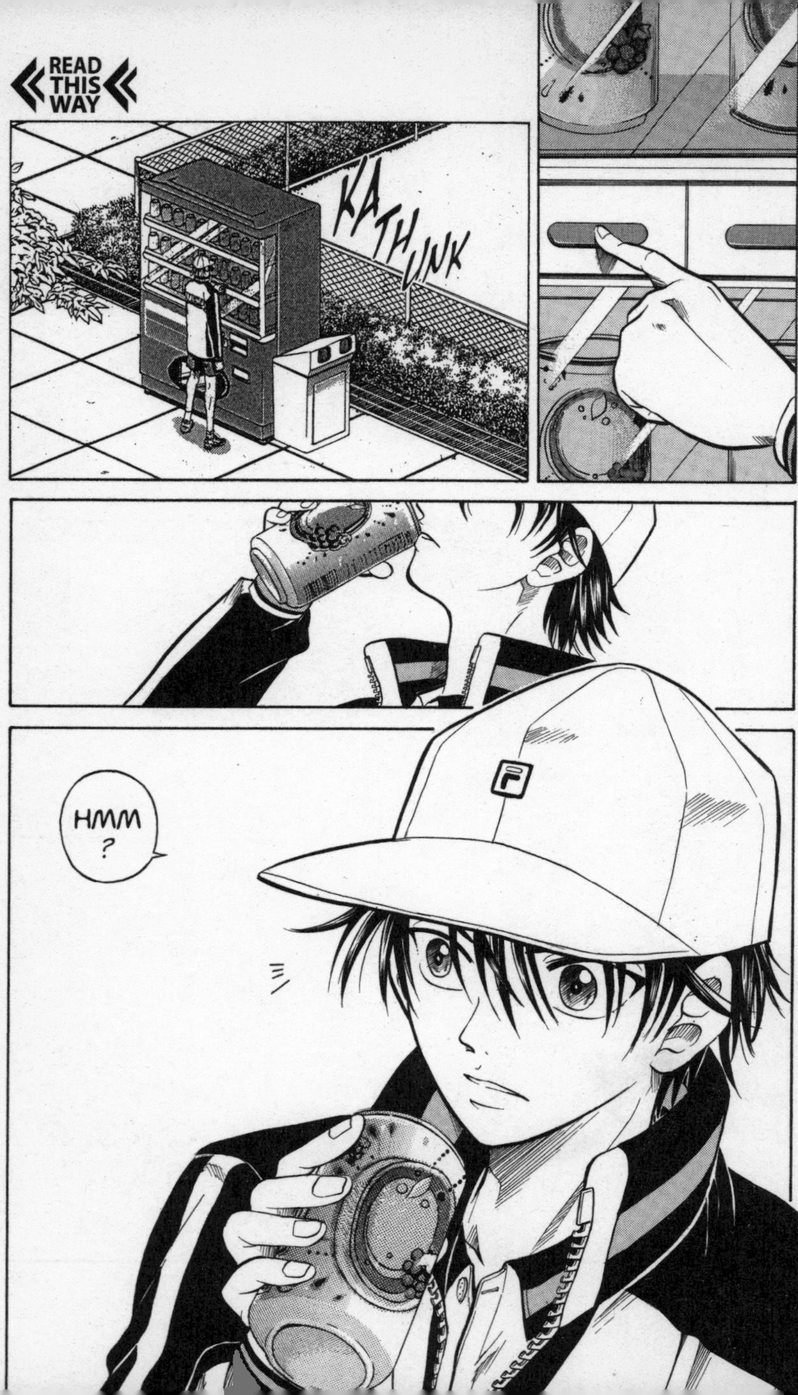
KATHUNK
HMM ?

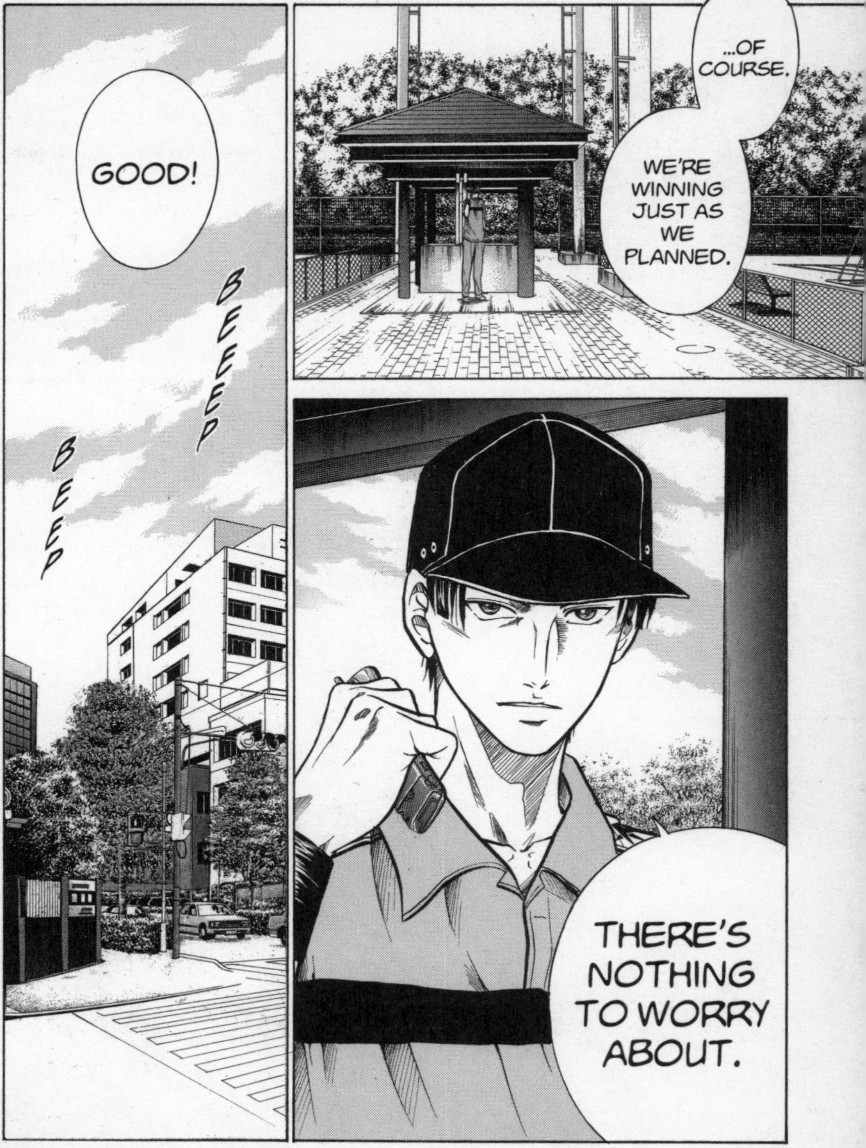
...OF COURSE.
WE'RE WINNING JUST AS WE PLANNED.
THERE'S NOTHING TO WORRY ABOUT.
GOOD!
BEEEP
BEEP

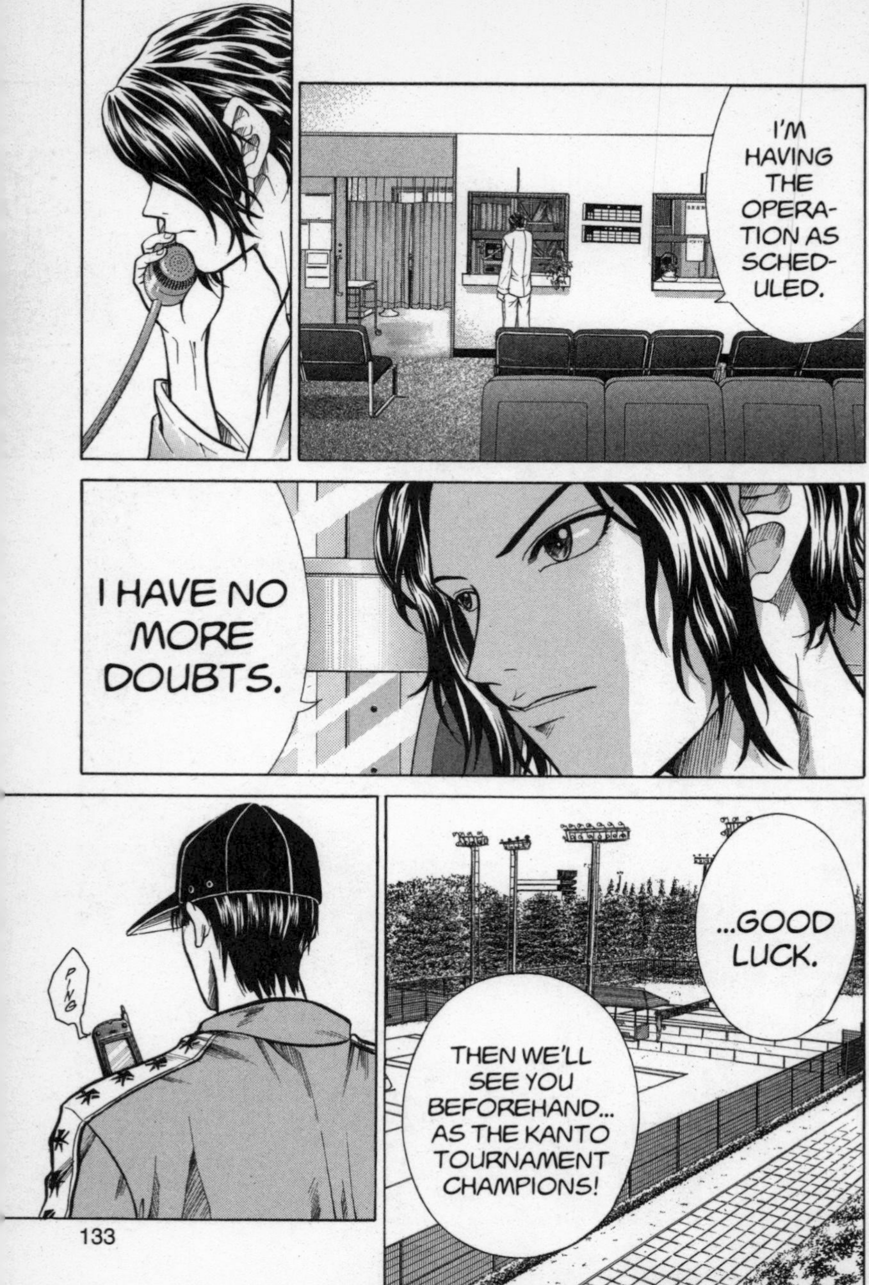
I'M HAVING THE OPERATION AS SCHEDULED.
I HAVE NO MORE DOUBTS.
...GOOD LUCK.
THEN WE'LL SEE YOU BEFOREHAND... AS THE KANTO TOURNAMENT CHAMPIONS!
PING

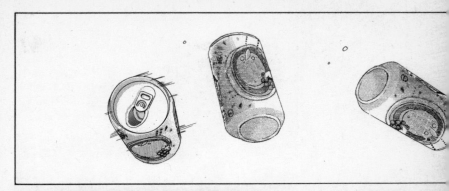

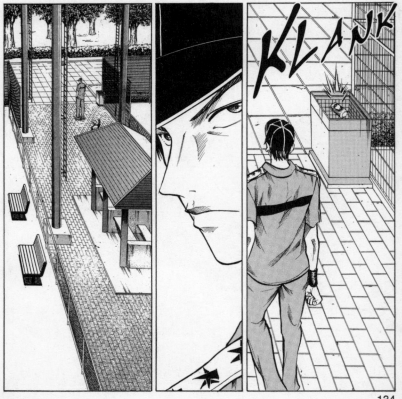

KLANK

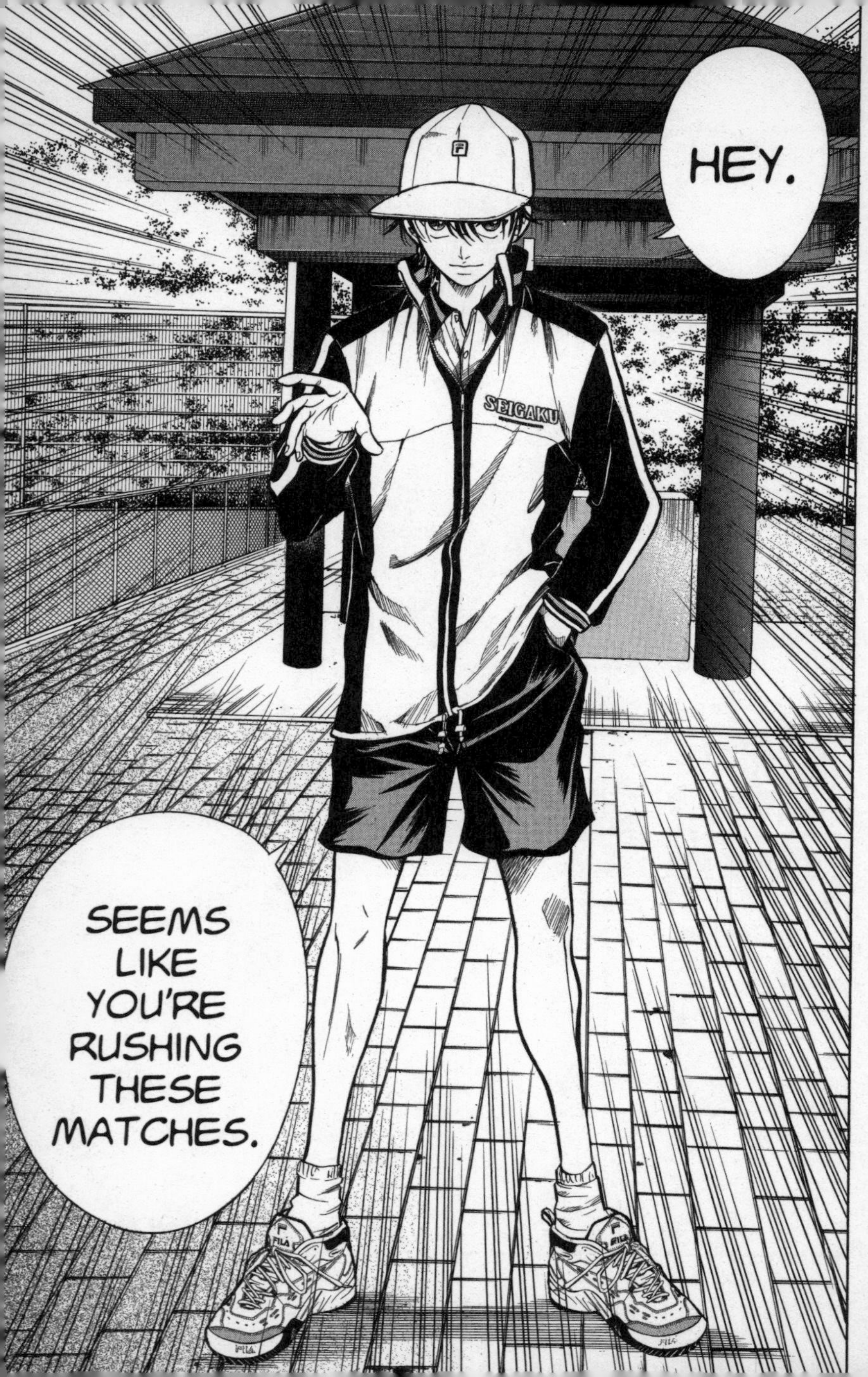
HEY.
SEIGAKU
SEEMS LIKE YOU'RE RUSHING THESE MATCHES.

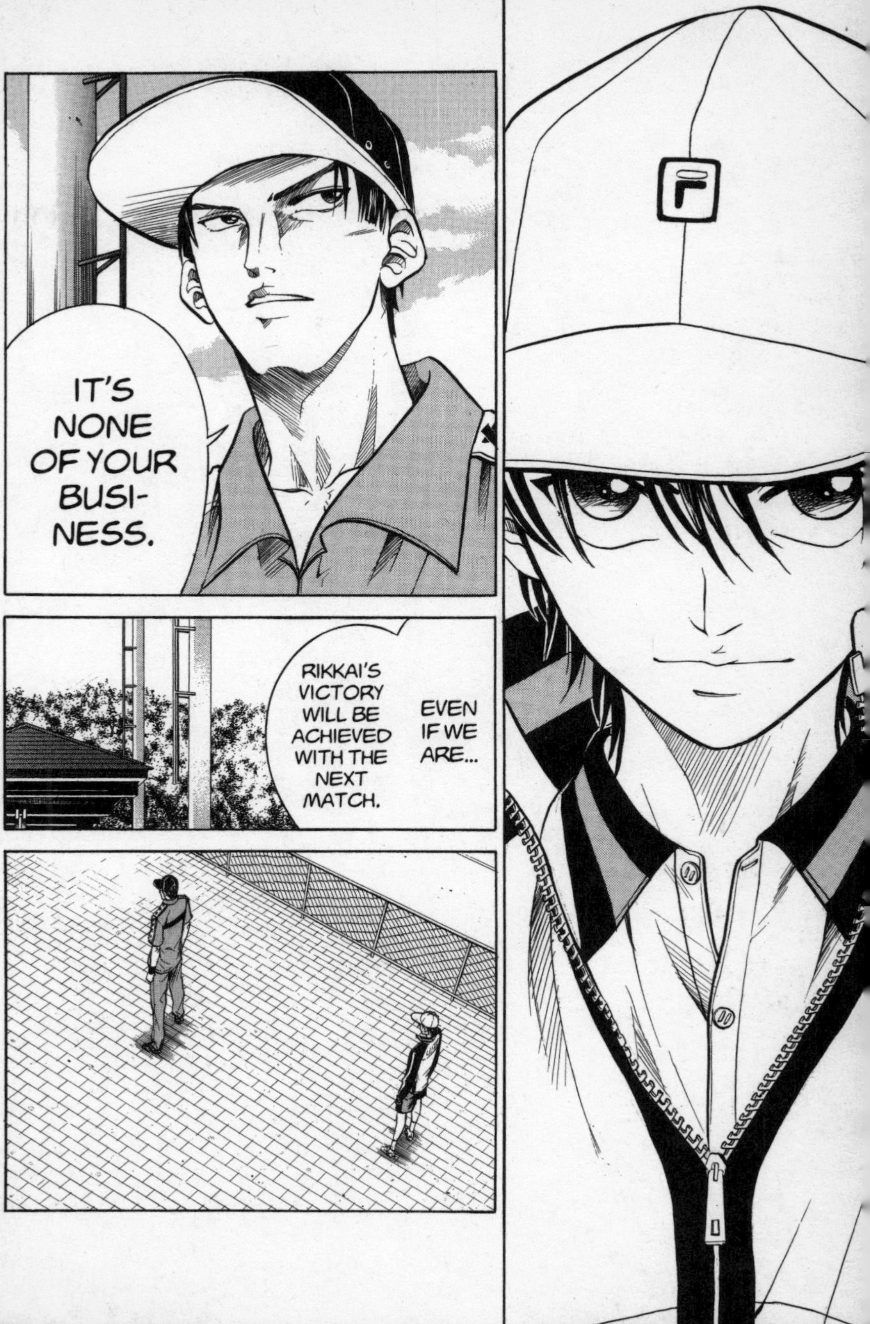
IT'S NONE OF YOUR BUSI- NESS.
EVEN IF WE ARE...
RIKKAI'S VICTORY WILL BE ACHIEVED WITH THE NEXT MATCH.

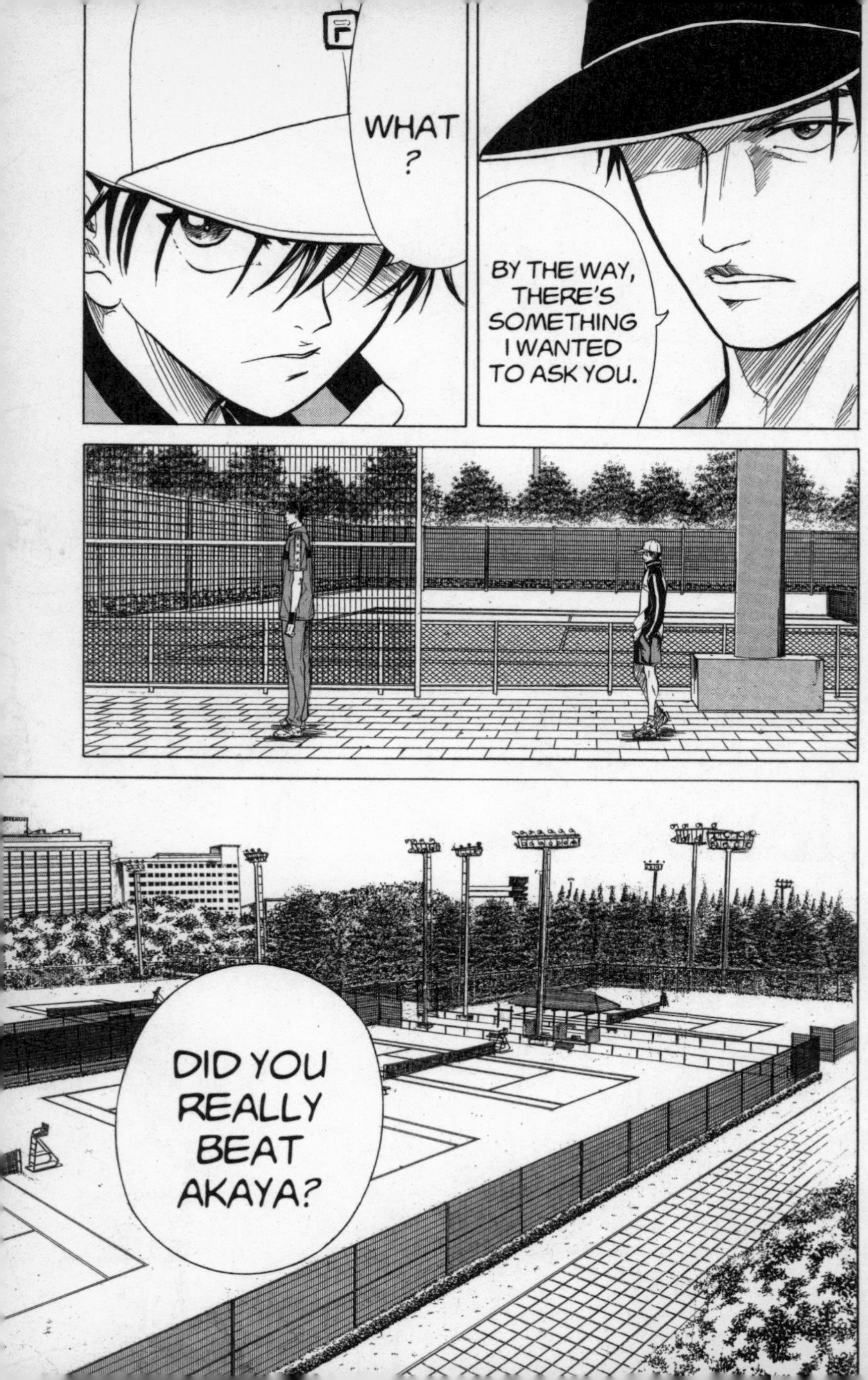
BY THE WAY, THERE'S SOMETHING I WANTED TO ASK YOU.
WHAT ?
DID YOU REALLY BEAT AKAYA?

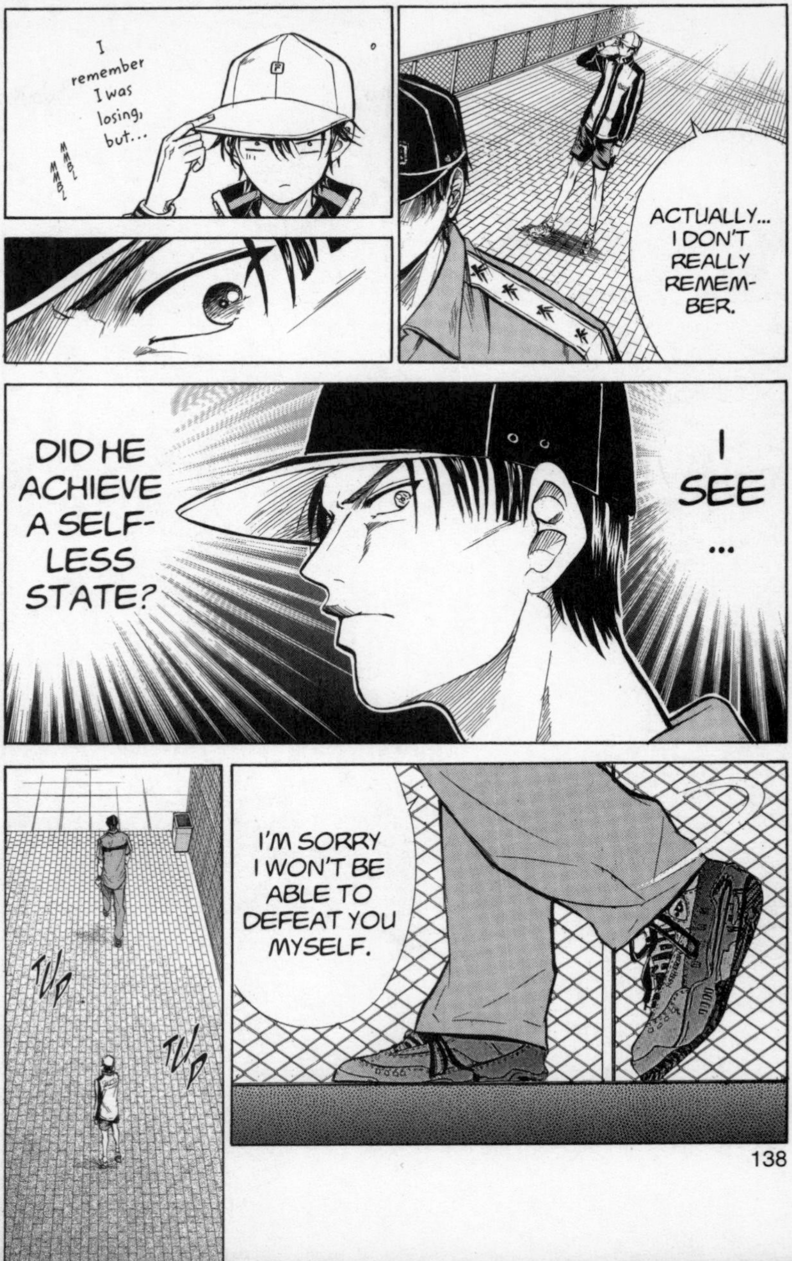

ACTUALLY... I DON'T REALLY REMEMBER.
I remember I was losing, but...
MMBL MMBL
I SEE...
DID HE ACHIEVE A SELF-LESS STATE?
I'M SORRY I WON'T BE ABLE TO DEFEAT YOU MYSELF.
TUD
TUD

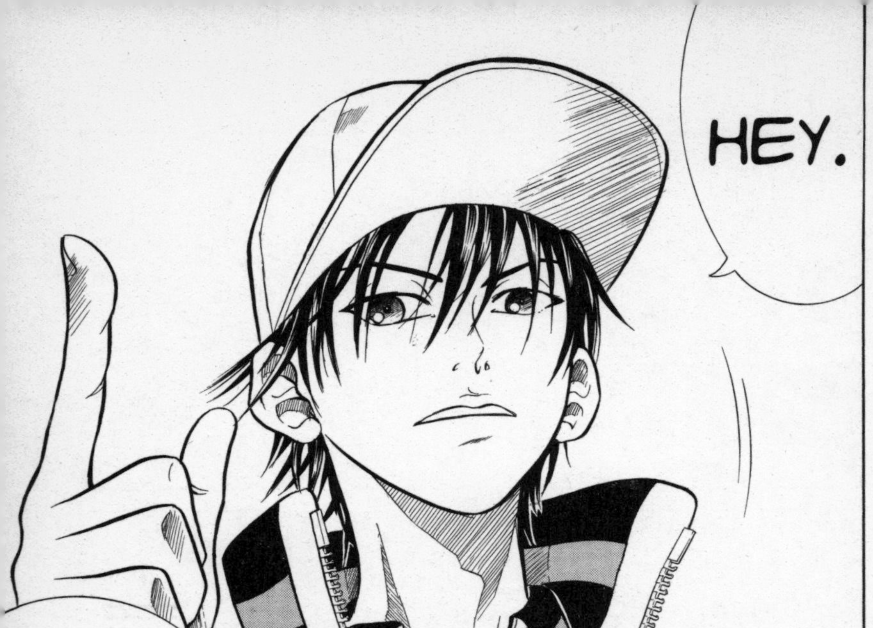
HEY.
IT'S DANGEROUS TO TAKE US TOO LIGHTLY.
SEIGAKU
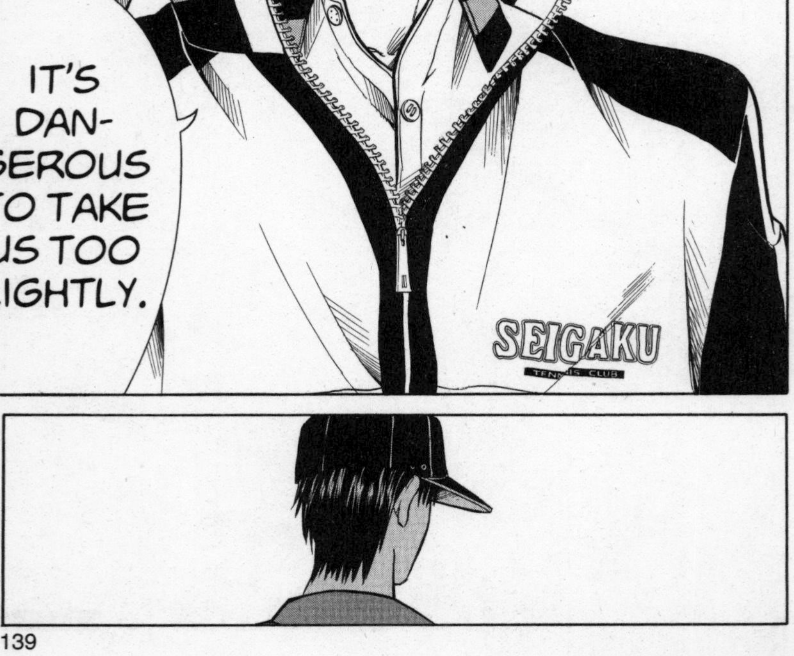

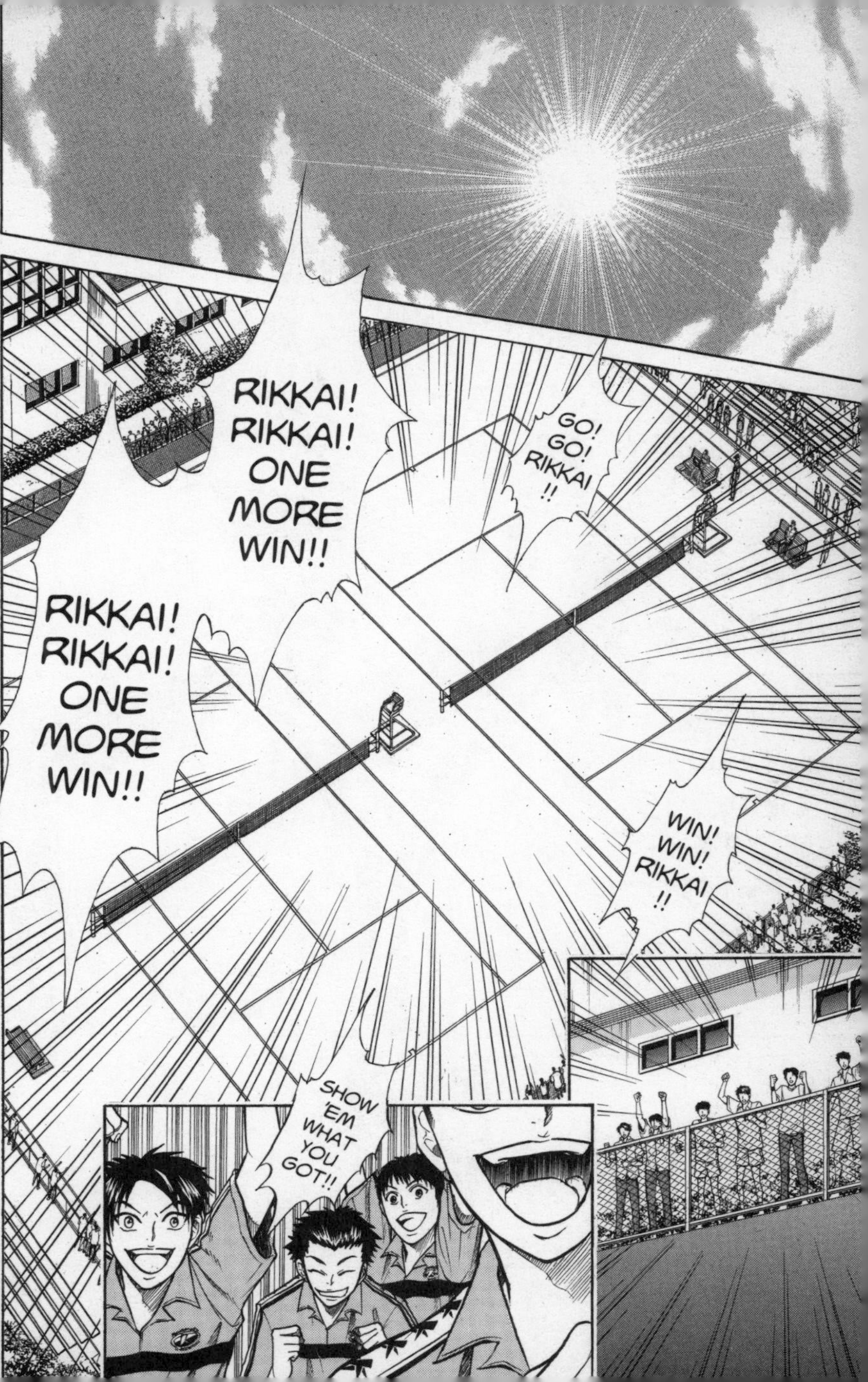
GO! GO! RIKKAI!!
RIKKAI! RIKKAI! ONE MORE WIN!!
RIKKAI! RIKKAI! ONE MORE WIN!!
WIN! WIN! RIKKAI!!
SHOW 'EM WHAT YOU GOT!!

READ THIS WAY

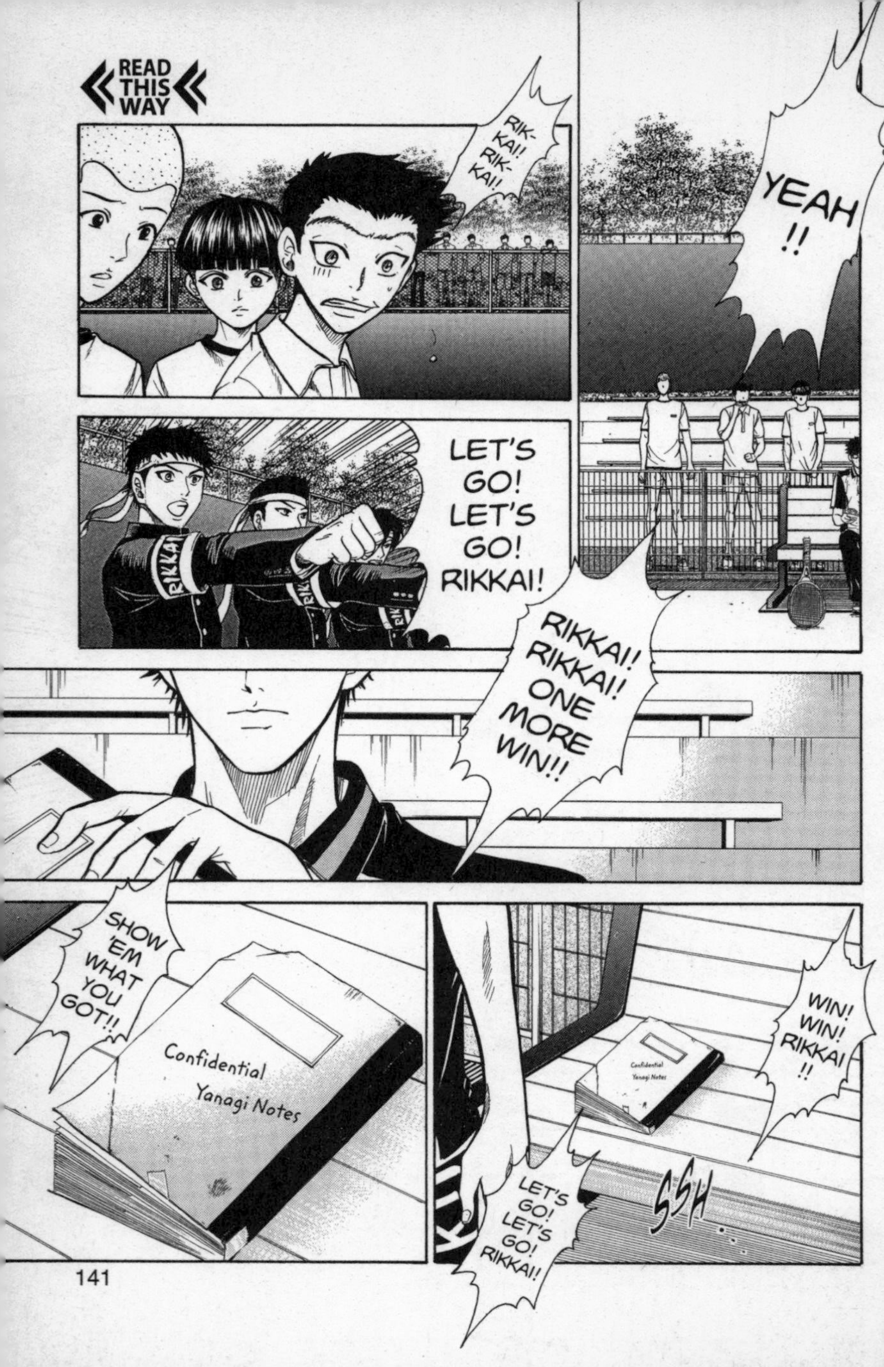

YEAH!!
RIK-KAI! RIK-KAI!
LET'S GO! LET'S GO! RIKKAI!
RIKKAI!! RIKKAI!! ONE MORE WIN!!
WIN! WIN! RIKKAI!!
Confidential Yanagi Notes
SSH
LET'S GO! LET'S GO! RIKKAI!
SHOW 'EM WHAT YOU GOT!!
Confidential Yanagi Notes

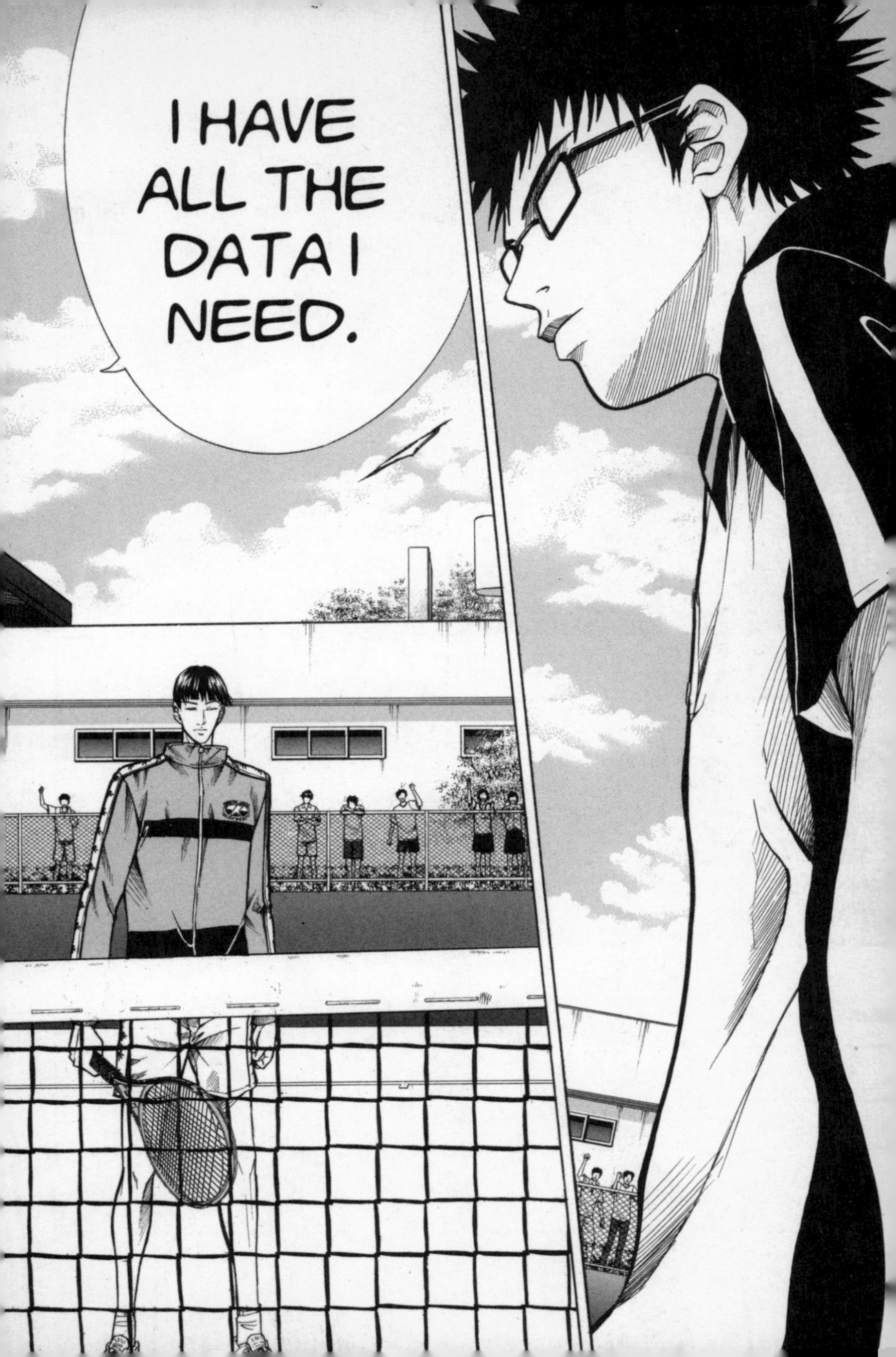
I HAVE ALL THE DATA I NEED.

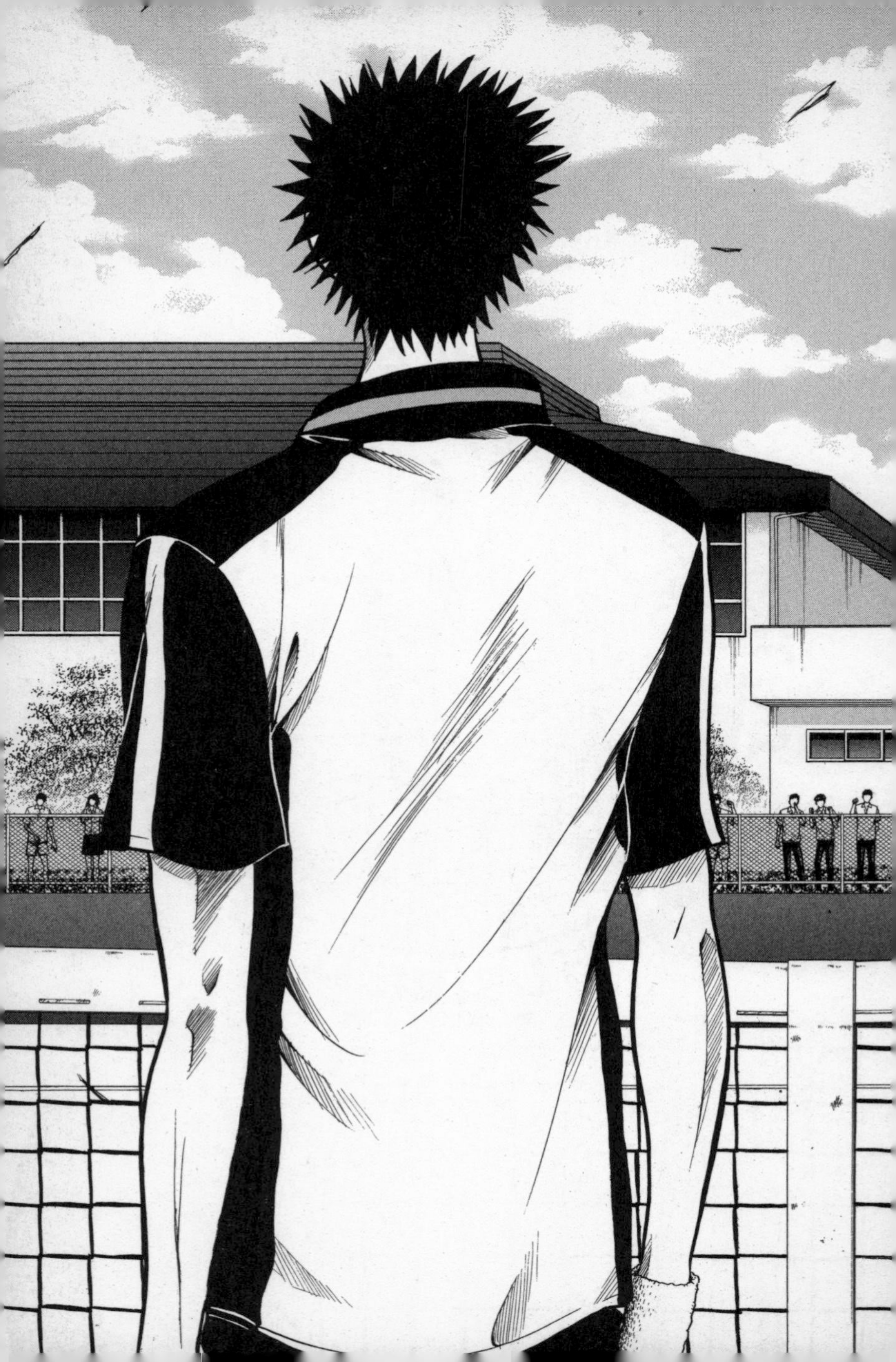

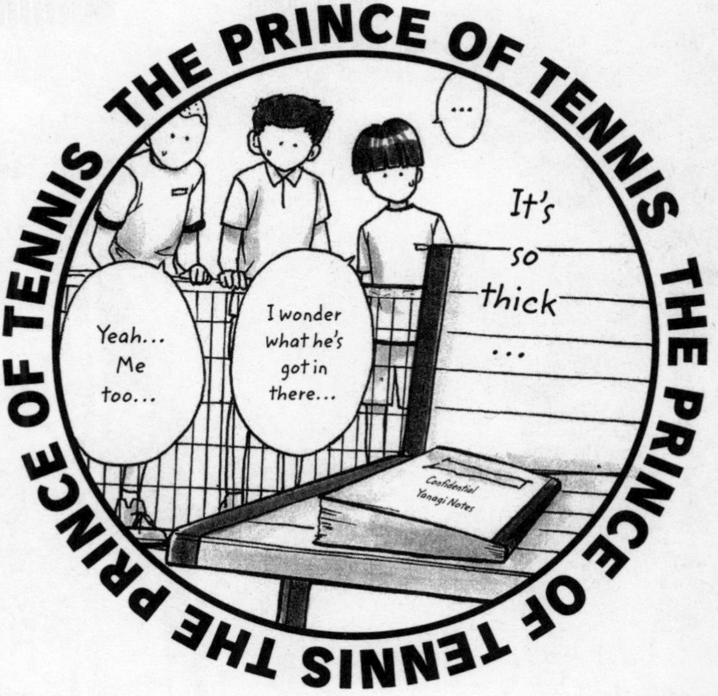
THE PRINCE OF TENNIS THE PRINCE OF TENNIS THE PRINCE OF TENNIS
...
It's so thick ...
I wonder what he's got in there...
Yeah... Me too...
Confidential Yanagi Notes

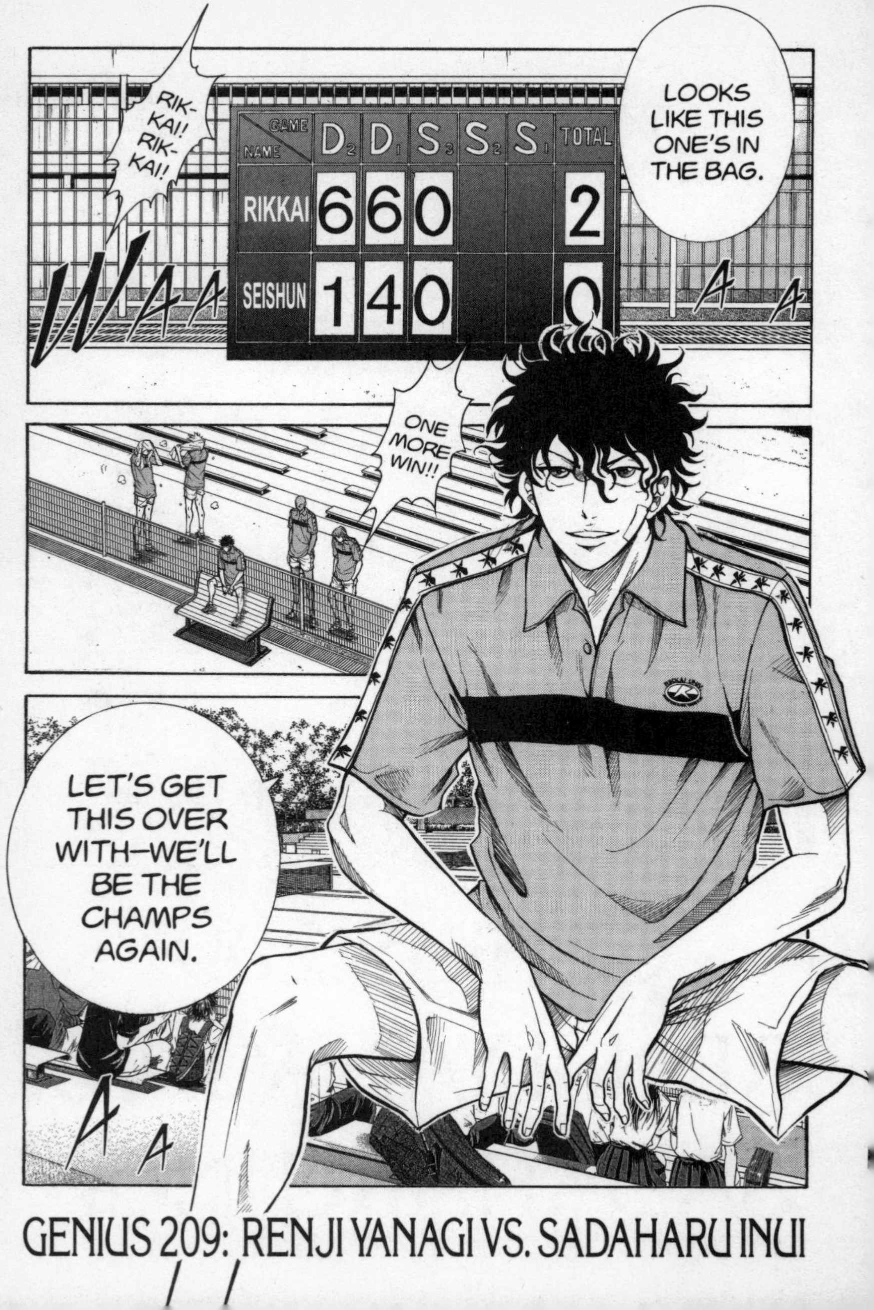
LOOKS LIKE THIS ONE'S IN THE BAG.
RIK-KAI!! RIK-KAI!!
GAME NAME D2 D1 S3 S2 S1 TOTAL
RIKKAI 6 6 0 2
SEISHUN 1 4 0 0
WAAAAA
ONE MORE WIN!!
LET'S GET THIS OVER WITH—WE'LL BE THE CHAMPS AGAIN.
AA

GENIUS 209: RENJI YANAGI VS. SADAHARU INUI

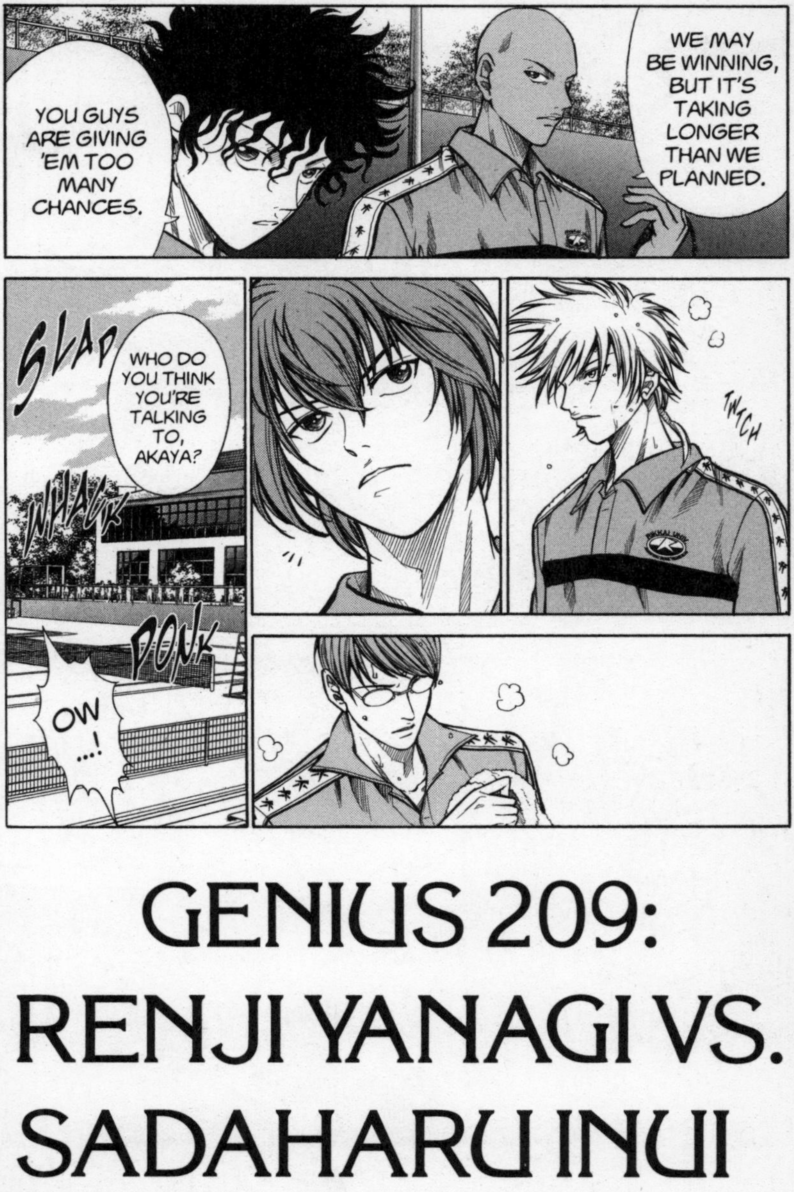
WE MAY BE WINNING, BUT IT'S TAKING LONGER THAN WE PLANNED.
YOU GUYS ARE GIVING 'EM TOO MANY CHANCES.
TWITCH
SLAP
WHO DO YOU THINK YOU'RE TALKING TO, AKAYA?
WHACK
PONK
OW ...!

GENIUS 209: RENJI YANAGI VS. SADAHARU INUI

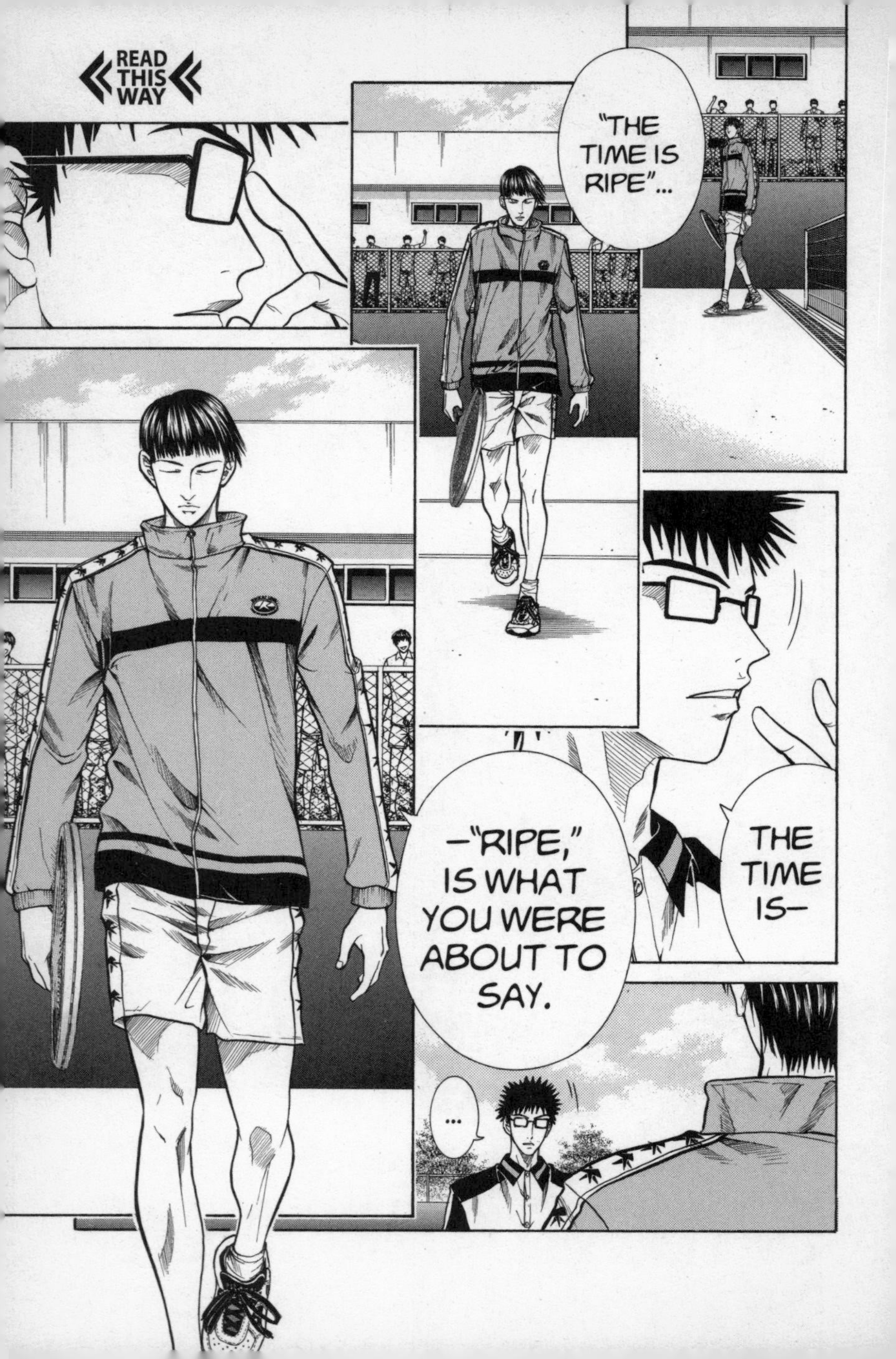
READ THIS WAY
"THE TIME IS RIPE"...
THE TIME IS—
—"RIPE," IS WHAT YOU WERE ABOUT TO SAY.
...

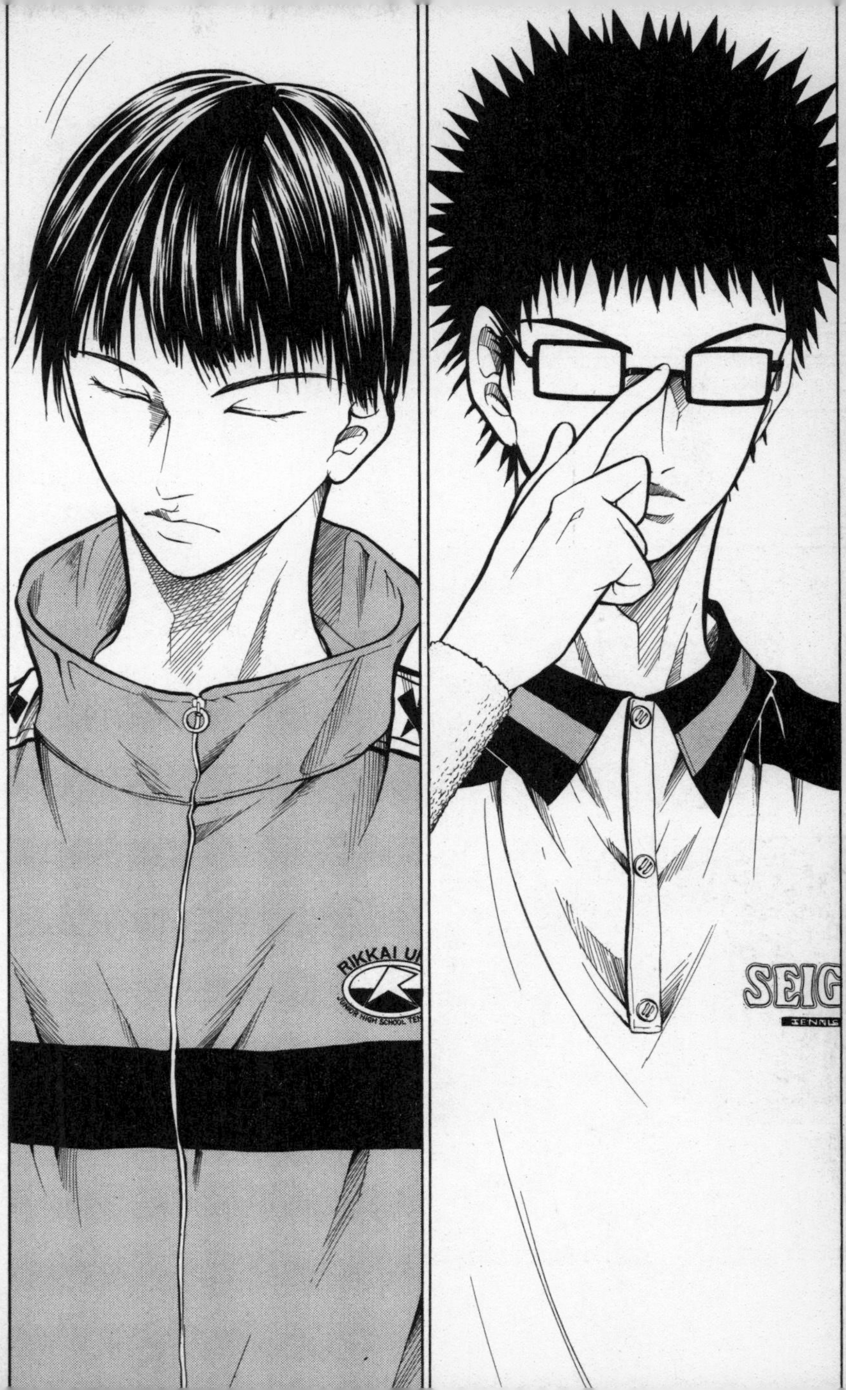

READ THIS WAY

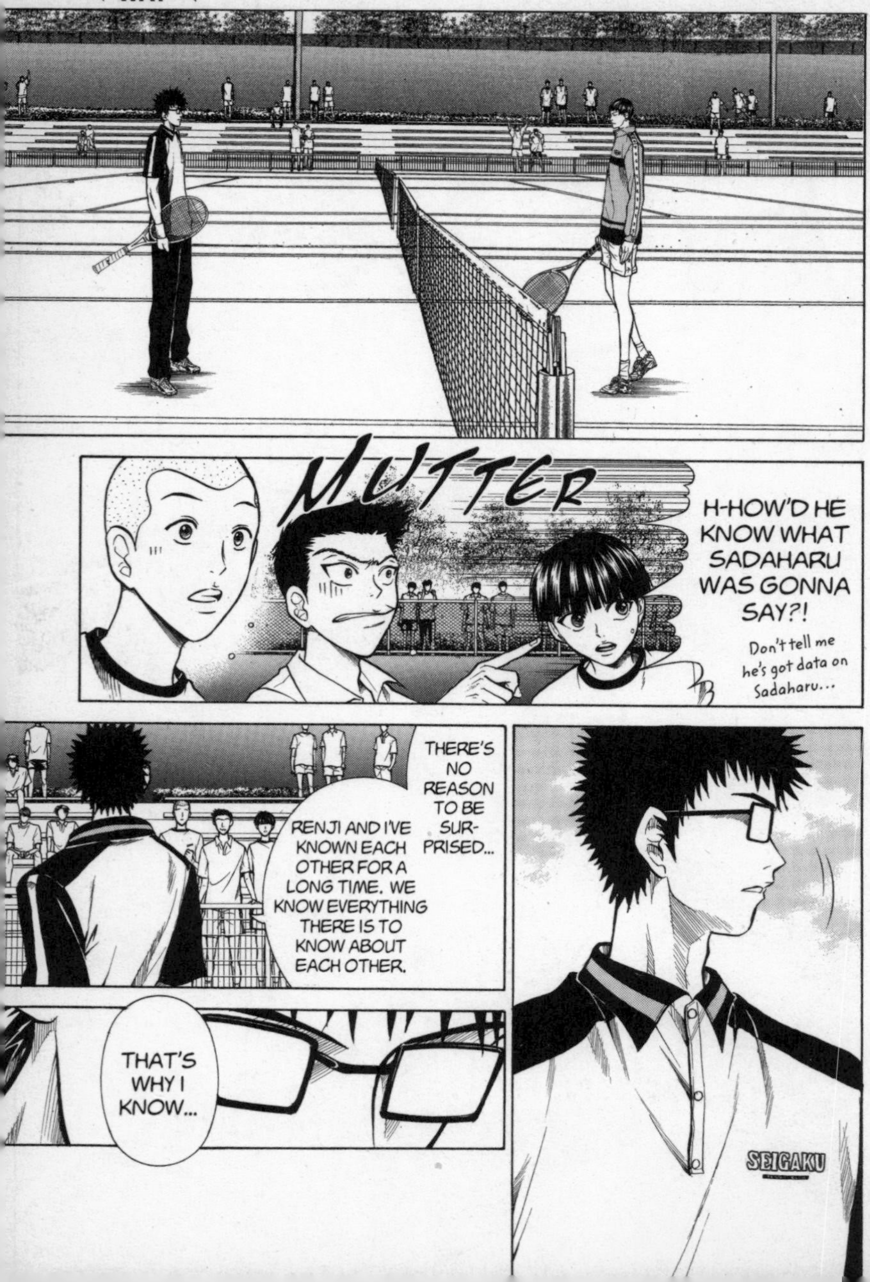
MUTTER
H-HOW'D HE KNOW WHAT SADAHARU WAS GONNA SAY?!
Don't tell me he's got data on Sadaharu...
SEIGAKU
THERE'S NO REASON TO BE SUR-PRISED...
RENJI AND I'VE KNOWN EACH OTHER FOR A LONG TIME. WE KNOW EVERYTHING THERE IS TO KNOW ABOUT EACH OTHER.
THAT'S WHY I KNOW...

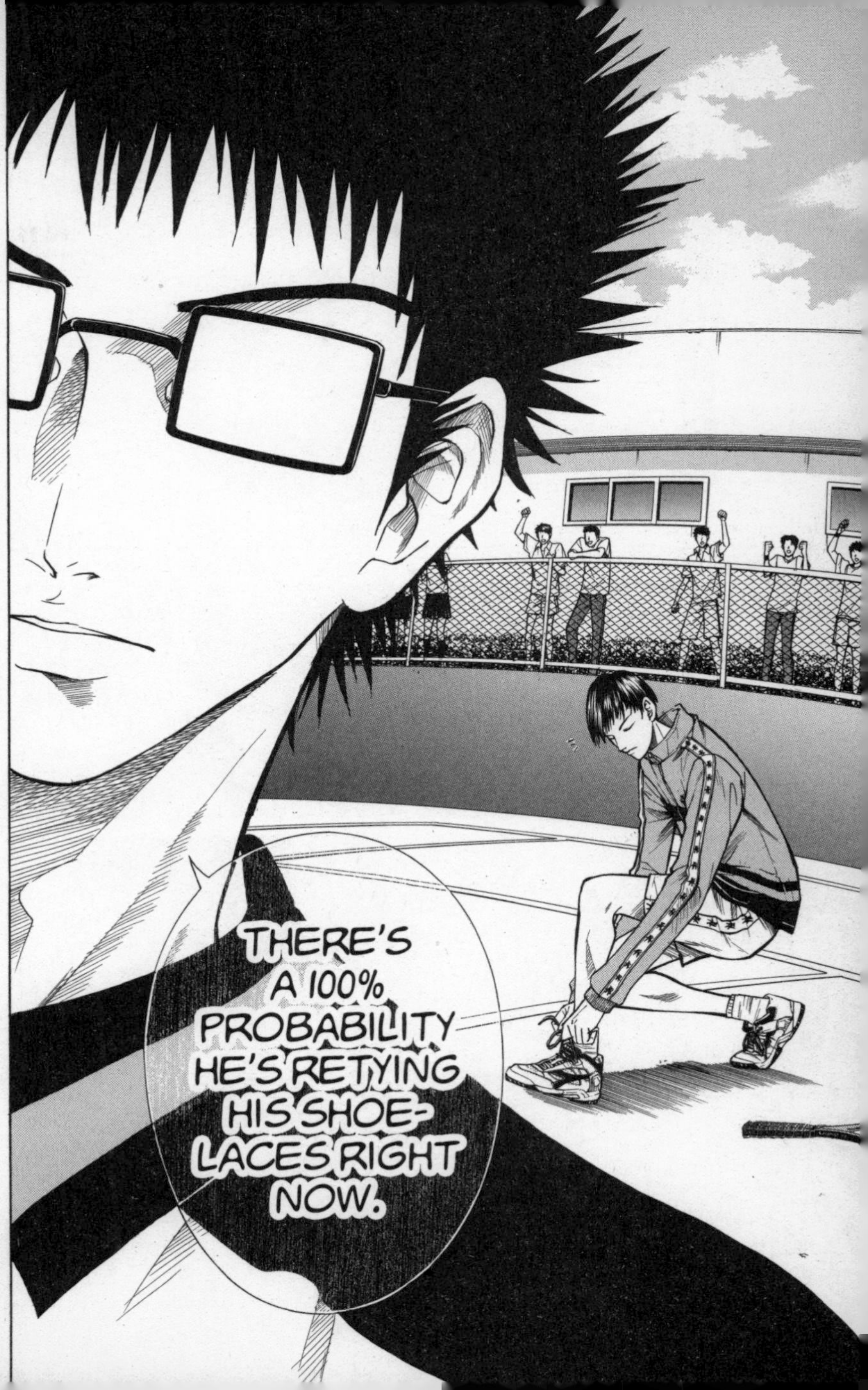
THERE'S A 100% PROBABILITY HE'S RETYING HIS SHOE-LACES RIGHT NOW.

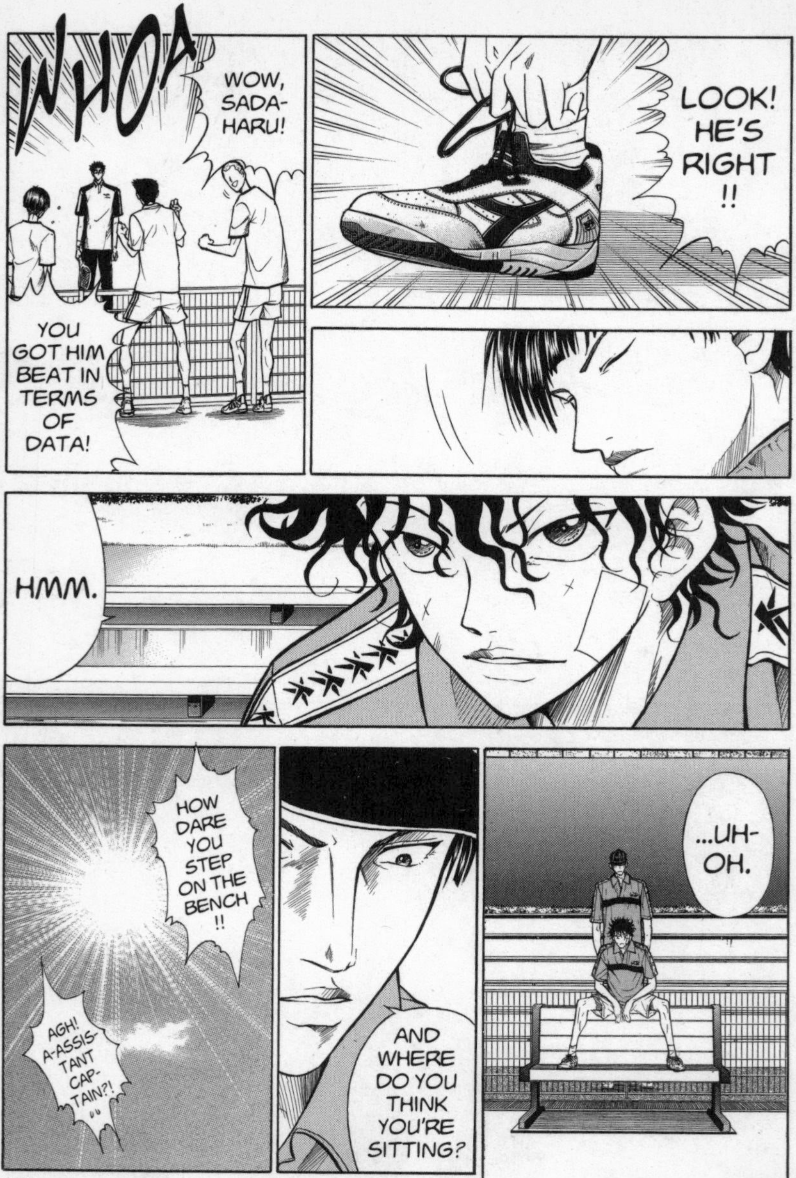
LOOK! HE'S RIGHT !!
WHOA
WOW, SADA-HARU!
YOU GOT HIM BEAT IN TERMS OF DATA!
HMM.
...UH-OH.
AND WHERE DO YOU THINK YOU'RE SITTING?
HOW DARE YOU STEP ON THE BENCH !!
AGH! A-ASSIS-TANT CAP-TAIN?!

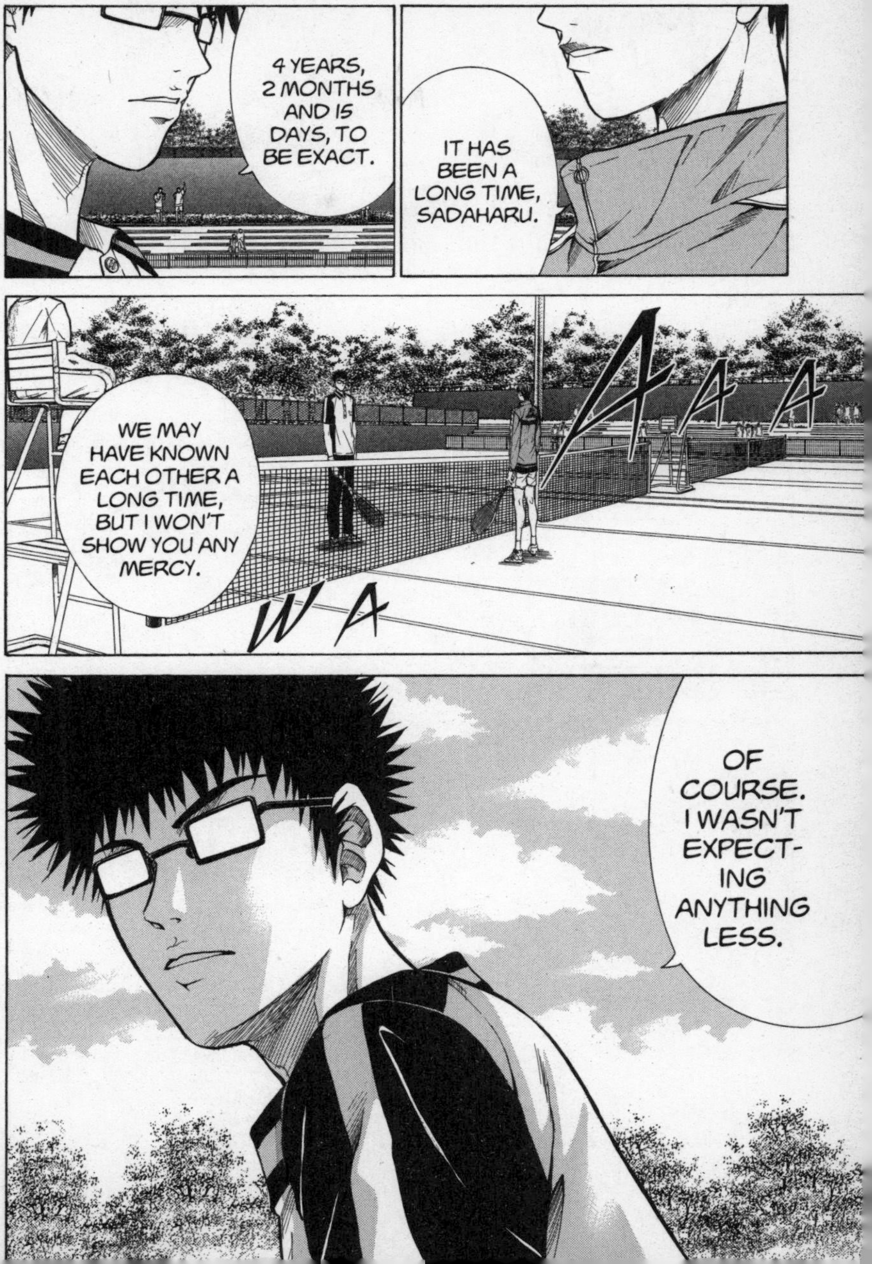
IT HAS BEEN A LONG TIME, SADAHARU.
4 YEARS, 2 MONTHS AND 15 DAYS, TO BE EXACT.
AAA
WA
WE MAY HAVE KNOWN EACH OTHER A LONG TIME, BUT I WON'T SHOW YOU ANY MERCY.
OF COURSE. I WASN'T EXPECT-ING ANYTHING LESS.

READ THIS WAY

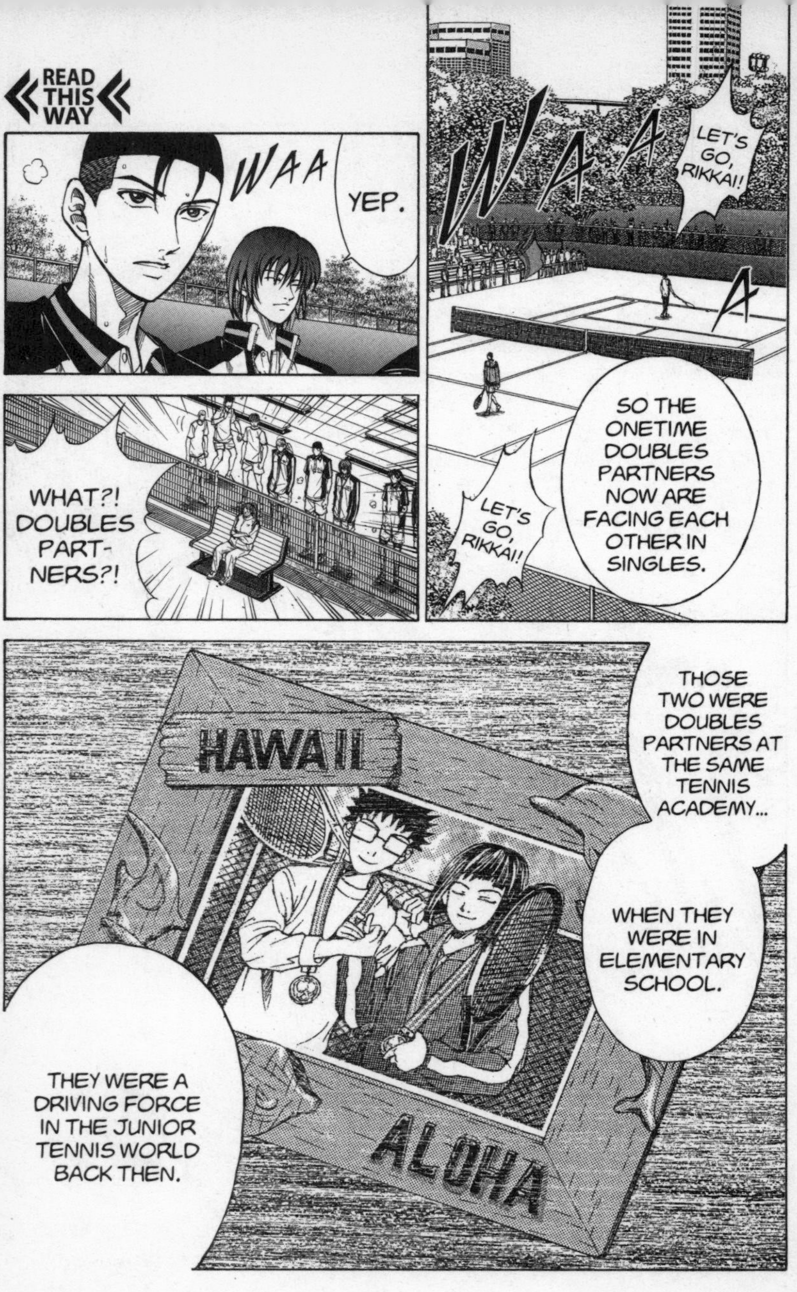
WAAA
LET'S GO, RIKKAI!
SO THE ONETIME DOUBLES PARTNERS NOW ARE FACING EACH OTHER IN SINGLES.
LET'S GO, RIKKAI!
WAA
YEP.
WHAT?! DOUBLES PART-NERS?!
HAWAII
THOSE TWO WERE DOUBLES PARTNERS AT THE SAME TENNIS ACADEMY...
WHEN THEY WERE IN ELEMENTARY SCHOOL.
THEY WERE A DRIVING FORCE IN THE JUNIOR TENNIS WORLD BACK THEN.
ALOHA

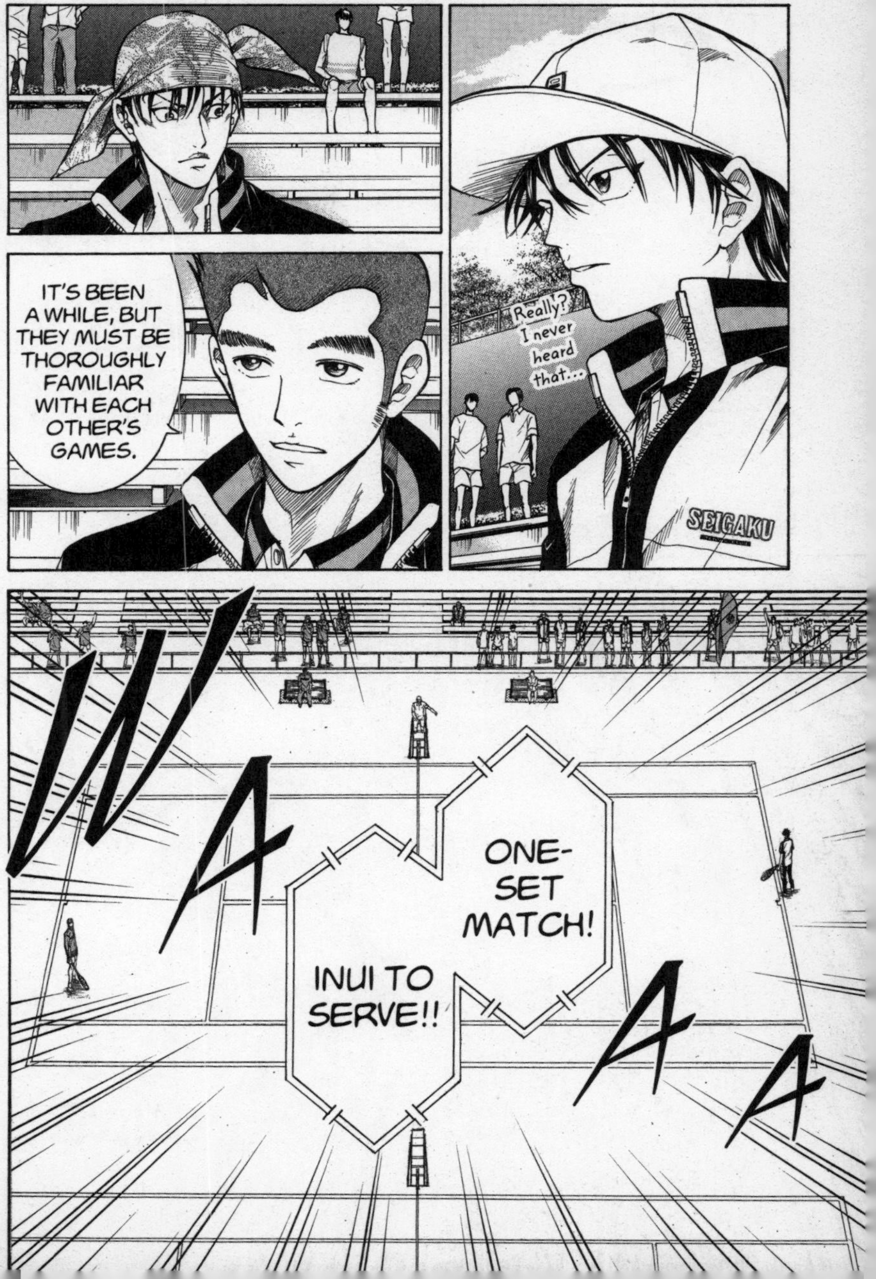
IT'S BEEN A WHILE, BUT THEY MUST BE THOROUGHLY FAMILIAR WITH EACH OTHER'S GAMES.
Really? I never heard that...
SEIGAKU
WAAA
ONE-SET MATCH!
INUI TO SERVE!!

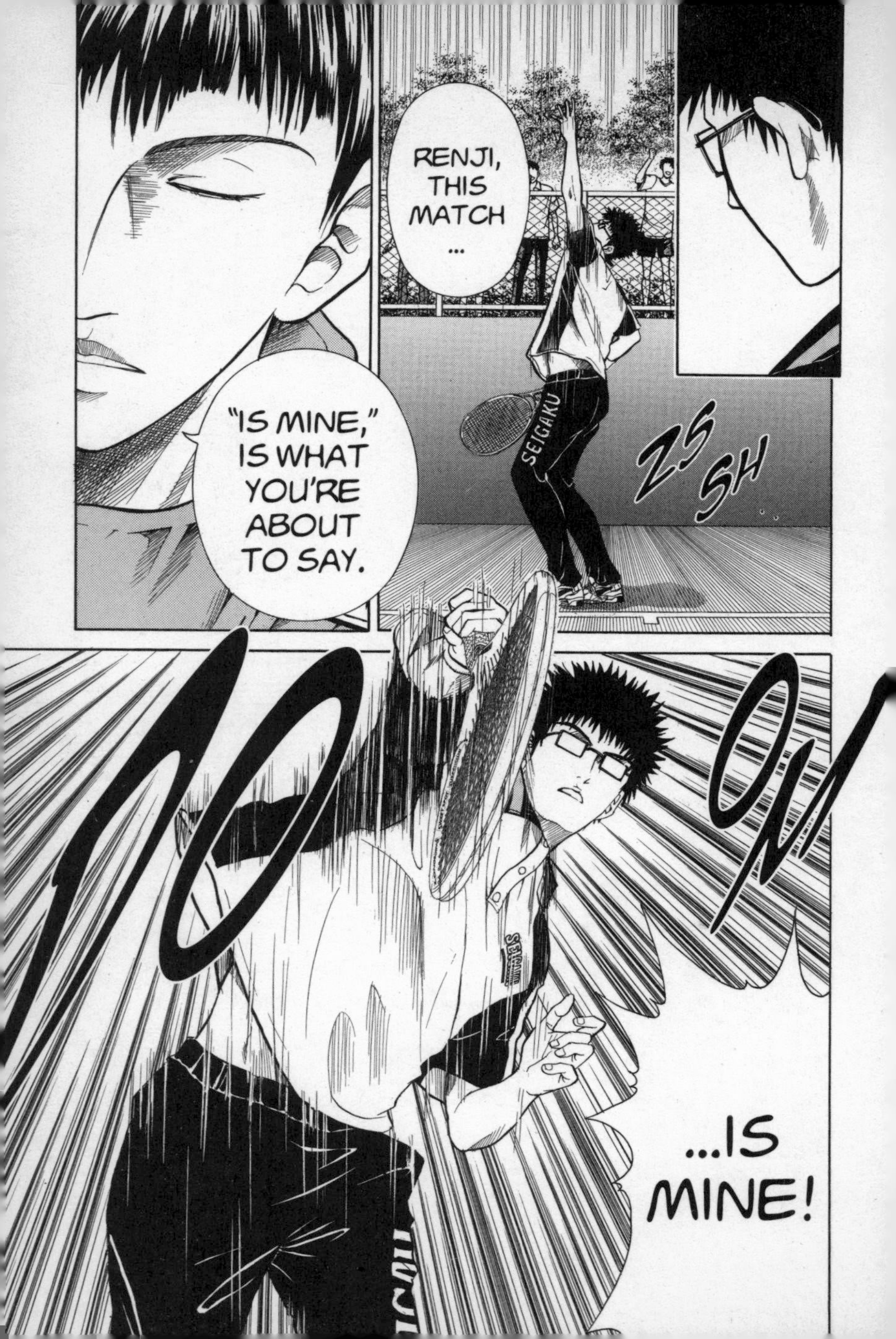
RENJI, THIS MATCH ...
ZSSH
"IS MINE," IS WHAT YOU'RE ABOUT TO SAY.
...IS MINE!

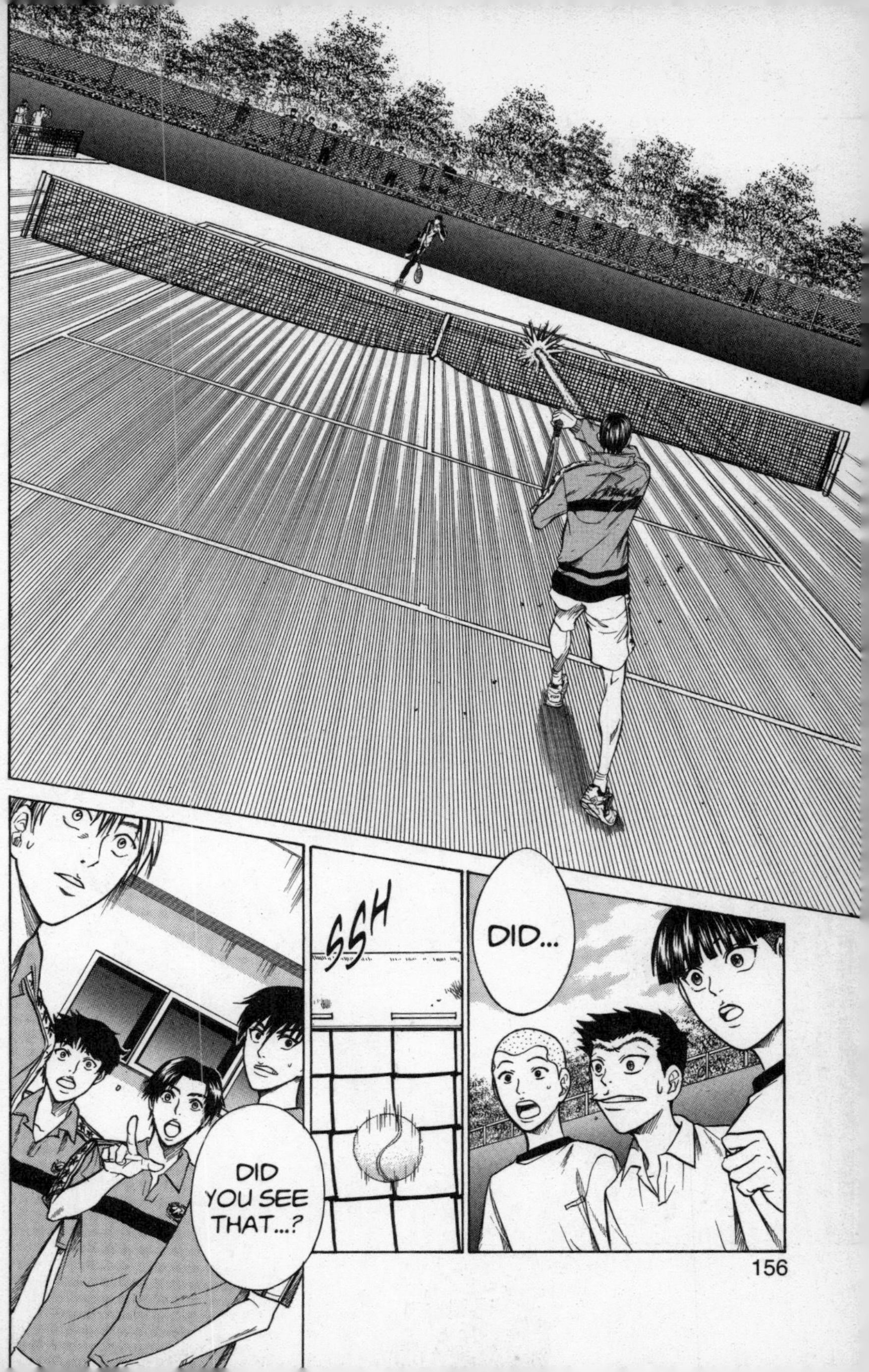
DID...
SSH
DID YOU SEE THAT...?

READ THIS WAY

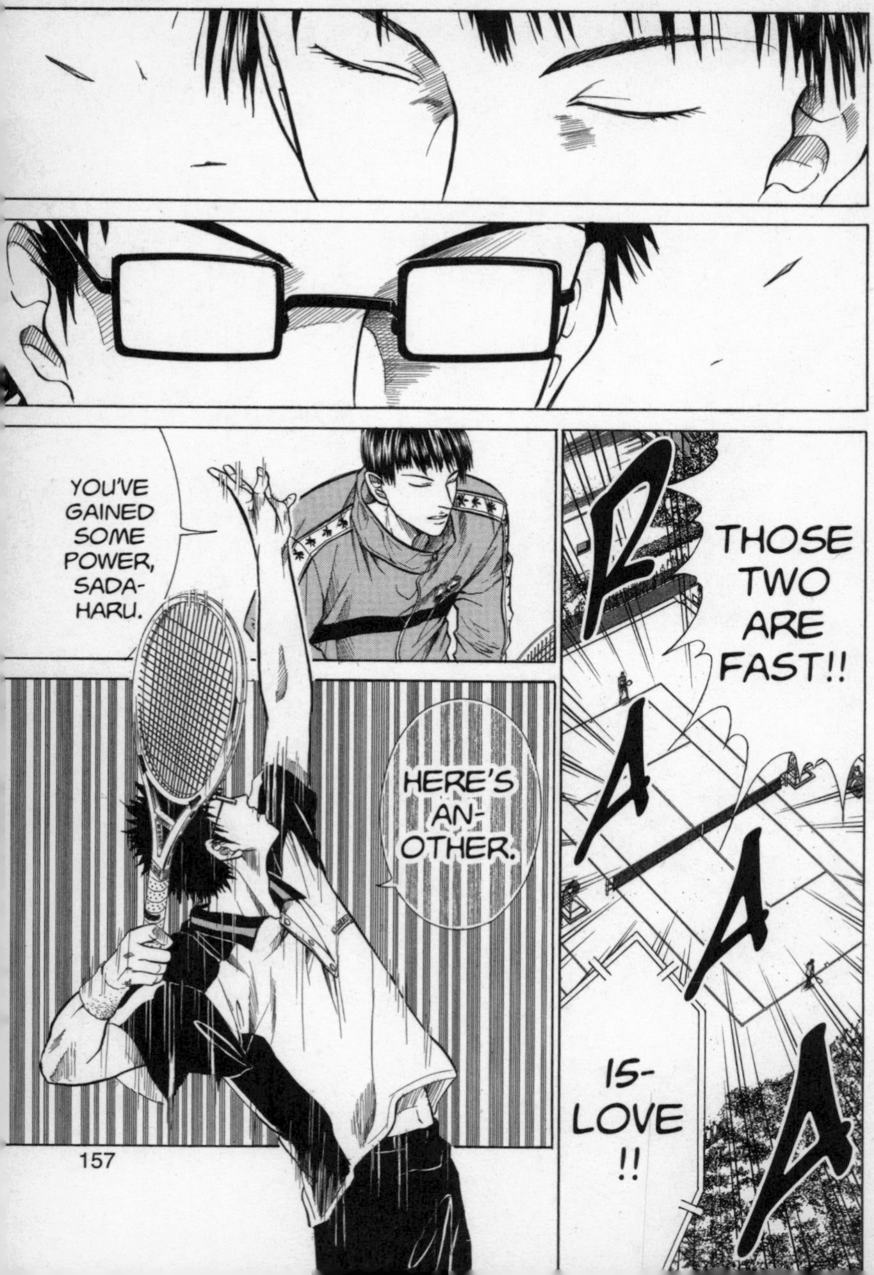

THOSE TWO ARE FAST!!
BAAA
15-LOVE!!
YOU'VE GAINED SOME POWER, SADA-HARU.
HERE'S AN-OTHER.

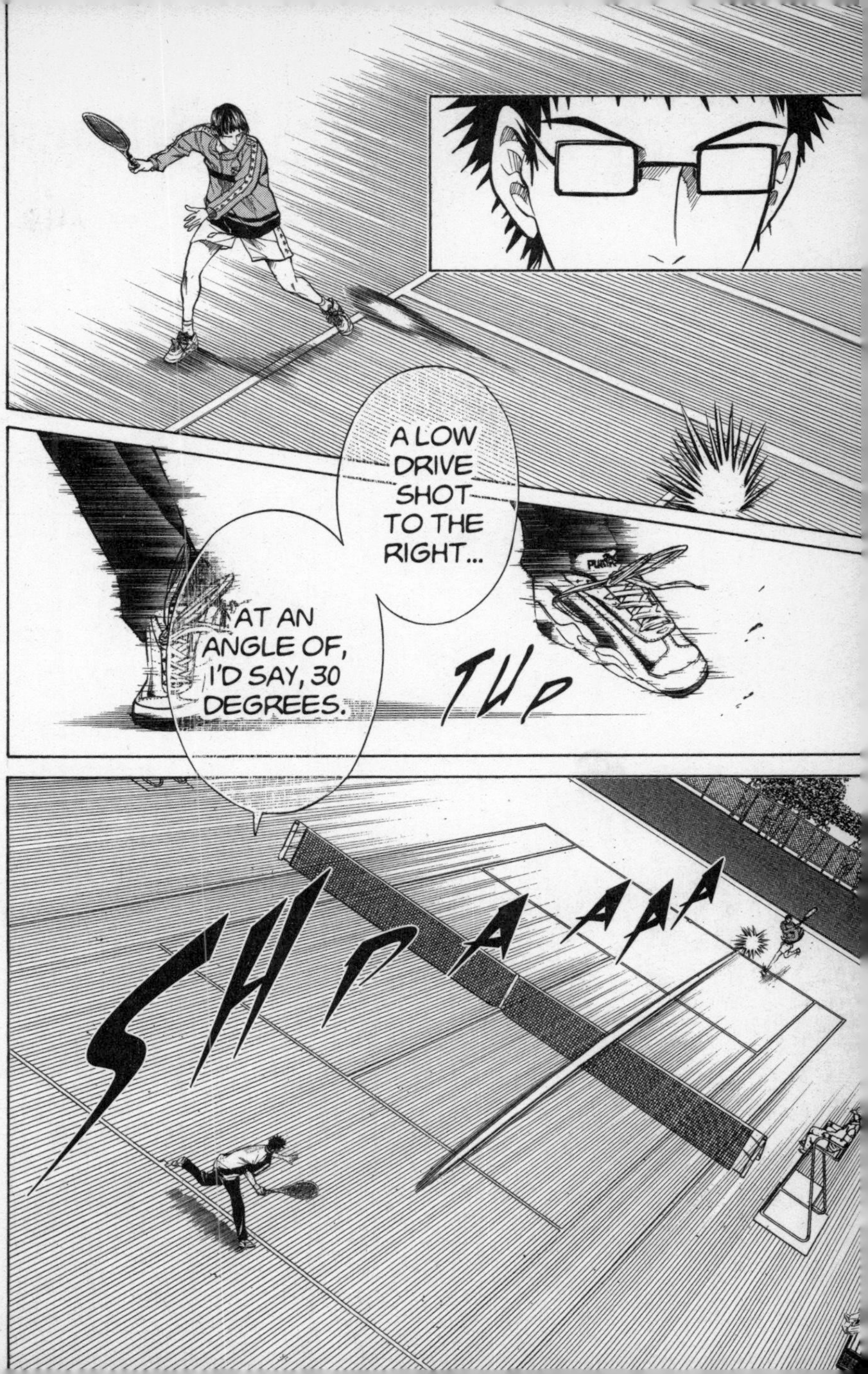
A LOW DRIVE SHOT TO THE RIGHT...
AT AN ANGLE OF, I'D SAY, 30 DEGREES.
TUP
SHPAAAA

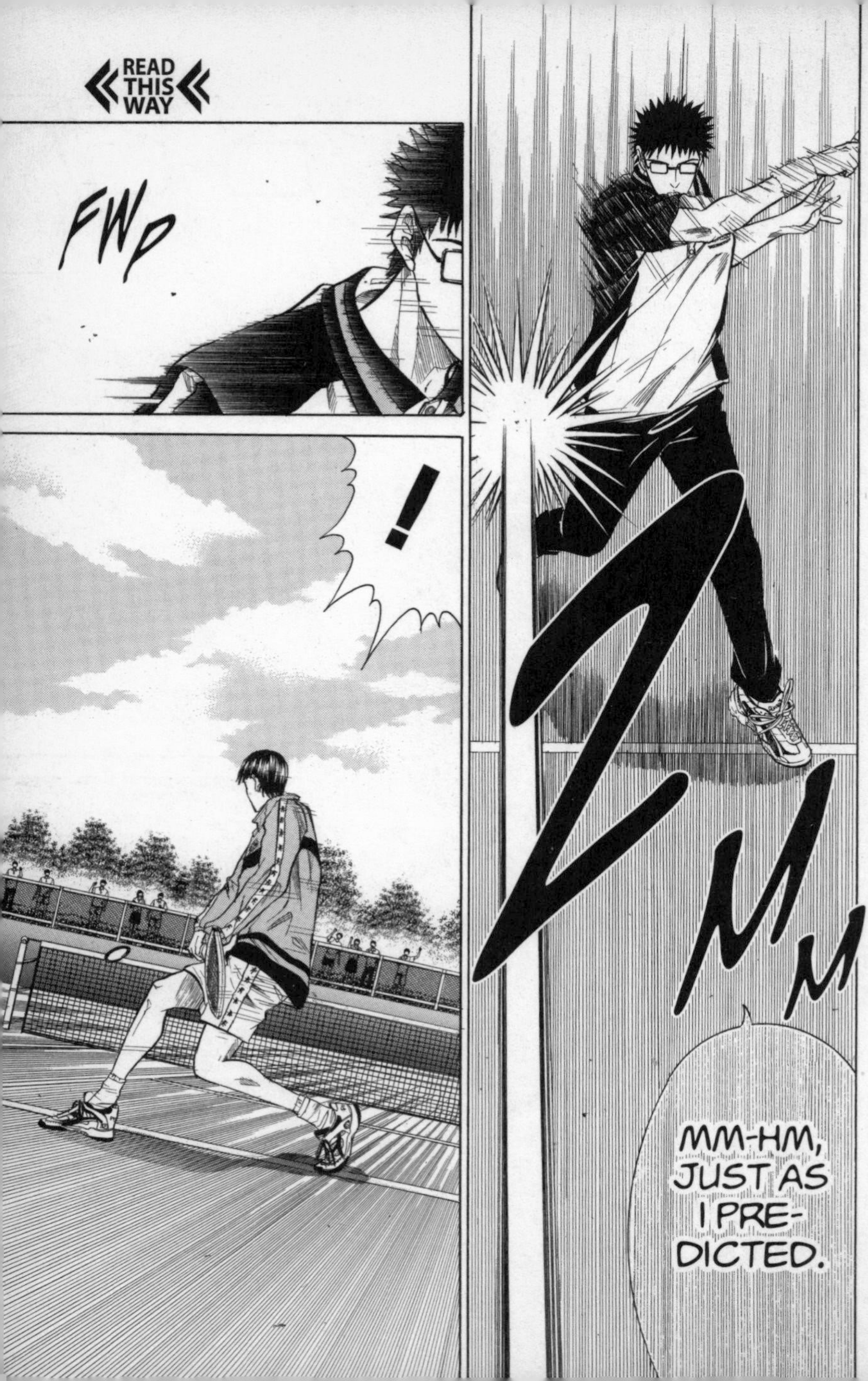
READ THIS WAY
ZMM
MM-HM, JUST AS I PRE-DICTED.
FWP
!

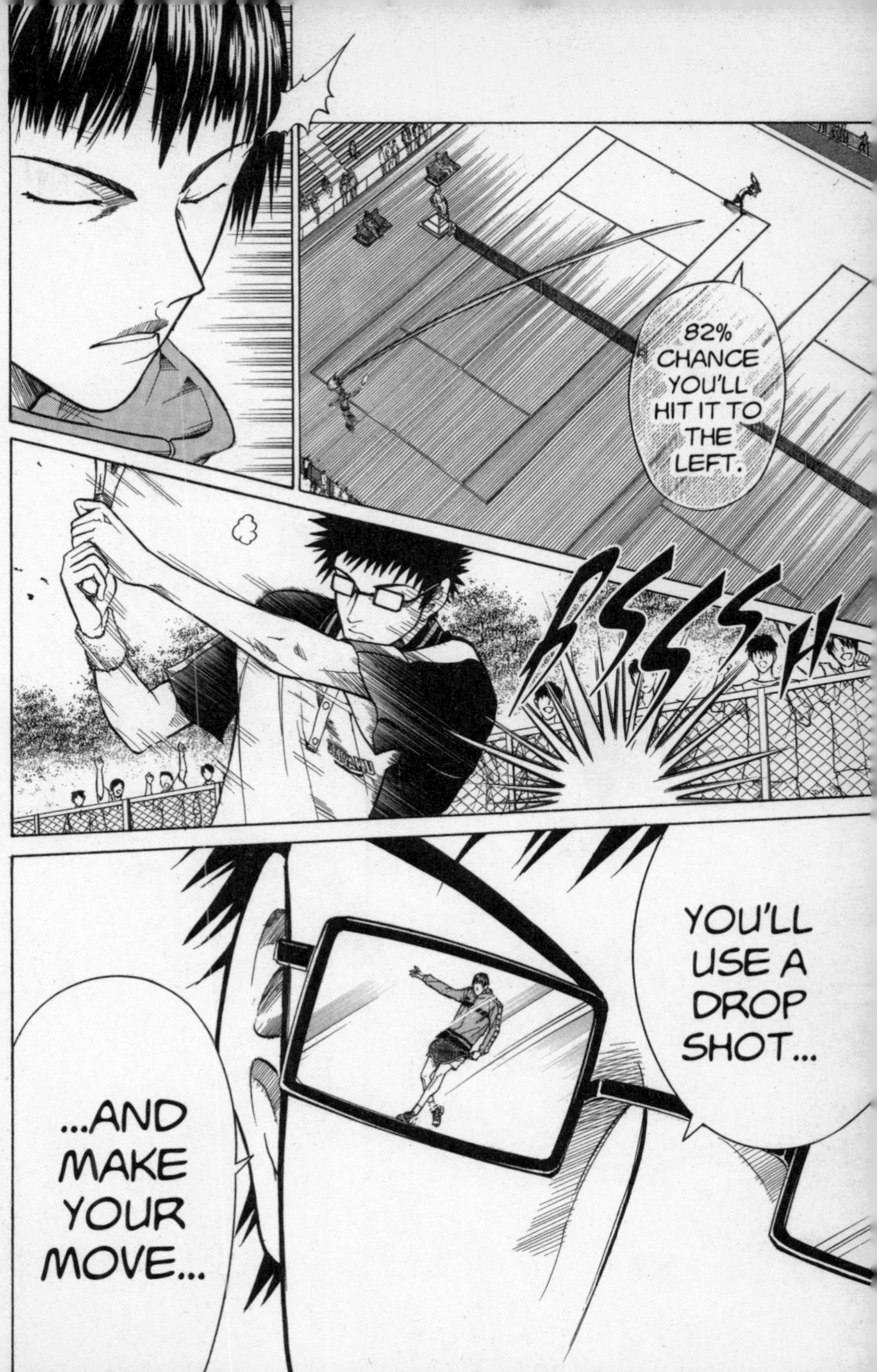
82% CHANCE YOU'LL HIT IT TO THE LEFT.
BSSSH
YOU'LL USE A DROP SHOT...
...AND MAKE YOUR MOVE...

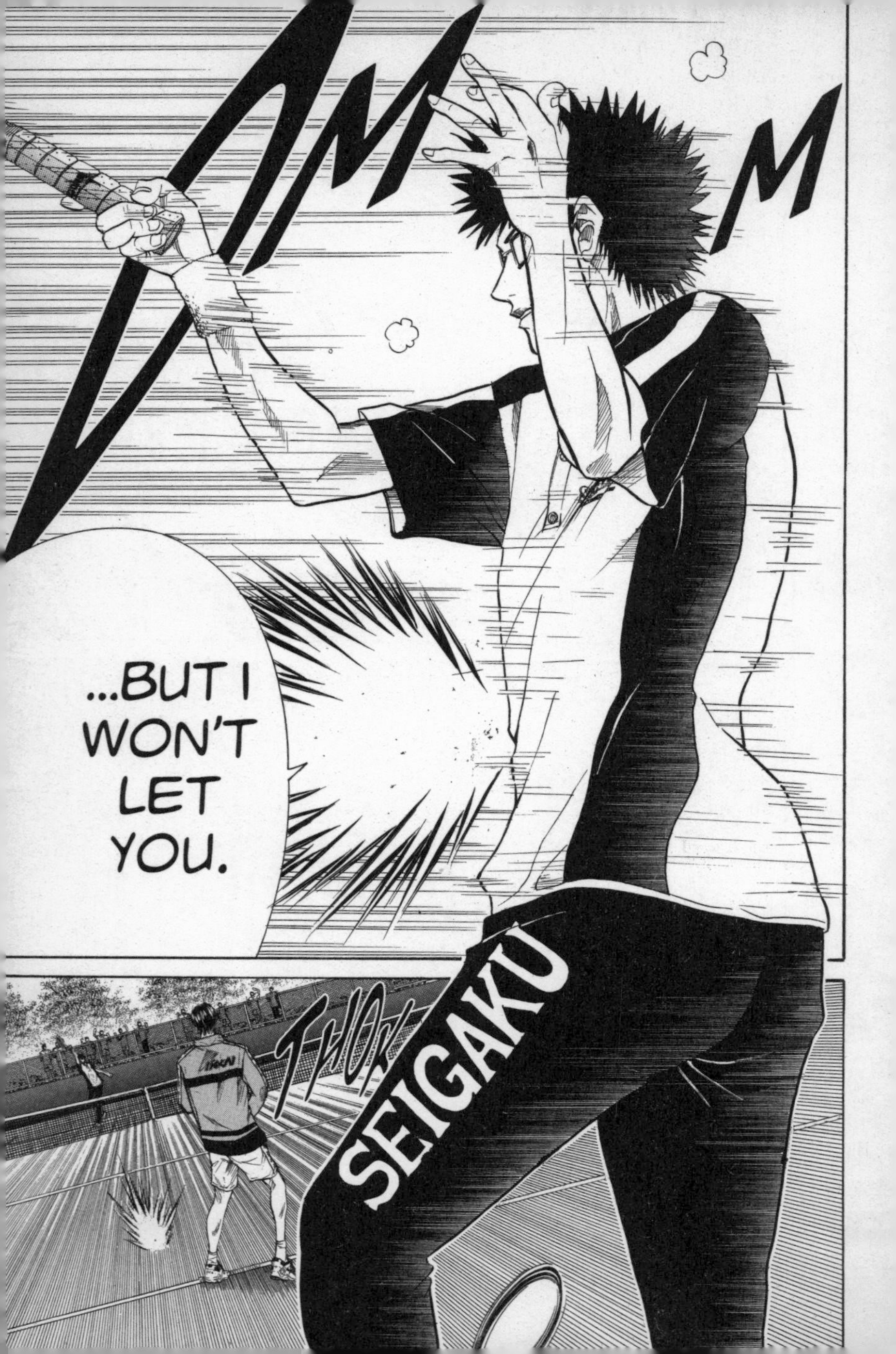
...BUT I WON'T LET YOU.
SEIGAKU

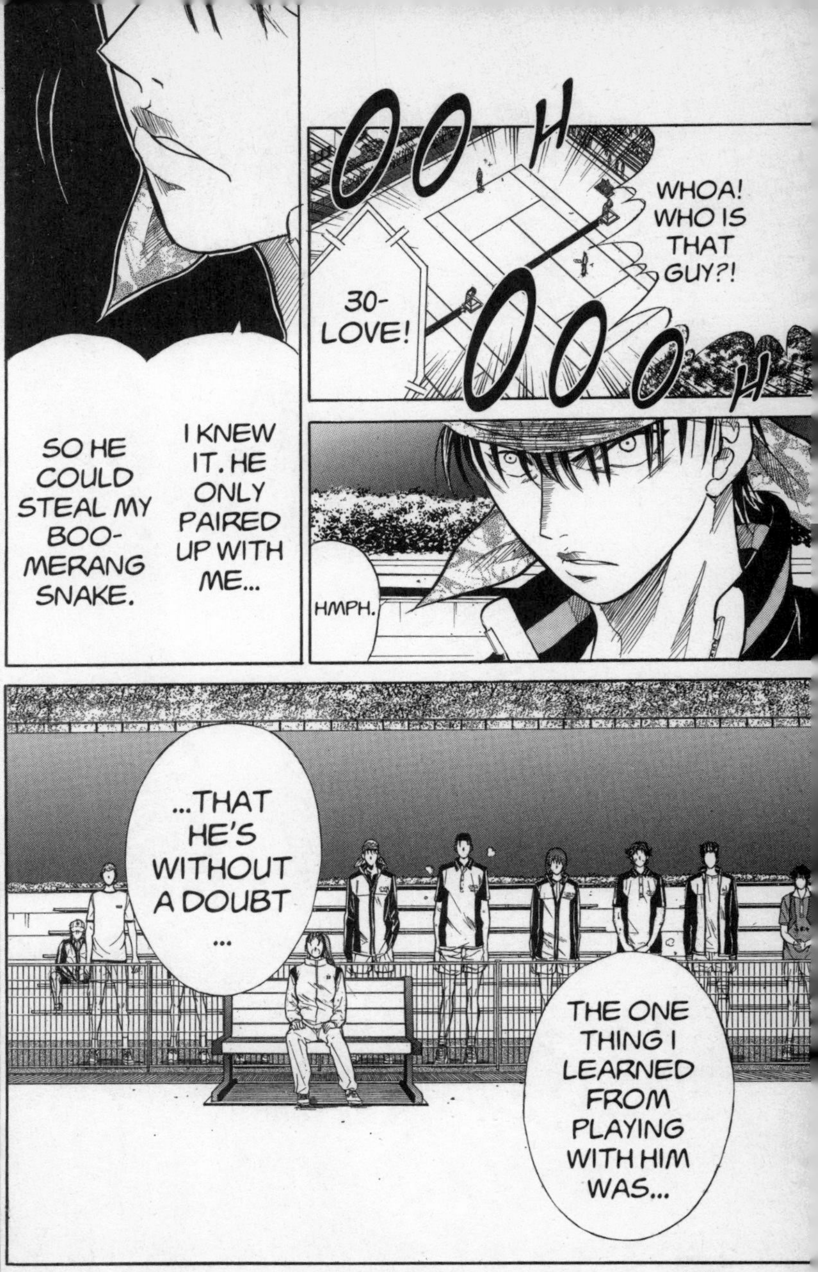
OOOH
WHOA! WHO IS THAT GUY?!
30-LOVE!
OOOOH
HMPH.
I KNEW IT. HE ONLY PAIRED UP WITH ME...
SO HE COULD STEAL MY BOOMERANG SNAKE.
THE ONE THING I LEARNED FROM PLAYING WITH HIM WAS...
...THAT HE'S WITHOUT A DOUBT ...

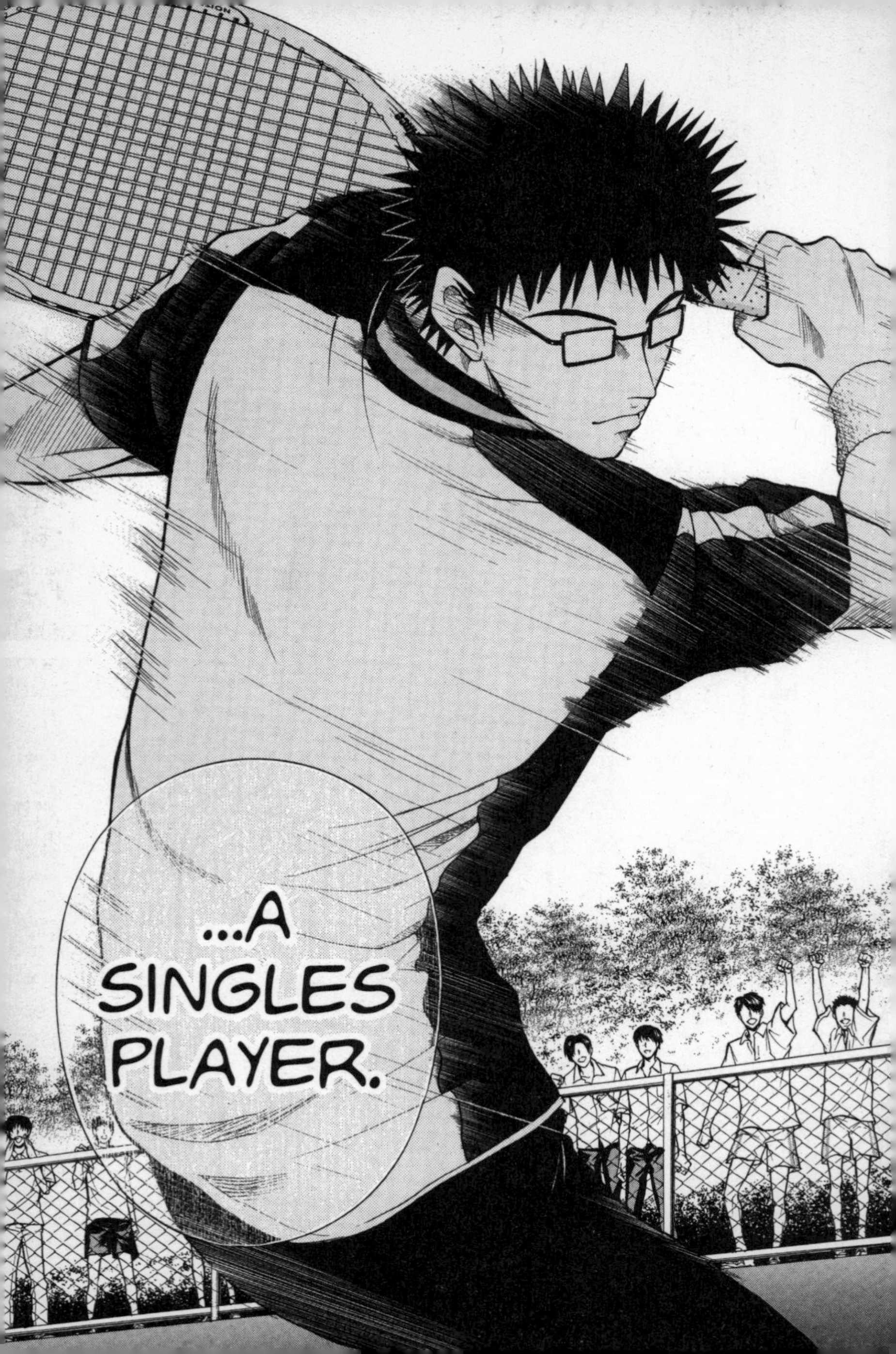
...A SINGLES PLAYER.

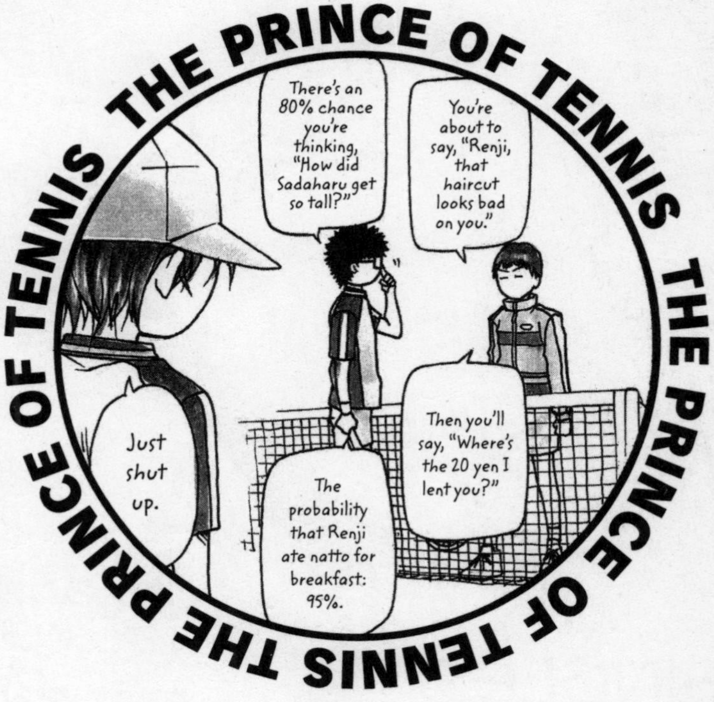
THE PRINCE OF TENNIS THE PRINCE OF TENNIS THE PRINCE OF TENNIS
You're about to say, "Renji, that haircut looks bad on you."
There's an 80% chance you're thinking, "How did Sadaharu get so tall?"
Then you'll say, "Where's the 20 yen I lent you?"
The probability that Renji ate natto for breakfast: 95%.
Just shut up.

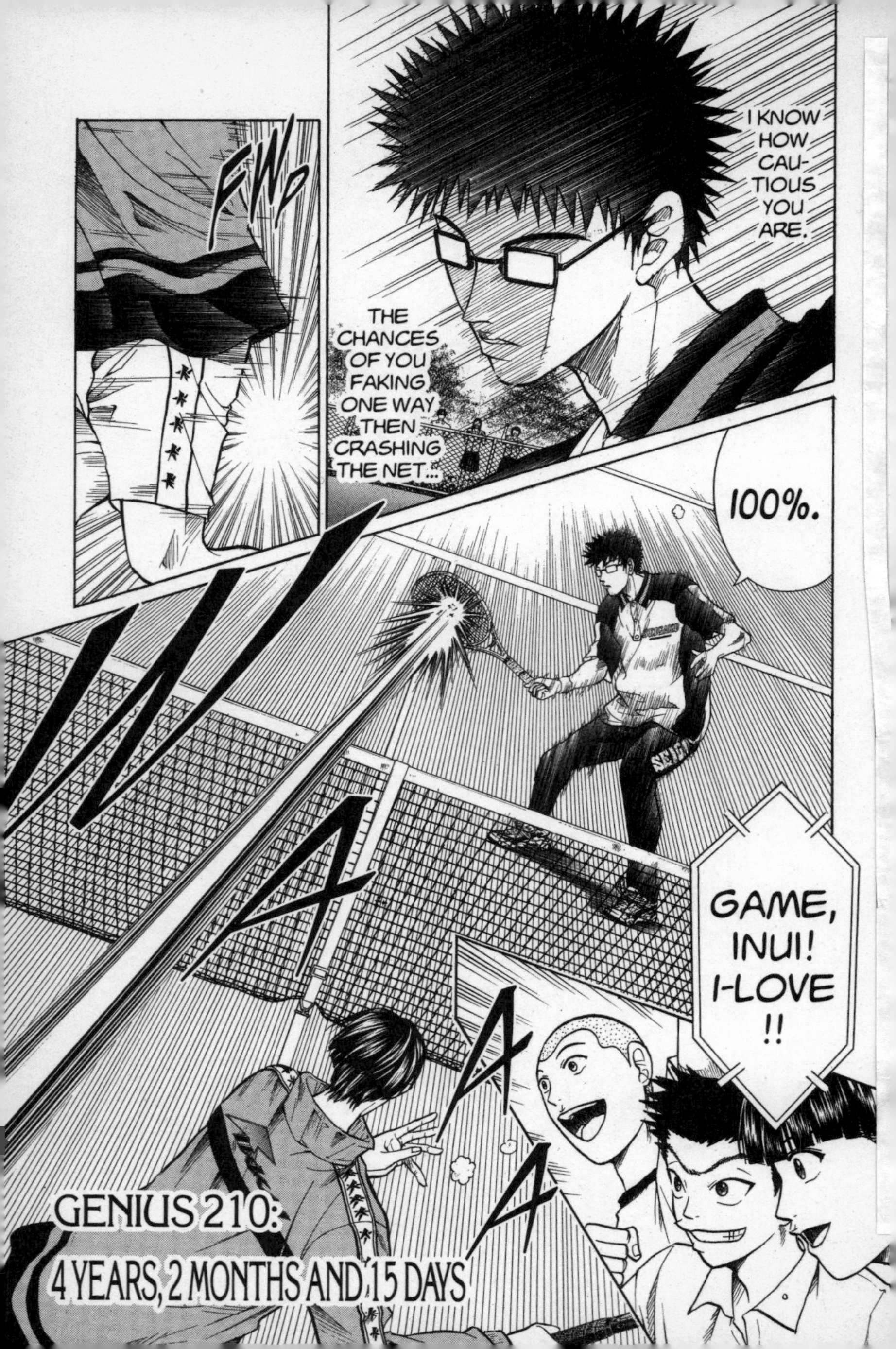
I KNOW HOW CAU-TIOUS YOU ARE.
THE CHANCES OF YOU FAKING ONE WAY THEN CRASHING THE NET...
100%.
GAME, INUI! I-LOVE !!
WAAAA

GENIUS 210: 4 YEARS, 2 MONTHS AND 15 DAYS

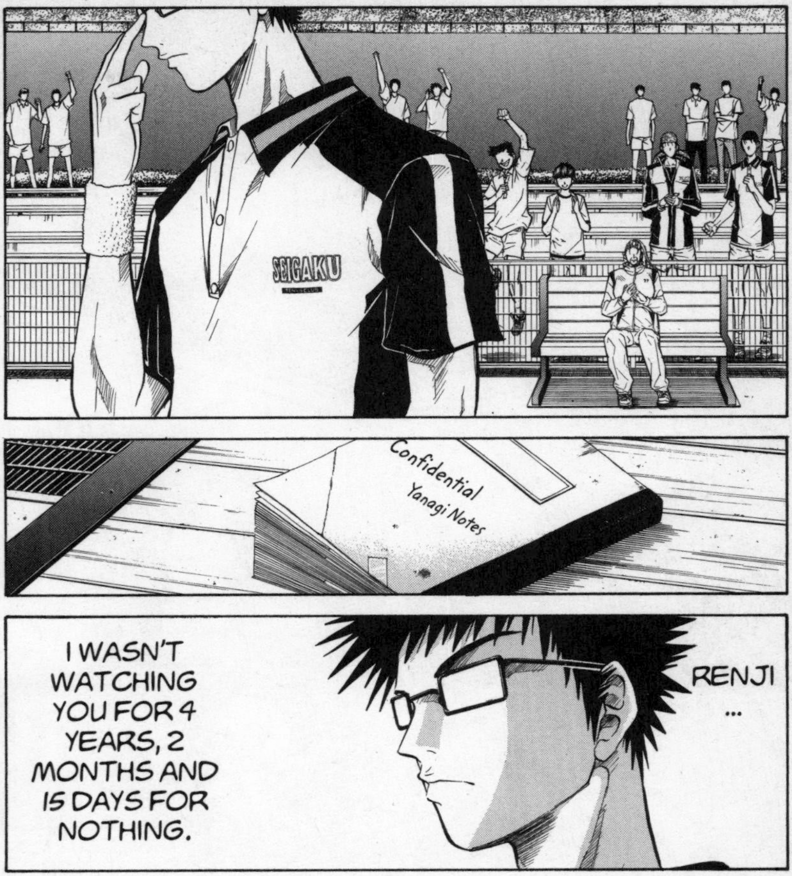
SEIGAKU
Confidential
Yanagi Notes
RENJI ...
I WASN'T WATCHING YOU FOR 4 YEARS, 2 MONTHS AND 15 DAYS FOR NOTHING.

GENIUS 210: 4 YEARS, 2 MONTHS AND 15 DAYS

READ THIS WAY

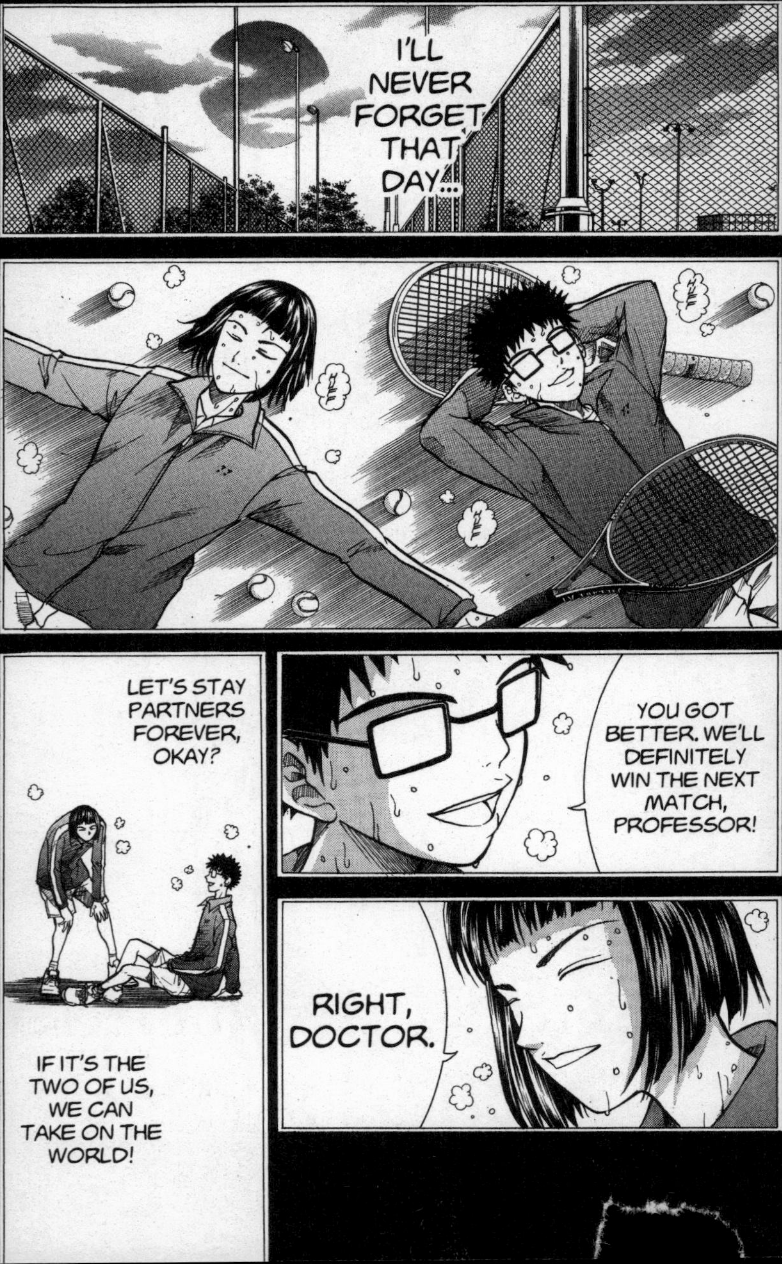
I'LL NEVER FORGET THAT DAY...
YOU GOT BETTER. WE'LL DEFINITELY WIN THE NEXT MATCH, PROFESSOR!
RIGHT, DOCTOR.
LET'S STAY PARTNERS FOREVER, OKAY?
IF IT'S THE TWO OF US, WE CAN TAKE ON THE WORLD!

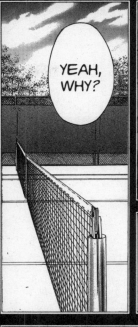

YEAH, WHY?

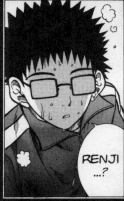

RENJI ...?

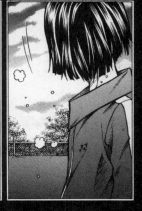

YOU KNOW HOW WE'VE NEVER PLAYED AGAINST EACH OTHER?

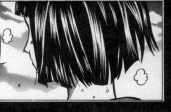

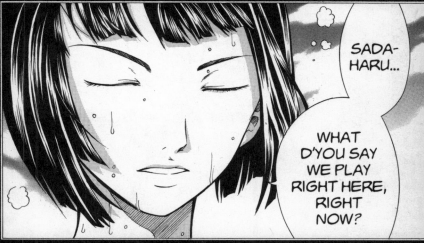

SADA-HARU...

WHAT D'YOU SAY WE PLAY RIGHT HERE, RIGHT NOW?

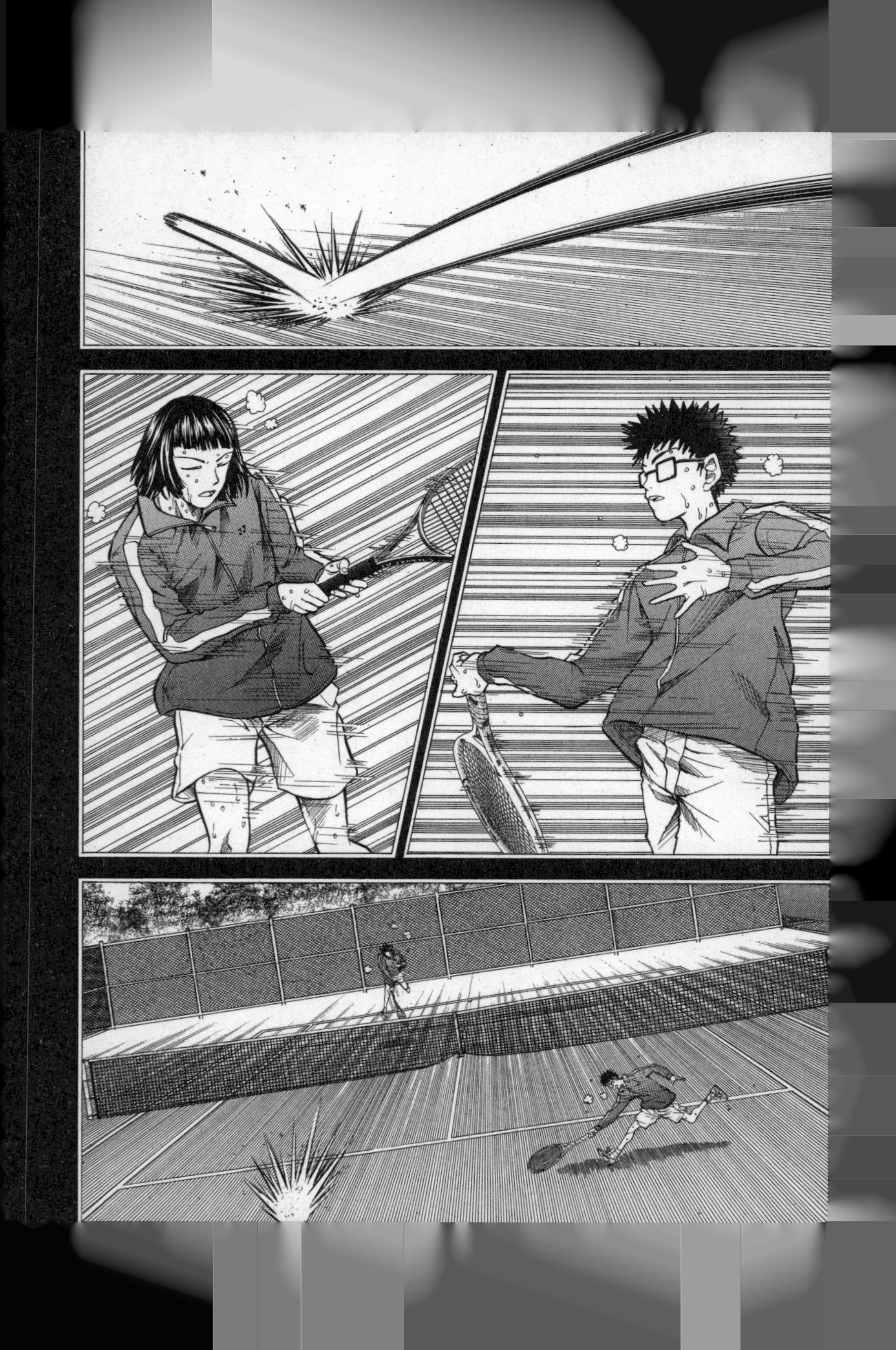

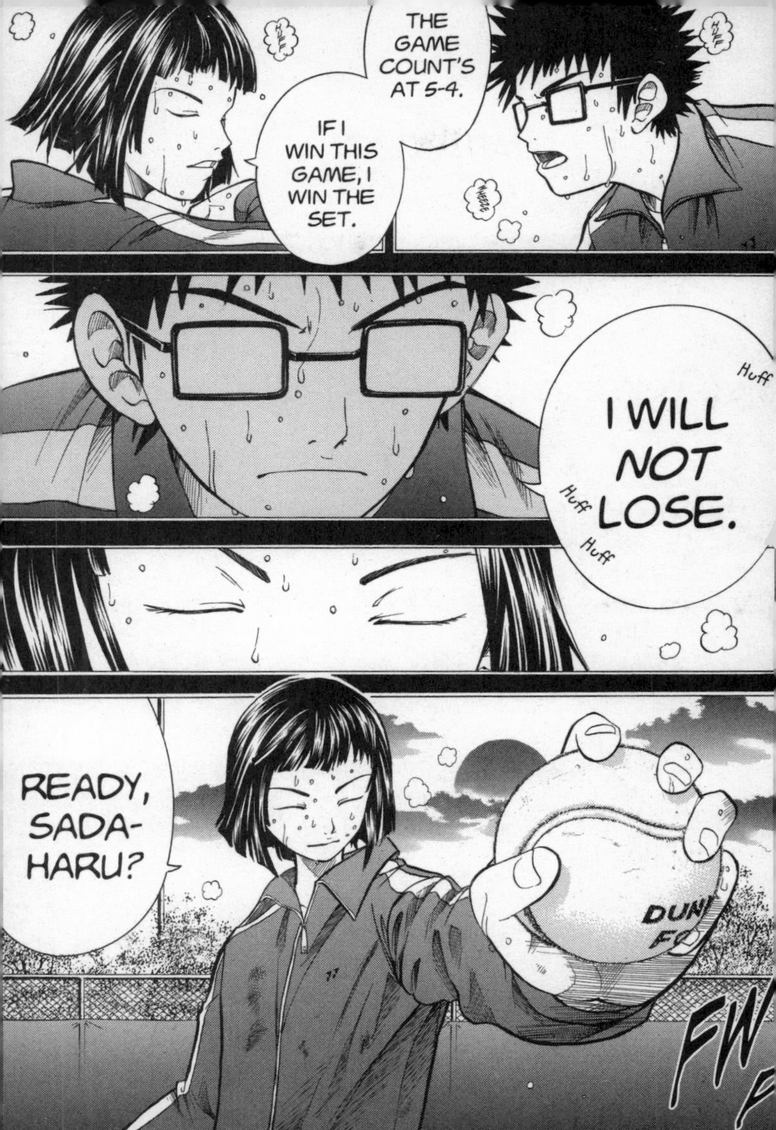
THE GAME COUNT'S AT 5-4.
IF I WIN THIS GAME, I WIN THE SET.
Huff
I WILL NOT LOSE.
Huff
Huff
READY, SADA-HARU?

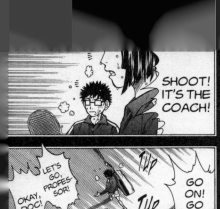

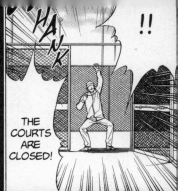

!!
THE COURTS ARE CLOSED!
SHOOT! IT'S THE COACH!
TUP
TUP
GO ON! GO HOME !!
LET'S GO, PROFES-SOR!
OKAY, DOC!
LET'S FINISH THIS GAME AFTER THE NEXT TOURNAMENT, OKAY? PROMISE?
SORRY. THAT'S A PROMISE I CAN'T KEEP...

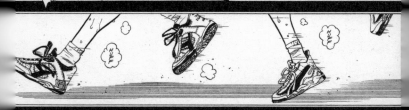

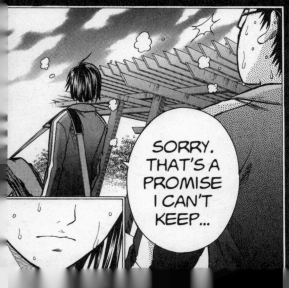

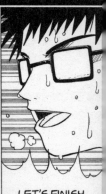

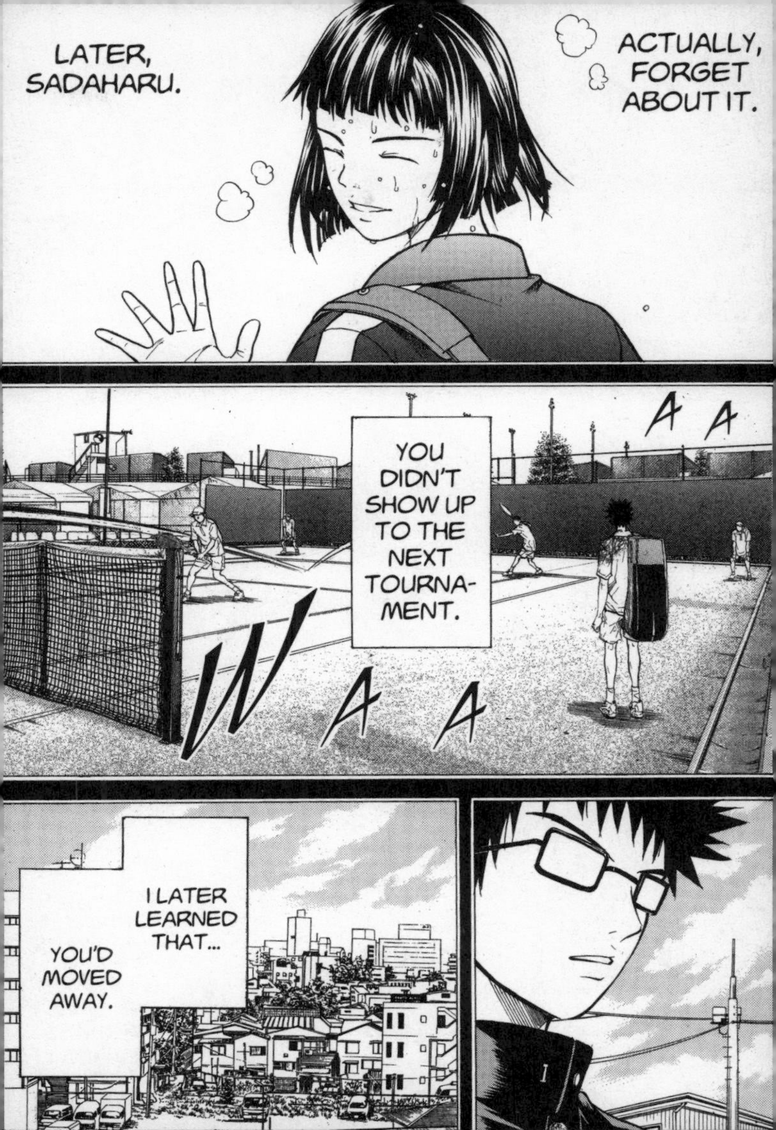
ACTUALLY, FORGET ABOUT IT.
LATER, SADAHARU.
AA
YOU DIDN'T SHOW UP TO THE NEXT TOURNA-MENT.
WAA
I LATER LEARNED THAT...
YOU'D MOVED AWAY.

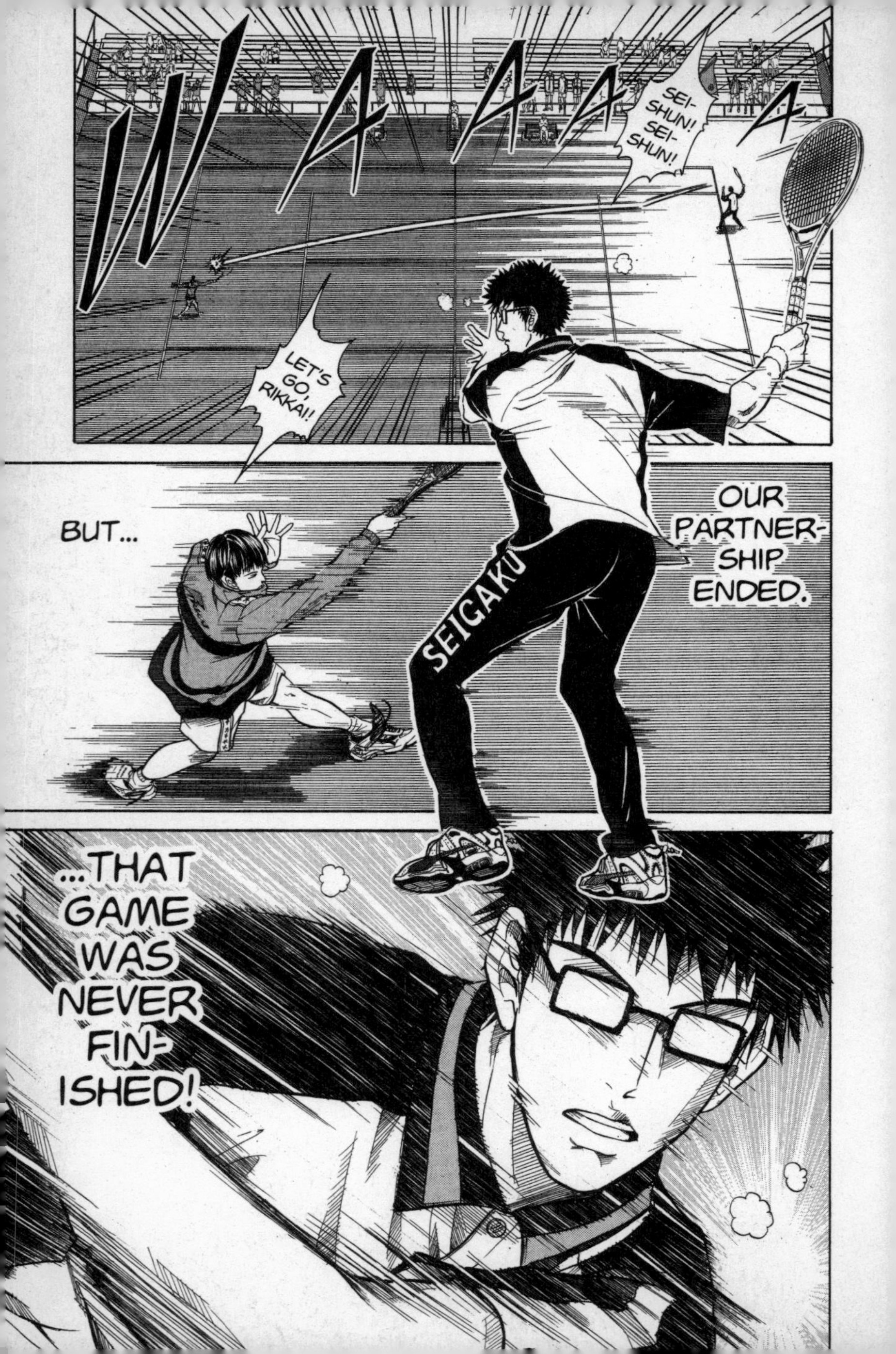
WAAAA
SEI-SHUN! SEI-SHUN!
LET'S GO, RIKKAI!!
OUR PARTNER-SHIP ENDED.
BUT...
...THAT GAME WAS NEVER FIN-ISHED!

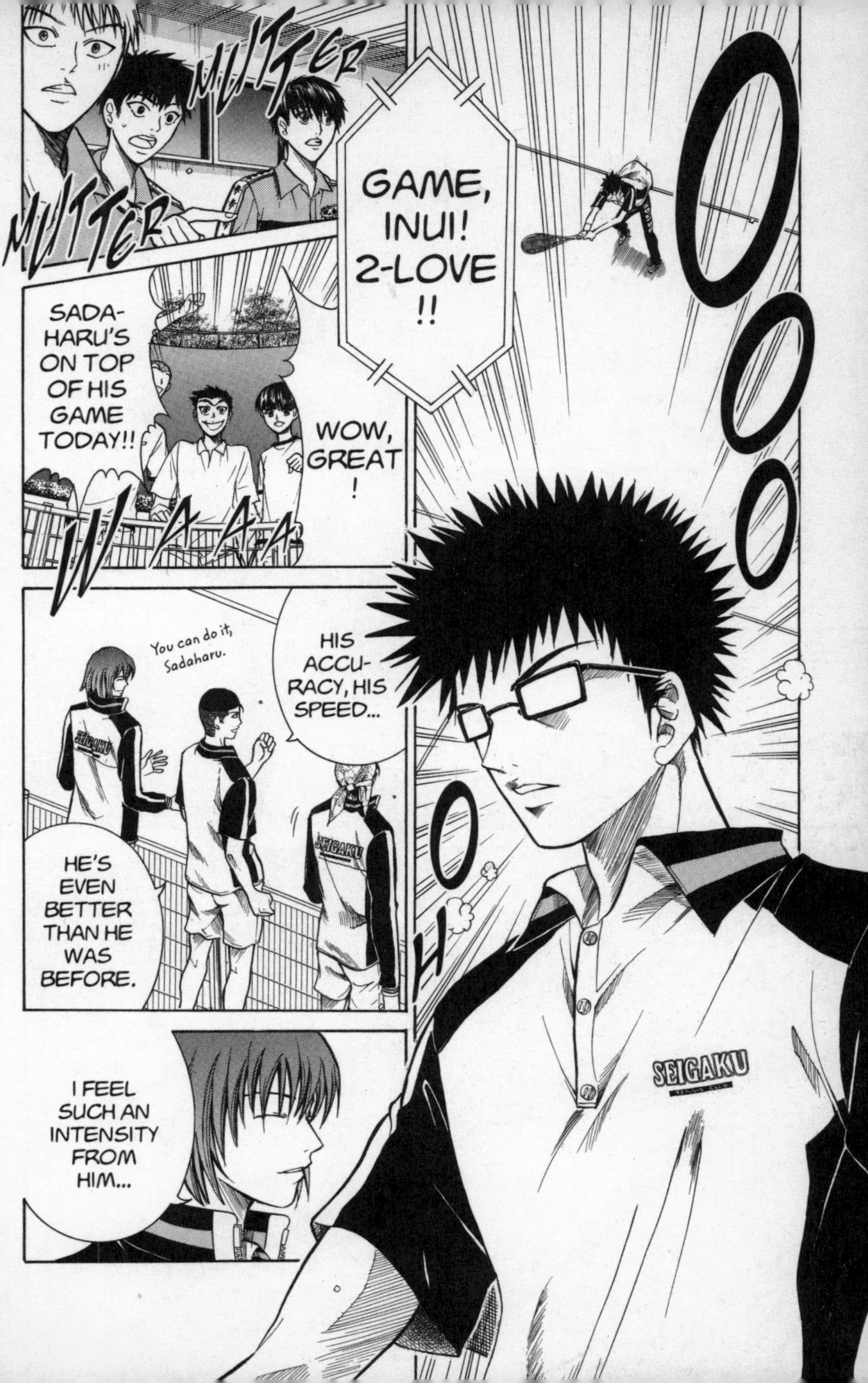
GAME, INUI! 2-LOVE!!
OOOOOH
MUTTER MUTTER
SADA-HARU'S ON TOP OF HIS GAME TODAY!!
WOW, GREAT!
WAAA
HIS ACCU-RACY, HIS SPEED...
You can do it, Sadaharu.
HE'S EVEN BETTER THAN HE WAS BEFORE.
I FEEL SUCH AN INTENSITY FROM HIM...

READ THIS WAY

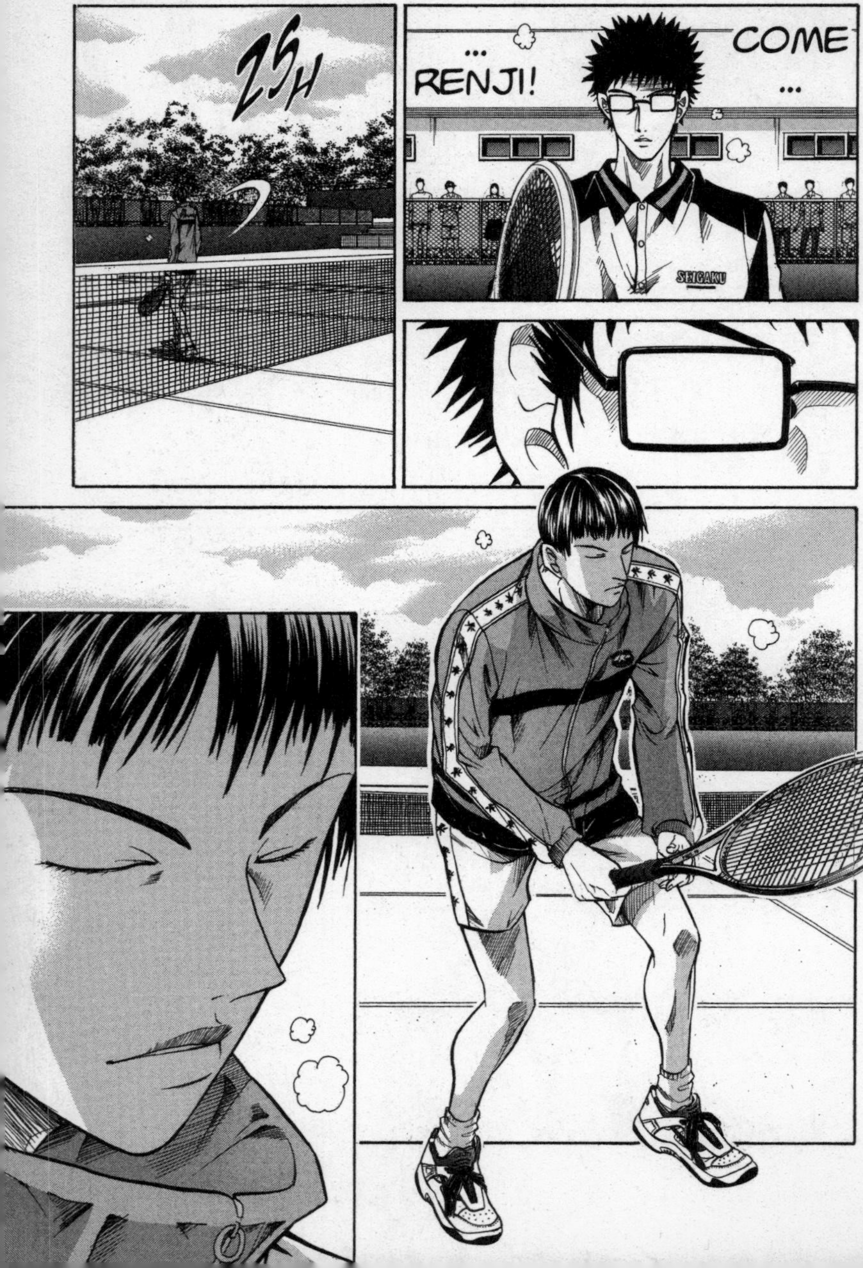
COME ...
... RENJI!
ZSH

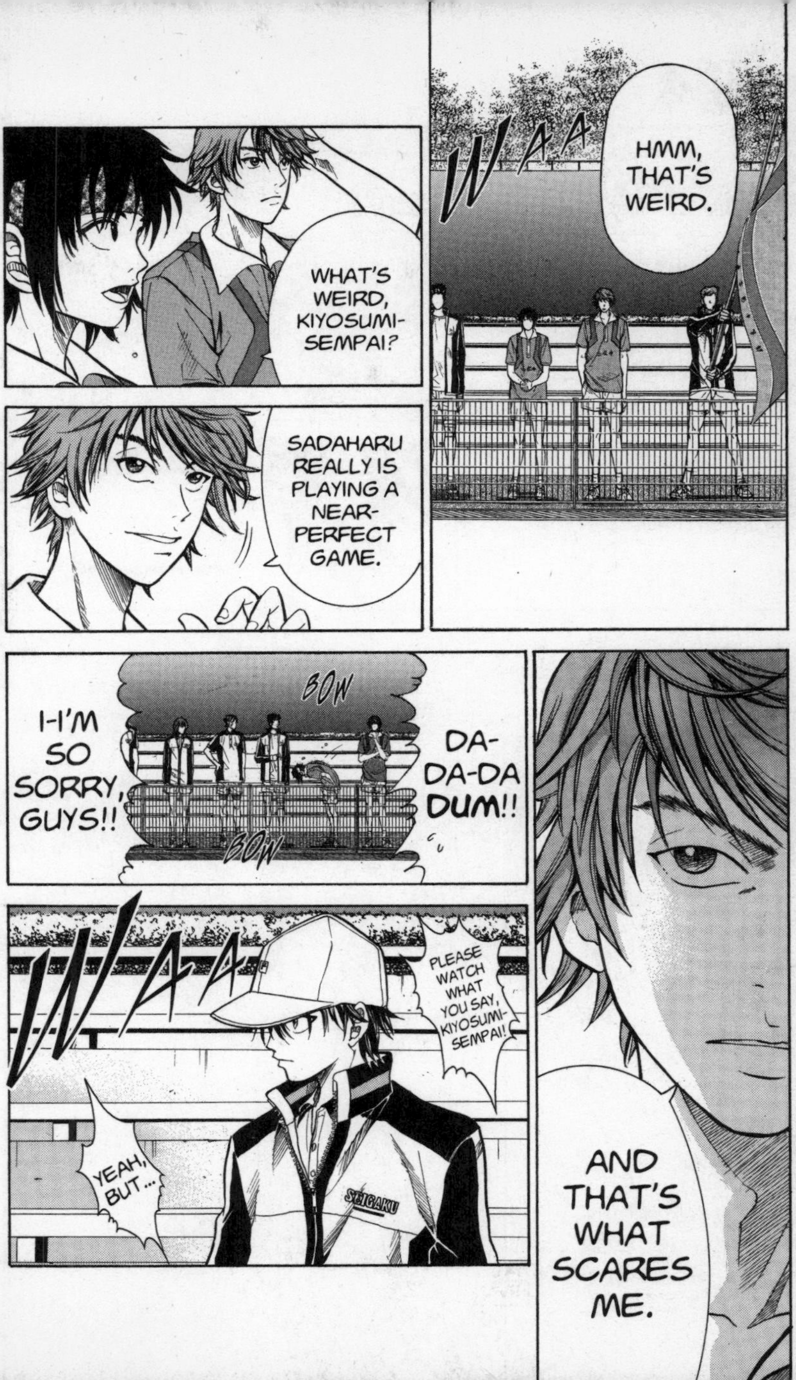
WAA
HMM, THAT'S WEIRD.
WHAT'S WEIRD, KIYOSUMI-SEMPAI?
SADAHARU REALLY IS PLAYING A NEAR-PERFECT GAME.
AND THAT'S WHAT SCARES ME.
DA-DA-DA DUM!!
BOW
I-I'M SO SORRY, GUYS!!
BOW
PLEASE WATCH WHAT YOU SAY, KIYOSUMI-SEMPAI!
WAA
SEIGAKU
YEAH, BUT...

READ THIS WAY

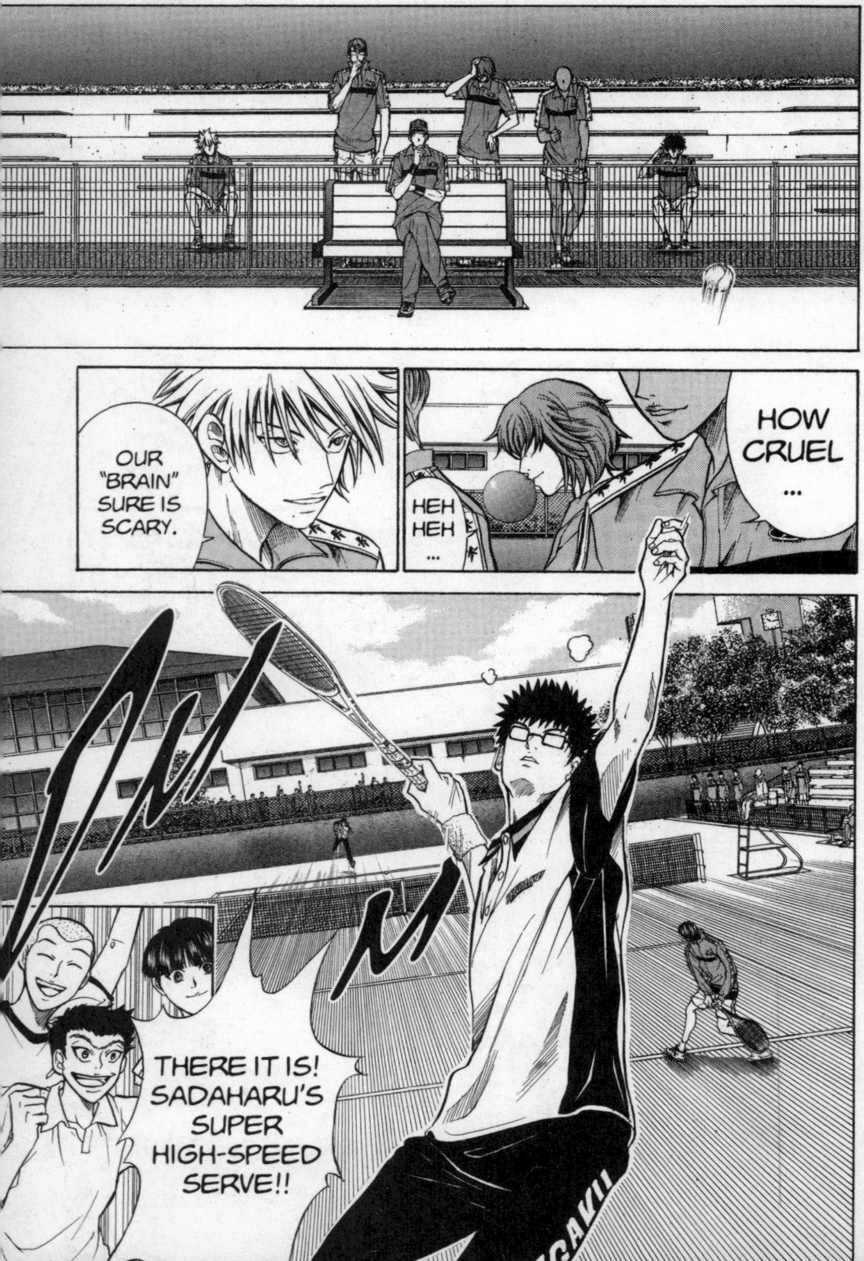
HOW CRUEL ...
HEH HEH ...
OUR "BRAIN" SURE IS SCARY.
THERE IT IS! SADAHARU'S SUPER HIGH-SPEED SERVE!!

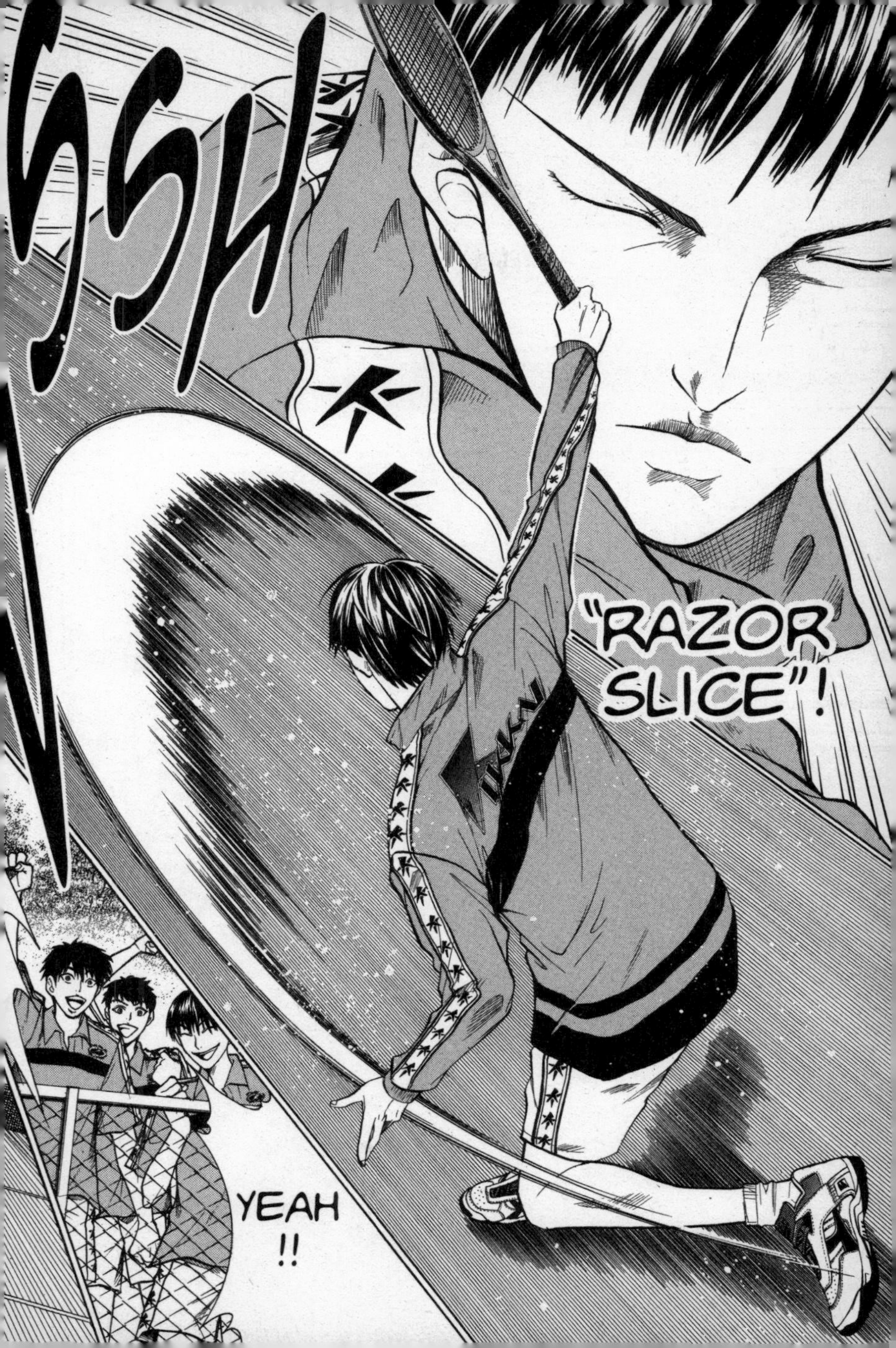
SSH
"RAZOR SLICE"!
YEAH !!

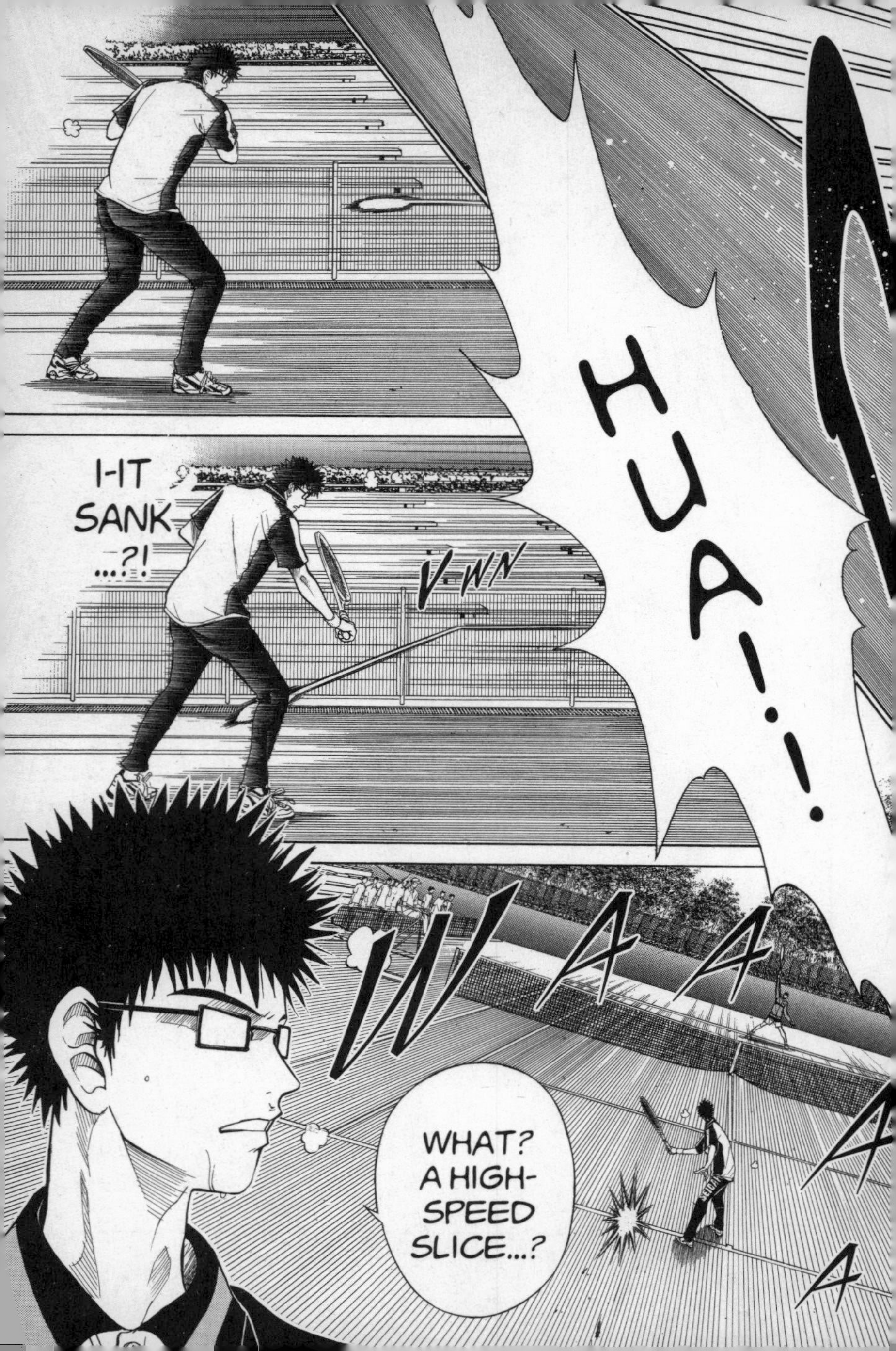
HUA-!!
I-IT SANK...?!
VWN
WAAAA
WHAT? A HIGH-SPEED SLICE...?

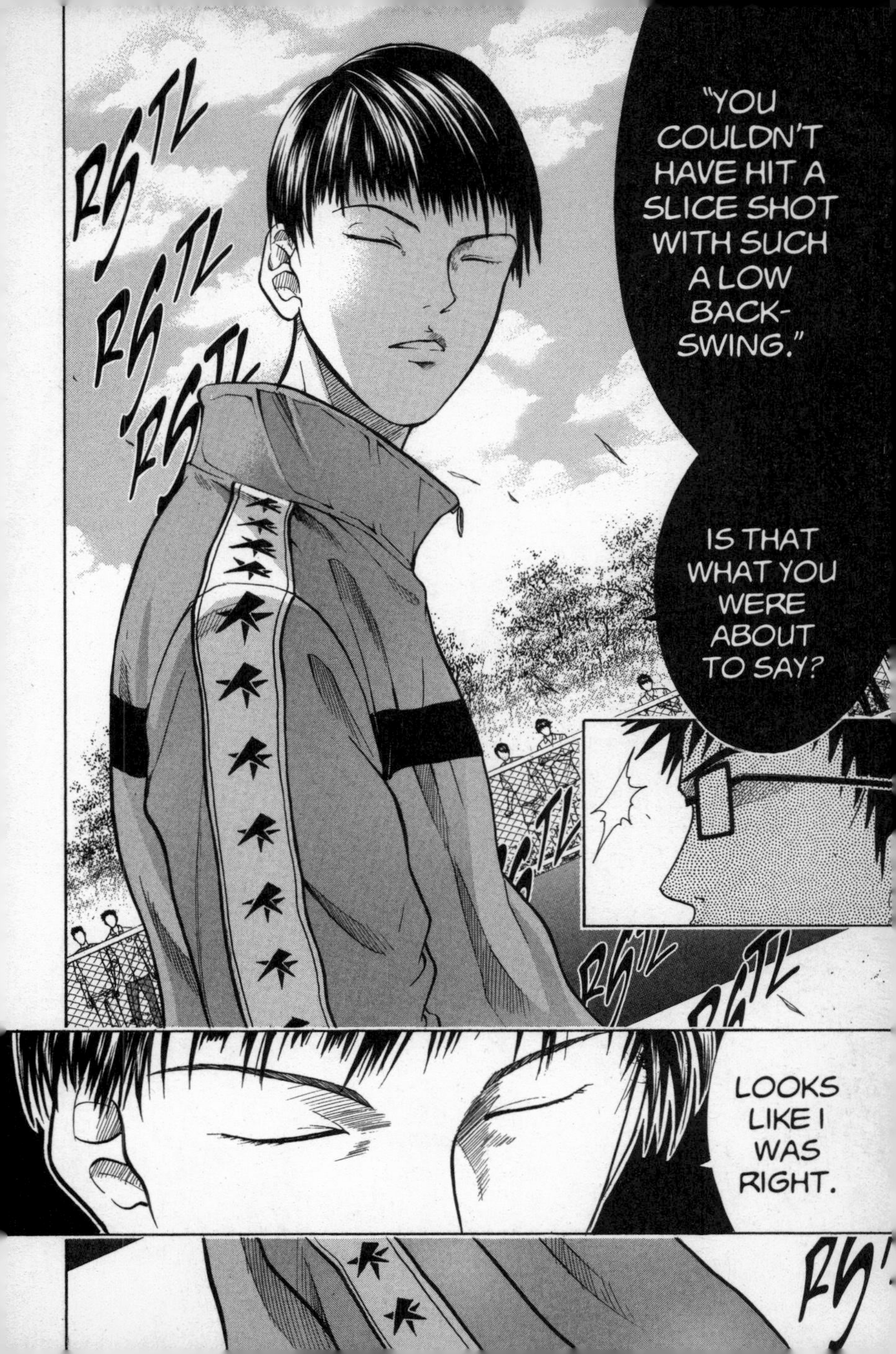
"YOU COULDN'T HAVE HIT A SLICE SHOT WITH SUCH A LOW BACK-SWING."
RSTL RSTL RSTL
IS THAT WHAT YOU WERE ABOUT TO SAY?
RSTL RSTL
LOOKS LIKE I WAS RIGHT.

READ THIS WAY

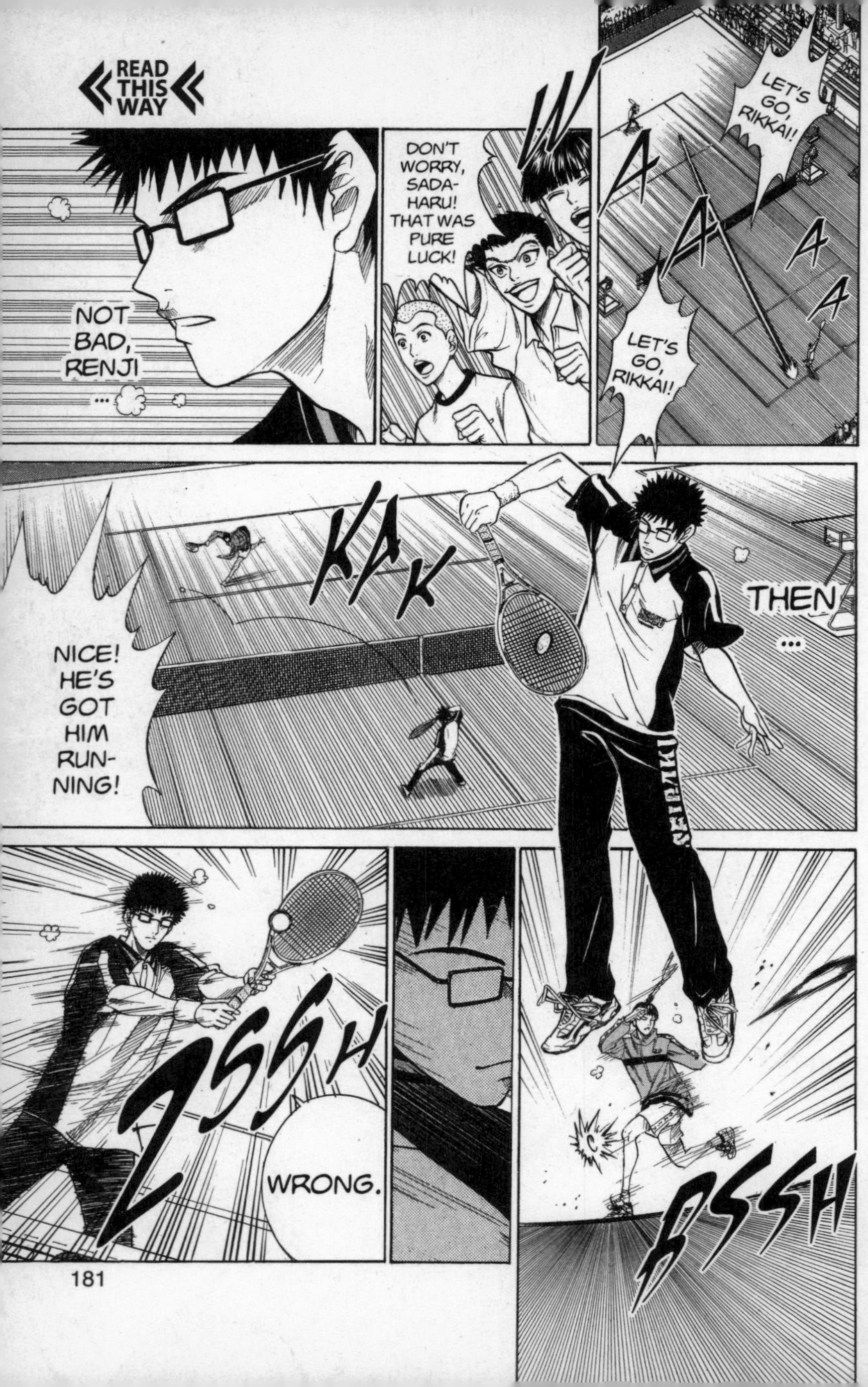
WAAAA
LET'S GO, RIKKAI!
LET'S GO, RIKKAI!
DON'T WORRY, SADA-HARU! THAT WAS PURE LUCK!
NOT BAD, RENJI ...
THEN ...
KAKK
NICE! HE'S GOT HIM RUN-NING!
SEIGAKU
BSSH
WRONG.
ZSSH

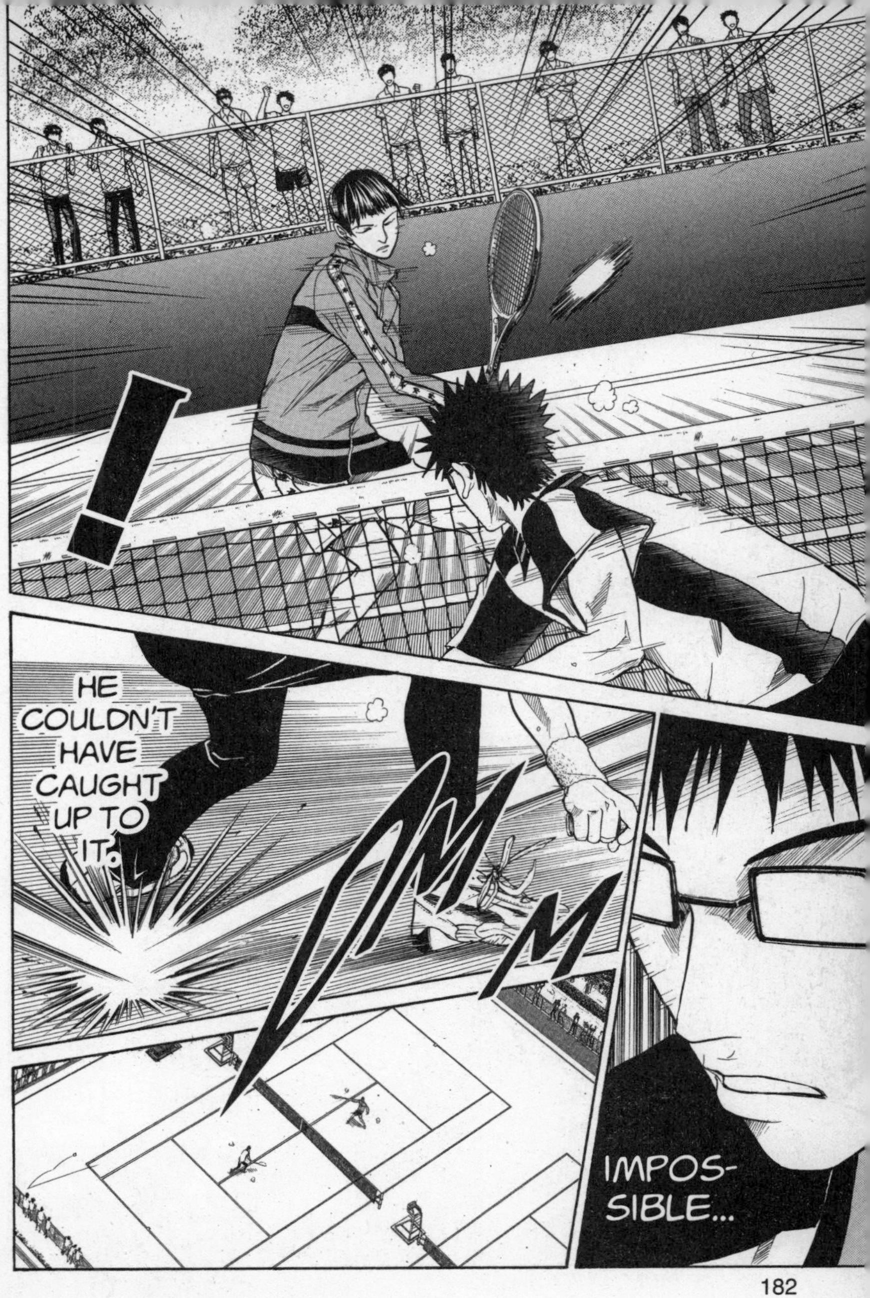
HE COULDN'T HAVE CAUGHT UP TO IT.
IMPOSSIBLE...

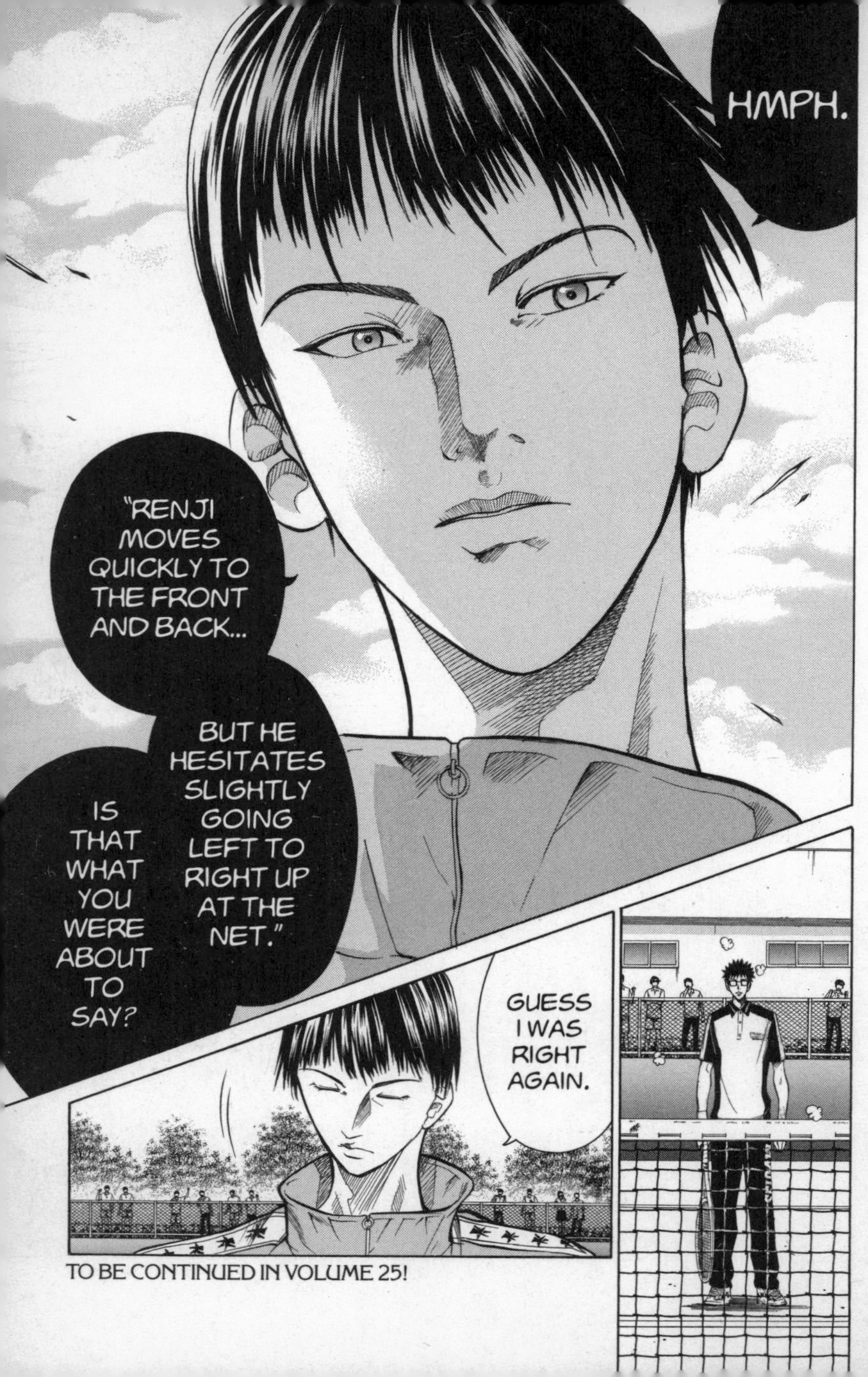
HMPH.
"RENJI MOVES QUICKLY TO THE FRONT AND BACK...
BUT HE HESITATES SLIGHTLY GOING LEFT TO RIGHT UP AT THE NET."
IS THAT WHAT YOU WERE ABOUT TO SAY?
GUESS I WAS RIGHT AGAIN.

TO BE CONTINUED IN VOLUME 25!

In the Next Volume...

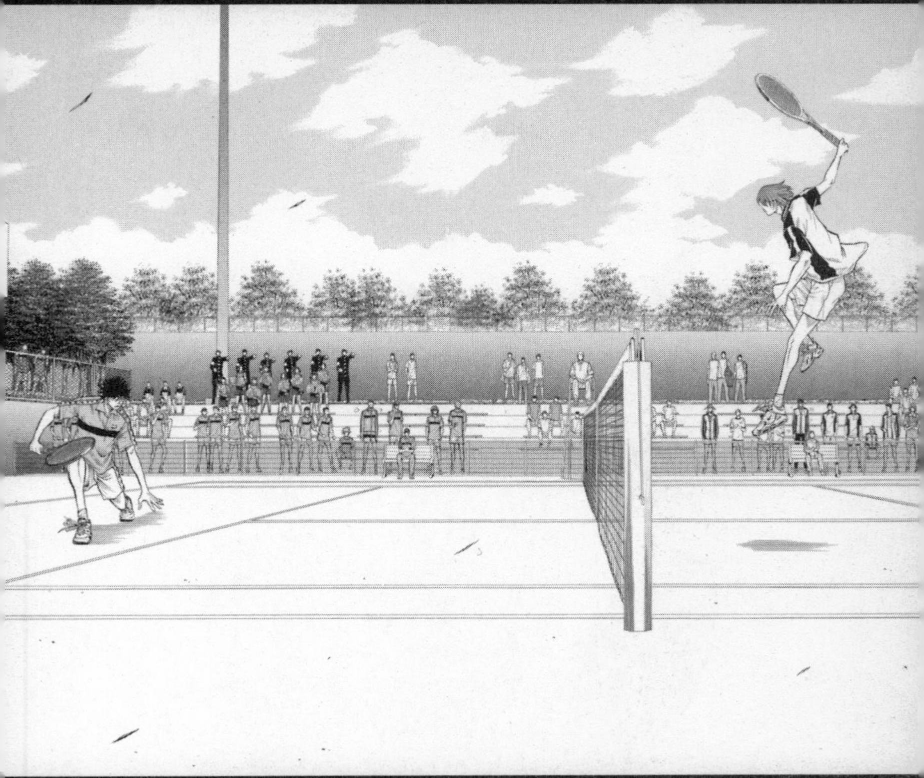

And Shusuke Smiles

The Kanto Tournament finals showdown between Seishun and Rikkai continues, and Seishun's in trouble. After losing consecutive doubles matches against Rikkai's powerhouse pairs, the team now pins its hopes on Sadaharu's and Shusuke's singles matches. But with their opponents being "The Master" Renji Yanagi and the fiery prodigy Akaya Kirihara, the Seishun players are facing their hardest battles yet.

Available May 2008!

テニスの王子様

THE PRINCE OF TENNIS

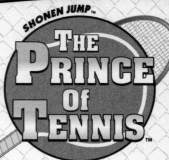

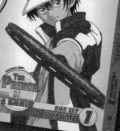

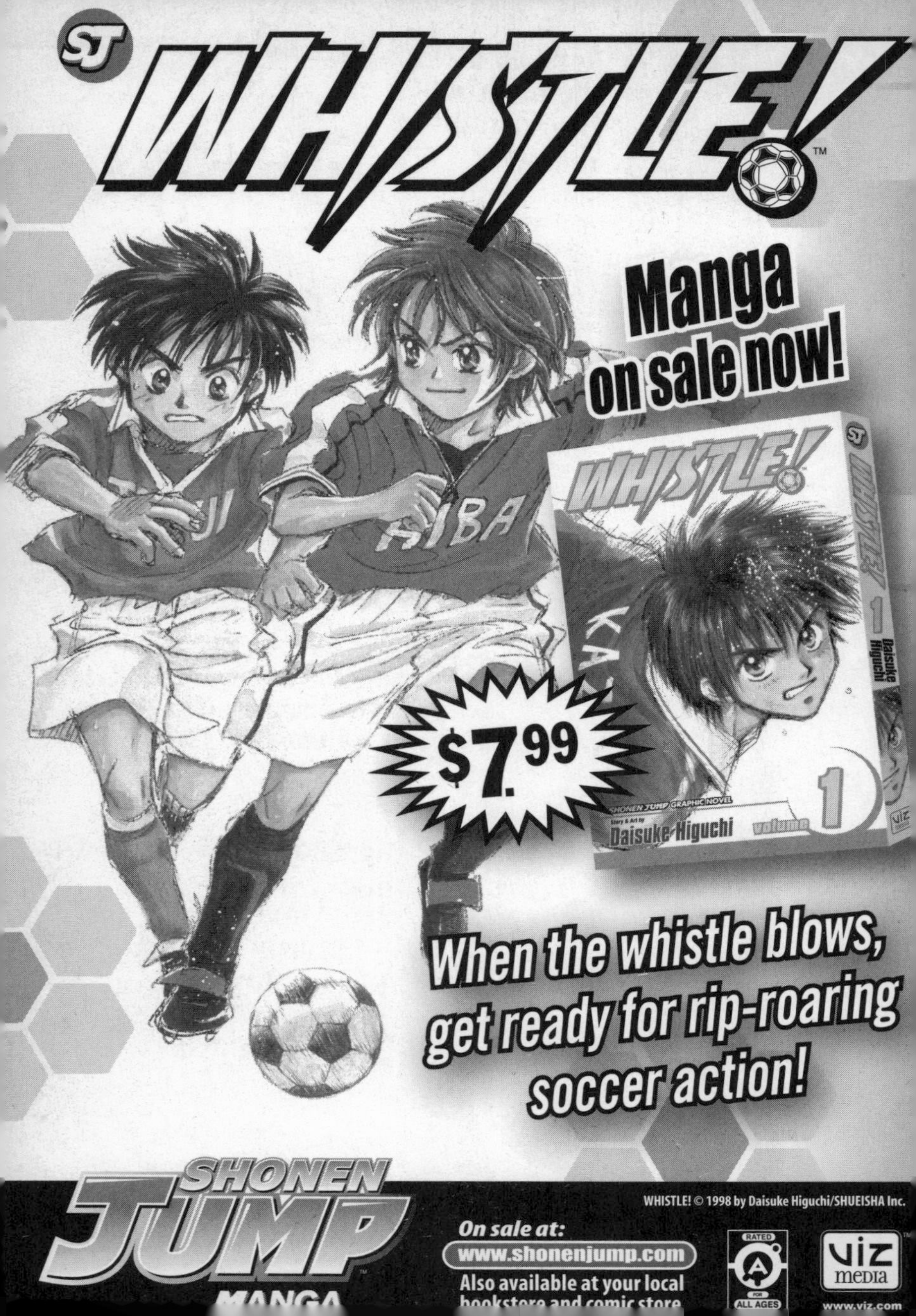
SJ
WHISTLE!™
Manga on sale now!
WHISTLE!
SHONEN JUMP GRAPHIC NOVEL
Story & Art by Daisuke Higuchi
volume 1
$7.99
When the whistle blows, get ready for rip-roaring soccer action!
SHONEN JUMP MANGA
WHISTLE! © 1998 by Daisuke Higuchi/SHUEISHA Inc.
On sale at:
www.shonenjump.com
Also available at your local
RATED A FOR ALL AGES
VIZ media
www.viz.com

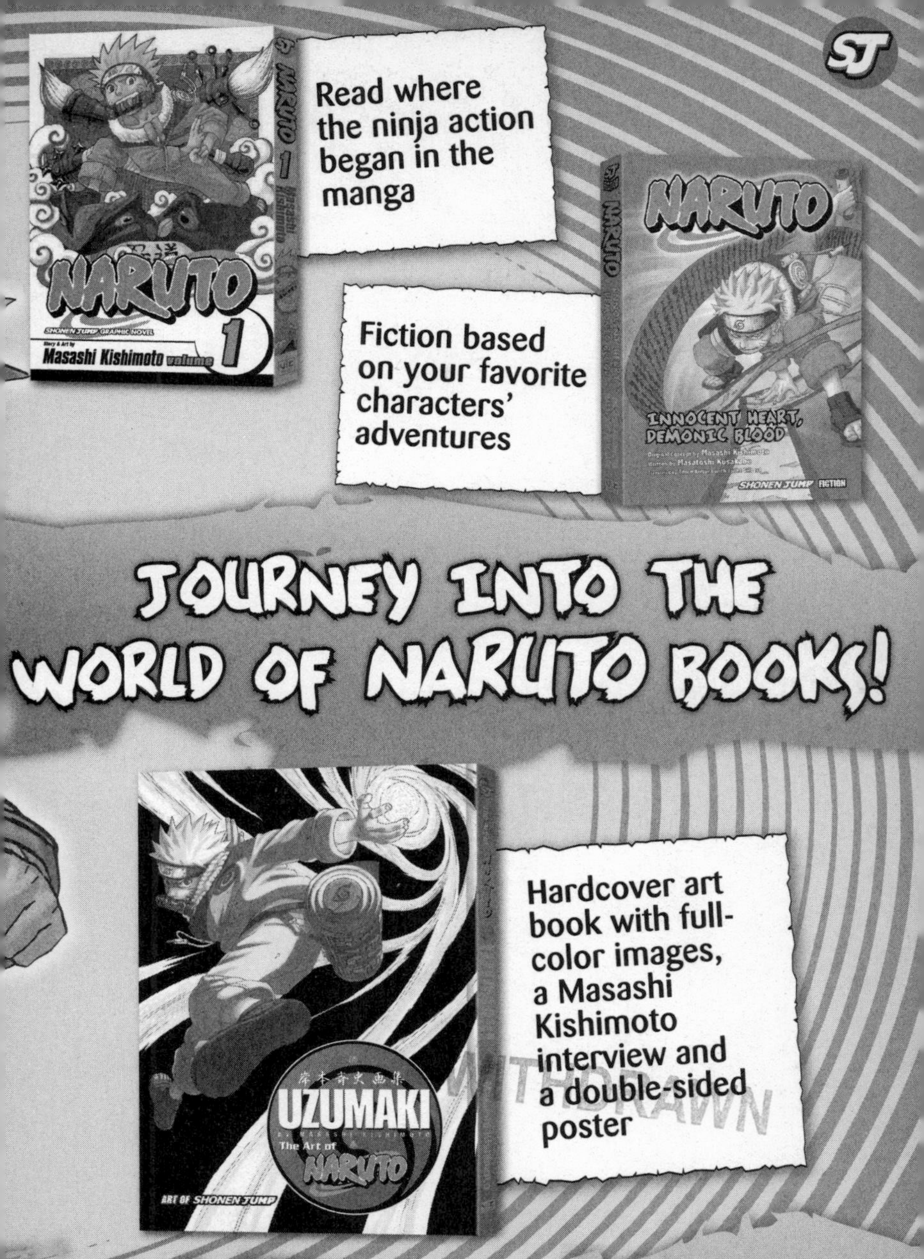

Read where the ninja action began in the manga
Fiction based on your favorite characters' adventures
JOURNEY INTO THE WORLD OF NARUTO BOOKS!
Hardcover art book with full-color images, a Masashi Kishimoto interview and a double-sided poster
NARUTO
SHONEN JUMP GRAPHIC NOVEL
Story & Art by Masashi Kishimoto volume 1
NARUTO
INNOCENT HEART, DEMONIC BLOOD
SHONEN JUMP FICTION
UZUMAKI
The Art of NARUTO
ART OF SHONEN JUMP
WITHDRAWN
RATED T FOR TEEN ratings.viz.com
VIZ MEDIA
www.viz.com

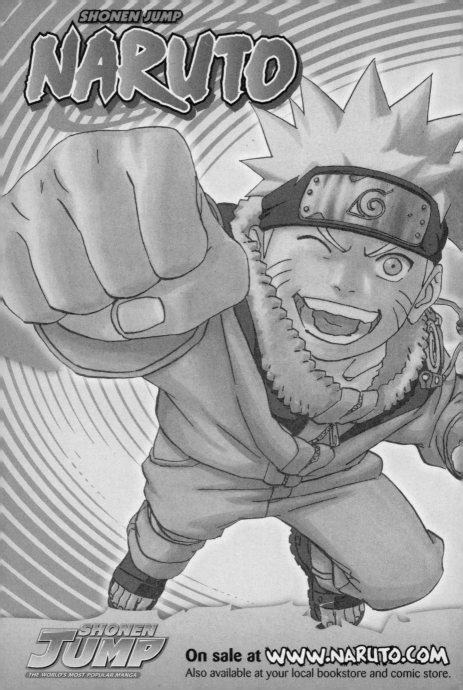

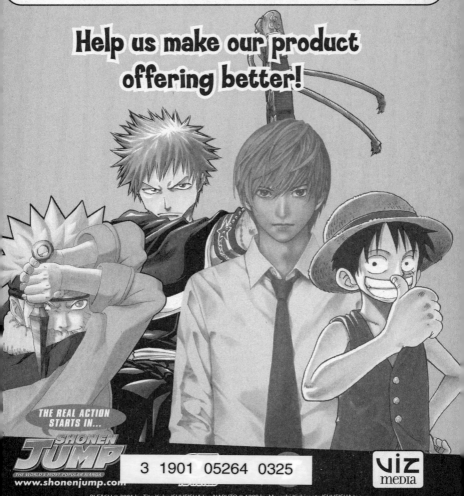

Tell us what you think about SHONEN JUMP manga!

Our survey is now available online.
Go to: www.*SHONENJUMP*.com/mangasurvey

Help us make our product offering better!

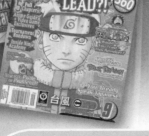
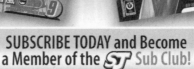

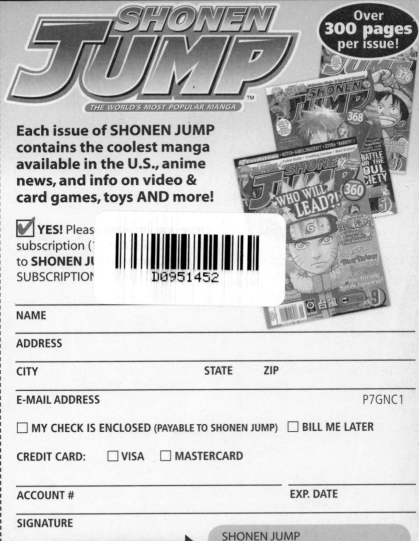